COPING WITH NEGATIVE LIFE EVENTS

Clinical and Social Psychological Perspectives

The Plenum Series on Stress and Coping

COPING WITH LIFE CRISES
An Integrated Approach
Edited by Rudolf H. Moos

COPING WITH NEGATIVE LIFE EVENTS
Clinical and Social Psychological Perspectives
Edited by C. R. Snyder and Carol E. Ford

DYNAMICS OF STRESS
Physiological, Psychological, and Social Perspectives
Edited by Mortimer H. Appley and Richard Trumbull

A Continuation Order Plan is available for this series. A continuation order will bring
delivery of each new volume immediately upon publication. Volumes are billed only upon
actual shipment. For further information please contact the publisher.

COPING WITH NEGATIVE LIFE EVENTS

Clinical and Social Psychological Perspectives

Edited by
C. R. Snyder
University of Kansas
Lawrence, Kansas

and
Carol E. Ford
University of Missouri
Columbia, Missouri

PLENUM PRESS • NEW YORK AND LONDON

Library of Congress Cataloging in Publication Data

Coping with negative life events.

(The Plenum series on stress and coping)
Includes bibliographies and index.
1. Life change events—Psychological aspects. 2. Adjustment (Psychology) I. Snyder,
C. R. II. Ford, Carol E. III. Series. [DNLM: 1. Adaptation, Psychological. 2. Life
Change Events. BF 335 C7828]
BF637.L53C66   1987   155.9   87-2483
ISBN 0-306-42432-0

This book is dedicated
to the memory of
Shirley Snyder
for endless lessons in coping

Contributors

Robert M. Arkin, Department of Psychology, University of Missouri, Columbia, Missouri

Ann H. Baumgardner, Department of Psychology, Virginia Polytechnic Institute and State University, Blacksburg, Virginia

Jack W. Brehm, Department of Psychology, University of Kansas, Lawrence, Kansas

Sharon S. Brehm, Department of Psychology, University of Kansas, Lawrence, Kansas

Carol E. Ford, Department of Psychology, University of Missouri, Columbia, Missouri

Jeff Greenberg, Department of Psychology, University of Arizona, Tucson, Arizona

Robert N. Harris, Department of Psychology, University of Kansas, Lawrence, Kansas

Jill M. Hooley, Department of Social Relations, Harvard University, Cambridge, Massachusetts

B. Kent Houston, Department of Psychology, University of Kansas, Lawrence, Kansas

Lina Jandorf, Department of Psychiatry, State University of New York, Stony Brook, New York

Ronnie Janoff-Bulman, Department of Psychology, University of Massachusetts, Amherst, Massachusetts

John M. Neale, Department of Psychology, State University of New York, Stony Brook, New York

Linda S. Perloff, Department of Psychology, University of Illinois, Chicago, Illinois

Tom Pyszczynski, Department of Psychology, University of Colorado, Colorado Springs, Colorado

Barry R. Schlenker, Department of Psychology, University of Florida, Gainesville, Florida

C. R. Snyder, Department of Psychology, University of Kansas, Lawrence, Kansas

Arthur A. Stone, Department of Psychiatry, State University of New York, Stony Brook, New York

Christine Timko, Department of Psychology, Yale University, New Haven, Connecticut

Thomas Ashby Wills, Departments of Psychology and Epidemiology, Ferkauf Graduate School of Psychology and Albert Einstein College of Medicine, Bronx, New York

Rex A. Wright, Department of Psychology, University of Missouri, Columbia, Missouri

Preface
"Like a Bridge over Troubled Waters"

The surge of current interest in the interface between clinical and social psychology is well illustrated by the publication of a number of general texts and journals in this area, and the growing emphasis in graduate programs on providing training in both disciplines. Although the benefits of an integrated clinical-social approach have been recognized for a number of years, the recent work in this area has advanced from theoretical extrapolations of social psychological models to clinical issues to theory and research that is based on social principles and conducted in clinical domains. It is becoming increasingly common to find social psychologists pursuing research with clinical populations and clinical psychologists investigating variables that have traditionally been in the realm of social psychology.

A major area of interface between the two disciplines is in research and theory concerned with how individuals respond to negative events. In addition to the trend toward an integrated clinical-social approach, the growing body of literature in this area reflects the explosion of current interest in the area of health psychology; work by clinical and social psychologists on the topics of stress and coping has been one of the major facets of this burgeoning field.

The purpose of the present volume is to provide a common forum for recent advances in the clinical and social literature on responses to negative life outcomes. In order to achieve this purpose, the book has been divided into six parts. In Part I, an introductory chapter examines the role of theoretical perspective in the analysis of coping with negative life events. Four case histories are described in this chapter in order to highlight how theoretical perspective influences the definition of negative life events and coping both for the insider (i.e., the person undergoing the negative life events) and outsiders (i.e., the observer in general, and mental health professional in particular). In order to give the reader a flavor of the common processes addressed by the chapters in the four major parts of the book, one case history is elaborated at the beginning of a section. In the next four parts of the book (Parts II, III, IV & V), chapters are grouped according to shared perspectives. For example, in Part II, there are four chapters involving the process of effort expenditure in coping with negative life events. In Part III, there are three chapters involving control/mastery issues. Part IV contains two chapters describing social comparison perspectives, and Part V includes three chapters revolving around the image maintenance process. In Part VI, a final chapter presents conclusions regarding a possible taxonomy for this research area.

Thanks are due to several people. First, our families and friends have patiently tolerated the extra hours that this project has necessitated. Our assistants, Judy Williams and Jane Niemeyer, have provided enthusiastic help at all phases. We also have had the privilege of working with Eliot Werner, senior editor at Plenum. Eliot and series editor Donald Meichenbaum provided excellent support for the completion of this project. Finally, the authors in this volume are to be congratulated for their continued good will and efforts at reaching the various deadlines.

The subtitle of this preface borrows from Paul Simon's song of a similar name. In this song, the lyrics tell the story of a person who offers assistance ("the bridge") in helping a friend to deal with the difficulties of life ("troubled waters"). In a slightly different vein, however, the refrain of "like a bridge over troubled waters" also can be applied to the authors of the present volume. These authors are architects, builders of sorts, who offer bridges or structures for understanding how we cope with negative life events.

C. R. SNYDER
CAROL E. FORD

Contents

PART VI. OVERVIEW PERSPECTIVE

Chapter 14: Stress and Coping

B. Kent Houston

I

Introductory Theoretical Viewpoint

Irrationally held truths may be more harmful than reasoned errors.

Thomas Henry Huxley, *Science and Culture,* xii, "The Coming of Age of the Origin of Species."

The great tragedy of Science—the slaying of the beautiful hypothesis by an ugly fact.

Thomas Henry Huxley, *Collected Essays,* viii, "Biogenesis and Abiogenesis."

1

The Effects of Theoretical Perspective on the Analysis of Coping With Negative Life Events

C. R. SNYDER, CAROL E. FORD, and ROBERT N. HARRIS

INTRODUCTION

Human beings are constantly trying to make sense out of the events in their lives. This searching for understanding makes *Homo sapiens* the most sophisticated theory or model generator among the multitude of living organisms. Although living organisms, for survival reasons, are intimately involved in unraveling the cause and effect relationships in their life arenas, humankind not only appears to generate the more intricate set of behaviors, but also develops the most complex explanations for the cause–effect sequences. These latter explanations of the cause–effect sequence are the essence of theory building. Much of the work of childhood is theory building and testing, and this process continues throughout the developmental sequence. Most people have a multitude of theories to explain the events in their lives and the lives of other people. A theory is a viewpoint or perspective, a way of looking at causality or the relationship between things. When theory is defined in

C. R. SNYDER AND ROBERT N. HARRIS • Department of Psychology, University of Kansas, Lawrence, KS 66045.   CAROL E. FORD • Department of Psychology, University of Missouri, Columbia, MO 65211.

these terms, even the most staunchly atheoretical people must be included in the human fold of theorizers. This is especially the case when people attempt to cope with the negative events in life. Theory is the very stuff by which life events and coping are defined.

EXAMPLES OF NEGATIVE LIFE EVENTS AND COPING

Having argued that theory is central in the processes of coping with negative life events, we would like to take a route that may be surprising to the reader. Namely, we will begin by presenting a series of case-histories. Such case histories serve to highlight the diversity of negative life events and coping endeavors, they vividly illustrate the real-life problems and solutions that are experienced by people and those who seek to help them, and lastly, they provide a rich context from which we can examine relevant definitions. These examples are fictitious, although practicing clinicians may find the vignettes to be familiar.

Case #1: Glory Days

Jack is much older looking than his 32 years. A single man, Jack has "given up on life." Jack says that he just can't seem to shake the bad breaks. "If I could just get a break" is a frequent phrase for Jack; he utters it to the guy on the next barstool, his landlady, and even his mother. The worst break of all appears to have been his inability to fulfill his life aspiration of becoming a professional baseball player. A pitcher, Jack was the star of his high school baseball team. His high school accomplishments took him to college, where he dropped out before the end of his second year. He found the competition to be too stiff, both on the ballfield and in the classroom.

Since age 20, Jack has had a series of manual labor jobs, and no relationships other than an occasional "one night stand." In recent years, he has become increasingly disinterested in relating to other people, except to recount his hardluck story. According to Jack, people don't seem to be very sympathetic to this story.

"I can remember my high school days," recounts Jack, "and I was so full of energy. I really got excited about things, and I felt I was going somewhere. That's why people noticed me. I had a future." This tale of an energetic past was told in a monotonic, self-effacing manner. The Bruce Springsteen songs about hard times are said to have special meaning to Jack, although he thinks there is too much hope in Springsteen's music. This music used to give Jack some sense of energy, but even it no longer was satisfying. Jack appeared depressed, although when asked about this, he said he hated the term.

These are the initial facts about Jack. He said he had no future, and the past was an ugly reminder of his failure. All of this information was given by Jack on the night that he was brought to the crisis intervention unit of a medical center after attempting suicide by the ingestion of sleeping pills.

Case #2: It's Over

Mary is a second semester freshman at a large Midwestern university. She notes the following events in an intake interview at a psychological clinic.

MARY: It's happened again . . .

INTERVIEWER: What's happened?

MARY (sobbing, but trying to regain her composure): I've been dumped. I thought that Ronnie was different.

INTERVIEWER: Who is Ronnie? Just slow down, and tell me what has happened.

MARY: Ronnie is my boyfriend. He's a sophomore. I've been dating him ever since I met him at a dorm party last August. I really need him. . . I love him. . . (breaks down crying). He's just been everything to me. We go everywhere together. I thought he was Mister Right. I mean, you know, he was so special. We were going to get married. Well, we never talked about it, but I just kind of hoped we would someday. What am I going to do? . . . (crying). I'm really lost, that's why I came in here today. I don't have any friends. I didn't think I needed anything but Ronnie. Why did he leave me?

INTERVIEWER: Can you tell me how he left you?

MARY: He said that we needed to talk, so I said 'sure.' Well, then he tells me this whole story about how I've just smothered him. And, he's just a regular guy. Doesn't want to get that serious now. Just have some good times. Said we were too tight . . . worse than being married. He even accused me of being dependent on him for too much.

INTERVIEWER: Are you?

MARY: Oh I don't know, what am I going to do now? I'm so alone. . . . (crying)

INTERVIEWER: What are you going to do?

MARY (Avoiding the question): Men always end up dumping on me. It hurts. . . I hurt. Why do they do it? Why did Ronnie leave me? Why? I can't even think straight. Please, please help me.

INTERVIEWER (repeating question): But, what are you going to do?

MARY: Oh, what I've done before when this happens. I'll throw myself into my studies and forget about men . . . (in a small voice) At least for a while.

INTERVIEWER: OK, let's talk about all of this more. . .

Case #3: The Survivor

It was a snowy and icy day when Jan had her car accident. Driving home after visiting her parents for Thanksgiving, her Subaru smashed into the side of a semi that had jack-knifed in front of her. Although she survived the wreck, she experienced extensive injuries, the most serious of which resulted in the amputation of her legs below the knee. Her recovery was long and painful, and there was some question whether Jan would resume her career as a social worker.

From the moment that Jan was brought into the emergency room, she insisted on looking at her crushed lower legs. She screamed at first because of the pain, but later cried just as hard when she learned that she would lose her legs. As the recovery period went into a few days, Jan became extremely interested, almost fascinated with the accident. She asked to see the police photographs of the wreck. Her smashed Subaru was difficult to recognize, and Jan's parents and friends were worried that this "morbid" preoccupation with viewing the wrecked auto would only make her suffering worse. When Jan had recovered sufficiently to travel, she asked to see the actual wreckage of her car. As with the pictures, she scrutinized the wrecked car, and especially the driver's front seat, very carefully. She even asked to talk with the state trooper who arrived at the scene of the accident. He told her, "Lady, I don't know how you survived that accident. I looked at that wreck, and said to myself 'that person is dead.' You are awfully lucky." Jan's response was "I know."

Thereafter, Jan talked of how others had not been as fortunate as she. "The cemeteries are full of accident victims, and I'm not one. Sure, I'm sorry about my legs and all, but I'll make it OK. I just feel lucky to be here." Subsequently, Jan's continued recovery was built on her basic perception that she "was lucky to be alive."

Case #4: The Booze Held Me Back

If it weren't for the bottle, Ray, a 47-year-old salesman, says that his life would be a huge success. Passed over repeatedly for the promotion from a territorial salesman to district manager, Ray felt stuck in his job. And although he admitted his discomfort with the seemingly endless sales pitches that he had to make to the druggists at every store (large and small) in his territory, he really didn't think that was the problem. Because, fortified with a few drinks of gin, he could do his job. However, Ray did report that he was drinking more now than ever before. In fact, he thought that his drinking had become a sufficient problem that he needed to talk with someone about it.

Ray began to talk with his wife about his drinking problem. This was exceedingly difficult, because he felt like a failure in his job and generally inadequate in his role as a husband. His wife, who had long wanted to talk things out, was delighted at this turn of events. She told him that he didn't have to be a district manager for her to love him. She even encouraged him to get a job where he wouldn't feel on the spot so much. Surely, she argued, that there must be jobs where he wouldn't feel so much performance pressure.

This husband and wife communication came to an end one evening when Ray watched a television production of Arthur Miller's "Death of a Salesman." Ray declared at the end that "Willie Loman was a weak man." The unsaid statement was that Ray wasn't like Willie Loman. Ray vowed that he would succeed in his sales job, and thereafter stopped talking with his wife. The bottle became his friend again. It was, to hear Ray, his major flaw. He would stop soon, and then everyone would see what he could really do.

The aforementioned details about Ray were told by his wife at a support group for relatives of alcoholics. At last record, Ray's drinking continued, but he steadfastly refused to talk with anyone, including his wife, about his problems.

NEGATIVE LIFE EVENTS AND COPING: THE INSIDE VIEW

In developing definitions of negative life events and coping, we believe that the perceptual process should play a central role. This conclusion is derived from examining how people actually define negative life events and coping and from considering the simplicity and power of such an analysis.

Negative Life Events

For our purposes, a *negative life event* is defined as an incident, or a sequence of incidents, that is perceived as being the cause (or primary antecedent) of physical and (or) psychological pain. All other factors being equal (e.g., controlling for coping), a more negative life event will be perceived as causing greater pain.

Consider each of our case histories in this regard. For Jack ("Glory Days"), the protagonist appears to view his early college period as a time where his inability to perform in the athletic arena (and perhaps the classroom) "caused" him to experience a psychological pain that endured over the years. For an outsider, it may be difficult to understand how such incidents could result in such trauma. This is a good example of how *in the eyes of the perceiver,* there is a recognizable set of experiences that generated considerable pain, whereas an observer may not truly understand this perception. Another aspect of this example is that the critical incidents happened 12 years earlier, and yet for the protagonist, these perceptions were still a driving source of pain. Logically, over time one might expect a negative life event to recede from perceptual vividness and accompanying pain, but one must "step into the shoes" of the person to test this inference. (One of the strengths of traditional psychoanalytic therapy was that the therapist is taught to be open to the fact that an event occurring years earlier may nevertheless play a central role in current functioning.)

In the case history of Mary ("It's Over"), the negative life event appears to be the boyfriend's breaking up with the protagonist. Although it may be tempting to dismiss this as a fairly typical response by college freshmen, the phenomenology of the protagonist may suggest otherwise. Dismissive statements, such as "Oh, she'll live through it," or "There are other fish in the sea" miss the point. For those who are familiar with the all too high rate of suicide among college students, as well as the number of breakup-related injuries, the "realness" of the pain is this case history must be taken seriously.

For Jan ("The Survivor"), the negative life event is the car accident that resulted in the amputation of her lower legs. During the early stages after the accident, Jan experienced intense physical pain and feelings of anger, loss, and general dysphoria about the magnitude of her injuries. Thereafter, because of Jan's coping strategies, the perception of the physical seriousness of her injuries and the general psychological disturbance abated. This case history illustrates how a physical incident can elicit a psychological response (pain and coping).

The last case history was of Ray ("The Booze Held Me Back"). Here, there does not appear to be one clearly identifiable incident that may be labeled the negative life event. Ray invokes his drinking as the cause of his problem, and it is undoubtedly the case that such a history of drinking has resulted in enormous pain. However, one also senses that Ray's discomfort in making the salesman pitch, and his possible shyness, may also represent the recurring negative events that drive him to drink.

Several points are worth highlighting in these comments on the case histories. In each case, the protagonists have personal theories or perspectives about the cause–effect sequences that have operated in their lives. Such personal theories are based on assumptions about reality; moreover, these assumptions serve to guide the way that people perceive the events in their lives. The idea that one's basic assumptions mold the perception of reality is not a new one, however. Adler (in Ansbacher & Ansbacher, 1964) called such assumptions "guiding fictions"; other writers have suggested similar ideas, including Bowlby's (1969) "world models", Epstein's (1984) "self-theory", and Marris' (1975) "structures of meaning" (see also Janoff-Bulman in this volume for an excellent discussion of people's assumptive worlds).

The persons described in the case histories, like the rest of us, have minitheories about why they are the way they are. In fact, should these persons ever reach the interview setting with a professional helper, the helpers will attempt to have the clients articulate their theories. What is obvious in this analysis is that idiosyncratic perception is a key in unraveling a person's theory. What may be a relatively benign event for one person, may be a negative life event of major proportions for another. Thus, the "size" of the negative life event depends as much upon the perception of the person as it does on some objective rating of the severity.

The perceptually based analysis also provides information concerning the temporal location of the negative life event (i.e., the precipitating event may be minutes, days, or years ago). Indeed, people appear to operate with a simple linear model about their lives by ascribing a previous cause to their pain. Although the temporal link may not follow strict notions of causality, these association-based perceptions take on near causal status when people develop their theories about their negative life events. As such, negative life events sometimes may be easily discerned by both the actor and observer (e.g., the case of Jan's automobile accident); however, in some instances the negative life event may be rather vague (e.g., Ray's drinking or sales pitch).

Coping

Coping represents attempts to lessen the physical and psychological pain that are associated with negative life events. All other things being equal (e.g., controlling for the severity of the negative life event), more successful coping will be perceived as producing less pain.

This definition of coping can be applied to our case histories. Whether Jack's suicide attempt was made in an effort to end his perceived suffering, or, to obtain support/secondary gain, in either case his perception probably was that his behavior would help assuage his pain. Similarly, in the case of Mary, she sought professional help as a means of coping. Her perception must have been that therapy might help to ease the pain she experienced due to her boyfriend's untimely departure.

Jan appears to have invoked an "I'm lucky to be alive" coping strategy. After experiencing the physical and psychological pain associated with her leg amputations, Jan accentuated how she was alive where most others would not be. Her perception turned from a grieving one to a hopeful one.

For Ray, the coping strategy appeared to be "blaming the bottle" and continued drinking. By drinking he appeared to lessen the pain associated with his inability to perform the necessary salesman-like behaviors. Ray seemingly perceived his drinking as a way of coping with his negative life events, but one wonders whether it did not just add to his pain. This is a case where the coping strategy may work in the short term, but backfire in the long run.

In these case histories, it would be instructive to ask explicitly each of the protagonists "How are you coping with your problems?" The good professional interviewer typically asks this question in order to get an idea of the client's perception about his or her coping. As may be obvious also, when one asks another to make his or her coping strategy explicit, then one also learns of that person's implicit theory of how coping behaviors diminish the pain of negative life events.

NEGATIVE LIFE EVENTS AND COPING: THE OUTSIDE VIEW

To this point, we have shown how laypersons use theory in their daily lives, especially in regard to negative life events and coping. In this analysis, we have emphasized the role of the protagonist's perceptual stance in defining the nature of the negative life event and coping. Obviously, such an analysis reflects the insider's view—what it is like from the viewpoint of the person undergoing the negative life event. Another perspective is also possible, however. In reading these case histories, for example, were you beginning to apply your own frameworks in order to understand these people? The answer is probably yes. Indeed, it is difficult to refrain from using one's personal perspectives when listening to other people. It is simply human nature to apply one's own perspectives to the lives of other people. The outsider view begins to color the insider view.

The definitions of negative life events and coping that are posited in the previous section apply to the insider and the outsider. For the professional, whether the prediliction is toward applied or empirical work, the key is to clearly articulate one's guiding theoretical perspective. Professional persons in the mental health field are taught various theoretical perspectives during their graduate education. These theoretical perspectives then serve to drive their evaluations of how people experience negative life events and cope with them. Like the insider's theory, which is specially derived for the person by the person, that is, tends to be idiosyncratic, the outsider's theories vary from one observer to the next. Whatever the outsider's theoretical perspective, however, it tends to be applied across people. Also, theoretical perspectives attempt to define cause–effect relationships that have predictive utility. The predictive utility pertains to an accurate understanding of the phenomenology and to overt behaviors of people undergoing a cause–effect sequence. Once an outsider's general theory about people is developed, refinements can be made in order to accomodate individual differences in the cause–effect chain; moreover, the situational subcomponents of the cause portion of the cause–effect chain can be differentiated. (This is the person-by-situation analysis that is increasingly gaining favor in psychology.)

Outsiders' theories about other people are based on assumptions about oneself and people in general. Just as these assumptions influence our perception of reality as it pertains to us, these assumptions also drive our perception of reality in others. The hallmark of science, however, is that the assumptions are made explicit as the outside observer attempts to explain and predict human behavior. When the assumptions are integrated into a larger theoretical framework, the outsider has a paradigm (see Kuhn, 1962) for examining other people and their lives.

The Power of Theoretical Perspective

Theoretical perspective can generate some fascinatingly accurate insights. Consider the following case reported by psychoanalyst Theodore Reik (1948):

> One session at this time took the following course. After a few sentences about the uneventful day, the patient fell into a long silence. She assured me that nothing was in her thoughts. Silence from me. After many minutes she complained about a toothache. She told me that she had been to the dentist yesterday; he had given her an injection and then had pulled a wisdom tooth. The spot was hurting again. New and longer silence. She pointed to my bookcase in the corner and said, "There's a book standing on its head." Without the slightest hesitation and in a reproachful voice I said, "But why did you not tell me that you had an abortion?" (p. 263)

From psychoanalytic theory regarding symbolism, Reik interpreted the upside down book as the inverted fetus and the toothpulling as the abortion. It was the theoretical perspective that facilitated this excellent piece of detective work.

Another psychoanalytic example may again illustrate the power of theory. Although the source (and therefore the veracity) of this example is not known to the authors, this vignette was making the rounds of clinical psychology graduate students in the late 1960s. The story goes as follows. A young man was seeing a psychoanalytically oriented psychotherapist. His recurring problem was a rash around his rectum. A long period of psychotherapy ensued in which the analyst interpreted the rash as anal retentiveness (the infantile stage in the Freudian approach characterized by a narcissistic interest in retaining feces, and a stubborness of sorts). At the beginning of one session, the man came in and said that he was cured. The rash was gone. The analyst was pleased, thinking that his theoretical perspective had helped the young man to correctly interpret his problem. However, the young man had a different view, as he noted, "Oh, my new girlfriend and I were taking a shower, and when we got out, she told me I hadn't washed off the soapy water from my butt. So, I washed it off. She also told me to be sure to dry off real good. Ever since then, I wash and dry off completely, and the rash has gone away."

The Fable of the Blind Men and the Elephant

The previous vignette reminds one of the Hindu fable of the blind men and the elephant. Six blind men approach an elephant in order to learn more about it. The first man touches the side of the elephant, and concludes that an elephant is like a wall. The second man feels the tusk, and deduces that the elephant is like a spear. A third man grabs the squirming trunk, and resolves that the elephant is like a snake. The fourth man reaches out and pats the huge leg, thereby determining that the elephant is like a tree. The fifth man touches the ear, and thus infers that the elephant is like a fan. Finally, the sixth man seizes the swinging tail, and judges an elephant to be like a rope. And, so the story goes, each man vehemently argued for the truth of his perception.

The obvious conclusion here is that one's theoretical perspectives can be very seductive. In the extent to which the practicing clinician or the researcher applies his or her theoretical perspective selectively to the data so that the theory is confirmed, then the theory naturally becomes "proven." Although it is tempting to discount the theory-driven approach because it may either give incorrect conclusions (e.g. the rectal rash story), or may lead the theoretician to validate his or her viewpoint in a self-fulfilling prophecy, we do not advocate such a pessimistic position. Rather, it is our belief that the process of theory development and testing against all the relevant data is the essence of the scientific approach. Eventually, some theories or models are revised. Happily, it is survival of the fittest in terms of what theories serve to best fit the data over time (see Kuhn, 1962, on "paradigm clashes").

A theoretical perspective is like a flashlight that we can shine on the data. There is obviously much that is dark and unknown about human behavior. In our estimation, however, we are not at the point of developing large-scale, comprehensive theories in the behavioral sciences. Although descriptive taxonomies are within the realm of possibility, we presently are more qualified to posit minitheories about some aspect of negative life events and the coping process. Used properly, such minitheories will guide us in perceiving portions of human behavior. Instead of the entire elephant, we would be well-advised to examine the various parts and know that we merely have hold of the trunk, leg, tail, ear, side, or tusk. Our theoretical flashlights can help us in this latter task.

REFERENCES

Ansbacher, H. L., & Ansbacher, R. R. (1964). *The individual psychology of Alfred Adler.* New York: Harper & Row

Bowlby, J. (1969). *Attachment and loss (Vol. 1): Attachment.* London: Hogarth.

Epstein, S. (1984). Controversial issues in emotion theory. In P. Shaver (Ed.), *Review of personality and social psychology: Emotions, relationships, and health* (pp. 64–88). Beverly Hills, CA: Sage.

Kuhn, T. S. (1962). *The structure of scientific revolutions.* Chicago, IL: University of Chicago Press.

Marris, P. (1975). *Loss and change.* Garden City, NY: Anchor/Doubleday.

Reik, T. (1948). *Listening with the third ear.* New York: Farrar, Straus, & Giroux.

II

Effort Expenditure Perspectives

For coping to occur, people must select a mode of response and somehow mobilize and sustain sufficient energy to pursue it. These facets of coping behavior—choice, intensity, and persistence—are the traditional topics that comprise the study of motivation.

The contribution of effort expenditure perspectives on coping is well illustrated by the first case example described in Chapter 1, the "Glory Days" case of Jack. During high school, Jack was a young man who felt like the world was at his fingertips. His success as a pitcher was the key factor leading his high school baseball team to the state championship two years in a row. His achievement on the playing fields brought him recognition and popularity among his peers. It also brought him opportunity when he graduated; Jack saw the full baseball scholarship he received as first a step toward his lifelong dream of playing professional ball.

Although not the star academically that he was athletically, Jack was a solid student in high school. It caught him by surprise, then, when he failed his first midterms at the university. Jack redoubled his efforts for the rest of the term; for the first time, doing well in the classroom seemed important to him. At the end of the semester, however, Jack had failed three classes, and his attitude toward scholastics changed dramatically. He told his teammates that the coursework at the university was unreasonable for someone who was going to be a professional athlete. Jack stopped studying after his first semester; the only subsequent surprise was that he somehow squeaked by with a passing grade in one of his classes.

Jack's comments about his future as a professional baseball player became the source of private derision among his teammates. Faced with stiffer competition than he had known in high school, Jack's success on the pitcher's mound dropped significantly. He continued to attend all the team practices through the Spring of his second year, trying to recapture his previous success, but his efforts were to no avail. Finally, faced with his fourth semester of failure in the classroom and on the ballfield, Jack left the university before the end of the term.

In the years that followed, Jack supported himself with a series of manual labor jobs, losing each of them after several months. Jack had trouble maintaining friendships and relationships as well. He often talked about his high school years, his problems at the university, and his lost dream of playing professional ball. Although people seemed initially sympathetic, before long they would begin to avoid him. When by himself, Jack spent most of his time thinking about what had gone wrong. As he lost friends and jobs over the years, the events of his life seemed to strengthen his belief that he was a loser.

Finally, at the age of 32, Jack was found unconscious with an empty bottle of sleeping pills by his bed. He was rushed to the medical center. When Jack's acquaintances heard what had happened, many felt his unsuccessful attempt at suicide might at least bring Jack the professional help they felt he needed.

The "Glory Days" case example depicts the important role that effort expenditure factors play in understanding responses to negative life events. This aspect of coping is addressed in the chapters in this section. In Chapter 2, Thomas Wills focuses on help-seeking efforts as a coping mechanism. Wills first reviews epidemiological findings on the prevalence and predictors of help-seeking. He notes, for example, that this behavior occurs frequently, and that people seem to show a preference for informal sources of help. Wills explores theoretical frameworks on help-seeking, with an emphasis on a functional approach to understanding this form of coping. He argues that in general the type of help that is sought may depend on the specific supportive functions (e.g., informational support) that are sought. In the "Glory Days" case, for example, Jack may have sought esteem support, motivational support, or even instrumental support in his attempts to talk about his life to any available audience. At the endpoint of the example, Jack may have given up completely; on the other hand, his suicide attempt may have been a means of turning to professional sources of help.

In Chapter 3, Rex Wright argues that a motivational analysis of responses to aversive situations may provide a useful alternative to traditional stress and coping theories. Wright reviews recent work on the determinants of motivational arousal, and draws on this research to develop predictions regarding physiological arousal, effort, and perceptions of stressors when people face a potential negative outcome. He asserts, for example, that both physiological arousal and perceptions of the aversiveness of a stressor should show a nonmonotonic relationship with perceptions of the difficulty of avoiding a negative outcome. To examine his predictions, Wright reviews relevant research concerned with cardiovascular reactivity and appraisals of potential negative outcomes, and concludes that the evidence is generally consistent with his motivational analysis. Wright might suggest in the case of Jack, for example, that the aversiveness of his experiences grew over the years because avoiding more failures seemed increasingly difficult.

In Chapter 4, Carol Ford and Jack Brehm discuss the effects of failure on subsequent motivation and performance. In recent years, learned helplessness theory has provided one of the dominant theoretical frameworks in this area. Ford and Brehm discuss this framework, concluding that to date it has raised more troublesome issues than provided understanding of failure effects. They argue that Brehm's recent work on the determinants of motivation suggests that responses to failure may be understood in terms of the effects of that outcome on the anticipated difficulty of subsequent tasks in conjunction with an individual's perceived ability and the upper limit to how hard he or she is willing to work for a given goal. In the case of Jack, for example, Ford and Brehm might argue that he gave up on academics sooner than athletics because his sense of ability and the amount of effort he was willing to invest were higher in the latter domain.

Finally, in Chapter 5, Tom Pyszczynski and Jeff Greenberg discuss the role of self-focused attention and self-regulatory processes in depressive responses to stressful life events. Pyszczynski and Greenberg review research that suggests that depressed individuals exhibit a unique pattern of self-focus; for example, depressives appear to persist in self-focus following failure longer than nondepressed individuals. To account for the maladaptive self-focusing style of depressives, Pyszczynski and Greenberg present a self-regulatory model; they argue that depressive episodes may be initiated when people experience a major loss and become stuck in a self-regulatory cycle that produces, exacerbates, and maintains depressive reaction. Pyszczynski and Greenberg thus might suggest that depression was a predictable outcome in the case of Jack; unable to disengage from his desire to achieve a career in baseball, Jack became stuck in a maladaptive cycle.

Taken together, as is illustrated in the "Glory Days" example, the perspectives presented in this section provide different frameworks for understanding the role that effort expenditure issues play in the coping process.

2

Help-Seeking as a Coping Mechanism

THOMAS ASHBY WILLS

INTRODUCTION

This chapter discusses how individuals can cope with negative life events through seeking help from other persons. When presented with adverse or demanding events, people can respond by seeking help from a husband or wife, from family members or relatives, or from members of larger community networks. Individuals may obtain help primarily within the context of informal social support; they may seek help from formal agencies or professional helpers; or they may combine formal and informal sources of help. In this chapter I discuss the variety of supportive resources that are potentially available to distressed persons, suggest some propositions about factors that influence help-seeking behavior, and delineate some functional mechanisms through which help-seeking may be related to adjustment and well-being.

The theoretical discussion in this chapter is based on an analysis of the coping demands presented by negative life events (Cohen & Wills, 1985; Wills & Langner, 1980). Stress is posited to develop when an event occurs that has important implications for an individual's adjustment, and when the demands posed by the event(s) exceed the current coping abilities and resources of the individual. Negative events are assumed to

THOMAS ASHBY WILLS • Departments of Psychology and Epidemiology, Ferkauf Graduate School of Psychology and Albert Einstein College of Medicine, 1300 Morris Park Avenue, Bronx, NY 10461.

be related to stress and psychological symptomatology because of several factors that are present in commonly studied life events: they create a strong threat to the individual's self-esteem and self-image; evoke perceptions of uncertainty or lack of self-efficacy; and present a need for continued problem-solving efforts to deal with changed conditions created by the event. A stress-coping model (Cohen & Wills, 1985; Wills & Shiffman, 1985) posits that psychological distress is reduced or ameliorated by coping processes or resources that counter the adverse consequences of the stressor. If a life event has a strong negative impact on self-esteem, for example, then effective helping resources would be those that served to enhance a person's feelings of self-worth; if an event has a major impact on uncertainty or confusion about appropriate coping efforts, then helping resources that provide cognitive guidance and assistance with appraising the stressor and the coping options would, in theory, be most effective. In general it can be assumed that a given life event probably creates multiple coping needs (Eckenrode, 1984; Pearlin, 1985); thus adjustment in the long term should be related to the number of coping abilities and resources applied by an individual in combination with the variety of helping functions and resources available from other persons.

Research on help-seeking is an area where several theoretical approaches are currently serving to guide investigations in laboratory and community settings. Studies of help-seeking behavior have been conceptualized in terms of instrumental or reinforcement theory (e.g., Gross & McMullen, 1983), social-psychological theories of equity or reciprocity (e.g., Greenberg, 1980), or the theory of social comparison and self-esteem maintenance (DePaulo, 1982; Wills, 1983). In considering the social context of help-seeking, theories of relationships (Clark, 1983) and social support functions (Cohen & Wills, 1985) are relevant for a fuller understanding of the help-seeking process. From a clinical standpoint, help-seeking may be construed within the framework of general coping theory (Lazarus & Folkman, 1984; Prochaska & DiClemente, 1985) and models of formal helping relationships (Goldfried, 1982; Wills, 1982b). As an avenue toward integration of this diverse body of work, in the present chapter I propose a functional analysis for conceptualizing the coping goals of help-seeking behavior (cf. Stone & Neale, 1984; Wills, 1985). Together with the background of research on factors that affect help-seeking, the functional analysis leads to a more specific model of help-seeking and suggests some commonalities in the supportive processes that occur in both informal social support and formal helping relationships.

The focus in this chapter is on psychological help-seeking for life events such as divorce, family problems, or job difficulties.[1] In the sections that follow, I begin by discussing epidemiological evidence on the prevalence of help-seeking in community settings. Then I discuss theoretical frameworks that have been applied to research on help-seeking. In following sections I develop functional analyses of processes involved in coping with negative events through help-seeking from (a) informal sources and (b) from professional helpers. In a final section I discuss some theoretical and empirical issues for further research on help-seeking as a coping mechanism.

PREVALENCE AND PREDICTORS OF HELP-SEEKING

Prevalence

For a broad view of the characteristics of help-seeking in community settings, data on prevalence rates of help-seeking behavior in various contexts are presented in Table 1. This selective summary focuses on studies that obtained data on more than one type of problem and/or type of help-seeking. The problem types vary widely, from minor worries ("If something is on your mind that is bothering you or worrying you") or times of continued distress ("How people face that unhappy period in their lives"—both from Veroff, Kulka, & Douvan, 1981), to indexes of major life crises (e.g., "The most stressful event experienced during the previous year"—McCrae, 1984). In most studies the samples were large and representative of either local or national populations, and the community studies are complemented by several projects that investigated help-seeking in specialized populations of particular interest. Overall, these studies show that help-seeking for psychological distress occurs with appreciable frequency in the community.

In traditional psychiatric epidemiology, the basic research design examines the percentage of defined cases who receive some type of formal treatment. In this research, a *case* is defined as an individual experiencing distress (i.e., depression/anxiety/demoralization) at a level comparable to that of clinical populations, as indicated either by self-report symptom inventories or by psychiatric interviews. In general-population studies the prevalence of symptomatology is found to be approximately 21% of the population, with the great majority of com-

---

[1]I do not address literature on medical help-seeking (see Kirscht, 1983; Ostrove & Baum, 1983). Research on seeking medical consultation for disease symptoms is an important area, but is less relevant for research on coping with psychological distress; although of course a major illness occurring to the self or a family member can be a severe stressor.

Table 1. Prevalence Rates of Help-Seeking, Community Studies

Reference	Sample	Problem type	Help-seeking index type	Rate(s)
Dooley & Catalano (1984)	Community $N = 500$	Emotional problem, help considered	Point prevalence (3 month)[a]	29% Formal / 46% Informal
Glidewell et al. (1983)	Specialized (teachers) $N = 121$	General teaching problems	Point prevalence (1 day)[b]	0.44/day Requests / 2.62/day Experience Swapping
Greenberg et al. (1983)	National $N = 60,000$	All crimes	Coping (used for event)	33% Formal (police)
Link & Dohrenwend (1980)	Community, 11 studies	Clinical maladjustment, all disorders	Lifetime prevalence[c]	27% Formal
McCrae (1984)	Community (elderly) $N = 255$	Stressful life event (most severe, 1 year)	Coping (used for event)	45% Formal / 68% Sought support
Norcross & Prochaska (1986)	Community (female) $N = 94$	Worst period of distress (3 years)	Coping (used for event)	28% Formal
	Specialized (therapists) $N = 191$	same	same	42% Formal

Study	Sample	Problem	Help-seeking index type	Results
Stone & Neale (1984)	Community (married) $N = 120$	Daily event (most bothersome)	Coping (used for event)[d]	15% Emotional support
Veroff et al. (1981)	National $N = 2,264$	Worries	Coping (used for problem)	2% Formal / 35% Informal
	same	Periods of unhappiness	same	2% Formal / 28% Informal
	same	Major life crises	same	3% Formal Only / 45% Informal Only / 39% Formal + Informal
Wilcox & Birkel (1983)	Specialized (divorced females) $N = 100$	Minor worries	Coping (used for problem)	9% Formal / 38% Informal
	same	Persistent depression	same	40% Formal / 27% Informal
	same	Any problem	Point prevalence (1 week)[e]	60% Sought Help

Note. For help-seeking index type, point prevalence = percent of cases seeking help during specified time period (1 day–3 months); lifetime prevalence = percent of cases who ever get help; coping index = percent of cases who seek help for specified problem. For rates of help-seeking, formal help = psychologist, psychiatrist, social worker, other mental health professional; informal help = spouse, relative, friend, other community member.

[a] Multiwave study, average over 12 waves.
[b] Repeated measures study, average over 10 days.
[c] Multistudy review, median over studies.
[d] Repeated measures study, average over 21 days.
[e] Repeated measures study, average over three 1-week periods.

munity cases characterized as neurosis or personality disorder (Neugebauer, Dohrenwend, & Dohrenwend, 1980). Link and Dohrenwend
(1980) noted that within this distressed population, the median percentage of individuals ever in treatment with members of the mental health
professions is 27%, that is, 73% had never sought professional help.[2]
These data, then, indicate that among the group of community-residing
persons experiencing serious psychological distress, some seek professional help but the majority do not come to the attention of professional
helpers.

More recent studies that have measured formal and informal help-
seeking present a somewhat different perspective, indicating relatively
high rates of help-seeking from informal sources such as spouse, friends,
and family. The difference between rates for formal and informal help-
seeking is substantial when open ended interview questions about coping
with worry or unhappiness are used (Veroff *et al.*, 1981) and narrow
somewhat when scenarios or recent help-seeking actions are used, but
even the smallest differences show approximately 2 : 1 ratios of infor-
mal:formal help-seeking.[3] Data on major life crises (McCrae, 1984; Veroff *et al.*, 1981) show that persons tend to utilize both formal *and* informal helping resources, but the data indicate that 45% to 55% of stressed
persons rely primarily on informal support. Studies examining help-
seeking for different types of problems suggest a trend for help-seeking
to increase with problem severity (Veroff *et al.*, 1981; Wilcox & Birkel,
1983) but there is little direct evidence on this issue from general-population studies.

Several studies are particularly informative because they obtained
comparative data on different types of help-seeking and other coping
mechanisms. Glidewell, Tucker, Todt, and Cox (1983) found in an observational study that the rate of explicit help-seeking requests was relatively low, but the rate of exchanging stories about problematic situations
(which the authors construed as a type of indirect help-seeking) was
substantial, producing approximately a 1 : 6 ratio of direct/indirect help-

[2]The authors suggested that this rate was probably an overestimate because the available
11 studies were dominated by urban research settings, where psychological services are
more available. Recent national-sample studies indicate rates closer to 20%, a figure that
the authors suggested was probably more representative.
[3]It should be noted that rates for formal and informal help-seeking are not necessarily
directly comparable because they may index different degrees of effort. Questions about
informal help only ask whether the respondent has talked with someone about a problem,
without assessing whether the time, effort, or involvement are comparable to those in
seeking professional help. Thus there is some reason for caution in comparing rates of
formal and informal help-seeking.

seeking. Norcross and Prochaska (1986) compared help-seeking rates in samples of female respondents and found that among a sample of laypersons 28% had sought formal treatment to cope with an episode of depression, whereas among a sample of professionals (clinical psychologists and counselors) 42% had sought formal help to cope with a depressive episode of their own. Studies that compared the relative use of help-seeking and other coping mechanisms (McRae, 1984; Norcross & Prochaska, in press; Prochaska & DiClemente, 1985; Stone & Neale, 1984; Veroff *et al.*, 1981) are virtually unanimous in finding help-seeking (primarily from informal sources) to be the first-ranked coping mechanism for psychological distress, compared with alternatives such as direct action, acceptance, cognitive mechanisms, or reinforcement control. The exception is a repeated-measure study by Stone and Neale (1984) that examined how people coped with the most bothersome problem of a particular day. This study found coping mechanisms such as problem solving and acceptance used most frequently over the range of daily problems, but informal support seeking was employed with appreciable frequency, used to 15% of the daily problems recorded.

To summarize, the evidence indicates that help-seeking behavior occurs with appreciable frequency in community settings. For coping with major life events, most individuals use some type of support during the course of the coping effort. There is an observed preference for informal sources of help, and many persons experiencing clinical-level maladjustment do not seek formal treatment (Link & Dohrenwend, 1980). The implication is that many distressed persons cope with emotional problems through self-help (Norcross & Prochaska, in press) and through informal social support (Cohen & Wills, 1985).

Predictors of Help-Seeking

Research on the predictors of help-seeking initially focused on demographic correlates (Gourash, 1978). From literature consisting primarily of cross-sectional studies that compared clinic and nonclinic samples, a fairly consistent set of findings emerged (see DePaulo, 1982; Fischer, Winer, & Abramowitz, 1983). These studies typically show help-seeking for psychological problems to be more likely among persons with college education; among younger and middle-aged persons (compared with elderly); among females; among divorced persons (compared with married or single); and among persons with no religious affiliation. Retrospective studies of community samples have provided general confirmation of these findings (Greenley & Mechanic, 1976; Kessler, Brown, & Bowman, 1981; Veroff *et al.*, 1981). Research on attitudes toward help-seeking has identified dimensions such as general favorability toward help-seeking, interpersonal openness, stigma tolerance, and confidence in mental health professionals (see Fischer *et al.*, 1983). Scores on these attitudinal dimensions are generally consistent with demographic findings on help-seeking, but to date there has been no direct test of the ability of attitudinal measures to predict help-seeking in a community sample.[4] Recent research on more specific predictors of help-seeking, bearing directly on a stress-coping model, are discussed in the following (see note 1).

Life Stress. Life stress has been implicated as an important factor in the onset of depression (Lewinsohn, Hoberman, Teri, & Hautzinger, 1985; Norcross & Prochaska, in press) and physical illness (Dohrenwend & Dohrenwend, 1981), hence it is plausible to predict a relationship between negative life events and help-seeking. Although there has been little direct investigation of this issue, confirming evidence is provided by studies comparing clinic and nonclinic groups within college populations (Goodman, Sewell, & Jampol, 1984; Greenley & Mechanic, 1976; Ostrow, Dark, & Poulton, 1982), which show higher levels of negative events experienced by the clinic sample. A community study based on telephone interviews (Dooley & Catalano, 1984) found a positive correlation between measures of life stress and an index of help-seeking (primarily from informal sources), both measures being assessed retrospectively over a 3-month period. Thus, there is some evidence that help-seeking is prompted by negative life events that strain the coping resources of the individual.

Symptomatology Level. A stress-coping model predicts that the effect of life events on help-seeking is mediated by increased subjective distress. Clinic versus control comparisons typically show the clinic samples as scoring higher on measures of psychological symptomatology (Greenley & Mechanic, 1976; Mechanic, 1978; Ostrow *et al.*, 1982) but these studies do not consider the distressed individuals who do not appear in clinic samples. Community studies show current symptom levels related to retrospective reports of formal help-seeking in some studies (Dooley & Catalano, 1984; Veroff *et al.*, 1981) but not in others (Norcross & Prochaska, in press); however, the retrospective design is particularly insensitive for detecting any such effects that may exist.[5] Thus, there is no

[4]Retrospective studies of attitudinal dimensions (e.g., Greenley & Mechanic, 1976) are suspect in this regard because attitudes about psychotherapy are strongly influenced by participation in a therapeutic relationship (see Beutler, 1981). Thus retrospective reports concerning attitudes toward therapy could be strongly skewed.

[5]Dooley and Catalano (1984) actually found that life events and symptomatology measures made independent contributions to the help-seeking index; this may have been due to the use of a composite index that combined formal and informal help-seeking.

evidence to contradict the proposition that problem severity increases the probability of help-seeking; but there is no prospective study that would provide a conclusive test of the issue.

Social Comparison. If people evaluate their own symptomatology through comparison with other persons (Sanders, 1982; Wills, 1981), then help-seeking may be affected by social comparison processes. Indirect support for this proposition is provided by laboratory studies that manipulated the perceived normativeness of help-seeking, implying that it is either common or uncommon in the population (Broll, Gross, & Piliavin, 1974; Gross, Fisher, Nadler, Stiglitz, & Craig, 1979; Nadler & Porat, 1978; Tessler & Schwartz, 1972); these studies all found help-seeking to be increased when perceived normativeness was high. Using manipulated information about the prevalence of symptoms in the population, Snyder and Ingram (1983) found that among nonsymptomatic subjects, low-consensus information (i.e., the problem is relatively rare) increased help-seeking intentions, apparently because this comparison information increased the perceived seriousness of the problem. However, among subjects previously affected by the target symptom, high-consensus information (i.e., the problem is common) increased help-seeking, apparently by reducing the ego-threatening aspects of the symptom information. Thus there is evidence that social comparison may increase help-seeking if it causes persons to see their symptoms as more serious, and there is some support for the proposition that social comparison is used differently by distressed versus nondistressed persons (Gibbons, 1986; Wills, 1983).[6]

Social Support. A stress-coping model (Cohen & Wills, 1985) predicts that having a high level of informal social support will reduce help-seeking from professional agencies. Some confirmation for this is provided by the college studies, which show clinic samples as having lower levels of available functional support even though they typically do not differ on measures of total network size (Bosmajian & Mattson, 1980; Goodman *et al.*, 1984; Ostrow *et al.*, 1982). For more elaborate structural measures results are complex (see Hall & Wellman, 1985); some studies suggest that less formal help-seeking occurs in networks with greater density (McKinlay, 1973; Wilcox & Birkel, 1983), whereas other studies suggest more professional help-seeking when a network is low in reciprocity (Tolsdorf, 1976). Because functional support measures are most relevant for stress-buffering (Cohen & Wills, 1985), these will probably be directly related to symptom-based help-seeking.

---

[6]When social network members give opinions to the effect that physical symptoms are more serious (Sanders, 1982; Strohmer, Biggs, & McIntyre, 1984) then help-seeking intentions are increased, but this is a different issue.

Source of Help. Experimental studies show general convergence with epidemiological findings in showing that subjects have a preference for seeking help from friends (vs. strangers or professionals). This has been found in both scenario studies (Christensen & Magoon, 1974; Corrigan, 1978; DePaulo, 1978; Tinsley, St. Aubin, & Brown, 1982) and laboratory studies (Shapiro, 1980). Some data suggest that friends are preferred both because of instrumental concerns (availability) and ego-related concerns (self-disclosure, trustworthiness). When specific knowledge and competence for dealing with serious problems is relevant, professionals may be preferred for this reason (Corrigan, Brown, de St. Aubin, & Lucek, 1984).

Cost. A final variable relevant for some models is the cost of help-seeking. One type of effort-expenditure cost is *financial,* and although it can plausibly be predicted that greater economic expense for medical or psychological services would decrease help-seeking (Gourash, 1978; McKinlay, 1972), there is little direct evidence on this point. At present the only controlled study in the psychological area is a randomized trial of service utilization in health maintenance organizations (Manning, Wells, Duan, Newhouse, & Ware, 1984); this study indeed found that utilization of outpatient mental health services increased as out-of-pocket economic costs were reduced in various insurance plans. In addition to financial cost, some models of help-seeking suggest that *psychological* costs, such as perceived indebtedness or threat to self-esteem, may serve to deter help-seeking (DePaulo, 1982). Laboratory studies show reduced help-seeking in conditions where a help request would cause greater effort by, or interference with, the helper (DePaulo, 1978; DePaulo & Fisher, 1980), suggesting that potential help-seekers are influenced by considering the helper's perspective. Another psychological cost is the potential self-esteem threat for the help-seeker because of perceived inadequacy (DePaulo, 1982; Rosen, 1983). Evidence for this position is largely inferential, based on laboratory studies with variables such as helper-recipient similarity or anonymity of the help request (see Clark, 1983; DePaulo, 1982), and several studies suggest that ego concerns or helper costs may not influence help-seeking in the context of close relationships (Clark, 1984; Shapiro, 1980). Thus at present the role of self-esteem concerns in help-seeking is unresolved.

THEORETICAL FRAMEWORKS

Help-seeking has been approached in terms of several theoretical frameworks. General models have proposed a series of stages in help-seeking action (Fischer *et al.,* 1983; Gross & McMullen, 1983). The first stage involves the cognitive labeling of a behavior or situation as problematic, through processes of social comparison and attributions about the locus of the problem (Batson, O'Quin, & Pych, 1982; Snyder & Ingram, 1983) the individual perceives that the current situation is problematic and it is appropriate to seek help. Next is a decision making stage in which the individual gathers information about potential help, weighs the costs and benefits of different alternatives, and generates commitment to a course of action (Lemkau, Bryant, & Brickman, 1982; Prochaska & DiClemente, 1985). The third stage is the act of help-seeking, which is posited to be influenced by the type of problem and the anticipated consequences of help-seeking. The fourth stage involves the development of a helping relationship, with processes of feedback (Snyder, Ingram, & Newburg, 1982), therapeutic relationship (Wills, 1982a,b), and reactions to help (Fisher & Nadler, 1982). It has been posited that different processes may be relevant for help-seeking at different levels of distress, with everyday help-seeking primarily guided by informational needs and instrumental assistance whereas at a high level of distress, emotional needs and self-esteem maintenance are most relevant (Wills, 1983). The major postulates of specific models of help-seeking, with a brief critique, are noted in the following (see note 1).

Instrumental Theory

Instrumental models view help-seeking as a straightforward social learning process in which a need exists, the individual is aware from previous modeling or learning experiences that the need can be resolved through help from other persons, and thus individuals will make a help-seeking request when the need arises (e.g., Gross & McMullen, 1983). This perspective leads to research that focuses on the effectiveness of various types of help-seeking requests, or on ways in which persons can ingratiate themselves with a potential helper. The major issue for instrumental theories is the typical finding in laboratory studies that a substantial proportion of subjects do not seek help when they could readily do so (see DePaulo, 1982). Although instrumental theory can countenance a reduction in help-seeking that is attributable to high financial or effort-expenditure costs, it can not easily explain a low level of help requests in conditions where the apparent costs of help-seeking are minimal.

Reciprocity Theories

Several models based on equity or social exchange theory delineate reciprocity concerns that create potential psychological costs of help-seeking. Equity theory predicts that the perception of indebtedness is a consequence of receiving help, because the recipient has a normative obligation to reciprocate the help at some time in the future (Greenberg, 1980). Several laboratory studies supported this model by showing that help-seeking was reduced in conditions where the help could not be reciprocated (Greenberg & Shapiro, 1971; Morris & Rosen, 1973). Although reciprocity theory had heuristic value in pointing out the potential indebtedness created by a help-seeking request, it was not clear how help-seeking would be influenced in ongoing relationships where the participants had repeated opportunities for help-giving or -receiving interactions.

Esteem Theories

Several models proposed that a psychological cost of help-seeking may occur because the act of requesting help creates a perception of personal inadequacy that is aversive to the potential help-seeker (DePaulo, 1982; Rosen, 1983). Perceived inadequacy may occur because of individual beliefs about independent achievement, or through anticipated negative evaluation because of unfavorable comparison with other persons who maintain comparable performance without help. These models derive support from studies previously discussed that show help-seeking in laboratory settings to be influenced by esteem-related variables, such as the visibility of the help-seeking request or the similarity of helper and recipient, all of which are interpreted as affecting the potential esteem threat in a helping transaction (DePaulo, 1982; Fisher & Nadler, 1982). Although esteem theories are valuable for delineating potential psychological costs of help-seeking, it was not clear how these models could explain the relatively high levels of help-seeking for esteem-related personal problems that occur in natural settings.

Relationship Theory

Several models that focus on the relationship context of help-seeking have emphasized the distinctive characteristics of long-term relationships. Theories of close relationships (Clark, 1983; Clark & Mills, 1979) have proposed that norms applying to exchange-oriented relationships may not apply for communal relationships (e.g., with a wife or husband), where normative structure emphasizes concern for the other's welfare rather than strict reciprocity. Models of social network structure and functional social support (Wills, 1985) note that individuals typically have a complex network of close and distant social relationships, which provides access to supportive transactions that may occur in the context of regular social interaction and with a background of previous reliability and trustworthiness. These models address the observed high prevalence rates of informal help-seeking that occur in community settings, as well as the laboratory evidence that help-seeking is not influenced by cost or reciprocity variables when the potential helper has a friendship or communal relationship with the subject (e.g., Clark, 1984; DePaulo & Fisher, 1980; Shapiro, 1980). Relationship models delineate several factors in social support relationships that may mitigate some of the esteem concerns that are found to be influential in laboratory studies (Clark, 1983; Wills, 1983).

Coping Theory

Help-seeking may also be approached from the perspective of general coping theory (Folkman & Lazarus, 1984; Moos & Billings, 1982; Pearlin & Schooler, 1978; Prochaska & DiClemente, 1985). These models propose basic dimensions of behavioral (or problem-focused) coping, in which persons actively attempt to change problematic environmental conditions, versus cognitive (or emotion-focused) coping, in which persons try to reduce subjective distress through reappraisal or minimization of the stressor. Recent formulations have also proposed different stages in the coping process, with different coping mechanisms applied in stages involving definition of the stressor, resolution of the problem, and maintenance of behavior change (Prochaska & DiClemente, 1985). In these formulations, help-seeking is viewed as one of several responses that could be used to cope with negative events. Although there is some empirical support for aspects of general coping models (e.g., Billings & Moos, 1981; Collins, Baum, & Singer, 1983), there has been less attention to the relative use and effectiveness of individualistic coping compared with socially oriented coping, that is, social support and help-seeking. Because many psychosocial stressors involve discord in interpersonal relationships, it is possible that socially oriented coping based on interpersonal discussion and negotiation operates in parallel with more individualistic coping processes, and that each contributes independently to reduction of stress.

FUNCTIONS AND EFFECTIVENESS OF INFORMAL HELP-SEEKING

As previously noted, the majority of help-seeking for psychological problems occurs within informal social networks. The following section develops a functional analysis of informal helping, addressing two questions: first, What are the psychological functions through which informal support has its effects? and second, How beneficial is informal helping?

Dimensions of Functional Support

Descriptive aspects of social support may be approached through social network analysis, which enumerates social relationships with individuals (friends, family, relatives, co-workers) and community organizations (clubs or lodges, service organizations, sports teams, religious attendance, cultural groups) and characterizes the social network on parameters such as size, density, and reciprocity (see Hall & Wellman, 1985). Complementary to research on network structure is a model of the supportive functions provided by network members that may serve to reduce the impact of negative life events (Cohen & Wills, 1985). Derived from a model of stress buffering, discussions of major supportive functions are presented in the following (see note 1).

Esteem Support. If an important element in the impact of negative life events is threat to self-esteem, then interpersonal transactions that serve to maintain or enhance a person's esteem would serve to counter the adverse impact of negative events. Esteem support describes the function of transactions showing that an individual is esteemed, accepted, and valued for his or her own worth as a person. This function (also termed emotional support or confidant support) may be provided through instances where someone listens attentively and sympathetically to a person's concerns or problems, shows understanding and sharing of personal experiences, and communicates that he or she accepts the person even though he or she is experiencing difficulty in some area. It is sometimes assumed that the support relationship is a reliable and enduring one, and this is measured explicitly in some scales (e.g., Henderson, Byrne, Duncan-Jones, Scott, & Adcock, 1980; Schaefer, Coyne, & Lazarus, 1981) and is implicit in some others (e.g., Cohen & Hoberman, 1983). The presumption is that this type of support has a direct effect on self-esteem when it is threatened, and several studies show esteem-support measures related to reduced depressive symptomatology primarily at a high level of negative events (see Cohen & Wills, 1985).

Informational Support. A different function of social support is the ability of other persons to provide help with problem definition, information about possible alternatives, and advice about decisions and courses of action. Conversations with helpful persons can reduce distress because they assist in clarifying the nature or locus of the problem and in correctly appraising the stressor with regard to its relative threat potential, severity, and longevity (Pearlin, 1985). When professional help might be appropriate, network members may be important sources of referral information either because of prior personal experience or through acquaintance with persons who were clients of the agency (Gourash, 1978; Wilcox & Birkel, 1983). Whether this type of support typically facilitates behavioral coping, versus an effect through primarily cognitive coping mechanisms, is not clear and may depend to a considerable extent on the type of problem; or both effects may typically be important.

Motivational Support. Conceptually distinct from enhancement of well-being through effects on self-esteem or information is the potential of close relationships to provide support for coping motivation: encouragement, reinforcement of positive expectancies, and reassurance that things will eventually improve. This aspect of support is important on theoretical grounds because many psychosocial stressors are long-term problems or enduring strains, hence a major coping demand is persistence in efforts at coping and problem solving (cf. Pearlin & Schooler, 1978). In addition, coping efforts may be strongly influenced by expectancies about the effectiveness or outcome of the coping process (cf. Bandura, 1977), so current expectancies and coping behavior may sometimes have a reciprocal relationship. From the perspective of either efficacy theory or learned helplessness models, the ability of close relationships to enhance motivation should be particularly helpful for persons under high stress, although at present there is no direct evidence on this point (cf. Scheier & Carver, 1985; Wills, 1985).[7]

Instrumental Support. For some types of life events, instrumental difficulties may be a major source of psychological distress (Pelton, 1982; Wills & Langner, 1980). In these conditions, social network members may be available to help with material aid (e.g., money, supplies or household furnishings) or assistance with instrumental tasks such as child care, housekeeping, or transportation. Instrumental support may reduce distress because of direct effects on depleted resources (e.g., financial aid to supplement lost income) or by reducing the cognitive overload of the stressed person by allowing more "released time" from burdensome tasks. Thus, instrumental help should be particularly relevant for persons currently experiencing a high level of negative events, and several studies have shown buffering interactions for specific mea-

---

[7]In current measures there is some potential confounding of esteem support and motivational support because scales that index confiding/supportive relationships may also tap the reliability/stability of the relationship. Separate assessment of these two aspects would help to clarify motivational dimensions of social support processes.

sures of instrumental support in relation to global measures of life events (Cohen & Hoberman, 1983; Paykel, Emms, Fletcher, & Rasaby, 1980).

Effectiveness of Informal Help

Several bodies of evidence are relevant for considering the effectiveness of informal social support in relation to psychological well-being. First is the simple matter of the observed prevalence rates of informal help-seeking (Table 1); because the rates of informal help-seeking seem high in absolute terms, it would be surprising if people did not derive some benefit from social support. Second is a body of literature determining the overall main effect of social support in relation to mortality rates (e.g., Broadhead *et al.,* 1983). Several prospective studies over 2-year to 10-year periods (Berkman & Syme, 1979; Blazer, 1982; House, Robbins, & Metzner, 1982) have found social support measures to predict lower rates of all-causes mortality, and have shown that this effect holds with control for pre-existing risk factors and health behavior patterns.

A related issue is what aspects of social support may serve to buffer the potentially adverse impact of negative life events. Here, results depend on the type of support measure used. Whereas buffering effects are typically not observed for structural network indexes, measures that index the availability of specific supportive functions (e.g., esteem support) consistently show stress-buffering interaction effects; that is, the effect of support on reduced symptomatology occurs primarily among persons with high levels of stress (Cohen & Wills, 1985). Thus it is evident that informal support may serve to reduce the stressful impact of adverse events, but this is only apparent when the social support measures assess functions that are relevant to the coping demands evoked by negative events. Correlations between structural network measures and functional support measures are typically rather low, indicating that the two approaches tap different aspects of social networks.

Several points about functional support measures are germane to the study of help-seeking as a coping mechanism. Stress-buffering effects have been observed for esteem support, informational support, and instrumental support and for more global measures of confidant relationships or total functional support (Henderson *et al.,* 1980; Wilcox, 1981). Thus, the contribution of informal support functions to well-being appears robust, and the suggestion is that the previously discussed functions may be useful for a wide range of negative life events. It should be noted that current functional measures assess the availability of supportive functions (e.g., Is there someone you could talk to if you have a personal problem?), the perception that if support is needed, then it will be available from someone. Direct links to help-seeking action are not made in these measures, but the presumption is that perceptions of adequate support originate in a previous history of supportive transactions, and that persons under stress do participate in supportive interactions. It has been suggested that in close or communal relationships, support does not necessarily involve an explicit help-seeking request because it occurs in the context of regular everyday interactions, and may be provided by sympathetic others even before it might be requested (Clark, 1983; Pearlin, 1985).

Some conceptual issues about the operation of social support still need to be clarified. It seems likely that different support functions would be most relevant at particular stages of the coping process, for example esteem support would be operative at early stages of event impact, informational or instrumental support operative during an intermediate period of problem definition and decision making, with motivational support more important during later phases of an extended coping effort. The fact that several functions have been found related to stress-buffering using global measures of life events as the stress index suggests that all functions may be relevant at some point in the stress-coping process, but sequential effects remain to be investigated (cf. DiClemente & Prochaska, 1985; Pearlin, 1985; Wills, 1983). Second, there are inferential suggestions that the majority of functional support may derive from one or a few close relationships, but there is little knowledge about the relative contribution of support functions from different sources. Third, there are notable suggestions of group and individual differences in support needs, with effects observed for age, gender, and some personality attributes (see Cohen & Wills, 1985), so it is likely that help-seeking under stress is related to these variables.

FUNCTIONS AND EFFECTIVENESS OF FORMAL HELP-SEEKING

Within the general population, a proportion of individuals are experiencing significant psychological distress, deriving in many cases from negative life events. Of these persons, approximately 25% will seek help from professionals: psychologists, psychiatrists, or other formal helping agencies. It can reasonably be said that at present, little knowledge is available to predict professional help-seeking within the group of distressed individuals. Beyond prediction based on the simple demographic correlates of help-seeking, there is some indication that professional help may be sought when problems are more serious; when available social support is low or social networks more diffuse; and when the distressed person knows someone who has received professional help. Among the various formal help sources, it is generally found that (a) physicians and (b) ministers are the most frequently consulted resources in help-seeking for psychological distress, with psychologists and other mental health professions lower in frequency (e.g., Schurman, Kramer, & Mitchell, 1985; Veroff *et al.*, 1981). The factors underlying this relative ranking of formal help sources are largely unknown.

The following sections address two issues: what functions are sought by distressed persons from professional helpers, and whether professional help improves the adjustment and coping ability of clients. I cannot attempt to cover the extensive literature on psychotherapy (see Garfield & Bergin, 1978; Gurman & Razin, 1977). The focus here is on the basic psychological processes that probably are operative in many types of formal helping relationships (Wills, 1982b). These processes are based on clinical and social-psychological research on interpersonal relationships, self-esteem maintenance, and psychological adjustment, and consider the helping relationship largely from the client's perspective.

Although there is a substantial literature on the psychotherapy process that focuses on technical aspects of therapist behavior, it is typically found in psychotherapy research that client vs. therapist perceptions of the psychotherapy are not highly correlated (see Wills, 1982b), and that client perceptions of therapy are significant and consistent predictors of outcome, whereas therapist behavior and perceptions often are not related to outcome (see Lambert, DeJulio, & Stein, 1978). In addition, systematic reviews of the psychotherapy outcome literature have found no observed difference in effectiveness when comparing professional therapists with nonprofessionals (Berman & Norton, 1985; Durlak, 1979). Thus, the functional analysis of formal helping relationships focuses on dimensions that appear in clients' perceptions of therapy and processes that are operative in many different types of helping relationships.

Dimensions of Formal Helping Relationships

Self-Esteem Enhancement. In clients' perceptions of psychotherapy, the most salient dimension is the perception that they are liked and respected by the therapist. Variously termed warmth, rapport, or positive regard, this dimension appears across several different studies and is a significant predictor of outcome in formal psychotherapy (Wills, 1982b). The nature of this dimension is quite similar to Cobb's (1976) original definition of esteem support: an interpersonal experience showing that the individual is esteemed and valued, and that reaffirms his or her sense of personal worth. The content of this dimension of clients' experience is consistent with social-psychological theories of esteem maintenance (e.g., Tesser & Campbell, 1983) and with clinicians' discussions of efficacious factors in psychotherapy (Brady *et al.*, 1982; Frank, 1982; Garfield, 1974). Also, analyses of psychotherapy outcome indicate that one of the strongest effects of formal helping relationships is on clients' self-esteem (Smith, Glass, & Miller, 1980). Thus, it is evident that self-esteem enhancement is one of the major functions provided by formal help.

Positive Expectancies. From studies of placebo effects and expectancy effects (Kazdin, 1979; Shapiro & Morris, 1978), it is apparent that restoring and enhancing positive expectancies is a major function of formal therapy. The beneficial effect of this function is posited to occur because a common element in many psychological disorders is a breakdown in motivation that includes manifestations of hopelessness and the feeling that things are not going to get better in the future (Dohrenwend, Shrout, Egri, & Mendelsohn, 1980; Frank, 1974). In terms of a stress-coping model, this function would serve to enhance motivation that had been reduced because of perceived coping inadequacy and continued subjective distress. As previously noted, expectancy and coping may have a reciprocal relationship, so that enhanced expectancies may lead to more sustained and effective coping efforts, which in turn will increase positive expectancies; thus a positive upward trend could be instituted to reverse the downward trend or vicious circle in coping-expectancy relationships that initially led to formal help-seeking.

Cognitive Changes. Although there has been relatively little attention given to cognitive factors in psychotherapy, there are suggestions that important cognitive changes may be occurring (Wills, 1982a,b). Convergence between counselor and client belief systems—with change largely occurring through clients' convergence on therapist's beliefs—is a significant predictor of psychotherapy outcome, and the convergence effect is independent of initial client–therapist attitude similarity (Beutler, 1981). Some cognitive change may be occurring because of increased self-focus, some because of feedback from the therapist about the client's feelings and behavior (Snyder *et al.*, 1982), and some because of direct explanation from the therapist concerning clients' decisions and coping goals. Some cognitive changes may derive from increased knowledge about the self, and perhaps some change occurs because of increased exploration of social comparisons and attention to other persons' problems and coping adequacy (cf. Wills, 1982b). To what extent cognitive factors have a direct effect on psychological well-being is not known; but it is clear that one of the major beneficial effects of formal therapy is on reduction in fear and anxiety (Smith *et al.*, 1980), and the suggestion is that stress reduction may be occurring in part because of cognitive factors that are operative in many different types of formal helping relationships.

Skill-Building. In addition to providing general esteem and motivation support, a professional helper may provide direct instruction in basic social skills, assertiveness, and techniques for coping with stress and interpersonal conflict. As previously discussed, persons may seek formal help because problems are more serious, and because social network members may be unable to label or modify particular skill deficits that are in need of improvement. Professional helpers may provide direct instruction in coping and social skills, or clients may arrive at changes in coping through a more subtle modeling of the therapist's general approach to problems and interpersonal interaction (Wills, 1982b). The predicted result is change in general coping adequacy as well as in social behavior and instrumental (school or work) performance. These changes are observed to a somewhat greater extent for therapies classified as behavioral, but substantial effects are found for many different therapy types (Ford, 1978; Smith *et al.*, 1980). Exactly how skill building is accomplished in formal helping relationships is largely unknown because psychotherapy process research has tended to focus on other variables.

Effectiveness of Formal Help

Research on the effectiveness of formal psychotherapy has been the subject of extensive reviews and meta-analyses (e.g., Berman, Miller, & Massman, 1985; Miller & Berman, 1983; Shapiro & Shapiro, 1982: Smith *et al.*, 1980). All reviews show formal psychological therapies to be effective for the broad range of psychological problems, with meta-analysis parameters showing an overall effect size of 0.85, that is, the average person receiving therapy is better off than 80% of the controls. Beneficial effects of formal help are found across various outcome dimensions and client groups (Smith *et al.*, 1980), so the effect of psychotherapy appears quite robust. Aside from the issue of overall effectiveness, there are several points about this effect that are notable for the present discussion. One point, often obscured in the meta-analyses, is the substantial degree of positive change that occurs in the control (untreated) groups (Luborsky, Singer, & Luborsky, 1975). How there can be such an amount of improvement in the untreated groups has not been extensively investigated, but discussions of the "spontaneous remission" of neurotic disorders have generally suggested that informal help and social support are a major factor in this process (Lambert, 1976; Lewinsohn et al., 1985). The other point is evidence showing that entry into formal therapy is accompanied by an increase in informal help-seeking as well (Cross, Sheehan, & Khan, 1980). This finding has profound implications for psychotherapy outcome research, for if professional help-seeking has the general consequence of stimulating an increase in informal help-seeking, then it is difficult to know how to attribute the observed therapy outcome effects to formal versus informal help.

Two other aspects of the research on psychotherapy outcome are worth discussing. One is the general failure to find any substantial difference in effectiveness between the major types of psychotherapy, that is, behavior therapy, cognitive therapy, psychoanalysis, and humanistic or client-centered therapies. How there can be comparable effectiveness for therapies that differ so drastically in recommended therapeutic methods, therapist training, and philosophy of human nature has not currently received a compelling theoretical or methodological explanation (see, e.g., Goldfried, 1982; Williams & Spitzer, 1984) and has been one reason for the increased attention to basic processes in helping relationships (Wills, 1982b).

Another noteworthy finding is from studies comparing the effectiveness of psychotherapy when conducted by trained professional therapists (Ph.D. level), and by untrained nonprofessionals. The conclusion from an extensive literature again has been quite consistent (Berman & Norton, 1985; Durlak, 1979): the evidence shows no observable difference, and the results are robust across different types of problems, therapies, and outcome measures. There has been no obvious explanation for the consistent finding of therapeutic effectiveness among nonprofessional helpers, and this provides reasons for increased attention to the common factors in formal psychotherapy and informal helping relationships.

In summary, there are notable similarities in the proposed functions of informal social support and of professional helping relationships. In both areas a confiding interpersonal relationship with a liked and respected person appears to have a major impact for maintaining self-esteem in the face of ego threats and uncertainties evoked by negative life events. Obtaining of supportive functions involving cognitive assistance (appraisal, information, or feedback) appears to be a supportive aspect of both formal and informal help-seeking, and motivational support also is a plausible common factor in both types of helping. If there are significant differences between formal and informal help-seeking, they may derive from the different types of problems addressed by informal networks and professional helpers, with some evidence suggesting that problems that are more severe or of longer duration are more likely to be taken to professionals.

GENERAL DISCUSSION

This chapter has painted a broad picture of help-seeking for psychological distress. Epidemiological research indicates that help-seeking occurs with substantial frequency in the general population and that help-seeking actions are part of a repertoire of coping responses that are used to cope with adverse life occurrences. From a functional model of coping and help-seeking several propositions were developed, and evidence from community settings indicates that they are supported as follows:

- Life stress is a precursor of help-seeking.
- The mechanism of help-seeking varies with the level of distress.
- The probability of help-seeking is influenced by social comparison.
- The type of help-seeking depends on the supportive function(s) that are sought from a potential helper.
- There is a preference for help-seeking in close relationships.
- Help-seeking through informal social support is effective for reducing psychological symptomatology.
- Help-seeking from professional therapists is effective for reducing psychological symptomatology.
- The types of supportive functions provided through informal help and professional help are similar.

Research on help-seeking as a coping mechanism is at the social-clinical interface where approaches taken by experimental social psychologists (e.g., DePaulo, 1982), stress-coping field researchers (e.g., Billings & Moos, 1981; Collins et al., 1983), and clinical research on helping relationships and self-change (e.g., Prochaska & DiClemente, 1985) provide methodological tools and substantive findings that may contribute to a better understanding of help-seeking for different kinds of distress. Considering the summary points noted previously, there is some support for each issue, but for many issues the available evidence is limited. Studies by social-clinical investigators are needed for questions such as how negative life events lead to help-seeking; how the match between environmental demands and available resources shapes help-seeking behavior; how the benefits and costs of help-seeking are perceived by persons of different age, race, and gender; and what ecological settings are the locus of helping interactions. All are basic issues concerning which more research is much needed. Some specific issues relevant for further research are discussed in the following (see note 1).

Issues for Further Research

Cognitive or Behavioral Coping. In theory, subjective distress could be reduced either through essentially cognitive changes or through behavioral coping processes that produce changes in environmental conditions or interpersonal relationships. Either cognitive or behavioral coping can plausibly be linked to stress reduction, but little research has examined exactly how coping in natural settings is enhanced through help-seeking. In formal psychotherapy research the relative contributions of cognitive and behavioral change to the overall effect of therapy on adjustment has not generally been explored, and in social support research it is not known whether the stress-buffering effect of functional support occurs more because of cognitive or behavioral factors. Each process may have an independent effect on outcome, but the issue can be resolved only when measures of cognitive and behavioral mediators are included in a multivariate study.

Social Comparison. Social comparison processes may be an important influence for either promoting or deterring help-seeking, and the way in which social comparison is pursued in naturalistic settings needs more research. The knowledge that other persons are having problems may lead persons in relatively nonthreatened conditions to assume that they themselves are relatively invulnerable to disease (cf. Perloff, Chap. 11, this volume); this may serve to reduce the likelihood of help-seeking or other preventive measures. For highly distressed persons, however, the type of information used for social comparison may differ, and given the diversity of information available to persons in naturalistic conditions there is considerable flexibility in the way comparison can be pursued. For threatened persons, it is possible to select comparison information that indicates they are relatively well off in comparison to others, which may reduce distress (cf. Wood, Taylor, & Lichtman, 1985) although its relation to help-seeking is unclear. Factors such as the perceived treatability or probable outcome of the disease may moderate the relation between social comparison and help-seeking, and the possible role of downward comparison for either reducing subjective distress or reducing self-esteem barriers to help-seeking needs further investigation.

Interface of Informal/Formal Help. At present little is known about factors that may affect the transition from informal to formal help-seeking. It is plausible to suggest that persons will be more likely to seek professional help if they have less social support, but there is little direct evidence for this issue; adequate tests must distinguish between structural network characteristics (e.g., size, density) and available functional support. Concerning entry into the professional help system it is apparent that nonpsychiatric personnel (particularly general practice physicians and ministers) are the primary source of initial help for a substantial proportion of distressed persons, but there is little understanding of the reasons for this; familiarity, empathy, problem labeling, and cost have all been suggested as relevant factors (Wills, 1983) but there is little knowledge about the operation of this major help resource. As with other aspects of help-seeking, prospective studies that follow a general population over time would be most informative for providing definitive findings about factors that predict various types of formal help-seeking.

Matching of Life Events and Help-Seeking. It has been suggested that research on stress and coping would be advanced by a theory of life events, that is, what are the dimensions of events that evoke psychological distress and what are the coping processes that are most appropriate for countering the effect(s) of the event (Wills, 1985). An integrative theory of help-seeking will have to address the match between life events and help-seeking choices, as there is considerable diversity both in the nature of negative life events (e.g., divorce, illness, bereavement) and in the range of potential coping options that have been delineated. By considering the matching between the dimensions of the adverse event, the available coping responses (self-change and social support), and other relevant resources (e.g., income, education, community integration) it may be possible to make more precise predictions about the course and outcome of help-seeking as a consequence of particular life events.

Commonalities of Informal/Formal Helping. Although research on professional psychotherapy has generally been pursued independently of research on social support, the high prevalence of informal help-seeking suggests renewed attention to the characteristics of informal helping relationships. Variables derived from formal psychotherapy research may be tested in community settings, and correspondingly, concepts derived from models of close relationships and clients' perceptions of psychotherapy (Clark, 1983; Elliott *et al.*, 1982) may be useful for research on formal psychotherapy. Such research may shed more light on the reasons for the effectiveness of nonprofessional helpers. Community-based studies may also suggest modifications of theoretical constructs from laboratory research by studying helping relationships in a context where support may occur in the context of regular activities where there is no obvious help-seeking request and where helping occurs in a context of previous acquaintance, self-disclosure, and previous supportive interactions. Through this kind of research the important commonalities in formal psychotherapy and informal helping relationships may be better developed at both the theoretical level and the empirical level.

WHAT IS COPING AND ADAPTATION WHEN VIEWED FROM THIS PERSPECTIVE?

A model of help-seeking as a coping mechanism posits that the ability of individuals to solve ongoing life problems can potentially be improved through helpful interactions with other persons. Epidemiological research has shown the great richness and diversity of helping resources available in the community, which may contribute to coping and adaptation if persons perceive that support is available, if conditions are conducive to requesting or receiving help, and if socially oriented coping is integrated with other ongoing coping efforts. Help-seeking may be beneficial through processes based on self-esteem maintenance, through processes that are more cognitive in nature, or sometimes through processes that improve instrumental resources or performance. These supportive functions may be provided by close relationships (spouse, family, friends) or by professional helpers, but the suggestion is that the processes of helping are similar for both formal and informal helping.

The study of help-seeking is a complex area where multiple options are available to a stressed individual, and the essential theoretical issue is to predict when persons would—or should—choose help-seeking in relation to other coping options. Depending on the conditions, problems may be resolved through self-change efforts or other coping options, through reliance on informal or formal help, or through a combination of coping methods, and a complete theory of coping through help-seeking would provide evidence on the effectiveness of different coping options for different types of problems. Individuals who could use help may sometimes be deterred from help-seeking because of attitudinal, normative, or psychological costs; or there may be conditions where an apparent lack of help-seeking occurs because coping is pursued through other, perhaps less visible approaches. Ambivalence at the individual level may be reflected in the current diversity of theoretical conceptualizations of help-seeking. Some models, pushed to their extreme, would portray help-seeking as an option pursued only when other alternatives have failed. Other models portray a rationalistic decision process in which various alternatives are considered in a logical, stepwise fashion. Still other models consider the interpersonal context of helping and the integration of supportive transactions with other aspects of an ongoing interpersonal relationship. Although I think that the latter model provides a better description of helping in naturalistic settings, each theoretical approach has identified variables that are relevant for help-seeking requests in some situations. This research should continue to inform clinical and social-psychological theory and show how supportive resources may best be made available to those who need them.

The present chapter has proposed a model of help-seeking based on a functional analysis of the stress-coping process. This model is consistent with current evidence on help-seeking and points out some connections among negative life events, social comparison and social support, and the probability of help-seeking behavior. This model of help-seeking is primarily a model of close relationships, because the evidence from field studies suggests that the majority of supportive transactions occur in the context of such relationships. More research is definitely needed to bridge the findings from laboratory studies of help-seeking, and the apparent barriers to help-seeking that are found in laboratory settings, with epidemiological evidence that shows relatively high rates of informal helping. At present, a model of help-seeking based on the distinctive properties of close relationships and social support functions seems to provide a useful approach to understanding help-seeking as it typically occurs in community settings.

REFERENCES

Abramowitz, S. I., Berger, A., & Weary, G. (1982). Similarity between clinician and client: Its influence on the helping relationship. In T. A. Wills (Ed.), *Basic processes in helping relationships* (pp. 357–379). New York: Academic Press.

Bandura, A. (1977). Self-efficacy: Toward a unifying theory of behavioral change. *Psychological Review, 84,* 191–215.

Batson, C. D., O'Quin, K., & Pych, V. (1982). Attribution-theory analysis of helpers' inferences about clients' needs. In T. A. Wills (Ed.), *Basic processes in helping relationships* (pp. 59–80). New York: Academic Press.

Berkman, L. F., & Syme, S. L. (1979). Social networks and mortality: A nine-year follow-up of Alameda County residents. *American Journal of Epidemiology, 109,* 186–204.

Berman, J. S., & Norton, N. C. (1985). Does professional training make a therapist more effective? *Psychological Bulletin, 98,* 401–407.

Beutler, L. E. (1981). Convergence in counseling and psychotherapy. *Clinical Psychology Review, 1,* 79–102.

Billings, A. G., & Moos, R. H. (1981). The role of coping responses and social resources in attenuating the stress of life events. *Journal of Behavioral Medicine, 4,* 139–157.

Blazer, D. G. (1982). Social support and mortality in an elderly community population. *American Journal of Epidemiology, 115,* 684–694.

Bosmajian, C. P., & Mattson, R. E. (1980). A controlled study of variables related to counseling center use. *Journal of Counseling Psychology, 27*, 510–519.

Brady, J. P., Davison, G. C., Dewald, P. A., Egan, G., Fadiman, J., Frank, J. D., Gill, M., Hoffman, I., Kempler, W., Lazarus, A. A., Raimy, V., Rotter, J. B., & Strupp, H. H. (1980). Some views on effective principles in psychotherapy. *Cognitive Therapy and Research, 4*, 269–306.

Broadhead, W. E., Kaplan, B. H., James, S. A., Wagner, E. H., Shoenbach, V. J., Grimson, R., Heyden, S., Tibblin, G., & Gehlbach, S. (1983). The epidemiologic evidence for a relationship between social support and health. *American Journal of Epidemiology, 117*, 521–537.

Broll, L., Gross, A. E., & Piliavin, I. (1974). Effects of offered and requested help on help-seeking. *Journal of Applied Social Psychology, 4*, 244–258.

Clark, M. S. (1983). Some implications of close social bonds for help-seeking. In B. M. DePaulo, A. Nadler, & J. D. Fisher (Eds.), *New directions in helping* (Vol. 2): *Help-seeking* (pp. 205–229). New York: Academic Press.

Clark, M. S. (1984). Record keeping in two types of relationships. *Journal of Personality and Social Psychology, 47*, 549–557.

Clark, M. S., & Mills, J. (1979). Interpersonal attraction in exchange and communal relationships. *Journal of Personality and Social Psychology, 37*, 12–24.

Christensen, K. C., & Magoon, T. M. (1974). Perceived hierarchy of help-giving sources for two categories of student problems. *Journal of Counseling Psychology, 21*, 311–324.

Cobb, S. (1976). Social support as a moderator of life stress. *Psychosomatic Medicine, 38*, 300–314.

Cohen, S., & Hoberman, H. (1983). Positive events and social supports as buffers of life stress. *Journal of Applied Social Psychology, 13*, 99–125.

Cohen, S., & Wills, T. A. (1985). Stress, social support, and the buffering hypothesis. *Psychological Bulletin, 98*, 310–357.

Collins, D. L., Baum, A., & Singer, J. E. (1983). Coping with chronic stress at Three Mile Island. *Health Psychology, 2*, 149–166.

Corrigan, J. D. (1978). Salient attributes of two types of helpers. *Journal of Counseling Psychology, 25*, 588–590.

Cross, D. G., Sheehan, P. W., & Khan, J. A. (1980). Alternative advice and counsel in psychotherapy. *Journal of Consulting and Clinical Psychology, 48*, 615–625.

DePaulo, B. M. (1978). Help-seeking from the recipient's point of view. JSAS *Catalog of Selected Documents in Psychology, 8*, 62. (MS No. 1721)

DePaulo, B. M. (1982). Social-psychological processes in informal help-seeking. In T. A. Wills (Ed.), *Basic processes in helping relationships* (pp. 255–279). New York: Academic Press.

DePaulo, B. M., & Fisher, J. D. (1980). The costs of asking for help. *Basic and Applied Social Psychology, 1*, 23–35.

DiClemente, C. C., & Prochaska, J. O. (1985). Processes and stages in self-change of smoking behavior. In S. Shiffman & T. A. Wills (Eds.), *Coping and substance use* (pp. 319–343). New York: Academic Press.

Dohrenwend, B. S., & Dohrenwend, B. P. (Eds.). (1981). *Stressful life events and their contexts.* New York: Prodist.

Dohrenwend, B. P., Shrout, P. E., Egri, G., & Mendelsohn, F. S. (1980). Nonspecific psychological distress and other dimensions of psychopathology. *Archives of General Psychiatry, 37*, 1229–1236.

Dooley, D., & Catalano, R. (1984). Why the economy predicts help-seeking: A test of competing explanations. *Journal of Health and Social Behavior, 25*, 160–176.

Durlak, J. A. (1979). Comparative effectiveness of paraprofessional and professional helpers. *Psychological Bulletin, 86,* 80–92.

Eckenrode, J. (1984). Impact of chronic and acute stressors on daily mood. *Journal of Personality and Social Psychology, 46,* 907–918.

Elliott, R., Stiles, W. B., Shiffman, S., Barker, C. B., Burstein, B.,& Goodman, G.The empirical analysis of help-intended communications. In T. A. Wills (Ed.), *Basic processes in helping relationships* (pp. 333–356). New York: Academic Press.

Fischer, E. H., Winer, D., & Abramowitz, S. I. (1983). Seeking professional help for psychological problems. In A. Nadler, J. D. Fisher, & B. M. DePaulo (Eds.), *New directions in helping* (Vol. 3, pp. 163–185). New York: Academic Press.

Fisher, J. D., & Nadler, A. (1982). Determinants of recipient reactions to aid. In T. A. Wills (Ed.), *Basic processes in helping relationships* (pp. 131–153). New York: Academic Press.

Folkman, S., & Lazarus; R. S. (1980). An analysis of coping in a middle-aged community sample. *Journal of Health and Social Behavior, 21,* 219–239.

Ford, J. D. (1978). Therapeutic relationship in behavior therapy: An empirical analysis. *Journal of Consulting and Clinical Psychology, 46,* 1302–1314.

Frank, J. D. (1974). *Persuasion and healing* (rev. ed.). New York: Schocken.

Frank, J. D. (1982). Therapeutic components shared by all psychotherapies. In J. H. Harvey & M. M. Parks (Eds.), *Psychotherapy research and behavior change* (pp. 9–37). Washington, DC: American Psychological Association.

Garber, J., & Seligman, M. E. P. (Eds.). (1980). *Human helplessness: Theory and applications.* New York: Academic Press.

Garfield, S. (1974). What are the therapeutic variables in psychotherapy? *Psychotherapy and Psychosomatics, 24,* 372–378.

Garfield, S. L., & Bergin, A. E. (Eds.). (1978). *Handbook of psychotherapy and behavior change* (2nd ed.). New York: Wiley.

Gibbons, F. X. (1986). Social comparison and depression: Company's effect on misery. *Journal of Personality and Social Psychology, 51,* 140–148.

Glidewell, J. C., Tucker, S., Todt, M., & Cox, S. (1983). Professional support systems: The teaching profession. In A. Nadler, J. D. Fisher, & B. M. DePaulo (Eds.), *New directions in helping* (Vol. 3, pp. 189–212). New York: Academic Press.

Goldfried, M. R. (Ed.). (1982). *Converging themes in psychotherapy.* New York: Springer.

Goodman, S. H., Sewell, D. R., & Jampol, R. C. (1984). Contributions of life stress and social supports to the decision to seek psychological counseling. *Journal of Counseling Psychology, 31,* 306–313.

Gourash, N. (1978). Help-seeking: A review of the literature. *American Journal of Community Psychology, 6,* 413–423.

Greenberg, M. S. (1980). A theory of indebtedness. In K. J. Gergen, M. S. Greenberg, & R. H. Willis (Eds.), *Social exchange: Advances in theory and research* (pp. 3–26). New York: Plenum.

Greenberg, M. S., & Shapiro, S. P. (1971). Indebtedness: An adverse aspect of asking for and receiving help. *Sociometry, 34,* 290–301.

Greenberg, M. S., Ruback, R. B., & Westcott, D. R. (1983). Seeking help from the police: The victim's perspective. In A. Nadler, J. D. Fisher, & B. M. DePaulo (Eds.), *New directions in helping* (Vol. 3, pp. 71–103). New York: Academic Press.

Greenley, J. R., & Mechanic, D. (1976). Social selection in seeking help for psychological problems. *Journal of Health and Social Behavior, 17,* 249–262.

Gross, A. E., & McMullen, P. A. (1983). Models of the help-seeking process. In B. M. DePaulo, A. Nadler, & J. D. Fisher (Eds.), *New directions in helping* (Vol. 2): *Help-seeking* (pp. 45–70). New York: Academic Press.

Gross, A. E., Fisher, J. D., Nadler, A., Stiglitz, E., & Craig, C. (1979). Correlates of help-utilization at a women's counseling service. *Journal of Community Psychology, 7*, 42–49.

Gurman, A. S., & Razin, A. M. (Eds.). (1977). *Effective psychotherapy: A handbook of research.* New York: Pergamon Press.

Hall, A., & Wellman, B. (1985). Social networks and social support. In S. Cohen & S. L. Syme (Eds.), *Social support and health.* (pp. 23–41). New York: Academic Press.

Henderson, S., Byrne, D. G., Duncan-Jones, P., Scott, R., & Adcock, S. (1980). Social relationships, adversity, and neurosis: A study of associations in a general-population sample. *British Journal of Psychiatry, 136*, 574–583.

House, J. S., Robbins, C., & Metzner, H. I. (1979). The association of social relationships and activities with mortality: Prospective evidence from the Tecumseh Community Health Study. *American Journal of Epidemiology, 116*, 123–140.

Kazdin, A. E. (1979). Nonspecific treatment factors in psychotherapy outcome research. *Journal of Consulting and Clinical Psychology, 47*, 846–851.

Kessler, R. C., Brown, R. L., & Bowman, C. L. (1981). Sex differences in psychiatric help-seeking. *Journal of Health and Social Behavior, 22*, 49–64.

Kirscht, J. P. (1983). Preventive health behavior: A review of research and issues. *Health Psychology, 2*, 277–301.

Lambert, M. J. (1976). Spontaneous remission in adult neurotic disorders. *Psychological Bulletin, 83*, 107–119.

Lambert, M. J., DeJulio, S. S., & Stein, D. M. (1978). Therapist interpersonal skills: Process, outcome, and methodological considerations. *Psychological Bulletin, 85*, 467–489.

Lazarus, R. S., & Folkman, S. (1984). *Stress, appraisal and coping.* New York: Springer.

Lemkau, J. P., Bryant, F. B., & Brickman, P. (1982). Client commitment to the helping relationship. In T. A. Wills (Ed.), *Basic processes in helping relationships* (pp. 187–207). New York: Academic Press.

Lewinsohn, P. M., Hoberman, H., Teri, L., & Hautzinger, M. (1985). An integrative theory of depression. In S. Reiss & R. Bootzin (Eds.), *Theoretical issues in behavior therapy* (331–359). New York: Academic Press.

Link, B., & Dohrenwend, B. P. (1980). Formulation of hypotheses about the ratio of untreated to treated cases in true prevalence studies of functional psychiatric disorders. In B. P. Dohrenwend, B. S. Dohrenwend, M. J. Gould, B. Link, R. Neugebauer, & R. Wunsch-Hitzig, *Mental illness in the United States: Epidemiological estimates* (pp. 133–149). New York: Praeger.

Luborsky, L., Singer, B., & Luborsky, L. (1975). Comparative studies of psychotherapies. *Archives of General Psychiatry, 32*, 995–1008.

Manning, W. G., Jr., Wells, K. B., Duan, H., Newhouse, J. P., & Ware, J. E., Jr. (1984). Cost sharing and the use of ambulatory mental health services. *American Psychologist, 39*, 1077–1089.

McCrae, R. R. (1984). Situational determinants of coping responses. *Journal of Personality and Social Psychology, 46*, 919–928.

McKinlay, J. B. (1972). Some approaches and problems in the use of services. *Journal of Health and Social Behavior, 13*, 115–152.

McKinlay, J. B. (1973). Social networks, lay consultation, and help-seeking behavior. *Social Forces, 51*, 275–292.

Mechanic, D. (1978). Effects of psychological distress on use of medical and psychiatric facilities. *Journal of Human Stress, 4*, 26–32.

Miller, R. C., & Berman, J. S. (1983). The efficacy of cognitive behavior therapies: A quantitative review. *Psychological Bulletin, 94*, 39–53.

Moos, R. H., & Billings, A. G. (1982). Conceptualizing and measuring coping resources and processes. In L. Goldberger & S. Breznitz (Eds.), *Handbook of stress* (pp. 212–230). New York: Macmillan.

Morris, S. C., & Rosen, S. (1973). Effects of felt adequacy and opportunity to reciprocate on help-seeking. *Journal of Experimental Social Psychology, 9,* 265–276.

Nadler, A., & Porat, I. (1978). Effects of anonymity and locus of need attribution on help-seeking behavior. *Personality and Social Psychology Bulletin, 4,* 624–626.

Neugebauer, R., Dohrenwend, B. P., & Dohrenwend, B. S. (1980). Formulation of hypotheses about the true prevalence of functional psychiatric disorders among adults. In B. P. Dohrenwend, B. S. Dohrenwend, M. S. Gould, B. Link, R. Neugebauer, & R. Wunsch-Hitzig, *Mental illness in the United States: Epidemiological estimates* (pp. 45–94). New York: Praeger.

Norcross, J. C., & Prochaska, J. O. (1986). The psychological distress and self-change of psychologists, counselors, and laypersons. *Psychotherapy, 23,* 102–114.

Norcross, J. C., & Prochaska, J. O. (in press). The self-initiated and therapy-facilitated change of psychological distress. *Psychotherapy.*

Ostrove, N., & Baum, A. (1983). Factors influencing medical help-seeking. In A. Nadler, J. D. Fisher, & B. M. DePaulo (Eds.), *New directions in helping* (Vol. 3, pp. 107–129). New York: Academic Press.

Ostrow, E., Dark, V. J., & Poulton, J. (1982). *Predicting health and help-seeking in high- and low-adjustment samples.* Paper presented at the American Psychological Association.

Paykel, E. S., Emms, E. M., Fletcher, J., & Rassaby, E. S. (1980). Life events and social support in puerperal depression. *British Journal of Psychiatry, 136,* 339–346.

Pearlin, L. I. (1985). Social structure and processes of social support. In S. Cohen & S. L. Syme (Eds.), *Social support and health* (pp. 43–60). New York: Academic Press.

Pearlin, L. I., & Schooler, C. (1978). The structure of coping. *Journal of Health and Social Behavior, 19,* 2–21.

Pelton, L. H. (1982). Workers' attributions and client perspectives in child welfare cases. In T. A. Wills (Ed.), *Basic processes in helping relationships* (pp. 81–101). New York: Academic Press.

Prochaska, J. O., & DiClemente, C. C. (1985). Common processes of self-change in smoking, weight control, and psychological distress. In S. Shiffman & T. A. Wills (Eds.), *Coping and substance use* (pp. 345–363). New York: Academic Press.

Rosen, S. (1983). Perceived inadequacy and help-seeking. In B. M. DePaulo, A. Nadler, & J. D. Fisher (Eds.), *New directions in helping (Vol. 2): Help-seeking* (pp. 73–105). New York: Academic Press.

Sanders, G. S. (1982). Social comparison and perceptions of health and illness. In G. S. Sanders & J. Suls (Eds.), *Social psychology of health and illness* (pp. 129–157). Hillsdale, NJ: Erlbaum.

Schaefer, C., Coyne, J. C., & Lazarus, R. S. (1981). The health-related functions of social support. *Journal of Behavioral Medicine, 4,* 381–406.

Scheier, M. F., & Carver, C. S. (1985). Optimism, coping, and health. *Health Psychology, 4,* 219–247.

Schurman, R. A., Kramer, P. D., & Mitchell, J. B. (1985). Treatment of mental illness by nonpsychiatrist physicians. *Archives of General Psychiatry, 42,* 89–94.

Shapiro, E. G. (1980). Is seeking help from a friend like seeking help from a stranger? *Social Psychology Quarterly, 43,* 259–263.

Shapiro, A. K., & Morris, L. A. (1978). Placebo effects in medical and psychological therapies. In S. I. Garfield & A. E. Bergin (Eds.), *Handbook of psychotherapy and behavior change* (2nd ed.). New York: Wiley.

Shapiro, D. A., & Shapiro, D. (1982). Meta-analysis of comparative therapy outcome studies: A replication and refinement. *Psychological Bulletin, 92,* 581–604.

Smith, M. L., Glass, G. V., & Miller, T. I. (1980). *The benefits of psychotherapy.* Baltimore, MD: Johns Hopkins University Press.

Snyder, C. R., & Ingram, R. E. (1983). The impact of consensus information on help seeking for psychological problems. *Journal of Personality and Social Psychology, 45,* 1118–1126.

Snyder, C. R., Ingram, R. E., & Newburg, C. L. (1982). The role of feedback in help seeking and the therapeutic relationship. In T. A. Wills (Ed.), *Basic processes in helping relationships* (pp. 287–305). New York: Academic Press.

Stone, A. A., & Neale, J. M. (1984). New measure of daily coping. *Journal of Personality and Social Psychology, 46,* 892–906.

Strohmer, D. C., Biggs, D. A., & McIntyre, W. F. (1984). Social comparison information and judgments about seeking counseling. *Journal of Counseling Psychology, 31,* 591–594.

Tesser, A., & Campbell, J. (1983). Self-definition and self-evaluation maintenance. In J. Suls & A. Greenwald (Eds.), *Psychological perspectives on the self* (Vol. 2, pp. 1–31). Hillsdale, NJ: Erlbaum.

Tessler, R., Mechanic, D., & Dimond, M. (1976). The effect of psychological distress on physician utilization: A prospective study. *Journal of Health and Social Behavior, 17,* 353–364.

Tessler, R. C., & Schwartz, S. H. (1972). Help-seeking, self-esteem, and achievement motivation. *Journal of Personality and Social Psychology, 21,* 318–326.

Tinsley, H. E. A., de St. Aubin, T. M., & Brown, M. T. (1982). College students' help-seeking preferences. *Journal of Counseling Psychology, 29,* 523–533.

Tinsley, H. E. A., Brown, M. T., de St. Aubin, T. M., & Lucek, J. (1984). Expectancies for a helping relationship and tendency to seek help from a campus help provider. *Journal of Counseling Psychology, 31,* 149–160.

Tolsdorf, C. (1976). Social networks, social support, and coping. *Family Process, 15,* 407–417.

Veroff, J. B., Kulka, R. A., & Douvan, E. (1981). *Mental health in America: Patterns of help-seeking from 1957 to 1976.* New York: Basic Books.

Wilcox, B. L. (1981). Social support, life stress, and psychological adjustment. *American Journal of Community Psychology, 9,* 371–386.

Wilcox, B. L., & Birkel, R. C. (1983). Social networks and the help-seeking process: A structural perspective. In B. M. DePaulo, J. D. Fisher, & A. Nadler (Eds.), *New directions in helping (Vol. 2): Help-seeking* (pp. 235–253). New York: Academic Press.

Williams, J. B. W., & Spitzer, R. L. (Eds.). (1984). *Psychotherapy research: Where are we, and where should we go?* New York: Guilford.

Wills, T. A. (1981). Downward comparison principles in social psychology. *Psychological Bulletin, 90,* 245–271.

Wills, T. A. (1982a). Directions for research on helping relationships. In T. A. Wills (Ed.), *Basic processes in helping relationships* (pp. 479–496). New York: Academic Press.

Wills, T. A. (1982b). Nonspecific factors in helping relationships. In T. A. Wills (Ed.), *Basic processes in helping relationships* (pp. 381–404). New York: Academic Press.

Wills, T. A. (1983). Social comparison in coping and help-seeking. In B. M. DePaulo, J. D. Fisher, & A. Nadler (Eds.), *New directions in helping (Vol. 2): Help-seeking* (pp. 109–141). New York: Academic Press.

Wills, T. A. (1985). Supportive functions of interpersonal relationships. In S. Cohen & S. L. Syme (Eds.), *Social support and health* (pp. 61–82). New York: Academic.

Wills, T. A., & Langner, T. S. (1980). Socioeconomic status and stress. In I. L. Kutash & L. B. Schlesinger (Eds.), *Handbook on stress and anxiety* (pp. 159–173). San Francisco: Jossey-Bass.

Wills, T. A., & Shiffman, S. (1985). Coping and substance use: A conceptual framework. In S. Shiffman & T. A. Wills (Eds.), *Coping and substance use* (pp. 3–24). New York: Academic Press.

Wood, J. V., Taylor, S. E., & Lichtman, R. R. (1985). Social comparison in adjustment to breast cancer. *Journal of Personality and Social Psychology, 49,* 1169–1183.

3

Coping Difficulty, Energy Mobilization, and Appraisals of a Stressor
Introduction of a Theory and a Comparison of Perspectives

REX A. WRIGHT

INTRODUCTION

It has been popular, in recent years, to conceptualize responses to negative events in terms of stress and coping theory (Lazarus, 1966; Mason, 1972; Selye, 1976). Definitions of stress vary (see Houston, this volume). However, the most commonly accepted view at this point is what usually is referred to as the interactionist approach. According to this viewpoint, stress is a psychological response that varies in magnitude with perceived threat. Threat, in turn, is believed to be a function of the severity of a potential negative event itself, and an individual's perception of his or her ability to cope with that event (Cox, 1978; Lazarus, 1966). The more severe the potential outcome, and the less the perceived ability to cope, the greater should be the stress response, which is proposed to be manifested physiologically, affectively, and behaviorally (Baum, Grunberg, & Singer, 1982).

An alternative way to conceptualize responses in aversive circum-

---

REX A. WRIGHT • Department of Psychology, 210 McAlester Hall, University of Missouri-Columbia, Columbia, MO 65211.

stances is in terms of motivation. Theoretically, when a potential negative outcome is perceived, motivation should be aroused to eliminate it or
reduce its effects. An increase in motivation should have specific physiologic, subjective, and behavioral consequences. Physiologically, motivation should be associated with increased energy mobilization (Elliott,
1969; Fowles, 1982, 1983; Malmo, 1958). Subjectively, motivation
should be associated with an increase in the magnitude of goal valence
(e.g., Lewin, 1935). In the case of avoidance, this means an enhanced
perception of the aversiveness of the outcome being dealt with. Finally,
behaviorally, motivation should be associated with an increase in effort,
which, among other things, may be indicated by such things as speed,
vigor, and directedness in action.

The main goal of this chapter is to introduce a theory of motivation
proposed recently by J. Brehm (J. Brehm, 1979; J. Brehm, Wright,
Solomon, Silka, & Greenberg, 1983; S. Brehm & J. Brehm, 1981, pp.
379–383) and explore ways that it may improve our understanding of
the way people respond when they are threatened. In discussing the
theory, I shall spell out what some implications might be, and review a
series of relevant research findings. In addition, I shall attempt to contrast predictions derived from this theory with some that may be derived
from the interactionist perspective on stress and coping, allowing for a
determination of which approach seems to best account for the data
being considered. The chapter will conclude with a summary and discussion of theoretical issues. Particular attention will be devoted to certain
responses that appear not to be interpretable in motivational terms
alone.

TASK DIFFICULTY AND MOTIVATION: BREHM'S
ENERGIZATION HYPOTHESIS

Basic Propositions

Brehm's formulation is perhaps clearest when it is presented in
juxtaposition to other theories of motivation. Reviews of past and current theories (Cofer & Appley, 1964; Pfaff, 1982; Stellar & Stellar, 1985;
Weiner, 1972) show that three general determinants have received primary attention: the state of the organism (i.e., biological, psychological,
or social needs), the value of the (positive or negative) incentive, and
expectancy of motive satisfaction. It is generally believed that motivation
increases directly with need state and incentive value. The exact effect of
expectancy is controversial (see Campbell & Pritchard, 1976). However,

most theorists would agree that motivation should be a positive function of the likelihood that a motive will be satisfied *upon the successful completion of instrumental activity*. Motivation should be higher, for example, when success is certain to result in motive satisfaction than when success increases the likelihood of motive satisfaction only slightly.

J. Brehm (J. Brehm, 1979; J. Brehm *et al.*, 1983; S. Brehm & J. Brehm, 1981, pp. 379–383) maintains that, rather than determining motivation, these factors combine to determine *potential* motivation. This is defined as the upper limit of motivation, or the maximum amount of effort an individual would be willing to exert in order to secure an outcome. The amount of effort that actually will be exerted, he argues, is determined by what the individual thinks is necessary, possible, and worthwhile to do to secure the outcome. If a motive is easy to satisfy, little effort is needed, and therefore little energy should be expended. This should be true regardless of the strength of the motive (potential motivation). Likewise, there should be little effort exerted if an outcome is impossible to attain or so difficult to attain that it does not warrant the effort it requires (see also, Kukla, 1972). It is only when instrumental activity is difficult, but possible, and justified by sufficiently important benefits, that a great deal of effort is expected.

Brehm accounts for the subjective and physiologic aspects of motivation by making two critical assertions. First, he contends that motivational arousal (energization) increases directly with the intention to try. Second, he proposes that the magnitude of goal valence is a positive linear function of energization level. Thus, if the satisfaction of an appetitive motive (e.g., the acquisition of food) is difficult, but possible and worth the effort required, energy mobilization and the attractiveness of the goal should be higher than if the motive is easy, too difficult, or impossible to satisfy. For the same reason, a negative event (e.g., impending surgery) should produce greater energization and be perceived as more aversive if coping activity is difficult, but possible and warranted, than if coping activity is easy, impossible, or unwarranted.

Energization and Motive Strength: When They Should Be Related

Although Brehm proposes that energization is a function of what can and must be done to satisfy a motive, he does not claim that energization and motive strength are always dissociated. To the contrary, it is implicit in his analysis that there will be relationship between these variables in at least two circumstances. One is where there is freedom with regard to the difficulty of instrumental activity that may be engaged in, and (a) the value of the incentive, or (b) the likelihood of motive satisfaction, increases with the difficulty of activity that is selected. Here, the difficulty of the activity chosen should be the maximum that is perceived as possible and warranted given considerations of need, incentive value at each level of task difficulty, and likelihood of motive satisfaction at each level of task difficulty. Once a task or activity level has been selected, energy should be mobilized in proportion to the perceived difficulty of the task or activity level.

To illustrate, first imagine a man who is told by his physician that he can minimize postoperative pain by performing ten sit-ups during the hour just prior to surgery. If he succeeds, the pain after surgery will be minimal; if he chooses not to exercise or fails, the pain will be undiminished. The energization hypothesis, of course, predicts that, so long as this task is viewed as possible and worthwhile, the fellow will expend as much energy as is required to do it, but no more than is required. As stated earlier, this should be true regardless of how much effort he would be willing to exert were it necessary or useful to do so. Now, by way of contrast, consider what would happen if the physician said there was a direct relationship between the amount of exercise the patient performed just before surgery and postoperative pain reduction. The more exercise, the less pain after the operation. Assuming the man can exercise as much as he likes, the present view suggests that he will perform as many sit-ups as he feels is justified, given his need to avoid pain, the amount of pain that each level of activity is likely to avoid, and so on.

Another circumstance in which energization and potential motivation should be correlated is where instrumental activity is needed, but task demands are ambiguous or unknown. If there is a perception of what is or will be necessary, but confidence in that perception is not complete, there should be a tendency to exert more effort than is estimated to be minimally required, in order to insure success. Presumably, the magnitude of this "overshoot" in terms of effort, and therefore energization, should be a function of (a) the degree of doubt about the perception of difficulty, and (b) motive strength. Thus, there should be a larger margin of safety—overshoot—when there is a 25% level of confidence in a perception of task difficulty than when there is an 85% level of confidence in a perception of task difficulty. Similarly, there should be a greater overshoot when the importance of success is high than when the importance of success is low. If task demands are completely unknown, energization should be the maximum warranted by considerations of need, incentive value, and expectancy of motive satisfaction upon completion of instrumental activity.

Comparison with the Interactionist View of Stress

What the energization hypothesis suggests about responses in aversive circumstances, then, may be compared and contrasted with what is suggested by the stress and coping view in at least three respects. The first concerns the impact of coping difficulty on energization. Both approaches predict that energy mobilization will be lower when it is easy to cope with a stressor than when it is moderately difficult to cope with a stressor. According to the energization hypothesis, this should occur because more effort is required when coping is moderately difficult than when coping is easy; stress and coping theory predicts this because energization—a part of the stress response (e.g., Baum *et al.*, 1982; Cannon, 1924)—should increase as adaptive demands approach an individual's perceived ability to cope.

The two perspectives make quite different predictions, however, about energy levels when coping is very difficult or impossible. The energization hypothesis predicts that energy mobilization will be low when nothing can be done to avert, terminate, or alleviate an aversive circumstance, or the effort required to do so is perceived as unjustified. Stress and coping theory, on the other hand, predicts that the stress response will be greatest when individuals believe they have little or no control over unpleasant outcomes.

The approaches also make different predictions concerning the impact of outcome severity on energization. The energization hypothesis postulates that when physiologic changes associated with the mobilization of energy occur, they should not necessarily vary as a function of (negative) incentive value. Instead, it is proposed that energy levels will be associated with this variable (as well as other variables that determine potential motivation) only in the special circumstances that were outlined earlier. This proposition conflicts with the prediction derived from stress and coping theory that, unless coping is so easy that there is no real threat, energization will increase directly with the severity of the negative outcome being dealt with.

Finally, the theoretical perspectives may be contrasted with respect to predictions concerning the impact of coping difficulty on perceptions of a stressor. According to the energization hypothesis, the perceived aversiveness of a negative outcome should vary (increase) with energy mobilized for instrumental activity, and therefore should be a nonmonotonic function of the difficulty of coping. Stress and coping theory makes no clear prediction in this regard. Perceptions of a stressor usually are assumed to be either static or affected by intrapsychic reappraisal processes, such as intellectualization or denial (e.g., Lazarus, 1966).

However, because stress and negative affect are proposed to be greatest when demands approach or exceed an individual's ability to cope, it might be speculated that appraisals of a stressor should be most negative in this situation as well.

RESEARCH

There are four lines of research that provide data that are directly pertinent to the contrasting hypotheses outlined earlier. These include (a) experiments examining cardiovascular reactivity under conditions where instrumental activity is more or less difficult, (b) experiments examining the impact of need and incentive value on cardiovascular reactivity, (c) experiments examining appraisals of potential outcomes as a function of the difficulty of obtaining or avoiding them, and (d) experiments designed to assess the effects of energization on the appraisals of potential negative outcomes directly, without manipulating the difficulty of avoiding the events. In this section, evidence from each type of study will be considered in turn. Readers interested in other kinds of data thought to be relevant to the energization hypothesis are referred to J. Brehm (1979), Ford and Brehm (this volume), Ford, Wright, and Haythornthwaite (1985), and Hill, Fultz, and Biner (1985).

Instrumental Task Difficulty and Cardiovascular Responsiveness

Among the most common and accessible indices of energy mobilization are measures of cardiovascular reactivity. The use of the measures for this purpose derives from functional considerations. That is, the main function of the cardiovascular system is to deliver oxygen, nutrients, and other vital substances to tissues, and to remove metabolic waste produce; the goal of cardiovascular adjustment (e.g., a change in heart rate, stroke volume, vascular resistance, etc.) is to maintain a rate of blood flow to tissues that is congruent with their needs (Cacioppo & Petty, 1982; Hassett, 1978; Surwit, Williams, & Shapiro, 1982). Although, as Obrist (e.g., 1976, 1981, 1982) and others have pointed out, measures of cardiovascular reactivity are not interchangeable indicators of sympathetic nervous system activity, when interpreted properly, they can provide considerable insight into an individual's physiologic state of readiness for action.

In the past 10 to 15 years, there seems to have been an especially large number of psychophysiological studies conducted that involve cardiovascular measures. Fortunately, many of these have included conditions that allow for the examination of hypotheses concerning the possible impact of coping difficulty on energization.

Avoidance Studies. Most directly relevant to the study of stress are experiments employing avoidance paradigms. For purposes of organization, these can be placed into two categories. In one category are studies in which subjects can avoid an aversive outcome by performing a task that is more or less difficult, or are not given the opportunity to avoid the outcome at all. Congruent with both stress and coping theory and the energization hypothesis, a number have shown that cardiovascular responses are less pronounced under easy avoidance conditions than under moderately difficult avoidance conditions. Light and Obrist (1980), for example, observed a greater increase in heart rate (HR) and systolic blood pressure (SBP) in subjects performing a moderately difficult reaction time (RT) task to avoid shock than in subjects performing an easy RT task to avoid shock. Similarly, Scher, Furedy, and Heslegrave (1984) found a greater acceleration HR, and a greater reduction in T-wave amplitude (a proposed measure of sympathetic influence on the heart) in subjects who could avoid noise by performing a "hard" memory task than in subjects who could avoid noise by performing an "easy" memory task.

Other experiments have included very difficult and impossible avoidance conditions, which allows for a test between the two theoretical perspectives. Obrist *et al.* (1978) told subjects they could avoid an electric shock by responding quickly enough on an RT task. Through experience, subjects learned that the task was easy, moderately difficult, or extremely difficult. In contrast to what would be predicted by the interactionist approach to stress—but consistent with Brehm's model—elevations in HR, SBP, and dP/dt (a measure of myocardial force) across trials were higher in the moderately difficult condition than in the easy and extremely difficult conditions, in which cardiovascular responses did not differ.

In a conceptually similar experiment by Wright (1984), subjects were threatened with the possibility of participating in an aversive learning experiment that would involve shock. Two thirds of the subjects were told they could avoid the session by performing a dynamometer grip they would be assigned; for approximately half of these the assigned grip turned out to be easy, and for the rest the grip turned out to be difficult. The other subjects were told they had been randomly assigned to a group that would not have the opportunity to avoid the session at all. Because the experiment was terminated before subjects actually performed the dynamometer exercise, measures of arousal during coping could not be taken. However, immediately before the period in which the task was to be performed, subjects in the difficult avoidance condition had faster HRs and greater digital vasoconstriction than subjects in the easy avoidance condition and subjects in the impossible avoidance condition.

Perhaps the most dramatic study of this kind was an experiment by Elliott (1969, Experiment 1), in which subjects were or were not given the opportunity to escape a series of electric shocks. In one condition, subjects could lessen the duration of each shock by quickly lifting their hands off the metal plate through which it was delivered. In the other condition, hands were strapped to the metal plate, thereby making escape impossible. Unexpectedly, from the investigator's point of view, HRs were lower when subjects could not escape the shock than when they could. This finding was later replicated by Malcuit (1973), and has been extended recently by Lovallo et al. (1985). Lovallo et al. found less reactivity on HR as well as a host of other cardiovascular measures (e.g., preejection period, contractility, peripheral resistance) in subjects who could not avoid shocks than in subjects who could avoid shocks by performing well on an (apparently difficult) RT task.

In the second type of avoidance study, subjects perform a task that they do or do not expect to be instrumental in allowing them to avoid a noxious stimulus. This paradigm also provides the opportunity to evaluate the predictive validity of the stress and coping and energization approaches. Stress and coping theory predicts that cardiovascular responsivity should be greatest when stimulation is presented irrespective of performance (when subjects have no control over the aversive outcome). The energization hypothesis, on the other hand, predicts that cardiovascular arousal will be proportional to task difficulty, but only when the effort required by a task is justified by the end it achieves. If the presentation of an aversive stimulus is not contingent on performance, subjects might be expected to manifest relatively low levels of reactivity because very little effort is warranted.

Once again, predictions derived from the energization model have been borne out. For example, Manuck, Harvey, Lechleiter, and Neal (1978) had subjects solve a series of easy or difficult concept formation problems, telling half of the subjects that success would prevent a "noise shock" from occurring after certain trials, and half that the noise shock would occur periodically regardless of how well they performed. Systolic blood pressure was greatest when the concept task was difficult and aversive stimulation was contingent on performance quality. When the task was easy and when stimulation was not related to performance, systolic elevations were uniformly low. Similar contingency effects have been reported by Contrada *et al.* (1982), Houston (1972), and Johnson (1963). Contrada *et al.* found greater SBP and diastolic blood pressure (DBP) reactivity in subjects who could avoid periodic presentations of noise and shock by performing well on a difficult RT task than in subjects who could not avoid noise and shock by performing well on the RT task. Houston and Johnson observed higher HRs in subjects who could avoid shock through performance on a difficult digit-span memory task and a tone discrimination task, respectively, than in subjects who could not avoid shock through performance on these tasks.

Only one study of this type yielded effects that are equivocal. Solomon, Holmes, and McCaul (1980) found greater digital vasoconstriction in subjects performing a difficult digit-span memory task than in subjects performing an easy digit-span memory task regardless of whether or not performance was related to the presentation of an electric shock. Whereas these results are open to different interpretations, one that is congruent with the energization analysis is that motives unrelated to the contingency manipulation (e.g., impression management) were involved in subjects' decisions of how hard to try. If so, the effort required by the difficult task may have appeared justified even in the noncontingent condition. On the other hand, it must be admitted that it is not at all clear why such motives would have been operating in this experiment if they were not operating in the other studies.

To summarize, the bulk of evidence from experiments in which subjects have or have not been allowed to avoid an aversive consequence by performing an easy or difficult experimental task suggests that energization is a nonmonotonic function of coping difficulty. As would be expected on the basis of Brehm's model, cardiovascular responsivity appears to be greatest when it is difficult, but possible and worthwhile, to avoid an aversive event. When negative outcomes are easy or impossible to avoid, such as in the Obrist *et al.* (1978) experiment, cardiovascular reactivity levels are relatively low. Similarly, when unpleasant outcomes are not contingent on quality of performance, as in the study by Manuck *et al.* (1978), reactivity levels tend to be low. Although these effects are quite consistent with the energization hypothesis, they would seem to contradict predictions based on stress and coping theory that the stress response will increase linearly as task demands approach or exceed an individual's perceived ability to cope.

Appetitive Studies. In addition to the avoidance studies, there are a few experiments involving difficulty manipulations that have employed appetitive paradigms. Although these are only indirectly related to the study of stress, they have clear relevance to questions concerning the proposed relationship between energization and the difficulty of goal attainment. Therefore, they will be reviewed briefly.

One of the earliest experiments was by Andreassi (1966). In it, HR was measured in subjects given the opportunity to earn money by performing either an easy or difficult paired-associate learning task. Apparently contradicting results of the avoidance studies, HR over trials was found to be greater in the easy task condition than in the difficult task condition.

The Andreassi findings could mean that, at least in an appetitive context, a low-effort task sometimes elicits greater cardiovascular responsiveness than a high-effort task. However, an alternative interpretation is possible. That is, subjects in the difficult condition may have stopped trying altogether if they perceived the monetary incentive as insufficient to justify the effort required by the experimental task. If these subjects exerted little to no effort, and subjects in the easy condition exerted a modest amount of effort, the data might be explanable in terms of the energization model.

Results of other appetitive experiments generally support this reasoning. For example, Elliott (1969, Experiment 2) told subjects they could earn a monetary incentive by correctly determining which of two tones more closely matched a standard tone presented earlier. Some subjects heard tones that were nearly identical, others heard tones that were moderately dissimilar, and still others heard tones that were highly dissimilar. When the tones were moderately difficult to discriminate, HRs increased steadily across trials. When the tones were extremely easy or extremely difficult to discriminate, however, HRs showed a steady decline over the course of the performance period.

In another study, by Light and Obrist (1983), subjects were offered money for success on a RT task that was designed to be easy, moderately difficult, or impossible. Those who were assigned the moderately difficult task had (a) shorter preejection periods and pulse transit times, and (b) higher SBP and DBP, than those who were assigned the impossible task. Cardiovascular responses in the easy RT condition did not differ from those in the difficult RT condition. However, ratings on a postexperimental questionnaire suggest that the easy/difficult manipulation probably was too weak to produce effects: estimates of task difficulty did not differ between the two conditions.

There were no such problems in recent experiments by Contrada, Wright, and Glass (1984) and Wright, Contrada, and Patane (1986), which included measures of anticipatory arousal. Contrada et al. told subjects they could earn three dollars by correctly solving 8 out of 10 math problems in an allotted time period. Half were assigned problems that were very easy, and half were assigned problems that were moderately difficult. As predicted, subjects expecting to work on the moderately difficult math problems showed greater anticipatory elevations in SBP than subjects expecting to work on the easy math problems. Wright *et al.* used trigram memorization as the experimental task. They found that subjects assigned a difficult memorization task to perform in order to earn a pen had higher anticipatory SBP elevations than subjects assigned an easy or impossible memorization task to perform to earn the pen.

Taken together, then, the appetitive studies provide additional support for the proposed nonlinear relation between coping difficulty and energization. With only minor, interpretable, exceptions, they show greater cardiovascular responsivity when attractive goals are difficult to obtain than when they are easy or impossible to obtain.

Incentive Value, Need, and Cardiovascular Reactivity

As noted earlier, stress and coping theory assumes that, unless coping is so easy that there is no real threat, stress and therefore cardiovascular reactivity will be proportional to the severity of an outcome being dealt with (i.e., incentive value). The possibility of a large cut in salary, for example, should be more threatening and produce more stress than the possibility of a small cut in salary. Though it has not been stated explicitly, it may be presumed also that stress should vary with need state. That is, an individual who has many mouths to feed, and therefore needs a full salary, should be more stressed by a possible paycut than an individual who must support only himself or herself.

The energization model, in contrast, views incentive value and need as determinants of potential motivation. Accordingly, it predicts that they will influence cardiovascular reactivity only when there is something to be done to cope with a stressor, and, then, only in two circumstances. To review, the first is where there is freedom to choose among tasks of different difficulties, and possible benefits increase with the difficulty of activity that is chosen. Here the organism is expected to engage in the most effortful behavior that is perceived to be justified by need and benefits at each level of difficulty. Once a level of activity is selected, energization should occur in proportion to the difficulty of that activity. The second circumstance is where task demands are vague or unknown. If there is not complete confidence in a perception of task difficulty, an individual is expected to exert more effort than is estimated to be minimally required. The magnitude of this effort overshoot should be a function of doubt × motive strength. If task demands are completely unknown, effort and energization should be the maximum allowed by the strength of the motive.

Several kinds of studies are relevant to these predictions. Perhaps most directly pertinent are those showing the potentiating effect of threat upon cardiovascular responsivity in college students. Exemplary are experiments by Houston (1972) and Solomon *et al.* (1980). In them, subjects performing digit-span memory tasks either were or were not threatened with electric shock for failure. Elevations in HR, and reductions in digital pulse volume, respectively, were substantially greater under threat than no threat conditions. Also relevant, though less directly so from a stress and coping point of view, are conceptually similar studies in which the value of positive incentives have been varied. Elliott (1969, Experiments 3, 4, & 5), for example, found that subjects performing a difficult RT task and Stroop's Color–Word Conflict task manifest HR increases that were directly proportional to the amount of money offered for good performance. Fowles and his colleagues (Fowles, Tranel, & Fisher, 1982; Tranel, Fisher, & Fowles, 1982) have obtained similar effects in subjects performing a demanding motor-coordination task.

This research usually is considered to support the stress and coping perspective, or at least the position that cardiovascular reactivity varies directly with incentives. However, a viable case can also be made for an energization interpretation of the effects. That is, it would appear that these studies represent the second circumstance described earlier, in which energization should be correlated with potential motivation. Tasks such as those used are not commonly encountered in everyday life, and the requirements for succeeding on them probably were not clear. Furthermore, subjects were not given the opportunity to practice before performance sessions began. If the subjects had an idea of how much effort would be needed, but were not certain of it, then an effort overshoot—of a magnitude determined, in part, by incentive value (degree of threat, amount of money offered)—would be expected. If the subjects had no idea about how much effort was needed, energization should have been the maximum warranted in the circumstance.

There appear to be no studies that directly test the hypothesis that energization and incentive value will be associated when task demands are vague, but dissociated when task demands are clear. Therefore, it is difficult to determine whether stress and coping theory or the energization hypothesis best accounts for such results. On the other hand, data from at least one experiment are highly consistent with the energization interpretation (Elliott, 1965). In it, subjects performed an RT task for one of three amounts of money over a series of 10 experimental sessions.

During early sessions (Sessions 1 to 4), when task requirements probably were ambiguous, findings were similar to those cited earlier: HR increases during performance were directly proportional to the value of the incentive. In the later sessions (Sessions 7 to 10), however, when demands should have been clear, HR was found to be unrelated to incentive value.

A second type of study that is relevant to predictions outlined at the beginning of this section involves the measurement of cardiovascular responses in animals working to obtain food or water under conditions of high or low deprivation. This research is well represented in classic work by Belanger and Feldman (1962) and Stern and his colleagues (e.g., Hahn, Stern, & McDonald, 1962). These investigators first deprived rats of liquid for periods ranging from 12 to 96 hours, and then monitored HRs while the animals bar-pressed for water. In general, results showed that HRs were higher the longer the animals had been deprived.

These experiments are often cited as documenting the direct effect of need on HR in the presence of an incentive, and, like the previous research using college students, may be viewed as generally consistent with stress and coping theory. Also like the previous studies, though, they can just as easily be interpreted in terms of the energization model. The circumstance represented here would seem to be the first in which energization and motive strength should be related. That is, the animals could bar-press at any speed, and the faster they pressed (i.e., the more effort they exerted), the faster they would obtain water. Because the willingness to exert effort under these conditions should increase with deprivation, so should energy levels during task performance.[1]

Interestingly, Belanger and Feldman (1962) and Hahn et al. (1962) measured the frequency of bar-pressing in their studies, and found that response frequency increased with deprivation up to a point (around 48 hours), but then decreased. Decreased responding at very high levels of deprivation would seem, at first blush, to contradict an analysis in terms of the energization hypothesis. However, an explanation for the effect suggested by Hahn et al. (1962) offers a possible resolution. They propose that when animals are deprived of water for a long time, they probably become weaker. As a result, the animals may have to exert more effort to execute relatively few bar-presses than less deprived animals do to execute many bar-presses. This interpretation of the Hahn et

---

[1] It is being assumed here that speed increases the value of the incentive. That is, a quantity x of water immediately is worth more to a thirsty animal than that same quantity of water some time later. It is possible, however, to conceive of time as a variable independent of incentive value that might determine potential motivation.

al. results is supported by additional data indicating significant weight loss in animals deprived of water for 72 or more hours.

Closely related to this research with animals are studies by Lipsitt and his associates concerned with the impact of incentives on HR in human neonates. Lipsitt, Reilly, Butcher, and Greenwood (1976) measured HR while infants sucked a bottle for 6 minutes receiving no fluid, and then sucked for 4 minutes receiving a 15% sucrose solution. Heart rates were higher in the sucrose condition than in the no fluid condition. Ashmead, Reilly, and Lipsitt (1980) extended this study by counterbalancing order, and including a condition in which infants received water. Half of the subjects sucked water-no fluid-sucrose, and half sucked sucrose-no fluid-water. When water was presented first to male infants, the Lipsitt *et al.* (1976) HR effects were replicated; however, when sucrose was presented first to males, HRs were relatively high in all fluid conditions. For females, HRs were relatively high in all fluid conditions, regardless of order. According to Lipsitt, results of the first study and in the male-subject, water-first conditions of the second study, show that HR can be used as an index of "pleasure" in infants. Effects in the sucrose-first conditions (for males), he contends, are a consequence of frustration aroused by the elimination of the sucrose solution.

Needless to say, these results are complicated. Interactions in the Ashmead *et al.* (1980) study involving order, and particularly gender, make a coherent interpretation of them especially difficult. Ignoring for the moment the gender effect, however, it would seem that the first set of findings could indicate that infants exerted more effort when receiving the sucrose solution than when receiving the nonsucrose solution or no fluid. Importantly, in both studies, sucking responses were more frequent and less spaced apart when there was sucrose than when there was not (although responses *within* a burst of sucking were more numerous in the nonsucrose conditions). An alternative explanation of HR effects in the nonsucrose conditions when sucrose was presented first is that they represent anticipatory arousal. Infants who had received the sucrose solution once may have expected the flow to resume at any time. If so, cardiovascular adjustments in preparation for effortful behavior would be expected.

By way of summary, a careful review of studies measuring cardiovascular reactivity under different levels of need and incentive value reveals primarily two things. First, as stress and coping theory would predict, there is considerable evidence that increases in threat and the value of positive incentives can serve to potentiate cardiovascular reactivity in subjects performing instrumental activity. Evidence of this comes from both the animal and human research literatures. Second, however, it also appears that studies showing these effects typically represent one or the other of the two circumstances in which, according to the energization hypothesis, energization and potential motivation should be related. Thus, at minimum, the findings cannot be viewed as contrary to that formulation. Indeed, an energization interpretation of the results is strengthened by results of one available study that apparently included conditions in which energization should and should not have been associated with energy levels (Elliott, 1965). When the experimental task was new, and presumably still unfamiliar to subjects, HRs were found to be positively related to incentives offered for good performance. Once the task had been performed for some time, and task demands should have been clearer, HRs and incentives were dissociated.

Instrumental Task Difficulty and the Magnitude of Goal Valence

Having established that at least one measure of energy mobilization, cardiovascular reactivity, varies in ways that are consistent with the energization hypothesis, we can now turn to studies examining subjective appraisals of potential outcomes under conditions where it is more or less difficult to cope. These studies, which have been carried out mainly by Brehm and his students at the University of Kansas, usually involve the following sequence: (a) the subject receives instructions describing the general purpose of the study and the nature of the task that can avert a negative outcome or lead to a positive outcome; (b) there is an anticipation period of variable length; (c) the experimenter interrupts just prior to the start of the task and has the subject complete a questionnaire assessing (among other things) perceptions of the outcome being sought or avoided; (d) the session ends. In an effort to prevent reactance (J. Brehm, 1966; S. Brehm & Brehm, 1981; Wicklund, 1974) and dissonance (J. Brehm & Cohen, 1962; Festinger, 1957; Wicklund & Brehm, 1976), the freedom to avoid a negative event or have a positive goal is not established prior to the introduction of the experimental task, and choice and commitment are minimized.

As stated previously, predictions based on the energization hypothesis are that the magnitude of goal valence (the perceived aversiveness or attractiveness of a potential outcome) will be high when instrumental activity is difficult, but possible and worthwhile, and relatively low when instrumental activity is easy, too difficult, or impossible. Stress and coping theory makes no clear predictions; however, it might be surmised on the basis of that perspective that the magnitude of goal valence would increase linearly with the perceived difficulty of instrumental activity.

Avoidance Studies. To date, four experiments employing avoidance paradigms have been published. In the first (Wright's first experiment, reported in J. Brehm *et al.* 1983), subjects were given the opportunity to avoid participating in an aversive shock experiment by doing well on a preliminary task. The task was to memorize two, four, or six nonsense trigrams within a 2-minute period, or to memorize 20 trigrams in 15 seconds. As expected, the potential shock was appraised as more aversive in the 4- and 6-trigram conditions than in the 2- and 20-trigram conditions. However, pair-wise comparisons involving the twenty trigram condition did not prove to be significant.

This study was followed by similar experiment in which the four trigram condition was dropped, and a timing manipulation was added (Wright's second experiment, reported in J. Brehm *et al.*, 1983). All subjects were told they would have to perform the 2-trigram, 6-trigram, or 20-trigram task in order to avoid the shock session. For half of the subjects, the procedure was the same as in the previous experiment, that is, the memorization task performance period was to occur immediately. For the other subjects, however, the task performance period was to occur approximately 30 minutes later. Reasoning that differences in energization as a function of task difficulty should occur only when instrumental task performance is imminent, the investigators predicted enhanced negative appraisals in the moderately difficult condition only when the task was to be performed right away. Results confirmed these expectations. The potential shock was rated significantly more aversive by subjects expecting to perform the 6-trigram task immediately than by subjects expecting to perform the 2- and 20-trigram memory tasks immediately. Unpleasantness ratings for subjects expecting to perform the preliminary task later were moderate and did not differ across difficulty conditions.

In the third experiment, the incentive was the same, but a different kind of avoidance task was used. As described earlier (see Instrumental Task Difficulty and Cardiovascular Responsiveness), Wright (1984) told subjects either that they could avoid an aversive shock session by making an easy or difficult dynamometer grip, or that they had been assigned to a group that could not avoid the shock session. Results indicated that subjects in the difficult avoidance condition thought it would be significantly more unpleasant to have to receive the shock than did subjects in the easy avoidance condition, and somewhat (not reliably) more unpleasant to have to receive the shock than did subjects in the impossible avoidance condition.

A dynamometer also was used in the fourth published experiment (Wright & Brehm, 1984). Subjects first listened to an unpleasant noise over headphones, and then were led to believe they could avoid a second presentation of it by making an easy, difficult, or impossible grip. As expected, unpleasantness ratings were higher in the difficult grip condition than in the easy grip condition. In the impossible grip condition, however, ratings were no different than those in the difficult grip condition.

Although high unpleasantness ratings in the impossible grip condition of this experiment were not predicted, and might be viewed as evidence contrary to the energization hypothesis, a word of caution is in order. As accounted in the research report, many subjects in the impossible condition stated after the study was over that they were prepared to forcibly remove the headphones if the noise became unbearable. If anticipatory energy mobilization took place for this reason, high unpleasantness ratings would make sense in terms of the theory.

Fortunately, this interpretation can be evaluated to an extent through results of a recent unpublished study (Wright, Solomon, Silka, & Brehm, 1986) in which subjects also were threatened with noise. In this case, the noise was to be presented over loud speakers in an anechoic chamber; therefore the extraexperimental means of escape present in the impossible condition of the Wright and Brehm study was not readily available. Under these circumstances, unpleasantness ratings were significantly lower in the impossible avoidance condition than in a difficult avoidance condition.

Appetitive Studies. Studies employing appetitive paradigms have involved a variety of tasks and goals. Two of the earliest were experiments by Vought (1977, Experiment 1) and Solomon and Silka (reported in J. Brehm *et al.*, 1983). Vought gave subjects the opportunity to win a one-dollar prize by successfully performing a dynamometer grip. For some subjects, the grip was half again as hard as an initial maximum grip they had taken at the beginning of the session, whereas for the rest, the grip was only three quarters as hard as the initial grip. As expected, subjects faced with the difficult grip rated the dollar more attractive than subjects faced with the easy grip. In the Solomon and Silka study, subjects could earn a dollar by successfully solving 8 out of 10 math problems designed to be easy, moderately difficult, or impossible. Consistent with predictions, again, ratings of the dollar were higher in the moderately difficult condition than in the easy and impossible conditions, where ratings did not differ.

These first experiments served as prototypes for a host of subsequent investigations. Toi (1980) told subjects they could qualify for an in-depth study of personality by solving the same math problems used by Solomon and Silka. Contrada *et al.* (1984) also used the Solomon and Silka problems, with three dollars as an incentive. In a study by Wright, Toi, and Brehm (1984), male subjects were led to believe they could work with an attractive female assistant if they passed a memory test that was easy, difficult, or impossible. Roberson (1985) used the same incentive, but a different kind of task. He told males they could work with a target female if they could convince her to choose them over another fellow, and then led them to believe this would be easy, difficult, or impossible. Finally, Wright, Contrada, and Patane (1986) gave subjects the opportunity to earn a pen by succeeding on a memory test that was easy, difficult, or impossible. In all but one of these experiments, results were in accordance with those obtained by Vought (1977) and Solomon and Silka (reported in J. Brehm *et al.*, 1983). The one exception was the study by Contrada *et al.* (1984), which yielded significant difficulty effects for SBP (see earlier description), but not goal attractiveness.[2]

A few investigators have moved beyond this basic format, and designed experiments with special conditions to assess the viability of specific alternative explanations of the goal attractiveness effects and predictions unique to the energization model. Again, Vought (1977, Experiment 2) was among the first. The aim of his research was to test the possibility that results such as those described earlier were due to between-condition differences in probability of goal attainment, rather than difficulty per se. Some subjects were told they could earn a dollar by performing a dynamometer grip, and other subjects were told they could win a dollar in a lottery. In the dynamometer conditions, the required grip was to be 50%, 120%, or 200% of an initial maximum grip that had been made at the start of the session. In the lottery conditions, the likelihood of success was either 50% or 80%. As predicted, goal attractiveness ratings were higher in the 120% dynamometer condition than in the 50% and 200% dynamometer conditions, but did not differ in the lottery conditions.

Solomon and Greenberg (reported in J. Brehm *et al.*, 1983) attempted to evaluate a dissonance interpretation of the goal attractiveness effects. As pointed out earlier, the goal valence studies have minimized choice and commitment, therefore, conditions thought to be necessary for the arousal of dissonance (Wicklund & Brehm, 1976) should not have been present. Furthermore, in most, subjects in the moderately difficult conditions were unsure about whether or not they would attain a goal or

---

[2]In the experiment by Toi (1980), participation ratings were higher in the moderately difficult qualifying condition than in the easy and impossible qualifying conditions for male subjects only. For females, ratings were low in all experimental conditions. Though the reason for the null effect for females is not certain, one possibility is that those in the moderately difficult condition gave up. Whereas the males in that condition reported that it was fairly likely that they could solve the problems, the females reported that they probably could not.

avoid an outcome. This is important, because Jecker (1964) has shown that dissonance reduction does not occur with probabilistic outcomes until the outcome is known. Nevertheless, it might be argued that choice in these studies was implicit, and that perhaps subjective estimates of the likelihood of goal attainment were different from the ones indicated publically on the dependent questionnaires. If so, a dissonance explanation would be plausible.

Solomon and Greenberg's strategy was to have subjects rate an incentive immediately before they began working on easy or difficult math problems, or 5 minutes after completing work on the problems (before performance feedback was provided). They reasoned that, if dissonance were operating, goal attractiveness differences as a function of task difficulty should be found both before and after task performance, because the tendency to justify effort should be at least as strong after work as before. If the effects are due to energization, on the other hand, goal attractiveness ratings should be higher in the difficult condition than in the easy condition only when measures are taken immediately before task performance. After a task is completed, energy levels in both difficulty conditions should return to baseline, and attractiveness ratings should be the same. Results supported the energization interpretation. The incentive was rated more valuable in the difficult/immediate performance condition than in all other conditions, in which ratings did not differ.

A final experiment, by Biner (1985), tested the hypothesis that incentive value will interact with task difficulty to determine goal attractiveness. Ratings of goal attractiveness were obtained immediately before a task performance period in which subjects could earn a modest incentive (one dollar) or a valuable incentive (a record album) by succeeding on a memory task that was easy, moderately difficult, or very difficult. Two primary results confirmed theoretical expectations. When incentive value was high, goal attractiveness ratings increased from the easy condition to the moderately difficult condition, and then remained high in the very difficult condition. When incentive value was low, on the other hand, goal attractiveness ratings increased from the easy to the moderately difficult condition, and then decreased in the very difficult condition.

Summary. The studies presented here constitute an impressive body of evidence in favor of the proposition that the magnitude of goal valence varies directly with energy mobilized for instrumental activity, and therefore is a nonmonotonic function of the difficulty of coping. Most obviously relevant are the avoidance studies. They indicate clearly that negative outcomes are appraised as less aversive when they are easy to avoid than when they are difficult to avoid. They also provide evidence that negative appraisals are reduced when avoidance is impossible relative to when avoidance is difficult, though findings are less clear in this regard. In contrast to what might be expected from stress and coping theory, there is virtually no evidence from these experiments that negative outcomes are perceived as most aversive when they are uncontrollable.

Studies using appetitive paradigms are even more consistent in confirming predictions derived from the energization hypothesis, and make strides toward ruling out alternative explanations of the results.

Residual Arousal and Appraisals of an Outcome's Being Avoided

The final studies we will consider represent attempts to examine the effects of energization on perceptions of a potential negative outcome directly, without manipulating the difficulty of avoiding the event. Their importance derives from the fact that studies such as those described so far show only that cardiovascular reactivity and outcome appraisals covary under different experimental conditions. For a causal relationship between energization and the magnitude of goal valence to be established, energy levels must be varied independent of task difficulty. There are only three of these experiments; each was conducted in the present author's laboratory.

The first (Wright, 1982, Experiment 1) was patterned roughly after an investigation by Cantor, Bryant, and Zillmann (1974), which was concerned with the effects of residual arousal on humor appreciation. Subjects were first asked to read passages that were erotic, violent, or educational, and then, shortly thereafter, were informed that they could avoid being in an aversive shock experiment by memorizing two trigrams. Predictions were that residual arousal from the high excitatory passages would transfer (Zillmann, 1983) and cause the potential shock to be appraised as more aversive than it would be otherwise. Consistent with these expectations, shock unpleasantness ratings were higher in the erotic and violent conditions than in the educational condition. Also as expected, the affective tone of the passages had no influence on unpleasantness ratings.

Although the major hypotheses were supported in this experiment, an energization interpretation of it was weakened by results on a manipulation check. Unexpectedly, ratings of how arousing the violent passage was were no different than ratings of how arousing the neutral passage was. Values in both of these conditions were significantly lower than those in the erotic passage condition. On the possibility that some subjects interpreted the question to ask how *sexually* arousing the passages were—which the violent passage clearly was not—a replication was conducted (Wright, 1982, Experiment 2). This time general arousal was specified. As predicted, subjects assigned the erotic and violent passages had higher arousal ratings than subjects assigned the educational passage, and the goal valence effects were replicated.

The other study of this type was carried out by Joy Weeks, Diane Burch, and Hilda Hernandez at the University of Texas-Austin under the author's supervision. Male subjects were told the investigators were interested in the relationships among fitness, intelligence, and personality type. The first task was to perform a stair-stepping exercise; for half of the subjects, this was made very easy, whereas for the others it was moderately difficult. To reinforce the cover story, the experimenter took each subject's pulse after the task was completed. Subjects were then taken to a cubicle to await instructions concerning what they were to do next. The experimenter returned, 1, 5, or 9 minutes later, telling subjects they would have 15 minutes to unscramble 15 anagrams. All subjects received the same anagrams, which had deliberately been made easy. Subjects were told that, if they unscrambled all of the anagrams, they could leave the session early, and thereby avoid reading a series of scientific articles. Immediately before subjects began working on the task, the experimenter interrupted with a questionnaire asking, among other things, how unpleasant subjects thought it would be to have to remain and read scientific articles.

Following work of Cantor, Zillmann, and Bryant (1975), it was predicted that arousal transfer effects like those in the Wright (1982) studies would be found only when subjects had performed a high-effort exercise, and waited 5 minutes before receiving instructions about the anagram task. The low-effort stepping exercise was expected to produce little residual arousal, regardless of how long the subject waited. In the high-effort conditions, subjects who waited one minute should have attributed the excess arousal to the just-completed exercise, and subjects who waited 9 minutes should have been back to baseline.

Unpleasantness ratings generally supported these predictions. In the high-effort conditions, the proportion of ratings above the group median in the 1-minute, 5-minute, and 9-minute conditions were .44, .80, and .25, respectively. In the low-effort conditions, proportions were .56, .44, and .44, respectively. An analysis of variance performed on the arc sine transformed proportions (see Langer & Abelson, 1972) yielded a marginally significant interaction ($p < .06$). A planned contrast of the high-effort/5-minute cell against all others was reliable at the 2% confidence level, with no significant residual.[3]

---

[3]Median splits were performed because distributions in some cells were highly skewed.

SUMMARY, CONCLUSIONS, AND COMMENTS

The question of how people respond in aversive circumstances is important for a variety of reasons. Perhaps principal among these are the linkages that have been established between "stress" and different physical and mental health disorders (Krantz, Glass, Contrada, & Miller, 1981). Typically, this problem is approached from the point of view of stress and coping theory, a perspective that emphasizes control and outcome severity as major determinants of potentially pathological subjective and physiologic reactions. In this chapter, I have presented a theory that offers a novel and interesting alternative framework for conceptualizing responses to threat. In my view, it warrants serious consideration by investigators studying stress.

The focus of the chapter has been on areas in which Brehm's energization hypothesis and conventional stress and coping theory differ. A review of four kinds of research related to contrasting predictions that may be derived shows that available evidence is largely supportive of, or at least not in conflict with, predictions from the energization model. Summarized, the studies indicate (a) that cardiovascular reactivity varies nonmonotonically with the difficulty of coping, (b) that the variables need and incentive value can potentiate cardiovascular reactivity, but (apparently) only in those special circumstances in which the energization hypothesis proposes that effort should increase with motive strength, (c) that the magnitude of goal valence varies nonmonotonically with instrumental task difficulty, and (d) that negative outcomes are perceived as more aversive under conditions that are conducive to arousal transfer effects (Zillmann, 1983) than under conditions that are not. These findings are highly consistent with the energization model, but are difficult to fit into a stress and coping theoretical analysis.

One explanation that could be offered for diminished cardiovascular reactivity and reduced appraisals of a stressor under impossible avoidance conditions stems from a distinction made by Folkman (1984) between two types of coping. She argues that so long as something can be done to deal with a stressor, efforts to cope will be problem focused, that is, directed toward removing or averting the stressor itself. When a negative outcome is unavoidable, however, she proposes that efforts to cope will be emotion focused, or aimed at managing one's affective/emotional response. One strategy for reducing an emotional response would be to reappraise the stressor as relatively benign; to the extent that this can be done, the stress response should be reduced.

Although it seems reasonable that people sometimes engage in strategies aimed at controlling negative emotional reactions, it is doubtful that this can explain the findings that have been reviewed here. For one thing, if such an interpretation is to be viable, we must assume that subjects are remarkably adept at reappraising outcomes. In a number of studies (e.g., Manuck et al., 1978; Obrist et al., 1978; Wright, 1982) cardiovascular responses were found to be no different when it was impossible to avoid a stressor than when it was easy to avoid a stressor. This suggests that subjects' reappraisals were effective not only in reducing stress, but in reducing it to nonthreat levels! Although this is conceivable, it seems like a lot to expect from subjects in the usually brief time frame available in an experimental session.

A second difficulty is that this explanation cannot easily account for results obtained in some of the goal valence studies. For example, in the second avoidance experiment by Wright (reported in J. Brehm et al., 1983) appraisals of the electric shock were different across difficulty conditions only when the instrumental task was to be performed right away. Does this suggest that reappraisal took place in all conditions in which there was to be a delay? Or perhaps that there was no stress in these conditions, because activity was not imminent? Both interpretations seem contrived, unwieldy, and not particularly satisfying. Similar questions can be raised concerning the residual arousal studies, which seem virtually unexplainable in purely cognitive terms.

Whereas the energization model would appear to provide a comprehensive and parsimonious accounting for a sizable body of data, it should be recognized that there are a number of questions of interest to stress-and-coping theorists that it does not speak to. One of the most important may be the question of anxiety. Although it is proposed that energization and negative appraisals of an aversive outcome vary as a function of coping difficulty, there is no reason, theoretically, to presume that anxiety will track these responses. Indeed, there is considerable empirical evidence suggesting that these variables are not always associated in an avoidance context. For example, self-reported anxiety has sometimes (e.g., Bloom, Houston, Burish, 1976; Bloom & Trautt, 1977; Johnson, 1963), but not always (e.g., Elliott, 1969, Experiment 1; Houston, 1972; Lovallo et al., 1985; Manuck et al., 1978; Solomon et al., 1980), been found to increase with cardiovascular reactivity. Similarly, reports of anxiety have sometimes (Wright, 1984; Wright & Brehm, 1984), but not always (Wright's first and second experiments, reported in J. Brehm et al., 1983), been found to increase with negative appraisals of a potential aversive outcome. Although inconsistencies in these results may be due, in part, to the inadequacies of self-report techniques (Spielberger, 1975), a point of theoretical significance may be indicated as well. That is, it seems reasonable that the determinants of motivation and anxiety simply are different.

There are, of course, many theories of anxiety, and it is beyond the scope of the present paper to review them here (see Epstein, 1972). Our own approach to this problem has been to distinguish between what may be considered two essential activities involved in coping, that is, the selection and execution of appropriate instrumental behavior. We have taken the position that motivation will vary (nonmonotonically) with the effortfulness of these activities, but that anxiety will occur only when there is behavioral uncertainty under threat (Wright, 1981). This hypothesis has received tentative support in two recent experiments. The first (Wright, 1984) showed greater cardiovascular arousal and anxiety in subjects who could avoid shock by making a difficult behavioral decision than (a) in subjects who could avoid shock by making an easy behavioral decision, and (b) in subjects who could only reduce their chance of getting shocked by 50% by making an easy behavioral decision.[4] This effect has been replicated and extended in a second study (Wright & Perez, 1986). As before, the difficulty of a behavioral decision subjects were required to make (to avoid noise) was found to be positively related to both cardiovascular reactivity and self-reported anxiety. However, the difficulty of a dynamometer grip that was also required was associated only with cardiovascular arousal. When behavioral uncertainty was low, anxiety was low, regardless of how difficult the grip had to be.

Another important question that the energization model does not address directly is that of depression. Learned helplessness theory (Seligman, 1975) suggests that the perception that one cannot control important outcomes should lead to dysphoria. Although there is evidence to substantiate this position (see Wortman & Brehm, 1975, for a review), it may be overstepping to say that helplessness per se is sufficient to produce depression. In the course of living, individuals encounter many significant outcomes that are impossible or not worthwhile for them to pursue (e.g., movie stardom, the presidency), and it seems unlikely that they always become depressed when considering these events. Indeed, this is borne out in the studies we have reviewed here. Measures of dysphoric affect were rarely included in the psychophysiological studies. However, affect was assessed in almost all of the studies examining outcome appraisals as a function of instrumental task difficulty. Although subjects faced with extremely difficult or impossible tasks usually reported feeling more helpless than did subjects faced with easy or moderately difficult tasks, they almost never reported feeling more tired, bored, depressed, or unhappy than did the other subjects (cf. Toi, 1980).

---

[4]These aspects of this experiment were not discussed earlier because they made the description of it unnecessarily complicated, and were not directly pertinent to the energization model.

What may be critical about these studies is the fact that, generally speaking, it is safe to assume that subjects did not feel free to attain or avoid outcomes prior to the introduction of instrumental tasks. As pointed out earlier, this was done in part to rule out reactance as an alternative explanation of goal attractiveness effects in the easy and moderately difficult conditions. The move may have had broader implications, however. In discussing the relationship between the energization model and depression, S. Brehm and J. Brehm (1981) distinguished two ways of becoming helpless. The first is to start out believing that motive satisfaction is too difficult or impossible, and never experience motivational arousal in regard to a motive. The second is to start out believing that an outcome is difficult to attain, but worthwhile and clearly within reach, and then learn that it is unattainable or too difficult to attain to be worth the effort. These investigators argue that the former circumstance should produce helplessness without depression. The latter circumstance is proposed to be associated with depression, but only if an individual has actually become energized for instrumental behavior. Implications of this hypothesis are manifold and warrant empirical attention.

ACKNOWLEDGMENTS

I would like to thank Jack W. Brehm, Arnold H. Buss, Richard J. Contrada, and the editors of this volume for their very helpful comments on earlier drafts of this manuscript.

REFERENCES

Andreassi, J. L. (1966). Some physiological correlates of verbal learning task difficulty. *Psychonomic Science, 6,* 69–70.

Ashmead, D. H., Reilly, B. M., & Lipsitt, L. P. Neonates' heart rate, sucking rhythm, and sucking amplitude as a function of sweet taste. *Journal of Experimental Child Psychology, 29,* 264–281.

Baum, A., Grunberg, N. E., & Singer, J. E. (1982). The use of psychological and neuroendocrinological measurements in the study of stress. *Health Psychology, 1,* 217–236.

Belanger, D., & Feldman, S. M. (1962). Effects of water deprivation upon heart rate and instrumental activity in the rat. *Journal of Comparative and Physiological Psychology, 55,* 220–225.

Biner, P. M. (1985). *The interactive effect of perceived task difficulty and motive value on motivational arousal.* Unpublished doctoral dissertation, University of Kansas, Lawrence, KS.

Bloom, L. J., & Trautt, G. M. (1977). Finger pulse volume as a measure of anxiety: Further evaluation. *Psychophysiology, 14,* 541–544.

Bloom, L. J., Houston, B. K., & Burish, T. G. (1976). An evaluation of finger pulse volume as a physiological measure anxiety. *Psychophysiology, 13,* 40–42.

Brehm, J. W. (1966). *A theory of psychological reactance.* New York: Academic Press.

Brehm, J. W. (1979). *Perceived difficulty and energization.* Grant proposal (Department of Psychology, University of Kansas, Lawrence, KS).

Brehm, J. W., & Cohen, A. R. (1962). *Explorations in cognitive dissonance.* New York: Wiley.

Brehm, J. W., Wright, R. A., Solomon, S., Silka, L., & Greenberg, J. (1983). Perceived difficulty, energization, and the magnitude of goal valence. *Journal of Experimental Social Psychology, 19,* 21–48.

Brehm, S. S., & Brehm, J. W. (1981). *Psychological reactance: A theory of freedom and control.* New York: Academic Press.

Cacioppo, J. T. & Petty, R. E. (Eds.). (1982). *Perspectives in cardiovascular psychophysiology.* New York: Guilford.

Campbell, J. P., & Pritchard, R. D. (1976). Motivation theory in industrial and organizational psychology. In M. D. Dunnette (Ed.), *Handbook of industrial and organizational psychology* (pp. 63–129). Chicago, IL: Rand McNally.

Cannon, W. B. (1924). *Bodily changes in pain, hunger, fear, and rage.* Boston, MA: Branford.

Cantor, J. R., Bryant, J., & Zillmann, D. (1974). Enhancement of humor appreciation by transferred excitation. *Journal of Personality and Social Psychology, 30,* 812–821.

Cantor, J. R., Zillmann, D., & Bryant, J. (1975). Enhancement of experienced sexual arousal in response to erotic stimuli through the misattribution of unrelated residual excitation. *Journal of Personality and Social Psychology, 32,* 69–75.

Cofer, C. N., & Appley, M. H. (1964). *Motivation: Theory and research.* New York: Wiley.

Contrada, R. J., Glass, D. C., Krakoff, L. R., Krantz, D. S., Kehoe, K., Isecke, W., Collins, C., & Elting, E. (1982). Effects of control over aversive stimulation and Type A behavior on cardiovascular and plasma catecholamine responses. *Psychophysiology, 19,* 408–419.

Contrada, R. J., Wright, R. A., & Glass, D. C. (1984). Task difficulty, Type A behavior pattern, and cardiovascular response. *Psychophysiology, 21,* 638–646.

Cox, T. (1978). *Stress.* Baltimore, MD: University Park Press.

Elliott, R. (1965). Reaction time and heart rate as functions of magnitude of incentive and probability of success. *Journal of Personality and Social Psychology, 2,* 604–609.

Elliott, R. (1969). Tonic heart rate: Experiments on the effect of collative variables lead to a hypothesis about its motivational significance. *Journal of Personality and Social Psychology, 12,* 211–228.

Epstein, S. (1972). The nature of anxiety with emphasis on its relationship to expectancy. In C. D. Spielberger (Ed.), *Anxiety: Current trends in theory and research* (pp. 291–337). New York: Academic Press.

Festinger, L. (1957). *A theory of cognitive dissonance.* Stanford, CA: Stanford University Press.

Folkman, S. (1984). Personal control and stress and coping processes: A theoretical analysis. *Journal of Personality and Social Psychology, 46,* 839–852.

Fowles, D. C. (1982). Heart rate as an index of anxiety: Failure of a hypothesis. In J. T. Cacioppo & R. E. Petty (Eds.), *Perspectives in cardiovascular psychophysiology* (pp. 93–126). New York: Guilford.

Fowles, D. C. (1983). Motivational effects on heart rate and electrodermal activity: Implications for research on personality and psychopathology. *Journal of Research in Personality, 17,* 48–71.

Fowles, D. C., Fisher, A. E., & Tranel, D. T. (1982). The heart beats to reward: The effect of monetary incentive on heart rate. *Psychophysiology, 19,* 506–513.

Ford, C. E., Wright, R. A., & Haythornthwaite, J. A. (1985). Task performance and the magnitude of goal valence. *Journal of Research in Personality, 19,* 253–260.

Hahn, W. W., Stern, J. A., & McDonald, D. G. (1962). Effects of water deprivation and bar pressing activity on heart rate of the male albino rat. *Journal of Comparative and Physiological Psychology, 55,* 786–790.

Hassett, J. (1978). *A primer of psychophysiology.* San Francisco: W. H. Freeman.

Hill, T., Fultz, J., & Biner, P. M. (1985). Incidental learning as a function of anticipated task difficulty. *Motivation and Emotion, 9,* 71–85.

Houston, B. K. (1972). Control over stress, locus of control, and responses to stress. *Journal of Personality and Social Psychology, 21,* 249–255.

Jecker, J. D. (1964). The cognitive effects of conflict and dissonance. In L. Festinger (Ed.), *Conflict, decision, and dissonance* (pp. 21–30). Stanford, Ca: Stanford University Press.

Johnson, H. J. (1963). Decision making, conflict, and physiological arousal. *Journal of Abnormal and Social Psychology, 2,* 114–124.

Krantz, D. S., Glass, D. C., Contrada, R. J., & Miller, N. E. (1981). Behavior and health. In the National Science Foundation's *Five year outlook on science and technology: 1981* (Source Materials, Vol. 2, pp. 561–588). Washington, DC: U.S. Government Printing Office.

Kukla, A. (1972). Foundations of an attributional theory of performance. *Psychological Review, 79,* 454–470.

Langer, E. J., & Abelson, R. P. (1972). The semantics of asking a favor: How to succeed without really dying. *Journal of Personality and Social Psychology, 24,* 26–32.

Lazarus, R. S. (1966). *Psychological stress and the coping process.* New York: McGraw-Hill.

Lewin, K. (1935). *A dynamic theory of personality.* New York: McGraw-Hill.

Light, K. C., & Obrist, P. (1980). Cardiovascular response to stress: Effects of the opportunity to avoid shock, shock experience, and performance feedback. *Psychophysiology, 17,* 243–252.

Light, K. C., & Obrist, P. (1983). Task difficulty, heart rate reactivity, and cardiovascular responses to an appetitive reaction time task. *Psychophysiology, 20,* 301–312.

Lipsitt, L. P., Reilly, B. M., Butcher, M. J., & Greenwood, M. M. (1976). The stability and interrelationships of newborn sucking and heart rate. *Developmental Biology, 9,* 305–310.

Lovallo, W. R., Wilson, M. F., Pincomb, G. A., Edwards, G. L., Tompkins, P., & Brackett, D. J. (1985). Activation patterns to aversive stimulation in man: Passive exposure versus effort to control. *Psychophysiology, 22,* 283–291.

Malcuit, G. (1973). Cardiac responses in aversive situation with and without avoidance possibility. *Psychophysiology, 10,* 295–306.

Malmo, R. B. (1958). Measurement of drive: An unresolved problem in psychology. In M. R. Jones (Ed.), *Nebraska Symposium on Motivation.* Lincoln, NE: University of Nebraska Press.

Manuck, S. B., Harvey, S. H., Lechleiter, S. L., & Neal, K. S. (1978). Effects of coping on blood pressure responses to threat of aversive stimulation. *Psychophysiology, 15,* 544–549.

Mason, J. W. (1972). Organization of psychoendocrine mechanisms: A review and reconsideration of research. In N. S. Greenfield & R. A. Sternbach (Eds.), *Handbook of psychophysiology* (pp. 3–91). New York: Holt, Rinehart, & Winston.

Obrist, P. A. (1976). The cardiovascular-behavioral interaction as it appears today. *Psychophysiology, 13,* 95–107.

Obrist, P. A. (1981). *Cardiovascular psychophysiology: A perspective.* New York: Plenum Press.

Obrist, P. A. (1982). Cardiac-behavioral interactions: A critical appraisal. In J. T. Cacioppo & R. E. Petty (Eds.), *Perspectives in cardiovascular psychophysiology* (pp. 265–295). New York: Guilford.

Obrist, P. A., Gaebelein, C. J., Teller, E. S., Langer, A. W., Grignolo, A., Light, K. C., &

McCubbin, J. A. (1978). The relationship among heart rate, carotid dP/dt, and blood pressure in humans as a function of type of stress. *Psychophysiology, 15*, 102–115.

Pfaff, D. W. (Ed.). (1982). *The physiological mechanisms of motivation.* New York: Springer-Verlag.

Roberson, B. F. (1985). *The effect of task characteristics and motivational arousal on the perceived valence of multiple outcomes.* Unpublished doctoral dissertation, University of Kansas, Lawrence, KS.

Scher, H., Furedy, J. J., & Heslegrave, R. J. (1984). Phasic T-wave amplitude and heart rate changes as indices of mental effort and task incentive. *Psychophysiology, 21*, 326–333.

Seligman, M. E. P. (1975). *Helplessness: On depression, development, and death.* San Fransisco: W. H. Freeman.

Selye, H. (1976). *The stress of life* (rev. ed.). New York: McGraw-Hill.

Solomon, S., Holmes, D., & McCaul, K. D. (1980). Behavioral control over aversive events: Does control that requires effort reduce anxiety and physiological arousal? *Journal of Personality and Social Psychology, 39*, 729–736.

Spielberger, C. D. (1975). The measurement of state and trait anxiety: Conceptual and methodological issues. In T. Levi (Ed.), *Emotions—Their parameters and measurement* (pp. 712–725). New York: Raven Press.

Stellar, J. R., & Stellar, E. (1985). *The neurobiology of motivation and reward.* New York: Springer-Verlag.

Surwit, R. S., Williams, R. B., & Shapiro, D. (1982). *Behavioral approaches to cardiovascular disease.* New York: Academic Press.

Toi, M. (1980). *The effect of perceived difficulty of cognitive task on goal attractiveness.* Unpublished master's thesis, University of Kansas, Lawrence, KS.

Tranel, D. T., Fisher, A. E., & Fowles, D. C. (1982). Magnitude of incentive effects upon the heart. *Psychophysiology, 19*, 514–519.

Vought, C. (1977). *The effect of physical difficulty on goal attractiveness.* Unpublished master's thesis, University of Kansas, Lawrence, KS.

Weiner, B. (1972). *Theories of motivation.* Chicago, IL: Markham.

Wicklund, R. A. (1974). *Freedom and reactance.* Hillsdale, NJ: Erlbaum.

Wicklund, R. A., & Brehm, J. W. (1976). *Perspectives on cognitive dissonance.* Hillsdale, NJ: Erlbaum.

Wortman, C. B., & Brehm, J. W. (1975). Responses to uncontrollable outcomes: An integration of reactance theory and the learned helplessness model. In L. Berkowitz (Ed.), *Advances in experimental social psychology* (Vol. 8, pp. 277–336). New York: Academic Press.

Wright, R. A. (1981). *Motivation, anxiety, and the difficulty of control.* Proposal for Individual National Service Award (National Institute of Mental Health).

Wright, R. A. (1982). Perceived motivational arousal as a mediator of the magnitude of goal valence. *Motivation and Emotion, 6*, 161–180.

Wright, R. A. (1984). Motivation, anxiety, and the difficulty of avoidant control. *Journal of Personality and Social Psychology, 46*, 1376–1388.

Wright, R. A., & Brehm, J. W. (1984). The impact of task difficulty upon perceptions of arousal and goal attractiveness in an avoidance paradigm. *Motivation and Emotion, 8*, 171–181.

Wright, R. A., & Perez, J. M. (1986). *The impact of effort, response uncertainty, and outcome uncertainty upon anticipatory cardiovascular responsiveness and subjective stress in an avoidance paradigm.* Manuscript submitted for publication.

Wright, R. A., Toi, M., & Brehm, J. W. (1984). Difficulty and interpersonal attraction. *Motivation and Emotion, 8*, 327–341.

Wright, R. A., Solomon, S. Silka, L., & Brehm, J. (1986). *Difficulty and availability of avoidance behavior as determinants of affect and the perceived unpleasantness of a potential negative outcome.* Manuscript submitted for publication.

Wright, R. A., Contrada, R. J., & Patane, M. J. (1986). Task difficulty, cardiovascular response, and the magnitude of goal valence. *Journal of Personality and Social Psychology, 52,* 837–843.

Zillmann, D. (1983). Transfer of excitation in emotional behavior. In J. T. Cacioppo & R. E. Petty (Eds.), *Social psychophysiology: A sourcebook* (pp. 215–235). New York: Guilford.

4

Effort Expenditure Following Failure

CAROL E. FORD and JACK W. BREHM

INTRODUCTION

There is a large body of research documenting the alternatively de-
leterious or beneficial effects of an experience with failure on subsequent
performance. Performance feedback on an achievement-oriented task is,
in fact, one of the most common independent variables to be found in
clinical and social psychological research. Work on the effects of failure
on subsequent performance has been used to examine a number of
theoretical models; failure induction studies have been conducted by
researchers interested, among other things, in test anxiety, depression,
attributional processes, achievement motivation, stress, and frustration
(Coyne, Metalsky, & Lavelle, 1980).

As would be expected given the amount of research using failure
paradigms, and the range in theoretical rationales, a variety of situational and individual differences variables have been shown to moderate
the relationship between failure and subsequent performance. Performance following failure has been affected, for example, by factors such
as the complexity of the failure-induction task as manipulated by the
experimenter (Douglas & Anisman, 1975) or perceived by the subject
(Levine, Rotkin, Pitchford, & Jankovick, 1977), prior experience with

CAROL E. FORD • Department of Psychology, University of Missouri, Columbia, MO
65211. JACK W. BREHM • Department of Psychology, University of Kansas, Lawrence, KS 66045.

success in the testing situation (Klee & Meyer, 1979; Klein & Seligman, 1976), the amount of failure feedback (Pittman & Pittman, 1979, 1980), the similarity between the failure experience and subsequent tasks or situations (Cole & Coyne, 1977; Pasahow, 1980), self-esteem (Shrauger & Sorman, 1977), generality of attributional style (Alloy, Peterson, Abramson, & Seligman, 1984), locus of control (e.g., Cohen, Rothbart, & Phillips, 1976; Gregory, Chartier, & Wright, 1979), and test anxiety (Lavelle, Metalsky, & Coyne, 1979).

In the last 15 years, a notable proportion of the work on the effects of failure on subsequent performance has been generated by, or discussed in terms of, learned helplessness theory (e.g., Seligman, 1975). Although theoretically concerned with responses to noncontingency, most of the research on helplessness in humans has employed some type of failure-induction, with subsequent task performance as the primary dependent measure (Coyne *et al.*, 1980). Based on the assumptions that failure experiences represent a subset of uncontrollable outcomes, and that subsequent deficits in performance may be considered manifestations of the postulated cognitive and motivational consequences of noncontingency, demonstrations of performance interference following failure have been obtained, or cited, as evidence for helplessness theory (e.g., Harris & Tyron, 1983; Hiroto, 1974; Hiroto & Seligman, 1975; Klein, Fencil-Morse, & Seligman, 1976; Peterson, 1985).

In addition to being the stimulus for much research using failure inductions, the topic of learned helplessness has been the subject of much criticism (e.g., Buchwald, Coyne, & Cole, 1978; Costello, 1978; Coyne *et al.*, 1980). Questions have been raised both regarding the adequacy of the methodologies used to test the theory and regarding the theory's ability to explain the findings it stimulated. Despite numerous attempts to expand or revise the original hypotheses of the theory (e.g., Abramson, Seligman, & Teasdale, 1978; Miller & Norman, 1979; Roth, 1980; Wortman & Brehm, 1975), a number of troublesome issues remain unresolved.

In the present chapter, we will briefly outline the history of the concept of learned helplessness in humans; given the number of comprehensive reviews that are available (e.g., Miller & Norman, 1979; Roth, 1980), our primary purpose will be to highlight the conceptual and methodological problems that seriously limit the usefulness of the theory as an explanation of the effects of failure on subsequent performance. In addition, we will argue that a more parsimonious account of the mechanisms involved in the motivational effects of failure is suggested by recent work by Brehm and his colleagues (e.g., Brehm, Wright, Solomon, Silka, & Greenberg, 1983) on the determinants of motivational arousal, or energization. Unlike helplessness theory, the energization model suggests a means of predicting and explaining both increases and declines in motivation following failure, and thus the enhancing and interfering performance effects that have been observed. The model also provides a unified framework for many of the specific processes that have been discussed by various researchers, and for understanding a number of the moderating variables that have been identified.

LEARNED HELPLESSNESS: CONCEPTS AND CRITICISMS

The Original Formulation

The phenomenon that came to be known as learned helplessness was first observed in Martin Seligman's laboratory in the latter half of the 1960s. While investigating avoidance learning in animals, Seligman and his colleagues (e.g., Overmier & Seligman, 1967; Seligman & Maier, 1967) noted that dogs that had been exposed to inescapable shocks displayed severe deficits in subsequent learning. The animals made few attempts to escape subsequent shocks and, when successful responses were made, showed little evidence of learning. In interpreting this effect, Seligman theorized that during the inescapable shocks the dogs learned that there was no relationship between their responses and outcomes. Seligman further developed a set of specific hypotheses regarding the cognitive and motivational consequences of learning that outcomes are uncontrollable. The term "learned helplessness" was used to refer to this framework,[1] and the theory soon was extended to consideration of the effects of noncontingency on humans (e.g., Hiroto, 1974; Seligman, 1975).

According to learned helplessness theory, when an individual is exposed to and perceives a lack of relationship between his or her responses and outcomes, this produces an expectation of future noncontingency. The expectation presumably interferes with the individual's ability to perceive response–outcome relationships (the "cognitive deficit"), and also results in reduced response initiation (the "motivational deficit"). These postulated deficits in turn are thought to interfere with performance in later situations in which control over outcomes actually is possible.

[1]In addition to the theory, the term "learned helplessness" also was applied to observed deficits in performance, and to specific components of Seligman's theory such as an expectation of noncontingency (Buchwald *et al.*, 1978). In an effort to avoid the ongoing problems in this area due to the multiple uses of the term (cf. Fincham & Cain, 1985; Peterson, 1985; Tyron, 1985), we will use the label *learned helplessness* only in reference to the theory (cf. Buchwald *et al.*, 1978).

The response of clinical and social psychologists to the concept of human helplessness, and the well-specified set of hypotheses that comprised Seligman's theory, was clearly one of great enthusiasm; an enormous amount of research was generated in the years following the initial formulation of the theory. Whereas some investigators attempted laboratory tests of the specific predictions provided by the theory, others pursued the application of the concept of helplessness to a variety of human difficulties (Alloy, 1982; Peterson, 1985; Peterson & Seligman, 1984). In the latter vein, a great deal of literature was devoted to the proposition put forth by Seligman and his associates (e.g., Seligman, Klein, & Miller, 1976) that learned helplessness provided a model of clinical depression.

Although generally beyond the scope of the present discussion, the applications of helplessness theory deserve brief comment. Some of the research that developed has been criticized for employing the concept of helplessness in a global sense, without adequate attention to the precise hypotheses that comprise the theory (cf. Peterson, 1985). The majority of the applied research, however, was devoted to helplessness as a model of depression, and based on relatively specific extrapolations of the components of the theory (although see, for example, Depue & Monroe, 1978, for a discussion of some problems with imprecision in the way depression was conceptualized in this work). The more exact applications of the theory, however, were vulnerable to criticism for the use of concepts that were not yet well established (cf. Buchwald *et al.*, 1978). Both issues are relevant to helplessness as a theory of responses to noncontingency because the sheer bulk of research that has, and continues to be, produced in applications of the theory, in particular in pursuit of helplessness as a model of depression, has the potential to create the illusion of proof for helplessness theory.

Meanwhile back in the laboratory, numerous attempts were made to verify the postulated effects of an experience with noncontingency. As noted at the outset, the primary source of data on the original hypotheses came from studies demonstrating the detrimental effects of failure on subsequent performance on laboratory tasks administered in the treatment situation (e.g., Hiroto & Seligman, 1975; Miller & Seligman, 1975).[2]

---

[2]Early laboratory investigations of learned helplessness also examined changes in expectancy as an index of perceived response–outcome relations (e.g., Miller & Seligman, 1976; Willis & Blaney, 1978). A number of subsequent writers questioned the relevance of these studies to helplessness theory, however, arguing that expectancy shift measures were better interpreted in terms of the stability of subjects' attributions rather than perceptions of control (e.g., Costello, 1978; Rizley, 1978).

The conclusion that this finding validates helplessness theory (e.g., Peterson & Seligman, 1984; Seligman, 1978), is clearly problematic, and indeed was subsequently subjected to much criticism (e.g., Buchwald *et al.*, 1978; Costello, 1978). In particular, problems were identified that related to the appropriateness and adequacy of the independent and dependent variables in the failure-induction research on helplessness. A number of writers questioned the assumption that an experience with failure is best conceptualized as an experience with noncontingency. In raising this issue, some critics noted the lack of consistent evidence for similar effects after an experience with noncontingent positive outcomes, and questioned the usefulness of the concept of noncontingency for understanding effects that apparently occurred primarily in failure situations (e.g., Buchwald *et al.*, 1978; Coyne *et al.*, 1980). Others noted the literature indicating the robustness with which people perceive themselves as having control, whether the perception was objectively correct or not (see, for example, Wortman, 1976 for a review of this literature), and questioned whether subjects in the failure-induction studies did in fact perceive the experience as one of noncontingency.

Concern over the use of performance as the primary dependent measure in the helplessness studies constituted the second critical problem that was identified. In essence, the assumption that performance deficits are manifestations of the predicted expectation of noncontingency, with resultant cognitive and motivational deficits, also was questioned. Any number of writers noted that demonstrations of performance interference alone, without direct evidence for the variables that presumably mediate this effect, do not constitute unambiguous proof for the theory (e.g., Buchwald *et al.*, 1978; Coyne *et al.*, 1980; Levine *et al.*, 1977; Wortman & Dintzer, 1978).

In addition to the two critical problems discussed above, a number of other troublesome issues for the original formulation of human helplessness were raised by various writers. It was noted, for example, that failure experiences sometimes enhance subsequent performance, a finding that was not readily accounted for by the original helplessness formulation (e.g., Wortman & Brehm, 1975). Concern was also voiced regarding the lack of evidence for generalization beyond the treatment situation of the effects that were being labeled learned helplessness (e.g., Roth & Kubal, 1975; Wortman & Brehm, 1975). By definition learned helplessness theory is concerned with inappropriate generalizations from an uncontrollable situation to one in which control is possible. Studies in which performance following failure was assessed in completely different situations, however, generally had not demonstrated performance deficits in the new setting (e.g., Cole & Coyne, 1977; Hanusa & Schulz, 1977; Kilpatrick-Tabak & Roth, 1978).

The Reformulation

By the late 1970s there was a growing disenchantment with help-lessness theory. Proponents as well as critics were recognizing and discussing a number of limitations and troublesome issues. In 1978, in response to what they identified as the major inadequacies in the original theory, Abramson, Seligman, and Teasdale published a reformulation. According to those authors, the major problem with the earlier model was the lack of boundary conditions for when the hypothesized effects of noncontingency should occur. Thus the new version of the theory retained the original tenets, but with the additional hypothesis that the attribution an individual makes for an experience with noncontingency determines the subsequent situations in which an expectation of noncontingency will be present as a result of that experience.

Specifically, Abramson *et al.* argued that the generalization of an expectation of noncontingency across time is a function of the stability of the attribution that is made; generalization across situations is determined by the generality of the attribution (i.e., whether the attribution is specific to a given situation or more global and applicable across situations). Overall, then, the more stable the attribution, the greater the likelihood an individual will expect noncontingency across time, and the more global the attribution, the greater the likelihood that noncontingency will be expected across situations.[3]

As with the original theory, a large amount of research was stimulated by the reformulated account of human helplessness. Much of the subsequent research was again focused on applications of the theory, most notably as a model of depression. A rapidly growing body of literature has been devoted to the corollary to the reformulation that a tendency to make internal, global, and stable attributions for negative outcomes may be a vulnerability factor for depression (e.g., Blaney, Behar, & Head, 1980; Cutrona, 1983; Golin, Sweeney, & Shaeffer, 1981; Seligman, Abramson, Semmel, & von Baeyer, 1979). The work on the relationship between depression and attributional style has produced problems in its own right, such as conflicting findings (cf. Coyne & Gotlib, 1983), difficulties with the construct of attributional style (e.g., Cutrona, Russell, & Jones, 1984; Krantz & Rude, 1984), and failures to support the interpretation of an association between the two factors as reflecting the causal impact of attributional styles on depression (e.g., Hamilton &

---

[3]The reformulation also included consideration of the locus of control of the attribution an individual selects. This dimension, however, was not viewed as a determinant of subsequent performance, but rather was used to derive predictions regarding the impact of noncontingency on self-esteem.

Abramson, 1983; Lewinsohn, Steinmetz, Larson, & Franklin, 1981). For the present purposes, however, the primary concern is that evidence for a relationship between attributions and depression typically has been obtained in isolation from information regarding perceptions (or expectations) of noncontingency, and yet has been interpreted as globally supporting the helplessness model (e.g., Peterson & Seligman, 1984). Even in the case of longitudinal studies that have suggested that attributional styles may be predictive of affective responses to negative life events (e.g., Metalsky, Abramson, Seligman, Semmel, & Peterson, 1982), the best evidence for the helplessness model, the relevance of these data for the process that is postulated by the theory has not been established. Again, then, there is a dangerous potential for a large, related literature to create a misleading air of proof for helplessness theory.

In terms of the reformulated version of the helplessness account of responses to noncontingency, the new theory provided a means, theoretically at any rate, of making more specific predictions about when the hypothesized effects of noncontingency will occur. Research on the role of attributions in the effects of failure on subsequent performance, in particular performance in new situations, has provided some support for Abramson *et al.*'s proposition that the stability and globality of attributions are important determinants of when performance effects will occur (e.g., Alloy *et al.*, 1984; Anderson, 1983; Anderson & Jennings, 1980; Hanusa & Schulz, 1977; Wortman, Panciera, Shusterman, & Hibscher, 1976).

This potential improvement in helplessness theory came, however, at the cost of several new problematic issues. In particular, the addition of the attributional component carried with it a loss in the falsifiability that was one of the major assets of the original theory (Huesman, 1978). Abramson *et al.* describe the stability and globality of attributions as determining when "the expectation of helplessness will be likely to recur." (1978, p. 59). The implication, apparent throughout their presentation, is that an experience with noncontingency always results in an expectation of future noncontingency, and that attributions merely delimit the situations in which this expectation will be operative. This hypothesis is particularly noteworthy because proponents of the theory have also asserted that there are no valid means of directly assessing expectations (Peterson & Seligman, 1984).

Taken together, there appears to be no way to verify the central prediction of the theory, that an experience with noncontingency produces an expectation of future noncontingency (cf. Fincham & Cain, 1985). A failure to demonstrate effects that theoretically occur when noncontingency is expected may be readily explained by assuming subjects did not make attributions that were stable or global enough for the necessary generalization to occur. This potential for tautology is especially problematic given the controversy in the attribution literature regarding people's ability to report accurately the causes of their behavior (e.g., Nisbett & Wilson, 1977; White, 1980).

Whereas it introduced new difficulties, the reformulation also failed to resolve most of the problems with the original version of the theory. Abramson et al. noted, for example, that facilitation effects have been observed following failure, but described this finding as poorly understood, and did not attempt to account for it within the mechanisms of helplessness theory. The lack of an adequate means of explaining performance enhancement is particularly noteworthy given that two of the studies that supported the role of attributions in moderating the effects of failure obtained solely facilitation effects (Hanusa & Schulz, 1977; Wortman et al., 1976).

The reformulation also did not address the critical problems with the assumptions that failure experiences are perceived in terms of uncontrollability and that subsequent deficits in performance reflect an expectation of noncontingency that has produced cognitive and motivational deficits. The failure to resolve these issues theoretically has become, if anything, increasingly important in light of research conducted since the reformulation. In terms of the presumed role of noncontingency, for example, researchers have attempted to assess more directly whether performance deficits in the helplessness paradigm are mediated by subjects' perceptions of control for the induction task (e.g., Oakes & Curtis, 1982; Tennen, Drum, Gillen, & Stanton, 1982); contrary to helplessness theory, however, perceptions of noncontingency have not been related to subsequent performance.

In response to the studies that failed to support the mediating role of perceived noncontingency, and the general concern over alternative explanations, proponents of the theory have argued that an expectation of noncontingency is a sufficient, not necessary, condition for the predicted effects (e.g., Alloy, 1982; Peterson & Seligman, 1984). Thus alternative explanations for performance interference effects are not seen as incompatible with helplessness theory. Although this distinction does provide a means of accounting for other mechanisms that may cause the predicted effects, it seems at best premature to address alternative explanations with the assertion that noncontingency is a sufficient condition for effects that have not yet been demonstrated unambiguously.

Recently, some researchers also have attempted direct tests of one of the hypothesized consequences of noncontingency that presumably intervenes between failure and performance interference, the postulated cognitive deficit (e.g., Alloy & Abramson, 1982; Ford & Neale, 1985).

These studies have not supported the proposition that an experience with failure results in a reduced ability to perceive response–outcome relations. For example, Ford and Neale (1985) exposed subjects to a failure-induction task, and then gave them a task in which they judged the amount of control their responses exerted over a designated outcome. Rather than displaying the postulated cognitive deficit and underestimating the contingency between their responses and the outcome, subjects who failed on the prior task made higher and more accurate judgments of control than subjects who had not had a failure experience.

The latter finding was interpreted as reflecting increased motivation as a result of the initial failure experience. This suggestion is especially noteworthy because a separate group of subjects who were exposed to failure in the study went on to complete an anagram task; consistent with previous studies (e.g., Hiroto & Seligman, 1975), the failure induction produced deficits in anagram performance. In discussing the potential incompatibility between the interpretation of the judgment of control findings in terms of motivational arousal and the observed deficits in anagram performance, Ford and Neale noted that motivational arousal can interfere with performance on some tasks. The implication that other demonstrations of performance deficits following failure could have reflected excessively high levels of motivation highlights the importance, already clear from the observation of facilitation effects, of an explanation of the motivational effects of failure that can account for increases in motivation as well as declines.

Summary and Current Status

In summary, despite more than a decade of research, including attempts to revise and expand the theory, there continue to be serious questions regarding the adequacy of the helplessness explanation of the effects of failure. The issues we have highlighted generally are not noteworthy on the basis of originality; what is noteworthy is that critical problems that were identified up to 10 years ago continue to plague this framework.

The lack of support for the one hypothesized consequence of failure that has been tested directly, the postulated cognitive deficit, has led some proponents of the theory to suggest that the current status of the model is one in which an expectation of noncontingency primarily results in motivational deficits (e.g., Alloy, 1982).[4] Given the results from

---

[4]Alloy (1982) also argued that an expectation of noncontingency can result in affective and self-esteem deficits. The latter consequences are excluded from the present discussion because they were not linked to subsequent performance (cf. Footnote 3).

the studies on judgments of contingency (e.g., Ford & Neale, 1985), de-emphasis of the specific cognitive deficit in the theory is clearly appropriate; a motivational account of the observed performance interference remains a viable alternative. In light of the conceptual problems we have reviewed, however, embedding a motivational interpretation within the helplessness constructs of an experience with, and expectation of, non-contingency to date appears to have raised more troublesome issues than provided understanding of the effects of failure.

A more parsimonious alternative account of the effect of failure on subsequent performance is suggested by recent work by Brehm and his colleagues (e.g., Brehm, Wright, Solomon, Silka, & Greenberg, 1983) on the determinants of motivational arousal, or energization. After reviewing the relevant tenets of the energization model, the straightforward explanation of the motivational effects of failure that is suggested will be examined.[5]

ENERGIZATION MODEL: BASIC TENETS

The model recently proposed by Brehm and his associates is concerned with the psychological factors involved in the mobilization of energy for some form of instrumental behavior, a process that these researchers refer to as energization (Brehm *et al.*, 1983). In addition, their model includes the proposition that the relative magnitude of goal valence (the attractiveness or unattractiveness of a potential outcome) varies as a direct function of energization level.

Determinants of Energization

Perceived Task Difficulty and Potential Motivation. One of the basic premises of the energization model is that the mobilization of energy for goal attainment is a function of an individual's perception of the task requirements. The model is conservational in nature. Energization is expected to occur in immediate anticipation of instrumental activity, to change in accordance with any immediately anticipated changes in task requirements, and to dissipate when the instrumental activity is completed. In addition, it is argued that an individual will mobilize energy only if goal attainment is viewed as possible and worth the required effort, and then only to the degree that is necessary for goal attainment.

[5]Detailed discussion of this formulation, including comparison with other theories of motivation and a review of the evidence in support of the energization model, may be found elsewhere in this volume (see Wright, this volume).

Consistent, then, with other models (e.g., Kukla, 1972) that have followed the tradition of the "difficulty law of motivation" formulated in the early part of this century (Brehm *et al.*, 1983), energization is expected to increase as perceptions of task difficulty increase.

Although it is argued that arousal will be an increasing function of perceived task requirements, as long as goal attainment is still viewed as possible, clearly there must be an upper limit to the amount of energy an individual will mobilize for a given goal. Some theorists have dealt with this issue by assuming there is an absolute limit to the amount of effort that an individual will intend to exert (e.g., Kukla, 1972). Consistent with their general conservational approach, Brehm and his associates argue, however, that the upper limit to energization for an instrumental activity is a function of the goal. More specifically, they assume that at any given time there is a level of potential motivation associated with a given goal; *potential motivation* refers to the maximum amount of energy that an individual will be willing to expend for the attainment of that goal. This ceiling on the amount of energy an individual will expend presumably is a function of an individual's need state and the value of the goal. For example, potential motivation for obtaining food should be higher immediately before a meal than immediately after one. Potential motivation also should be higher for earning one hundred dollars than for earning one.

Energization is not expected if a task is perceived as requiring a level of effort that exceeds potential motivation. Theoretically, the mobilization of energy for an instrumental behavior thus is determined not only by what an individual believes he or she can and must do, but also by what the individual is willing to do for goal attainment.

According to the model, then, energization will be a nonmonotonic function of the perceived difficulty of goal attainment. As perceived task difficulty increases, energization is expected to increase until the task is perceived as either impossible or as requiring more energy expenditure than the goal is worth. When the task requirements are perceived as impossible or as exceeding potential motivation, low energization is expected.

Role of Perceived Ability. This formulation of the determinants of energization includes an implicit assumption that an individual's perception of the requirements for goal attainment are determined by both perceptions regarding the task and regarding his/her ability. If, for example, two people have similar views of the objective difficulty of a task, but differing senses of their ability, the person with lower perceived ability should view the task as requiring greater effort than the one with relatively high perceived ability (cf. Kukla, 1972).

The implications for energization of this expected difference in perceptions regarding task requirements depend on where the difficulty levels anticipated by low or high perceived ability individuals fall relative to potential motivation. It is possible for two people differing in perceived ability both to view a given task as requiring a level of effort that the goal is worth; consequently, the relatively greater anticipated effort expected for the individual with lower perceived ability should result in a relatively higher level of energization. For more objectively difficult tasks, however, the greater effort anticipated by low perceived ability individuals may exceed potential motivation, whereas the lower anticipated effort expected for high perceived ability individuals for the same task may still be within the range of potential motivation; in this case, higher perceived ability should be associated with high energization, low perceived ability with low energization. Finally, a task may be so difficult that the requirements anticipated by both groups exceed potential motivation, and no energization would be predicted regardless of perceived ability.

In summary, then, when faced with a relatively easy task, greater energization should occur for low perceived ability individuals. For objectively more difficult tasks, the opposite pattern would be expected, with greater energization predicted for people with higher perceived ability. Finally, when a task is extremely difficult, equally low levels of energization may occur across levels of perceived ability (see Kukla, 1972, 1974, for more detailed discussion and evidence regarding the role of perceived ability in performance intensity).

ENERGIZATION FOLLOWING FAILURE: THEORETICAL APPLICATION

Having outlined the relevant tenets of the energization model, we can now consider a theoretical application to the more specific situation in which an individual has failed and is facing another task. According to this framework, motivational arousal for the approaching task will be a nonmonotonic function of anticipated task difficulty. The motivational work conducted by Brehm and his colleagues thus suggests that an experience with failure will affect subsequent motivation when the failure affects the expected difficulty of the impending task.

The specific predictions regarding the impact of failure on motivation that may be derived from the energization model follow from this general assumption that motivational effects are mediated by changes in anticipated difficulty. Before examining in more detail the implications of the energization framework and considering some of the factors that have been shown to affect performance following failure in terms of this model, two other assumptions should be noted. First, it is assumed that there is a direct, linear relationship between performance intensity, or effort expenditure, and motivational arousal (cf. Kukla, 1972). Accordingly, it is also assumed that the level of performance provides an index of motivational arousal. In making the latter assumption, however, the complexities in the relationship between intensity of effort and actual performance alluded to earlier must be acknowledged. High effort may not always result in superior performance; clearly other variables (e.g., attention, or task strategy) are also involved in the level of performance an individual achieves. Thus although our forthcoming discussion of the congruence between the predictions derived from the energization model and the literature on the performance following failure provides some support for this formulation, verification is limited not only by the post hoc nature of the application but also by the fact that performance provides an imperfect index of the central construct, motivational arousal.

The Occurrence of Motivational Effects

The assumption that the motivational effects of failure are mediated by alterations in anticipated difficulty implies two necessary conditions for motivational changes to be predicted by the energization framework.[6] First, variations in motivation that are due to failure should occur only if the failure feedback provides information that is relevant to anticipated difficulty. In other words, for failure on one task to alter motivation regarding a second task, the experience must provide information that is applicable to the expected requirements of the impending task. When anticipated difficulty is affected, motivation should be as well. If failure feedback has no relevance to the anticipated difficulty of a subsequent task, this appraisal, and in consequence motivation, should be unaffected by the prior outcome.

A number of variables may affect the relevance of failure feedback on one task to the anticipated difficulty of a subsequent task. In general, however, relevance may be viewed as a function of the interaction between the causal attribution that is made for the failure and situational

---

[6]It should be emphasized that the focus of Brehm et al.'s model is on the psychological component of energization. The conditions delineated are not intended as an exhaustive explanation of the factors that can affect arousal. For example, fatigue may attenuate energization; conversely, the ingestion of stimulant drugs may result in a higher level of energization than would be predicted solely on the basis of Brehm et al.'s model.

variables (cf. Pasahow, West, & Boroto, 1982). If, for example, a student attributes failure on an exam in a college course to a relatively unstable cause (e.g., fatigue), that outcome should have little relevance to future exams; if the failure also is attributed to a specific cause (e.g., boredom with the particular subject material), the failed exam should have little relevance for exams in other courses.

The stability and generality of causal attributions, in this view, thus establish the parameters for relevance, whereas situational characteristics determine where a forthcoming task falls relative to those parameters. The proposition that these factors delimit the conditions under which an experience with failure will affect motivational arousal is consistent with research documenting their moderating effects on the relationship between failure and subsequent performance. Performance deficits following failure have been observed, for example, when task instructions were used to promote global attributions for the failure, but not when specific attributions were suggested (Pasahow, 1980). Investigations of the importance of the similarity between the situations in which subjects failed and in which subsequent performance was assessed have demonstrated performance interference in the same setting as the failure experience, not in a completely new one (e.g., Cole & Coyne, 1977).

The conjoint importance of attributions and situational variables is illustrated by research in which attributions for failure to stable or global factors were not predictive of performance assessed in the same setting (e.g., Tennen, Gillen, & Drum, 1982; the nondepressed subjects in Klein *et al.*, 1976). In addition, perhaps the best support for the present proposition regarding relevance comes from studies in which performance following failure was assessed in a new setting for subjects who had been identified as tending to make global versus specific attributions for negative outcomes, or for subjects who had been exposed to task instructions designed to manipulate attributions for the failure experience. In the former case, performance deficits have been observed for subjects who tend to make global relative to specific attributions (Alloy *et al.*, 1984). Performance enhancement in a new setting has also been observed for subjects who received task instructions promoting an ability attribution for failure, a global (and stable) causal factor, whereas subjects induced to make more specific, unstable attributions, such as task difficulty, did not evidence any performance effects in the new situation (Hanusa & Schulz, 1977; Wortman *et al.*, 1976).

The present view of the conditions that establish relevance is, of course, analogous to the boundary conditions for helplessness that were suggested by Abramson *et al.* (1978) as well as other investigators working within a helplessness framework (e.g., Miller & Norman, 1979; Roth, 1980). According to the helplessness framework, however, attributions determine the generalization of an expectation of noncontingency; in the present formulation, they determine the relevance of the failure experience for the anticipated difficulty of a subsequent task. The energization framework thus suggests a different, more parsimonious, mechanism for understanding the documented role of these factors in the relationship between failure and subsequent performance.

Although relevance is a necessary condition for failure to affect subsequent motivation according to this framework, it is not a sufficient one. Failure on one task can have relevance to the difficulty of a subsequent task without altering how the later task is appraised. If failure feedback is expected, it may provide confirmation of the anticipated difficulty of the task, and thus have no impact on the expected requirements of a related task. Thus a *change* in anticipated difficulty may be viewed as a second necessary condition for the occurrence of motivational effects due to failure. In addition, it may be argued that the congruence between outcome expectations and performance is a primary determinant of whether failure feedback alters the difficulty level that is anticipated for ensuing tasks; a change in anticipated difficulty should occur when outcome expectations and feedback are incongruent.

The importance of initial expectations in failure induction paradigms has been suggested by other writers (e.g., Douglas & Anisman, 1975; Harris & Tryon, 1983; Roth & Kubal, 1975; Wortman & Dintzer, 1978), and is supported by research in which performance following failure was affected by variables that should impact on initial expectations. For example, Thornton and Jacobs (1971) and Thornton and Powell (1974) did not observe performance deficits in subjects who failed to escape an aversive noise; these researchers, however, told subjects that there would be nothing they could do to control the aversive noise. In an explicit attempt to examine the importance of expectation incongruency, Douglas and Anisman observed performance deficits following failure on a simple task, (i.e., one that presumably subjects expected to solve), but not a complex one.

Although the general finding of performance deficits in the Douglas and Anisman (1975) study is consistent with the energization formulation, more detailed consideration of their observations also serves to illustrate the inherent complexity in applying a motivational explanation to performance findings. Douglas and Anisman noted that the failure manipulation in their experiments did not affect the speed with which subjects initiated or performed responses on a subsequent task; they also reported that the subjects appeared agitated rather than passive. These

observations seem incompatible with an interpretation of the performance deficits that were obtained in terms of low motivation. They do
not rule out a motivational explanation in general, however, but impli-
cate excessively high, rather than reduced, levels of arousal as the possible motivational mechanism.

In summary, the relevance of a failure experience to perceptions of
the difficulty of an ensuing task, as determined by the interaction of
attributions and situational characteristics, may be viewed as a necessary
condition for the experience to impact on that appraisal and potentially
affect motivation. In addition, a change in anticipated difficulty, as a
function of expectation incongruency, is also a necessary, and sufficient,
condition for the occurrence of motivational effects due to failure.

The Nature of Motivational Effects

In considering the direction of motivational effects, it is assumed
that when an experience with failure alters anticipated difficulty, the
next task will be perceived as more difficult. Having failed may, in fact,
result in a perception that the ensuing task will be impossible; in this
case, motivational arousal should decline. The work on the energization
model, however, indicates that a belief that an ensuing task is impossible
is a sufficient but not a necessary condition for low motivation; low
energization also should occur if a task is viewed as more difficult than
successful performance is worth to the individual. In other words, when
a more difficult, although not impossible, task is expected after a failure
experience, the resultant degree of arousal will be a function of how
anticipated difficulty interacts with potential motivation. Motivation
should *decline* if anticipated difficulty increases to a level that exceeds
potential motivation; an *increase* in motivation is expected if anticipated
difficulty increases but does not go beyond potential motivation.

The direction and degree of motivational change following failure
thus should be determined by the amount of increase in anticipated
difficulty and the level of potential motivation for success on the impending task. Accordingly, factors that affect the amount of increase in
anticipated difficulty or that affect potential motivation should in turn
affect the level of motivation that occurs after an experience with failure.
When anticipated difficulty increases as a function of failing on one task,
the higher the level of potential motivation for the next task, the greater
the likelihood anticipated difficulty will not exceed potential motivation,
and motivation will increase. Conversely, when potential motivation on
the second task does not exceed that of the first, the greater the increase
in anticipated task difficulty, the greater the likelihood that perceived

task requirements will be greater than potential motivation, and energization will decline.

Consistent with this analysis, many of the situational variables that have been shown to affect the relationship between failure and subsequent performance may be interpreted as impacting on anticipated difficulty. Pittman and Pittman (1980), for example, found that subsequent performance was enhanced by failure on two problems whereas failure on six problems resulted in deficits in subsequent performance. One viable explanation for the impact of the amount of failure feedback on subsequent performance (see also Pittman & Pittman, 1979; Roth & Kubal, 1975) is that anticipated difficulty increases with increasing amounts of failure feedback.

A number of researchers have demonstrated that failure experiences do not affect subsequent performance if subjects receive either prior or intervening success feedback (e.g., Klein & Seligman, 1976; Prindaville & Stein, 1978; Teasdale, 1978). This finding also is consistent with the possibility that changes in anticipated difficulty mediate motivational changes due to failure; that is, the inclusion of success feedback may attenuate the impact of failure on anticipated difficulty. In a similar vein, Coyne et al. (1980) found that failure did not affect the subsequent performance of subjects who received an intervening experience with an imagination exercise described as an effective procedure for coping with stress and "permitting greater efficiency in problem solving." The possibility that this manipulation affected subjects' perceptions of the effort required for the ensuing task is strengthened by the fact that subjects who experienced failure and then engaged in the imagination task without the explanation did show deficits in subsequent performance.

Research conducted by Williams and Teasdale (1982) provides additional support for the role of perceived task difficulty in responses to failure. Basing their work on an expectancy-value analysis, these authors also suggested that the alternatively facilitative or detrimental effects of failure may be linked to variations in anticipated difficulty in conjunction with the subjective importance of successful performance. Consistent with their analysis, Williams and Teasdale (1982, Experiment 2) observed deficits in subsequent performance on a "high importance" task for subjects given instructions indicating the task was difficult and who initially received failure feedback, but not for subjects who received failure feedback after instructions indicating the task was easy. This finding is consistent with the possibility that the failure feedback increased anticipated difficulty to a level beyond potential motivation for subjects who began with a high level of perceived difficulty. However, Williams and Teasdale did not obtain the expected increase in performance following failure on the presumably easy task; they speculated that the subjects who expected an easy task may have exerted little energy at the outset and that this attenuated the impact of the failure feedback.

Individual Differences in Motivational Effects

The concept of anticipated difficulty that is central to the energization model implicitly involves perceptions regarding both objective task characteristics and an individual's assessment of his or her capabilities for successful performance. One's perceived ability thus should affect motivation following failure, given the necessary conditions for motivational effects to occur.

In general, individuals who perceive their own ability as low should expect a higher level of required effort for a given task than individuals with high perceived ability. Accordingly, a decrease in motivation following failure is more likely for individuals with a low sense of their ability, relative to individuals with high perceived ability.

As noted at the outset, research on individual differences in response to failure has implicated a number of variables. Poor performance following failure has been observed for individuals with low relative to high self-esteem (Shrauger & Sorman, 1977), external rather than internal locus of control (e.g., Cohen et al., 1976; Pittman & Pittman, 1979; although see, Gregory, Chartier, & Wright, 1979 for conflicting findings), high relative to low test anxiety (Lavelle et al., 1979), and low relative to high grade point averages (Means & Means, 1971). Although it is possible to postulate independent mechanisms that may account for these affects (e.g., as suggested by Lavelle et al., 1979, reduced attentional capacity for high test anxious individuals), the energization framework clearly suggests that the observed differences in performance may be a function of differences in perceived ability that are associated with each of the individual differences variables.

Perhaps the clearest evidence in support of the interpretation of individual differences according to the energization framework is provided by Pittman and Pittman (1979). These researchers examined the effects of amount of failure feedback on the subsequent performance of subjects with internal or external locus of control. Consistent with the present formulation, failure on two problems produced deficits in subsequent performance for subjects with an external locus of control, whereas the subsequent performance of subjects with an internal locus of control was enhanced. Failure feedback on six problems, however, resulted in poor performance for both groups.

SUMMARY

Following a review of the conceptual problems with the learned helplessness account of the performance effects of failure, we concluded that the helplessness framework appeared to bring more troublesome issues than clarity to the literature in this area. One set of difficulties with the theory revolve around conceptual problems with (and the lack of support for) the postulated cognitive mechanisms. In addition, the helplessness framework is only able to account for declines in motivation. Clearly, however, failure also may result in increased arousal; an adequate analysis of motivational reactions should include mechanisms that can explain changes in either direction.

Given these considerations, we suggested that a more parsimonious and comprehensive explanation of the effects of failure on subsequent motivation is provided by Brehm and associates' recent formulation of the determinants of energization. In general, it is hypothesized that energization is a function of the anticipated difficulty of an impending task and potential motivation; the latter is defined as the upper limit to the effort an individual is willing to expend for successful task performance.

Accordingly, we argued that the occurrence and direction of motivational changes due to failure are mediated by the impact of the prior outcome on anticipated difficulty in conjunction with potential motivation. Consideration of the specific hypotheses that may be derived from this model suggested that it provides a unified framework for many of the situational and individual differences variables that have been identified in the work on performance following failure.

ACKNOWLEDGMENTS

The authors wish to thank Robert G. Frank for his helpful comments on an earlier version of this chapter.

REFERENCES

Abramson, L. Y., Seligman, M. E. P., & Teasdale, J. D. (1978). Learned helplessness in humans: Critique and reformulation. *Journal of Abnormal Psychology, 87*, 49–74.

Alloy, L. B. (1982). The role of perceptions and attributions for response-outcome noncontingency in learned helplessness: A commentary and discussion. *Journal of Personality, 50*, 443–479.

Alloy, L. B., & Abramson, L. Y. (1982). Learned helplessness, depression, and the illusion of control. *Journal of Personality and Social Psychology, 42*, 1114–1126.

Alloy, L. B., Peterson, C., Abramson, L. Y., & Seligman, M. E. P. (1984). Attributional style and the generality of learned helplessness. *Journal of Personality and Social Psychology, 46,* 681–687.

Anderson, C. A. (1983). Motivational and performance deficits in interpersonal settings: The effect of attributional style. *Journal of Personality and Social Psychology, 45,* 1136–1141.

Anderson, C. A., & Jennings, D. L. (1980). When experiences of failure promote expectations of success: The impact of attributing failure to ineffective strategies. *Journal of Personality, 48,* 393–407.

Blaney, P. H., Behar, V., & Head, R. (1980). Two measures of depressive cognitions: Their association with depression and with each other. *Journal of Abnormal Psychology, 89,* 678–682.

Brehm, J. W., Wright, R. A., Solomon, S., Silka, L., & Greenberg, J. (1983). Perceived difficulty, energization, and the magnitude of goal valence. *Journal of Experimental Social Psychology, 19,* 21–48.

Buchwald, A. M., Coyne, J. C., & Cole, C. S. (1978). A critical evaluation of the learned helplessness model of depression. *Journal of Abnormal Psychology, 87,* 180–193.

Cohen, S., Rothbart, M., & Philips, S. (1976). Locus of control and the generality of learned helplessness in humans. *Journal of Personality and Social Psychology, 34,* 1040–1056.

Cole, C. S., & Coyne, J. C. (1977). Situational specificity of laboratory-induced learned helplessness. *Journal of Abnormal Psychology, 86,* 615–623.

Costello, C. G. (1978). A critical review of Seligman's laboratory experiments on learned helplessness and depression in humans. *Journal of Abnormal Psychology, 87,* 21–31.

Coyne, J. C., & Gotlib, I. H. (1983). The role of cognition in depression: A critical reappraisal. *Psychological Bulletin, 94,* 472–505.

Coyne, J. C., Metalsky, G. I., & Lavelle, T. L. (1980). Learned helplessness as experimenter induced failure and its alleviation with attentional redeployment. *Journal of Abnormal Psychology, 89,* 350–357.

Cutrona, C. E. (1983). Causal attributions and perinatal depression. *Journal of Abnormal Psychology, 92,* 161–172.

Cutrona, C. E., Russell, D., & Jones, R. D. (1984). Cross-situational consistency is causal attributions: Does attributional style exist? *Journal of Personality and Social Psychology, 47,* 1043–1058.

Depue, R. A. & Monroe, S. M. (1978). Learned helplessness in the perspective of the depressive disorders: Conceptual and definitional issues. *Journal of Abnormal Psychology, 87,* 3–20.

Douglas, D., & Anisman, H. (1975). Helplessness or expectation incongruency: Effects of aversive stimulation on subsequent performance. *Journal of Experimental Psychology: Human Perception and Performance, 1,* 411–417.

Fincham, F. D., & Cain, K. M. (1985). Laboratory-induced learned helplessness: A critique. *Journal of Social and Clinical Psychology, 3,* 238–243.

Ford, C. E., & Neale, J. M. (1985). Learned helplessness and judgments of control. *Journal of Personality and Social Psychology, 49,* 1330–1336.

Golin, S., Sweeney, P. D., & Shaeffer, D. E. (1981). The causality of causal attributions in depression: A cross-lagged panel correlational analysis. *Journal of Abnormal Psychology, 90,* 14–22.

Gregory, W. L., Chartier, G. M., & Wright, M. H. (1979). *Learned helplessness and learned effectiveness: Effects of explicit response cues on individuals differing in personal control expectancies. Journal of Personality and Social Psychology, 37,* 1982–1992.

Hamilton, E. W., & Abramson, L. Y. (1983). Cognitive patterns and major depressive disorder: A longitudinal study in a hospital setting. *Journal of Abnormal Psychology, 92,* 173–184.

Hanusa, B. H., & Schulz, R. (1977). Attributional mediators of learned helplessness. *Journal of Personality and Social Psychology, 35,* 602–611.

Harris, F. A., & Tyron, W. W. (1983). Some necessary and sufficient conditions for the experimental induction of learned helplessness. *Journal of Social and Clinical Psychology, 1,* 15–26.

Hiroto, D. S. (1974). Locus of control and learned helplessness. *Journal of Experimental Psychology, 102,* 187–193.

Hiroto, D. S., & Seligman, M. E. P. (1975). Generality of learned helplessness in man. *Journal of Personality and Social Psychology, 31,* 311–327.

Huesman, R. L. (1978). Cognitive processes and models of depression. *Journal of Abnormal Psychology, 87,* 194–198.

Kilpatrick-Tabak, B., & Roth, S. (1978). An attempt to reverse performance deficits associated with depression and experimentally induced helplessness. *Journal of Abnormal Psychology, 87,* 141–154.

Klee, S., & Meyer, R. G. (1979). Prevention of learned helplessness in humans. *Journal of Consulting and Clinical Psychology, 47,* 411–412.

Klein, D. C., & Seligman, M. E. P. (1976). Reversal of performance deficits and perceptual deficits in learned helplessness and depression. *Journal of Abnormal Psychology, 85,* 11–26.

Klein, D. C., Fencil-Morse, E., & Seligman, M. E. P. (1976). Learned helplessness, depression and the attribution of failure. *Journal of Personality and Social Psychology, 33,* 508–516.

Krantz, S. E., & Rude, S. (1984). Depressive attributions: Selection of different causes or assignment of dimensional meanings? *Journal of Personality and Social Psychology, 47,* 193–203.

Kukla, A. (1972). Foundations of an attributional theory of performance. *Psychological Review, 79,* 454–470.

Kukla, A. (1974). Performance as a function of resultant achievement motivation (perceived ability) and perceived difficulty. *Journal of Research in Personality, 7,* 374–383.

Lavelle, T. L., Metalsky, G. I., & Coyne, J. C. (1979). Learned helplessness, test anxiety, and acknowledgment of contingencies. *Journal of Abnormal Psychology, 88,* 381–387.

Lewinsohn, P. M., Steinmetz, J. L., Larson, D. W., & Franklin, J. (1981). Depression-related cognitions: Antecedent or consequence. *Journal of Abnormal Psychology, 90,* 213–219.

Levine, M., Rotkin, L., Jankovick, I. N., & Pitchford, L. (1977). Impaired performance by adult humans: Learned helplessness or wrong hypotheses? *Cognitive Therapy and Research, 1,* 275–285.

Means, R. S., & Means, G. H. (1971). Achievement as a function of the presence of prior information concerning aptitude. *Journal of Educational Psychology, 62,* 185–187.

Metalsky, G. I., Abramson, L. Y., Seligman, M. E. P., Semmel, A., & Peterson, C. (1982). Attributional styles and life events in the classroom: Vulnerability and invulnerability to depressive mood reactions. *Journal of Personality and Social Psychology, 43,* 612–617.

Miller, I. W., & Norman, W. H. (1979). Learned helplessness in humans: A review and attribution theory model. *Psychological Bulletin, 86,* 93–119.

Miller, W. R., & Seligman, M. E. P. (1975). Depression and learned helplessness in man. *Journal of Abnormal Psychology, 84,* 228–238.

Miller, W. R., & Seligman, M. E. P. (1976). Learned helplessness, depression, and the perception of reinforcement. *Behavior Research and Therapy, 14,* 7–17.

Nisbett, R. E., & Wilson, T. D. (1977). Telling more than we can know: Verbal reports on mental processes. *Psychological Review, 84,* 231–259.

Oakes, W. F., & Curtis, N. (1982). Learned helplessness: Not dependent upon cognitions, attributions, or other such phenomenal experiences. *Journal of Personality, 50,* 387–408.

Overmier, J. B., & Seligman, M. E. P. (1967). Effects of inescapable shock upon subsequent escape avoidance learning. *Journal of Comparative and Physiological Psychology, 63,* 23–33.

Pasahow, R. J. (1980). The relation between an attributional dimension and learned helplessness. *Journal of Abnormal Psychology, 89,* 358–367.

Pasahow, R. J., West, S. G., & Boroto, D. R. (1982). Predicting when uncontrollability will produce performance deficits: A refinement of the reformulated learned helplessness hypothesis. *Psychological Review, 89,* 595–598.

Peterson, C. (1985). Learned helplessness: Fundamental issues in theory and research. *Journal of Social and Clinical Psychology, 3,* 248–254.

Peterson, C., & Seligman, M. E. P. (1984). Causal explanations as a risk factor for depression: Theory and evidence. *Psychological Review, 91,* 247–374.

Pittman, N. L., & Pittman, T. S. (1979). Effects of amount of helplessness training and internal-external locus of control on mood and performance. *Journal of Personality and Social Psychology, 37,* 39–47.

Pittman, T. S., & Pittman, N. L. (1980). Deprivation of control and the attribution process. *Journal of Personality and Social Psychology, 39,* 377–389.

Prindaville, P., & Stein, N. (1978). Predictability, controllability, and inoculation against learned helplessness. *Behavior Research and Therapy, 16,* 263–271.

Rizley, R. (1978). Depression and distortion in the attribution of causality. *Journal of Abnormal Psychology, 87,* 32–48.

Roth, S. (1980). A revised model of learned helplessness in humans. *Journal of Personality, 48,* 103–133.

Roth, S., & Kubal, L. (1975). The effects of noncontingent reinforcement on tasks of differing importance. *Journal of Personality and Social Psychology, 32,* 680–691.

Seligman, M. E. P. (1975). *Helplessness: On depression, development and death.* San Francisco: W. H. Freeman.

Seligman, M. E. P. (1978). Comment and integration. *Journal of Abnormal Psychology, 87,* 165–179.

Seligman, M. E. P., & Maier, S. F. (1967). Failure to escape traumatic shock. *Journal of Experimental Psychology, 74,* 1–9.

Seligman, M. E. P., Klein, D. C., & Miller, W. R. (1976). Depression. In H. Leitenberg (Ed.), *Handbook of behavior modification and behavior therapy* (pp. 168–210). Englewood Cliff, NJ: Prentice-Hall.

Seligman, M. E. P., Abramson, L. Y., Semmel, A., & von Baeyer, C. (1979). Depressive attributional style. *Journal of Abnormal Psychology, 88,* 242–247.

Shrauger, J. S., & Sorman, P. B. (1977). Self-evaluations, initial success and failure, and improvement as determinants of persistence. *Journal of Consulting and Clinical Psychology, 45,* 784–795.

Teasdale, J. D. (1978). Effects of real and recalled success on learned helplessness and depression. *Journal of Abnormal Psychology, 87,* 155–164.

Tennen, H., Gillen, R., & Drum, P. E. (1982). The debilitating effect of exposure to noncontingent escape: A test of the learned helplessness model. *Journal of Personality, 50,* 409–425.

Tennen, H., Drum, P. E., Gillen, R., & Stanton, A. (1982). Learned helplessness and the detection of contingency: A direct test. *Journal of Personality, 50,* 426–442.

Thornton, J. W., & Jacobs, P. D. (1971). Learned helplessness in human subjects. *Journal of Experimental Psychology, 87,* 367–372.

Thornton, J. W., & Powell, G. D. (1974). Immunization to and alleviation of learned helplessness in man. *American Journal of Psychology, 87,* 351–367.

Tryon, W. W. (1985). Suggestions regarding future research on the effects of noncontingent consequences. *Journal of Social and Clinical Psychology, 3,* 244–247.

White, P. (1980). Limitations on verbal reports of internal events: A refutation of Nisbett and Wilson and of Bem. *Psychological Review, 87,* 105–112.

Williams, J. M. G., & Teasdale, J. D. (1982). Facilitation and helplessness: The interaction of perceived difficulty and importance of a task. *Behavior Research and Therapy, 20,* 161–171.

Willis, M. H., & Blaney, P. H. (1978). Three tests of the learned helplessness model of depression. *Journal of Abnormal Psychology, 87,* 131–136.

Wortman, C. B. (1976). Causal attributions and personal control. In J. H. Harvey, W. J. Ickes, & R. F. Kidd (Eds.), *New directions in attribution research* (Vol. 1, pp. 23–52). Hillsdale, NJ: Erlbaum.

Wortman, C. B. & Brehm, J. W. (1975). Responses to uncontrollable outcomes: An integration of reactance theory and the learned helplessness model. In L. Berkowitz (Ed.), *Advances in experimental social psychology* (Vol. 8, pp. 277–336). New York: Academic Press.

Wortman, C. B., & Dintzer, L. (1978). Is an attributional analysis of the learned helplessness phenomenon viable? A critique of the Abramson-Seligman-Teasdale reformulation. *Journal of Abnormal Psychology, 87,* 75–90.

Wortman, C. B., Panciera, L., Shusterman, L., & Hibscher, J. (1976). Attributions of causality and reactions to uncontrollable outcomes. *Journal of Experimental Social Psychology, 12,* 301–316.

5

Depression, Self-Focused Attention, and Self-Regulatory Perseveration

TOM PYSZCZYNSKI and JEFF GREENBERG

The tendency of depressed individuals to dwell excessively on their current and past negative life experiences has been noted by a wide variety of clinically oriented theorists, from Sigmund Freud to Aaron Beck. Depressed individuals have been characterized as self-obsessed or self-preoccupied, and as sinking into the self (cf. Abraham, 1911; Arieti & Bemporad, 1978; Beck, 1967, 1976; Mollon & Parry, 1984). In addition, it has often been noted that depressives tend to be especially critical of themselves and to engage constantly in comparisons of themselves with unrealistic and unattainable standards (e.g., Abramson & Sackheim, 1977; Arieti & Bemporad, 1978; Beck, 1967; Bibring, 1953; Freud, 1917/1957). Interestingly, recent theory and research on the consequences of self-focused attention (cf. Carver & Scheier, 1981; Duval & Wicklund, 1972; Wicklund, 1975) suggests that these self-obsessive tendencies are likely to have serious negative consequences, especially for persons who have recently experienced a major loss or failure.

We have recently developed a theory of the role of self-focused attention and self-regulatory processes in the development, maintenance, and exacerbation of reactive depression (Pyszczynski & Greenberg, in press-a). Self-regulatory perseveration theory builds on prior theory and research on the determinants and consequences of self-

TOM PYSZCZYNSKI • Department of Psychology, University of Colorado, Colorado Springs, CO 80933-7150.   JEFF GREENBERG • Department of Psychology, University of Arizona, Tucson, AZ 85721.

focused attention (Carver & Scheier, 1981; Duval & Wicklund, 1972) and is an attempt to explain the psychological processes involved in major depressions for which precipitating stressful life events seem to be involved (i.e., unipolar reactive depressions). However, the maintenance components of the theory may apply to other DSM-III categories of depression as well. Because the theory employs a psychological level of analysis, we focus primarily on accounting for psychological rather than somatic symptoms of depression.

Interest in the effects of focusing attention on the self was initially stimulated by Duval and Wicklund's (1972) influential book, A *Theory of Objective Self-Awareness*. More recently, Carver and Scheier (1981; Carver, 1979) have integrated self-awareness theory with a cybernetic perspective on the self-regulation of behavior. According to self-awareness theorists, conscious attention can be focused either inward toward the self or outward toward the environment. When attention is focused on the self, it sets off a self-evaluative process in which one's current state on whatever dimension is most salient at the time is compared with the standard for that dimension that is currently most salient. Exceeding the standard produces positive affect; falling short of the standard produces negative affect and instigates behavior aimed at either reducing the self-standard discrepancy or escaping the self-focused state. A broad range of empirical investigations have shown that, when a negative discrepancy is salient, self-focus leads to intensified efforts at reducing the discrepancy, unless successful discrepancy reduction appears unlikely (for reviews, see Carver & Scheier, 1981; and Wicklund, 1975).

Self-awareness theories posit that when there is a low probability of successfully reducing a negative discrepancy, self-focus is aversive. Research has shown that in such instances, stimuli that draw attention to the self, such as mirrors, cameras, or tape-recordings of one's own voice, are actively avoided (e.g., Duval, Wicklund, & Fine, cited in Duval & Wicklund, 1972; Gibbons & Wicklund, 1976; Steenbarger & Aderman, 1979). Interestingly, depressed individuals do not seem to find self-focus on negative discrepancies aversive. In fact, in several recent studies, we obtained evidence suggesting that depressed persons exhibit a unique *depressive self-focusing style* in which they find self-focus after positive outcomes more aversive than self-focus after negative outcomes.

EMPIRICAL SUPPORT FOR A DEPRESSIVE SELF-FOCUSING STYLE

In our first study of the self-focusing tendencies of depressed individuals (Pyszczynski & Greenberg, 1985), mild to moderately depressed and nondepressed college students were led to succeed or fail a supposed test of verbal abilities. They were then taken to a second room and given 3 minutes in which to work on each of two sets of puzzles. One of the puzzle sets was positioned in front of a large mirror so that when subjects worked on it they were confronted with their mirror images; the other puzzle set was positioned in front of a blank wall. Subjects were then taken back to the original room and asked to rate which of the two puzzles they liked best and to indicate which one they would choose, if given the opportunity, to work on for an additional 10 minutes. Because which of the two puzzles was worked on in the presence of the mirror was counterbalanced, any differential liking for the mirror-associated puzzle as a function of subjects' outcome on the prior test was taken as an indication of subjects' affective response to the self-focused state brought on by the mirror. Significant depression × outcome interactions were obtained on both measures. As may be seen in Table 1, nondepressed subjects exhibited the typical pattern of preferring self-focus after positive outcomes to self-focus after negative outcomes. Depressed subjects clearly did not; in fact they tended toward a reversal of the typical pattern, actually liking the mirror-associated puzzle more after failure than after success ($p < 10$).

Stronger evidence of a unique depressive self-focusing style was obtained in a second study in which we used a behavioral measure of mirror avoidance in the same general paradigm (Pyszczynski & Greenberg, 1986). Depressed subjects clearly spent less time in front of the mirror after success than after failure. Relative to a no-outcome control group, depressed success subjects spent less time in front of the mirror

Table 1. Mean Ratings of Liking for the Self-Focusing Puzzle and Proportion of Subjects Choosing the Self-Focusing Puzzle as a Function of Depression and Performance Outcome[a]

	Performance outcome	
	Success	Failure
Liking for Self-focusing puzzles[b]		
Nondepressed Ss	6.07	4.14
Depressed Ss	4.79	6.43
Proportion of subjects choosing Self-focusing puzzle		
Nondepressed Ss	.71	.50
Depressed Ss	.29	.57

[a]From Pyszczynski & Greenberg (1985).
[b]Scores reflect liking for the mirror associated puzzle, with higher scores indicating greater liking.

and depressed failure subjects tended to spend more time in front of the mirror. These data suggest that depressed individuals actively avoid self-focus after success.

Our first two studies demonstrated clear differences between the responses of depressed and nondepressed subjects to self-focus enhancing stimuli. In our next study we attempted to ascertain whether these differences would generalize to the extent of self-focus in such individuals' spontaneously generated thoughts (Greenberg & Pyszczynski, 1986). To do this, depressed and nondepressed subjects were again induced to either succeed or fail a supposed test of verbal intelligence. Their spontaneous self-focusing tendencies were then assessed with the Exner (1973) Sentence Completion Task. This task required subjects to complete a set of sentence stems; their completions were then scored for extent of self-focus. Rather surprisingly, both depressed and nondepressed subjects tended to spontaneously self-focus more after failure than after success.

Although initially unexpected, this effect is actually quite consistent with Carver and Scheier's (1981) model of the role of self-focus in self-regulation. Their model suggests that self-focus serves a self-regulatory function. Thus disruptions, such as frustrations and failures, may encourage self-focus and a comparison of self with standards, as part of a self-regulatory cycle aimed at keeping one "on track" in one's goal-directed activity. Although self-focus on a negative discrepancy may be aversive, people may tolerate this negative affect because it serves a useful self-regulatory function. But why, then, have previous studies shown that nondepressed persons tend to avoid self-focus enhancing stimuli, such as mirrors, after failure? Perhaps such stimuli are avoided because they increase one's already elevated level of self-focus beyond a tolerable and useful level.

If increasing one's level of self-focus after failure serves an adaptive self-regulatory function, it follows that with the passage of time and the diminishing of self-regulatory concerns, nondepressed persons may shift to the more hedonically beneficial pattern of greater self-focus after positive than after negative outcomes. If depressed persons, on the other hand, find self-focus after positive but not negative outcomes aversive, they may maintain an elevated level of self-focus after failure and a low level of self-focus after success, even after their self-regulatory concerns have diminished. To assess this possibility, we replicated the procedures of our prior study and assessed spontaneous self-focus immediately before the outcome, immediately after the outcome, and again after a delay during which subjects read 10 pages of involving fiction. Data from this study are presented in Table 2.

Table 2. Self-Focus as a Function of Depression, Outcome, and Time of Measurement

Outcome:	Success depressed	Success non-depressed	Failure depressed	Failure non-depressed
Time of measurement: Posttest	$.280_a$	$.303_a$	$.459_b$	$.469_b$
Poststory	$.016_c$	$.202_{ad}$	$.198_d$	$.046_c$

Note: Data taken from Greenberg & Pyszczynski (1986), Study 2. High means represent high self-focus. Pairwise t tests revealed that means that do not share subscripts differ at $p < .05$.

Consistent with our previous findings, immediately after the outcome, both depressed and nondepressed subjects were more self-focused in the failure than in the success condition. However, after the delay, nondepressed subjects showed the opposite pattern, becoming more self-focused after success than after failure; depressed subjects, on the other hand, persisted in exhibiting higher levels of self-focus after failure than after success even after the delay. Furthermore, after the delay, compared to nondepressed subjects, depressed subjects were higher in self-focus after failure and lower in self-focus after success. Thus it appears that although the initial response of nondepressed persons to negative outcomes is an elevation of their levels of self-focus, once a short period of time has passed and their self-regulatory concerns have diminished, their spontaneous self-focusing tendencies are guided by the affective implications of the self-focused state. Depressed persons, on the other hand, continue to engage in high levels of self-focus after failure and low levels of self-focus after success even after a delay and distraction.

Taken together, these studies suggest clear differences in the way depressed and nondepressed persons allocate attention to themselves after performance outcomes. Although nondepressed persons exhibit a brief elevation in level of self-focus immediately after a negative outcome, they appear to find self-focus after negative outcomes aversive and avoid self-focus enhancing stimuli after such outcomes when successful discrepancy reduction is unlikely. Depressed persons also exhibit elevated levels of self-focus after negative outcomes; it appears, however, that they tend to persist in focusing attention on themselves after failure even after a delay and distraction. In addition, it appears that depressed persons find self-focus after success more aversive than self-focus after failure and actively avoid self-focus enhancing stimuli after success. According to the self-regulatory perseveration theory of depression, this depressive self-focusing style plays a major role in the maintenance and exacerbation of depression.

CONSEQUENCES OF THE DEPRESSIVE SELF-FOCUSING STYLE

Previous research on the consequences of self-focused attention suggests that the depressive self-focusing style could provide an elegant explanatory mechanism for integrating a wide range of characteristics commonly associated with depression. Generally, such a pattern of self-focus allocation would be expected to maximize the psychological costs associated with negative outcomes and minimize the psychological benefits associated with positive outcomes. In particular, we suggest that a depressive self-focusing style has a detrimental effect on the depressed person's affective state, attributions, self-esteem, expectancies, motivation, and performance.

Affect

Depression is, by definition, an affective disorder. Extreme negative affect and an inability to experience positive affect are central features of all types of depression. When awareness is focused on the self, the individual becomes more aware of his or her internal state; consequently, emotions are experienced more vividly. Consistent with this proposition, research has shown that self-focus intensifies both positive and negative affective states (e.g., Gibbons, Smith, Ingram, Pearce, & Brehm, 1985; Scheier, 1976; Scheier & Carver, 1977). A depressive self-focusing style would then be expected to facilitate greatly the continued dysphoria that depressed persons experience. To the extent that depressed persons seek self-focus after negative outcomes and avoid self-focus after positive outcomes it follows that the negative affect that they experience after failures will be intensified and the positive affect they experience after successes will be minimized. Consistent with this reasoning, we recently found that relative to nondepressed subjects, depressed subjects were more displeased with failure and less pleased with success (Pyszczynski & Greenberg, 1985).

Attributions

Research on the causal attributions that depressed person's make for their performance outcomes indicates that they tend to be rather even-handed in their attributions; that is, they fail to exhibit the self-serving attributional bias that is commonly observed in nondepressed persons. Relative to the attributions made by nondepressed persons, depressed persons attributions tend to be more internal for failure and less internal for success (e.g., Kuiper, 1978; Pyszczynski & Greenberg, 1985; Rizley, 1978). The self-regulatory perseveration theory of depression posits that this attributional difference between depressed and nondepressed persons is mediated by differences in their self-focusing tendencies after performance outcomes. Research has shown that self-focus increases the tendency to make internal or dispositional attributions for one's behavior and outcomes (e.g., Duval & Wicklund, 1973; Fenigstein & Levine, 1984). As social and cognitive psychologists have suggested, increasing the salience of any object increases the extent to which it influences inferential processes (cf. Taylor & Fiske, 1978; Tversky & Kahneman, 1973). Thus, when attention is focused on the self, it follows that the self should become a more likely candidate for causal attribution. A tendency on the part of depressed persons to seek self-focus after negative outcomes and avoid self-focus after positive outcomes would thus be expected to increase the internality of their attributions for failures and decrease the internality of their attributions for successes.

We recently obtained evidence supportive of this proposition in a study in which we attempted to control subjects' self-focusing tendencies (Greenberg et al., 1985). Depressed and nondepressed subjects succeeded or failed a supposed test of verbal ability and were then induced to focus their attention either internally or externally via a story writing technique recently developed and shown to influence attributions by Fenigstein and Levine (1984). Their attributions for their performance on the verbal intelligence test were then assessed. The data revealed main effects for both performance outcome and focus of attention. Positive outcomes led to more internal attributions than did negative outcomes and self-focus led to more internal attributions than did external-focus. In addition, consistent with the theory, when self-focus was controlled, no depression-related differences in attributions emerged. More importantly, planned comparisons of the conditions analogous to the pattern of self-focus typically found in nondepressed subjects (self-focus success vs. external-focus failure) revealed a strong self-serving bias in both nondepressed and depressed individuals. Conversely, planned comparisons of the conditions analogous to the depressive self-focusing style (external-focus success vs. self-focus failure) revealed an absence of self-serving bias in depressed and nondepressed individuals. These findings are highly consistent with the hypothesis that differences in the attributions that depressed and nondepressed persons make for performance outcomes are mediated by differences in the way they allocate attention to the self. Apparently the depressive self-focusing style interferes with the tendency to make self-serving attributions for performance outcomes.

Self-Schema and Self-Esteem

Low self-esteem and a negative self-schema are central to many theories of depression (e.g., Beck, 1967; Bibring, 1953; Freud, 1917/1957; Kuiper, Derry, & MacDonald, 1982). Consistent with such perspectives, depression has been shown to be associated with perceptions of large discrepancies between real and ideal self (Laxer, 1964; Nadich, Gargan, & Michael, 1975). A series of studies conducted by Kuiper et al. (1982), in which depressed persons' incidental recall of previously presented information was assessed, are also supportive of the notion that the self-schemata of depressed persons are more negative than those of nondepressed persons. Self-regulatory perseveration theory posits several mechanisms through which a negative self-schema and low self-esteem might be created and maintained.

First, the depressive self-focusing style is likely to have a detrimental effect on self-esteem by virtue of its effect on the attributions depressives makes for their behavior and outcomes. As suggested earlier, this style of self-focus allocation is likely to decrease the internality of their attributions for positive outcomes and increase the internality of their attributions for negative outcomes (cf. Greenberg et al., 1985). To the extent that self-esteem is maximized when people make internal attributions for their positive outcomes and external attributions for their negative outcomes (cf. Bowerman, 1978), it follows that depressed persons should experience relatively little boost to self-esteem after positive outcomes but a definite drop in self-esteem after negative outcomes. Indeed, a subsidiary finding of our initial study of depressed persons' self-focusing tendencies was that whereas the self-esteem of nondepressed persons was unaffected by performance feedback, depressed persons exhibited a significant loss of self-esteem after failure (Pyszczynski & Greenberg, 1985).

In addition, self-focus may have a more direct effect on self-esteem by virtue of the self-evaluative process it sets into motion. To the extent that self-focus increases the salience of discrepancies between current and desired states, a tendency to seek self-focus after failure would be expected to increase one's awareness of one's shortcomings; likewise, a tendency to avoid self-focus after success would be expected to decrease one's awareness of one's positive qualities. Thus the depressive self-focusing style is likely to increase the loss of self-esteem associated with negative outcomes and interfere with the increase in self-esteem that could follow from positive outcomes.

Finally, the depressive self-focusing style can influence self-esteem by affecting depressed persons' tendency to draw general inferences on the basis of specific outcomes. Beck (1967) described the tendency to overgeneralize as one of the basic logical errors to which depressed persons are prone. Consistent with Beck's observations, Carver and Ganellen (1983) have presented correlational evidence linking the tendency to overgeneralize from one's failure to depression. To the extent that self-focus encourages individuals to consider the implications of events for the self (cf. Hull & Levy,1979), a depressive self-focusing style is likely to lead them to draw overly general inferences from their failures and insufficiently general inferences from their successes.

Expectancies for the Future

Beck (1967) describes depressed persons as pessimistic about themselves, their futures, and their world. Recent research documents the tendency of depressed individuals to be generally more pessimistic than nondepressed persons in their judgments of the likelihood of a variety of future life events (e.g., Pietromonaco & Markus, 1985; Pyszczynski, Holt, & Greenberg, in press, Study 1). Although there has been little in the way of systematic research on the effects of self-focused attention on probability judgments, we recently obtained evidence suggesting that these differences between depressed and nondepressed persons may be mediated by the depressive self-focusing style (Pyszczynski et al., in press, Study 2).

In the preliminary study (Pyszczynski et al., in press, Study 1), we asked depressed and nondepressed college students to estimate the likelihood of a series of positive and negative life events, both for themselves and for the typical college student. We found that depressed subjects rated negative events as more likely to happen to themselves than did nondepressed subjects; in addition, whereas nondepressed subjects rated negative events as less likely to occur to themselves than to the typical college student, depressed subjects showed no such difference. In a follow-up study (Pyszczynski et al., in press, Study 2) we varied self-focus by using Fenigstein and Levine's (1984) story writing technique and again assessed subjects' expectancies regarding future life events. In this second study, in which self-focus was controlled, the differences in probability estimates between depressed and nondepressed subjects that was obtained in the previous study emerged only when depressed subjects were self-focused. When attention was externally focused, the depressed subjects were no more pessimistic than the nondepressed subjects. These data suggest that the pessimism commonly associated with depression may be at least partially mediated by depressed individuals' generally high levels of self-focus.

Motivation and Performance

Depressed persons are routinely described as passive and unmotivated (e.g., Beck, 1967; Seligman, 1975). Consistent with these observations, research has shown that depressed persons perform poorly on a wide variety of cognitive tasks (for a review, see Miller, 1975) and in social interactions (e.g., Coyne, 1976; Gotlib, 1982). There are several ways in which a depressive self-focusing style might produce deficits in performance.

To the extent that depressed persons perseverate in focusing on previous negative outcomes, they may have diminished cognitive capacity for working on current tasks. Indeed, Kuhl and Helle (1984) demonstrated that, for depressed persons, an unfinished task produces a deficit in short-term memory. In addition, Strack, Blaney, Ganellen, and Coyne (1985) demonstrated that, by encouraging depressed subjects to focus on the task at hand, their performance was improved. It may be that the depressive tendency to focus on prior negative outcomes is at least partially responsible for the performance differential between depressed and nondepressed persons.

Another factor likely to interfere with the motivation and performance of depressed individuals is their pessimistic expectancies for future success. Given that expectancy of success is considered to be a central determinant of motivation by many theorists (e.g., Atkinson, 1964; Bandura, 1977; Lewin, 1935), a pessimistic outlook is likely to have a detrimental effect on motivation and performance. As suggested above, the self-focusing tendencies of depressed persons are likely to encourage such a pessimitic outlook.

Finally, Carver and Scheier's (1981) cybernetic model posits that self-focus amplifies the effect of outcome expectancies on subsequent motivation. Research has shown that self-focus interferes with performance when outcome expectancies are low but facilitates performance when outcome expectancies are high (e.g., Brockner, 1979; Carver, Blaney, & Scheier, 1979). To the extent that depressed persons seek self-focus after failure, when outcome expectancies are likely to be especially low, and avoid self-focus after success, when outcome expectancies should be higher, subsequent motivation and performance is likely to be minimized.

To summarize, previous research on the consequences of self-focus suggests that the depressive self-focusing style is likely to lead to (a) decreased positive affect after successes and increased negative affect after failures, (b) a decreased tendency to make internal attributions for successes and an increased tendency to make internal attributions for failures, and (c) an inhibition of the increase in self-esteem, expectancies, and motivation that could result from successes and a facilitation of the decrease in self-esteem, expectancies, and motivation that could result from failures. We suggest, then, that the depressive self-focusing style plays a central role in the maintenance and exacerbation of a wide variety of depressive symptoms.

But what accounts for this rather unusual and maladaptive pattern of self-focus deployment? What psychological functions might it serve? Before attempting to answer these very important questions we must consider the role played by self-focused attention and self-regulatory processes in the development of depression. By so doing, we may arrive at some insights into the nature of depression that help explain why such a counterhedonic pattern of self-focus allocation emerges.

SELF-REGULATORY PERSEVERATION AND THE DEPRESSIVE SPIRAL

Both clinical observations and more rigorously controlled empirical research suggests that depressive episodes are often precipitated by impactful personal losses (e.g., Aneshensel & Frerichs, 1982; Arieti & Bemporad, 1978; Beck, 1976; Brown & Harris, 1978; Freud, 1917/1957; Lloyd, 1980). For example, Arieti and Bemporad (1978) observe that the types of losses that most commonly precipitate depression are the loss of a central social or romantic relationship, the death of a loved one, and the failure in the pursuit of a central self-defining goal. From the self-regulatory perseveration perspective, depression occurs when the value of the lost object interferes with the normal functioning of the self-regulatory system. Our analysis of the initiation of depressive episodes builds from Carver and Scheier's (1981) cybernetic model of self-regulation.

According to Carver and Scheier, any event that disrupts ongoing behavior initiates a self-regulatory cycle, the purpose of which is to facilitate the individual's progress towards various goals. The self-regulatory cycle consists of a self-focus phase, in which current and desired states are compared and any discrepancies noted, and a discrepancy reduction phase, in which behavior is engaged in, in an attempt to minimize discrepancies between current and desired states. Thus self-focus is a necessary component of the self-regulatory cycle because it provides information needed for effective coping with disruptions. Carver and Scheier posit that when self-focus makes negative discrepancies salient, the preferred response is to attempt to reduce the discrepancy. However, if the individual perceives that the probability of successfully reducing the discrepancy is very low, self-focus is avoided and further attempts at discrepancy reduction are abandoned. Research by Carver *et al.* (1979), Steenbarger and Aderman (1979), and others has been generally supportive of the model.

Withdrawal from the self-regulatory cycle when successful discrepancy reduction is unlikely is a very adaptive response, because, besides being a fruitless waste of energy, continued self-focus on an irreducible negative discrepancy is likely to be highly aversive and produce a wide range of negative consequences. We propose that depression develops when the person is unable or unwilling to exit the self-regulatory cycle. This is likely to occur when what was lost functioned for the individual as a central source of self-esteem, emotional security, or identity. In such instances, he or she may simply be unable to accept the absence of the object because without it life becomes terrifying and unliveable (cf. Greenberg, Pyszczynski, & Solomon, 1986). Withdrawal from the cycle might normally be facilitated by the availability and pursuit of substitute goals (cf. Lewin, 1938; Mahler, 1933; Wicklund & Gollwitzer, 1982) or by the use of defensive strategies in which the lost object is derogated (cf. Brehm, Wright, Solomon, Silka, & Greenberg, 1983; Festinger, 1957). However, to the extent that the individual had centered his or her life around the lost object and used the object as source of meaning and value, such strategies are likely to be both unappealing and ineffective.

The self-regulatory perseveration theory of depression is essentially a diathesis-stress model. An irrevocable loss or failure will result in depression only if the individual is unable to exit the self-regulatory cycle that would normally function to help him or her minimize discrepancies between current and desired states. A person is likely to be unable to exit such a cycle to the extent that (a) the lost object previously functioned as a source of self-esteem, security, and value in life, and (b) few alternate objects that could substitute for the function of the lost object are available. Perseveration in focusing attention on the lost object then instigates a spiral of events that produces the wide range of symptoms that generally accompany the depressive state.

As a result of his or her inability to exit the self-regulatory cycle, the individual is faced with a virtually constant confrontation with the discrepancy between current and desired states. Although such confrontations may be adaptive when instrumental behaviors capable of reducing the discrepancy are available, they are clearly maladaptive when the loss is irrevocable. As discussed previously, self-focus on a negative discrepancy is likely to intensify the negative affect one experiences, increase one's tendency to blame oneself for the loss, lead to high levels of self-criticism and a loss of self-esteem, lower one's expectancies for positive outcomes in the future, and decrease one's motivation and performance in other situations. Because the person is attending to this one central domain of his or her life, functioning in other areas is bound to suffer. In essence, self-regulatory perseveration on the lost object creates a spiraling process that culminates in a state of depression.

We propose that it is this unwillingness to give up the lost object, along with the mounting psychological consequences produced by perseveration in self-focus concerning the lost object, that leads to the emergence of the depressive self-focusing style. This generalized pattern of avoiding self-focus after positive outcomes and seeking self-focus after negative outcomes may initially emerge because of the impact of such later outcomes on the person's self-regulatory attempts to recover the lost object. Positive outcomes in other domains may be seen as distractions that interfere with the individual's attempts to deal with the "real issues" that are troubling him or her. Thus, in contrast to the tremendous negative affect the individual is experiencing in response to the recent loss of a major source of emotional security, the positive affect that most other positive outcomes could generate seems trivial. Indeed, dwelling on such outcomes would violate the person's sense of the tragic nature of his or her situation. Stated simply, depressed individuals do not want to be temporarily cheered up; they want their problems to be solved. Because self-focus after positive outcomes interferes with their attempts to cope with their real problems, it becomes aversive and is avoided.

Negative outcomes, on the other hand, may be viewed as symptoms of and contributors to the person's overall problem. Recall that the person has just lost a central source of identity and self-worth; thus his or her self-image is likely to be especially malleable at this time. Given that self-regulatory perseveration on the lost object is likely to lead the person to blame him or herself for the loss, view the loss as the result of some very general personal shortcoming, suffer detriments in self-esteem, and have difficulties functioning in other domains, the emergence of a negative self-image seems quite likely. As a result, other negative outcomes that occur may also encourage self-focus because they are seen as part of the problem through which the person lost the prior object.

Once a negative self-image is established, the individual may actually become motivated to maintain it because it begins to provide him or her with several beneficial consequences. Initially, accepting a negative self-image may provide the individual with a sense of relief from his or her increasingly futile attempts to preserve a positive self-image. In the face of the spiral of effects produced by self-regulatory perseveration, normal defensive efforts to cope with the loss are unlikely to be successful. Because ineffective defensive maneuvers are likely to be aversive, a negative self-image may eventually be accepted as the lesser of two evils; it provides the individual with a simple parsimonious explanation for his or her aversive experiences (cf. Becker, 1973) and does not require the elaborate control of self-relevant information that is sometimes necessary to maintain a positive self-image (cf. Pyszczynski, Greenberg, & Holt, 1985; Pyszczynski, Greenberg, & LaPrelle, 1985).

In addition to the relief from attempts to maintain a positive self-image, a negative self-image may be maintained because, after a tragic loss, it is preferred to the alternative of viewing the world as an unpredictable, unjust, and absurd place in which to live. Several theorists have argued that people have a need to believe that the world is fair and just, or at least not meaningless, chaotic, and terrifying (e.g., Becker, 1962; Greenberg et al., 1986; Lerner, Miller, & Holmes, 1976). Research has shown that when people witness the misfortune of others they often derogate the victim, presumably in an attempt to preserve their belief that the world is just. Perhaps when faced with an extreme personal loss, people prefer to derogate themselves, believing that they in some way deserve what has happened, because this preserves such a benign view of the world. A literary example of this can be seen in Hardy's *Jude the Obscure*, in which, when faced with the tragic death of her children, an unmarried woman decides that she is being punished by God for her sin of having children out of wedlock; although this interpretation of the tragedy caused her great suffering, it was preferrable to concluding that life is a meaningless and godless nightmare.

Finally, a negative self-image may be maintained because it minimizes demands on the individual for successful and competent behavior in the future and minimizes the potential for disappointment. Rothbaum, Weisz, and Snyder (1982) have recently argued that when people are unable to exert control over their outcomes, they then switch to attempts to control their emotional responses to their outcomes. Adopting a negative self-image may be a way of minimizing the potential for devastating losses in the future. Because the tremendous pain brought on by the precipitating loss was made possible by the person's dependence on the lost object as a source of self-worth and emotional security, he or she may adopt a negative self-image because it enables him/her to avoid investment in other sources of self-value. By viewing oneself as a loser, one can avoid endeavors where additional failures are likely to occur. In addition, when negative outcomes do occur, they may have less impact because they are expected (cf. Pyszczynski, 1982). Thus a negative self-image provides the person with a relatively safe, unassailable perspective from which to interact with the world, and consequently he or she may strive to preserve it.

In summary, a negative self-image may be actively maintained because it (a) provides relief from increasingly difficult and aversive attempts to maintain a positive self-image, (b) may be preferred over accepting the world as an unjust and chaotic place in which to exist, and (c) enables the individual to minimize demands for future positive outcomes and the potential for future disappointment. The depressive self-focusing style functions to maintain the negative self-image by minimizing the psychological consequences of positive outcomes and maximizing the psychological consequences of negative outcomes. Generally speaking, the deeper the depression and the more firmly entrenched the negative self-image, the greater will be the adherence to the depressive self-focusing style.

To summarize the theory, a depressive episode is instigated after a major loss when the value attached to the lost object interferes with the normal functioning of the individual's self-regulatory mechanisms. Essentially, the individual becomes stuck in a self-regulatory cycle in which successful discrepancy reduction is impossible. The resulting high levels of self-focus lead to an intensification of negative affect, an increased tendency to blame oneself for the loss, an enhancement of self-evaluative tendencies, interference with motivation and performance in other areas, a loss of self-esteem, and the emergence of a depressive self-focusing style. The depressive self-focusing style then maintains and exacerbates the depressive state.

EXISTING EMPIRICAL SUPPORT AND DIRECTIONS FOR RESEARCH

The self-regulatory perseveration theory of depression is an attempt to integrate the role played by a variety of processes that seem to play central roles in depression. It is generally consistent with what is currently known about depression and can be used to generate a variety of testable hypotheses. Although a thorough review of the support for the theory provided by the existing literature on depression is beyond the scope of this chapter, we now briefly point to several findings that seem particularly relevant.

Thus far the research generated by the theory has been focused on determining the self-focusing preferences of currently depressed individuals (Greenberg & Pyszczynski, 1986; Pyszczynski & Greenberg, 1985, 1986) and the effect of the depressive self-focusing style on various "symptoms" of depression (Greenberg et al., 1985; Pyszczynski et al., 1986). Although the results of these studies (described previously in this chapter) have been encouraging, future research on these issues will be required before the importance of the role played by depressive self-focusing tendencies can adequately be assessed. Thus far, these processes have been investigated in only mild to moderately depressed individuals. Thus studies addressing the role of self-focus in more severe forms of depression would be especially useful. In addition, studies investigating the hypothesized functions of the depressive self-focusing style are needed.

We are just now beginning to conduct studies assessing the role of self-regulatory perseveration in the onset of depression. However, a variety of clinical observations and findings from previous research are consistent with the theory. Clinical observations and more rigorously controlled descriptive studies suggest that depression tends to follow significant self-related losses (e.g., Anehensel & Frerichs, 1982; Arieti & Bemporad, 1978; Beck, 1976; Billings & Moos, 1982; Paykel et al., 1969). It also appears that such losses are especially likely to lead to depression when the person lacks alternate sources of what was provided by the lost object. For example, Brown and Harris (1978), Anehensel and Frerichs (1982), and Paykel et al. (1969) have shown that individuals who lack close relationships with persons other than those associated with the loss are especially prone to depression. Furthermore, cross-cultural studies suggest that persons who live in cultures in which people are encouraged to value only a narrow range of significant others seem to be especially prone to depression (e.g., Parker, 1962).

As noted earlier, theorists, researchers, and clinical observers from a wide variety of orientations have all noted the tendency of depressed individuals to dwell excessively on past losses (e.g., Beck, 1967; Brown & Harris, 1978; Coyne, Aldwin, & Lazarus, 1981; Kanfer & Hagerman, 1981) and to become self-preoccupied and self-obsessed (e.g., Abraham, 1911; Arieti & Bemporad, 1978; Beck, 1976; Freud, 1917/1957). Indeed, a number of recent correlational studies have shown that depression and self-focus are positively associated (e.g., Ingram & Smith, 1984;

Smith & Greenberg, 1981; Smith, Ingram, & Roth, 1985). Our studies of the depressive self-focusing style suggest that although depressed individuals may be highly self-preoccupied, they actively avoid self-focus after positive outcomes. From the present perspective, this preoccupation with self and one's losses plays a central role in the development of depression.

Clearly, further research designed to test more directly the central propositions of the theory is needed. Especially important would be studies assessing the effect of the ego relevance of a goal object on the amount of time individuals remain in a self-regulatory cycle where the probability of successful discrepancy reduction is low. Also important would be prospective research assessing the relationship between ego investment in an object, loss of the object, perseveration in focusing on the lost object, self-preoccupation, and the development of depressive symptomology (e.g., affect, attributions, negative self-image, etc.). Additional studies of the determinants and consequences of the depressive self-focusing style are also needed.

GENERAL IMPLICATIONS FOR THE PREVENTION AND TREATMENT OF DEPRESSION

The theory suggests that the fewer sources of self-esteem an individual has and the more readily these sources may be lost, the more vulnerable that individual is to depression. Therefore, a society concerned with minimizing depression should encourage and provide a wide range of stable sources of self-esteem and discourage exclusive investment in any one particular source. Of course, an alternative would be to provide one extremely powerful source of self-esteem that could not be lost. Perhaps for truly devout religious persons, their beliefs may provide such stable bases for value.

However, once a person suffers the loss of a primary source of self-esteem, some degree of depression is likely to result. Whether this state becomes severe enough to be categorized as major depression depends on the extent to which the individual perseverates in self-focus concerning the loss. Therefore, therapy should be directed at helping the individual disengage from self-regulatory perseveration. To accomplish this, the individual must give up his or her dependence on the lost object for self-esteem and establish alternative sources.

To begin to reduce the individual's preoccupation with the loss, client–therapist contracts and homework assignments that encourage external focus might be useful (e.g., Beck, Rush, Shaw, & Emery, 1979). Such interventions can also be used to show the individual that alternative bases of self-value do exist. Change in environment and daily routines may also contribute to these goals. Perhaps in some cases, expression of anger at and devaluation of the lost object may also facilitate shifting the individual's attention sufficiently to disengage the self-regulatory cycle and establish alternative bases of self-worth.

Of course the individual may be quite reluctant to invest in other sources of self-esteem because it was just such an investment that led to his or her extreme pain and anxiety when the object was lost. Further investments may be seen as simply setting up the potential for additional devastating losses. In such cases, the individual would probably reinvest in new sources of self-value only if he or she felt reasonably certain that such negative experiences would not occur again. Thus an acceptable alternative would have to be sufficiently different from the prior source to appear convincingly as permanent, or at least incapable of being lost in the manner in which the previous object was lost. For example, a person who has experienced a devastating divorce may be able to shift investments from relationships to career pursuits if he or she is confident that the latter is a more reliable and enduring source of self-value. The person may also be encouraged to shift investment if multiple sources could be established, thereby minimizing the likelihood of devastation should any one source be lost.

In order to facilitate accomplishing such goals, it may also be necessary to reverse the depressive self-focusing style that is likely to have emerged by the time the individual seeks therapy. Once a depressive self-focusing style has been established, the resulting negative effects are likely to interfere with any attempts to encourage the client to reinvest in other sources of self-value and prevent him or her from reaping the psychological benefits from potential new sources that do emerge. Thus, as Schmitt (1983) and Smith and Greenberg (1981) have previously suggested, it may be important to discourage self-focus concerning negative experience, a recommendation that runs counter to the approach advocated by many insight-oriented therapies. It may be equally important to encourage self-focus concerning positive outcomes, to enhance positive affect, motivation, and self-esteem. Of course depressed individuals may not experience many positive outcomes and are likely to resist focusing on those that do occur. Therefore, special steps may be necessary to structure the person's environment so that such experiences become more frequent (cf. Lewinsohn, 1975) and attention is directed to them when they do occur (cf. Beck, 1976).

RELATIONSHIP TO OTHER THEORIES OF DEPRESSION

Interestingly, a number of other recent analyses of depression have independently begun to consider self-awareness and self-regulatory processes as important factors (e.g., Kanfer & Hagerman, 1981; Lewinsohn, Hoberman, Teri, & Hautzinger, 1985). We find this convergence on the notion that self-focus contributes to the maintenance and exacerbation of depression to be quite encouraging, especially given the divergent perspectives from which these theorists approach this idea. Kanfer and Hagerman approach the problem of depression from the perspective of behavioral self-regulation theory. Although they do not explicitly take the self-awareness literature into account, they do give self-monitoring and comparison of current and desired states a central role in their analysis. The Lewinsohn *et al.* model is a more explicit application of self-awareness theory to the problem of depression and is generally quite consistent with our analysis. They take more of an epidemiological approach and use the self-awareness literature to account for a variety of empirically demonstrated characteristics of depression. Although both of these analyses are generally compatible with self-regulatory perseveration theory, neither provides an explanation of why depressed individuals persist in high levels of self-focus concerning negative outcomes in spite of the negative affect that is engendered. In addition, these analyses do not posit a depressive self-focusing style. As we have argued earlier such a pattern of self-focus allocation best characterizes the state of depression and can be used to account for a wide range of depressive symptomology.

For the most part, our theory is quite compatible with other psychological theories of depression. It is an attempt to outline a sequence of interrelated cognitive, emotional, and motivational events that occur when an individual is faced with the loss of a central source of self-worth, emotional security, or identity. It incorporates a variety of variables emphasized by other theories (e.g., attributions, self-schemata, expectancies, affect, contingencies for self-worth) and organizes them around a framework provided by basic theory and research on self-focused attention and self-regulatory processes. We believe that one of the strengths of the theory is that it provides a framework that can be used to integrate the role played by a variety of processes emphasized by other theories of depression.

For example, in their revised learned helplessness theory of depression, Abramson, Seligman, and Teasdale (1978) posited that internal, stable, and global attributions for negative outcomes influence one's expectancies for future outcomes, which in turn influence one's motivation and performance in other domains. However, the revised helplessness model does not explain how such depressive attributional tendencies emerge. From the helplessness perspective, relatively stable individual differences in attributional style are assumed to interact with experience of uncontrollable outcomes to produce the cognitive, motivational, and emotional deficits typically associated with depression.

Unfortunately, the literature on the relationship between attributions and depression is inconsistent with respect to the question of whether stable differences in attributional style interact with life experiences to cause depression (cf. Peterson & Seligman, 1984) or, alternatively, the attributional characteristics of depression are a consequence rather than a cause of depression (cf. Lewinsohn, Steinmetz, Larson, & Franklin, 1981). From the present perspective, the attributional characteristics of depression result from the self-focusing tendencies that emerge as a result of the individual's inability to let go of a lost source of self-regard. Although further research on this possibility is needed, the findings of Greenberg et al. (1985) are highly consistent with this interpretation.

Similarly, Beck's (1967) more general cognitive perspective posits that depression occurs as the result of a negative self-schema that biases the individual toward increasingly negative thoughts about oneself, one's future, and the world. Self-regulatory perseveration theory provides an explanation of how significant losses can contribute to the development of such self-schemata and how attentional processes can play a central role in a wide range of self-referent thoughts. An additional advantage of the self-regulatory approach is that it provides a useful conceptual framework for discussing the relationship between cognitive variables and their effect on subsequent motivation and emotion.

Psychodynamic approaches also generally focus on negative views of the self, with an emphasis on self-blame and heightened self-criticism (e.g., Arieti & Bemporad, 1979; Becker, 1973; Bibring, 1953; Freud, 1917/1957). Freud viewed depression as a condition in which the superego becomes very active in producing guilt and self-deprecation. To the extent that the superego is viewed as functioning to compare one's behavior and characteristics to idealized standards (the ego ideal), self-focus could be viewed as an activation of the superego. More generally, the phenomenology of the depressive self-focusing style can be viewed as a direct manifestation of the self-critical characteristics emphasized by psychodynamic theories of depression. The present framework is useful because it provides a paradigm for investigating some of the psychodynamically based hypotheses that had previously eluded experimental verification.

Finally, a number of theorists (e.g., Coyne, 1976; Strack & Coyne, 1983) have focused on the role of social difficulties in depression. Depressed individuals often appear shy, awkward, distant, and uninterested in their social encounters. Jacobson and Anderson (1982) have shown that depressed persons often interrupt their conversations with inappropriate reference to themselves. We suggest that such individuals' self-preoccupation is largely responsible for their social difficulties. This preoccupation may encourage the expression of negative affect and frequent discussions of one's problems; research has shown that these characteristics of depressed persons' conversations are often aversive to others (Coyne, 1976, Strack & Coyne, 1984). In addition, as suggested earlier, high levels of self-focus after negative outcomes are likely to lead to low motivation and withdrawal (Carver & Scheier, 1981; Schlenker & Leary, 1982), making it more difficult for depressed persons to maintain their social contacts.

Although the theory is not in conflict with other theories in most respects, there is one central point of divergence from other approaches. From the perspective of many other theories, depression is viewed as a phenomenon in which an individual experiences losses or difficulties in attaining or maintaining an important goal, gives up on that goal, and then generalizes this loss of motivation to other goals and other domains (e.g., Abramson *et al.,* 1978; Bowlby, 1980; Kanfer & Hagerman, 1981; Klinger, 1975; Seligman, 1975; Wortman & Brehm, 1975). From these perspectives a generalized loss of motivation is synonymous with depression. In contrast, self-regulatory perseveration theory posits that it is an inability or unwillingness to give up on an unattainable goal when it would be adaptive to do so that instigates the spiral of events that produce depression. Certainly depressed persons do indeed often appear to be passive and unmotivated. We argue, however, that this passivity in other realms is the result of self-regulatory perseveration concerning a significant loss. We would argue that if the lost object suddenly became available to the individual, he or she would show a remarkable level of interest in resuming his or her relationship with it.

In conclusion, although our theory diverges from many other theories of depression in this important way, it provides a framework that can be used to integrate a broad range of processes emphasized by these other perspectives. The theory is based on a clear and well-supported conceptual framework, it is quite consistent with a broad range of clinical observations and systematic research concerning depression, and it can be used to generate a variety of novel hypotheses concerning the relationship among a broad range of depressive phenomena.

REFERENCES

Abraham, K. (1927). Notes on the psychoanalytic investigation and treatment of manic-depressive insanity and allied conditions. In *Selected papers on psycho-analysis* (pp. 137–156). London: Hogarth. (Originally published in 1911).

Abramson, L. Y., & Sackheim, H. A. (1977). A paradox in depression: Uncontrollability and self-blame. *Psychological Bulletin, 84,* 838–851.

Abramson, L. Y., Seligman, M. E. P., & Teasdale, J. D. (1978). Learned helplessness in humans: Critique and reformulation. *Journal of Abnormal Psychology, 87,* 49–74.

Aneshensel, C. S., & Frerichs, R. R. (1982). Stress, support, and depression: A longitudinal causal model. *Journal of Community Psychology, 10,* 363–376.

Arieti, S., & Bemporad, J. (1978). *Severe and mild depression.* New York: Basic Books.

Atkinson, J. W. (1964). *An introduction to motivation.* Princeton, NJ: Van Nostrand.

Bandura, A. (1977). Self-efficacy: Toward a unifying theory of behavior change. *Psychological Review, 84,* 191–215.

Beck, A. T. (1967). *Depression: Clinical, experimental, and theoretical aspects.* New York: Hoeber.

Beck, A. T. (1976). *Cognitive therapy and the emotional disorders.* New York: International Universities Press.

Beck, A. T., Rush, A., Shaw, B., & Emery, G. (1979). *Cognitive therapy of depression.* New York: Guilford.

Becker, E. (1962). *The birth and death of meaning.* New York: The Free Press.

Becker, E. (1973). *The denial of death.* New York: The Free Press.

Bibring, E. (1953). The mechanism of depression. In P. Greenacre (Ed.), *Affective disorders* (pp. 14–47). New York: International Universities Press.

Billings, A. G., & Moos, R. N. (1982). Psychosocial theory and research on depression: An integrative framework and review. *Clinical Psychology Review, 2,* 213–237.

Bowerman, W. R. (1978). Subjective competence: The structure, process and function of self-referent causal attributions. *Journal for the Theory of Social Behavior, 8,* 45–75.

Bowlby, J. (1980). *Loss, sadness and depression.* London: Hogarth.

Brehm, J. W., Wright, R. A. Solomon, S., Silka, K., & Greenberg, J. (1983). Perceived difficulty, energization and the magnitude of good valence. *Journal of Experimental Social Psychology, 19,* 21–48.

Brockner, J. (1979). The effects of self-esteem, success-failure, and self-consciousness on task performance. *Journal of Personality and Social Psychology, 37,* 1732–1741.

Brown, G. W., & Harris, T. (1978). *Social origins of depression: A study of psychiatric disorder in women.* New York: Free Press.

Carver, C. (1979). A cybernetic model of self-attention processes. *Journal of Personality and Social Psychology, 37,* 1251–1281.

Carver, C. S., & Ganellen, R. J. (1983). Depression and components of self-punitiveness: High standards, self-concept and overgeneralization. *Journal of Abnormal Psychology, 92,* 330–337.

Carver, C. S., & Scheier, M. F. (1981). *Attention and self-regulation: A control-theory approach to human behavior.* New York: Springer.

Carver, C. S., Blaney, P. H., & Scheier, M. F. (1979). Reassertion and giving up: The interactive role of self-directed attention and outcome expectancy. *Journal of Personality and Social Psychology, 37,* 1895–1870.

Coyne, J. C. (1976). Depression and the responses of others. *Journal of Abnormal Psychology, 85,* 186–193.

Coyne, J. C., Aldwin, C., & Lazarus, R. S. (1981). Depression and coping in stressful episodes. *Journal of Abnormal Psychology, 90,* 439–447.

Duval, S., & Wicklund, R. (1972). *A theory of objective self-awareness.* New York: Academic Press.

Duval, S., & Wicklund, R. (1973). Effects of objective self-awareness on attributions of causality. *Journal of Experimental Social Psychology, 9,* 17–31.

Exner, J. E. (1973). The self-focus sentence completion: A study of egocentricity. *Journal of Personality Assessment, 37,* 437–455.

Fenigstein, A., & Levine, M. P. (1984). Self-attention, concept activation, and the causal self. *Journal of Experimental Social Psychology, 20,* 231–245.

Festinger, L. (1957). *A theory of cognitive dissonance.* Evanston, IL: Row & Peterson.

Freud, S. (1957). Mourning and melancholia. In J. Strachey (Ed. & trans.), *The complete psychological works of Sigmund Freud* (Vol. 14). London: Hogarth Press. (Original work published 1917)

Gibbons, F. X., & Wicklund, R. (1976). Selective exposure to self. *Journal of Research in Personality, 10,* 98–106.

Gibbons, F. X., Smith, T. W., Ingram, R. E., Pierce, X., Brehm, S. S., & Schroeder, D. (1985). Self-awareness and self-confrontation. Effects of self-focused attention on members of a clinical population. *Journal of Personality and Social Psychology, 48,* 662–675.

Gotlib, I. H. (1982). Self-reinforcement and depression in interpersonal interaction: The role of performance level. *Journal of Abnormal Psychology, 91,* 3–13.

Greenberg, J., & Pyszczynski, T. (1986). Persistent high self-focus after failure and low self-focus after success: The depressive self-focusing style. *Journal of Personality and Social Psychology, 50,* 1039–1044.

Greenberg, J., Pyszczynski, T., Kelly, C., Burling, J., Byler, E., & Tibbs, K. (1985). *Depression, self-focus, and the self-serving attributional bias.* Unpublished manuscript, University of Arizona.

Greenberg, J., Pyszczynski, T., & Solomon, S. (1986). The causes and consequences of a need for self-esteem: A terror management theory. In R. Baumeister (Ed.), *Public self and private self* (pp. 189–212). New York: Springer-Verlag.

Hull, J. G., & Levy, A. S. (1979). The organizational functioning of the self: An alternative to the Duval and Wicklund model of self-awareness. *Journal of Personality and Social Psychology, 37,* 756–768.

Ingram, R. E., & Smith, T. W. (1984). Depression and internal versus external locus of attention. *Cognitive Therapy and Research, 8,* 139–152.

Jacobson, N. S., & Anderson, E. A. (1982). Interpersonal skill and depression in college students: An analyses of the timing of self-disclosures. *Behavior Therapy, 13,* 271–282.

Kanfer, F. H., & Hagerman, S. (1981). The role of self-regulation. In L. Rehm (Ed.), *Behavior therapy for depression: Present status and future directions* (pp. 143–180). New York: Academic Press.

Klinger, E. (1975). Consequences of commitment to and disengagement form incentives. *Psychological Review, 82,* 1–25.

Kuiper, N. A. (1978). Depression and causal attributions for success and failure. *Journal of Personality and Social Psychology, 36,* 236–246.

Kuiper, N. A., Derry, P. A., & MacDonald, M. R. (1982). Self-reference and person perception in depression: A social cognition perspective. In G. Weary & H. Mirels (Eds.), *Integration of social and clinical psychology* (pp. 79–103). New York: Oxford University Press.

Kuhl, J., & Helle, P. (1984). *Motivational and volitional determinants of depression: The degenerated intentions hypothesis.* Unpublished manuscript, Max Planok institute for Psychological Research, Munich, West Germany.

Laxer, R. (1964). Self-concept changes of depressed patients in general hospital treatment. *Journal of Consulting Psychology, 28,* 214–219.

Lerner, M. J., Miller, D. T., & Holmes, J. G. (1976). Deserving and the emergence of forms of justice. In L. Berkowitz & E. Walster (Eds.), *Advances in experimental social psychology.* (Vol. 9, pp. 133–162). New York: Academic Press.

Lewin, K. (1935). *A dynamic theory of personality.* New York: McGraw-Hill.

Lewinsohn, P. M. (1975). Engagement in pleasant activities and depression level. *Journal of Abnormal Psychology, 84,* 729–731.

Lewinsohn, P. M., Hoberman, H., Teri, L., & Hautzinger, M. (1985). An integrative theory of depression. In S. Reiss & R. Bootzin (Eds.), *Theoretical issues in behavior therapy.* New York: Academic Press.

Lewinsohn, P. M., Steinmetz, J. L., Larson, D. W., & Franklin, J. (1981). Depression-related cognitions: Antecedents or consequence? *Journal of Abnormal Psychology, 90,* 213–219.

Lloyd, C. (1980). Life events and depressive disorder reviewed: Events as predisposing factors. *Archives of General Psychiatry, 37,* 529–535.

Mahler, V. (1933). Ersatzhandlungen verschiedenen. Realitätsgrads. *Psychologische Forschung, 18,* 27–89.

Miller, W. R. (1975). Psychological deficit in depression. *Psychological Bulletin, 82,* 238–260.

Mollon, P., & Parry, G. (1984). The fragile self: Narcissistic disturbance and the protective function of depression. *British Journal of Medical Psychology, 57,* 137–145.

Nadich, M., Gargan, M., & Michael, L. (1975). Denial, anxiety, locus of control, and the discrepancy between aspirations and achievements as components of depression. *Journal of Abnormal Psychology, 84,* 1–9.

Parker, S. (1962). Eskimo psychopathology in the context of Eskimo personality and culture. *American Anthropologist, 64,* 76–96.

Paykel, E. S., Myers, J. K., Dienelt, M. N., Klerman, G. L., Lindenthal, J. J., & Pepper, M. P. (1969). Life events and depression: A controlled study. *Archives of General Psychiatry, 21,* 753–760.

Peterson, C., & Seligman, M. E. P. (1984). Causal explanations as a risk factor for depression: Theory and evidence. *Psychological Review, 91,* 347–374.

Pietromonoco, P. R., & Markus, H. (1985). The nature of negative thoughts in depression. *Journal of Personality and Social Psychology, 48,* 791–798.

Pyszczynski, T. (1982). Cognitive strategies for coping with uncertain outcomes. *Journal of Research in Personality, 16,* 236–399.

Pyszczynski, T., & Greenberg, J. (1985). Depression and preference for self-focusing stimuli following success and failure. *Journal of Personality and Social Psychology, 49,*

Pyszczynski, T., & Greenberg, J. (1986). Evidence for a depressive self-focusing style. *Journal of Research in Personality, 20,* 95–106.

Pyszczynski, T., & Greenberg, J. (in press). The role of self-focused attention in the development, maintenance, and exacerbation of depression. In K. Yardley & T. Honess (Eds.), *Self and identity Psychosocial perspectives,* Chicester: Wiley.

Pyszczynski, T., & Greenberg, J., & Holt, K. (1985). Maintaining consistency between self-serving beliefs and available data: A bias in information evaluation following success and failure. *Personality and Social Psychology Bulletin, 11,* 179–190.

Pyszczynski, T., Greenberg, J., & LaPrelle, J. (1985). Social comparison after success and failure: Biased search for information consistent with a self-serving hypothesis. *Journal of Experimental Social Psychology, 21,* 195–211.

Pyszczynski, T., Holt, K., & Greenberg, J. (in press). Depression, self-focused attention, and expectancies for positive and negative future life events for self and others. *Journal of Personality and Social Psychology.*

Rizley, R. (1978). Depression and distortion in the attribution of causality. *Journal of Abnormal Psychology, 87,* 32–48.

Rothbaum, F., Weisz, J. R., & Snyder, S. S. (1982). Changing the world and changing the self: A two-process model of perceived control. *Journal of Personality and Social Psychology, 42,* 5–37.

Scheier, M. F. (1976). Self-awareness, self-consciousness and angry aggression. *Journal of Personality, 44,* 627–644.

Scheier, M. F., & Carver, C. S. (1977). Self-focused attention and the experience of emotion: Attraction, repulsion, elation, and depression. *Journal of Personality and Social Psychology, 35,* 625–636.

Schlenker, B. R., & Lear, M. R. (1982). Audiences' reaction to self-enhancing, self-demigrating, and accurate self-presentations. *Journal of Experimental Social Psychology, 18,* 89–104.

Schmitt, J. P. (1983). Focus of attention in the treatment of depression. *Psychotherapy: Theory, Research, and Practice, 20,* 457–463.

Seligman, M. E. P. (1975). *Helplessness: On depression, development, and death.* San Francisco, CA: W. H. Freeman.

Smith, T. W., & Greenberg, J. (1981). Depression and self-focused attention. *Motivation and Emotion, 5,* 323–331.

Smith, T. W., Ingram, R. E., & Roth, D. (1985). Self-focused attention and depression. Self-evaluation and life stress. *Motivation and Emotion, 9,* 381–390.

Steenbarger, B. N., & Aderman, D. (1979). Objective self-awareness as a nonaversive state. Effect of anticipating discrepancy reduction. *Journal of Personality, 47,* 330–339.

Strack, S., Blaney, P. H., Ganellen, R. J., & Coyne, J. C. (1985). Pessimistic self-preoccupation, performance deficits, and depression. *Journal of Personality and Social Psychology, 49,* 1076–1085.

Strack, S., & Coyne, J. C. (1983). Social confirmation of dysphoria: Shared and private reactions. *Journal of Personality and Social Psychology, 44,* 796–806.

Taylor, S. E., & Fiske, S. T. (1978). Salience, attention, and attribution: Top of the head phenomena. In L. Berkowitz (Ed.), *Advances in experimental social psychology* (Vol. 2, pp. 250–288). New York: Academic Press.

Tversky, A., & Kahneman, D. (1973). Availability: A heuristic for judging frequency and probability. *Cognitive Psychology, 5,* 207–232.

Wicklund, R. (1975). Objective self-awareness. In L. Berkowitz (Ed.), *Advances in experimental social psychology* (Vol. 8, pp. 233–275). New York: Academic Press.

Wickland, R. A., & Gollwitzer, P. M. (1982). *Symbolic self-completion.* Hillsdale, NJ: Erlbaum.

Wortman, C. B., & Brehm, J. W. (1975). Responses to uncontrollable outcomes: An integration of reactance theory and the learned helplessness model. In L. Berkowitz (Ed.), *Advances in experimental social psychology* (Vol. 8, pp. 277–336). New York: Academic Press.

III

Control/Mastery Perspectives

Much of the work in clinical and social psychology is based on the assumption that a need to establish control over the environment is one of the fundamental human motives. The importance of people's perceptions of—and attempts to achieve—control is especially salient when considering the topic of coping with negative life events. Appraisals of control may be an integral part of perceiving events as negative; conversely, the experience of negative life events can represent an inherent threat to an individual's sense of control. In considering coping, by definition we are examining attempts to control or master the painful consequences of negative occurrences; coping behaviors can, in fact, represent specific attempts to restore a lost or threatened sense of control and mastery.

The "It's Over" case outlined in Chapter 1 provides an example of the relevance of control/mastery factors. Mary always expected that one day she would meet the right man, marry, and live happily ever after. She rarely articulated this belief, anymore than she might have articulated a belief that the seasons change, although it was a major aspect of the way Mary organized and directed her life.

When Mary was a sophomore in high school, she began to date Doug. By their senior year, she no longer wondered if they might get married someday, but whether they should wait until after college. School did not seem very important to Mary, but she made plans to attend college because Doug thought she should do so.

Mary was stunned when Doug told her a month before graduation that he thought it was time for them to go their separate ways. At first she did not believe he was serious; it was not until she was going to college in August that Mary finally acknowledged that the relationship was over. By that time, Mary had convinced herself that she had been wrong in her feeling that Doug was the man with whom she was destined to spend her life.

Mary met Ronnie at a party in her dorm the first week of classes, and they began to date. From the beginning, Mary felt sure that with Ronnie she had found a mature love. While others in her dorm were getting to know each other, Mary spent as much of her time as she could with Ronnie.

When the second semester started and Ronnie told her they needed to talk, Mary thought perhaps he was going to propose. At first she could not believe what she was hearing when instead Ronnie said he did not want to go out anymore. Ronnie told her he could not deal with her demands on his time, or her reliance on his opinions and advice. He said that she was just too intense for him; he was too young to settle down.

Mary felt like her world had caved in. For the second time she had been wrong when she thought she had found her once-in-a-lifetime relationship; she did not understand how any of it could have happened. She knew she needed to talk to someone, but the only friends she had made since going to college were Ronnie's friends. Finally, Mary made an appointment to see a psychologist at the university clinic.

The case of Mary provides an illustration of the potential usefulness of control/mastery perspectives on coping. The chapters in this section include discussions of some of the issues that arise from this perspective. In Chapter 6, Ronnie Janoff-Bulman and Christine Timko discuss people's personal theories of reality, and the coherence and stability that is provided by "assumptive worlds." They argue that traumatic events create a crisis in which the individual's assumptive world is threatened. Contrary to the traditional notion of denial as inherently maladaptive, Janoff-Bulman and Timko suggest that denial may provide people with the necessary time to rebuild their beliefs while maintaining some stability and coherence. In the case of Mary, for example, her initial denial when her high school relationship ended may have been an effective means of coping with the threat to her personal theory regarding relationships. When the second breakup occurred, Mary was overwhelmed; Janoff-Bulman and Timko's discussion suggests the possibility that Mary was facing a crisis from the threat to her assumptive world.

In Chapter 7, John Neale, Jill Hooley, Lina Jandorf, and Arthur Stone examine in detail the relationship between daily life events and mood. These authors first outline the development of their instrument for the assessment of daily experiences, and discuss the meaning of mood ratings for an entire day. They then explore a number of questions regarding daily experiences and mood, such as the validity of the common belief in "Blue Mondays," the differential impact on mood of different types of experiences, and the occurrence of lagged mood effects. In the latter vein, the authors describe a series of studies in which they did not obtain evidence in support of lagged mood effects. However, their data do reveal synchronous associations between mood and daily events. In examining the role appraisals play in this relationship, they argue that a simple index of the total number of undesirable events predicts mood about as well as schemes based on a number of appraisal dimensions such as meaningfulness, change, and control. It is possible, for example, that the impact of the breakups on Mary's mood in the "It's Over" case could have been predicted on the basis of the number of undesirable things that were happening to her as well as on the basis of her feelings of upheaval and lack of control.

In Chapter 8, Sharon Brehm discusses the practical, psychological, and social factors that may be involved in the amount of disruption people experience at the end of relationships. There is some indication, for example, that emotional reactions to the end of a relationship may be related to the amount of practical assistance that is lost with the breakup. Psychologically, anticipation and preparation may be important variables, as may perceptions of responsibility. Brehm also discusses the role of social support in the context of breakups; recent work on this topic suggests the importance of factors such as the fit between people's social network and their supportive needs, and their attributions for the receipt of support. In the case of Mary, for example, her devastation over her breakup might have been lessened had she developed an independent social network. This suggestion regarding the case of Mary also highlights one of Brehm's critical points; after discussing the various factors that are involved in reactions to breakups, Brehm emphasizes that the most important implications are in terms of how to construct better relationships, and how best to pursue our lives while involved, rather than how to cope better when relationships end.

Although varying in the explicitness with which control/mastery issues are identified, this aspect of coping is a consistent theme in the chapters of this part, especially in relationship to the amount of distress that follows in the wake of negative events.

6

Coping with Traumatic Life Events

The Role of Denial in Light of People's Assumptive Worlds

RONNIE JANOFF-BULMAN and CHRISTINE TIMKO

Through our work with a number of populations that have experienced traumatic negative events (e.g., rape victims, cancer patients, paralyzed accident victims) we have come to recognize the extent to which we ordinarily take for granted our very basic assumptions about ourselves and our world. These assumptions play a significant role in the emotional trauma and the coping process following severe negative events. In what follows we will consider the process of denial in light of the existence of people's assumptive worlds, in hopes of providing a richer framework for considering the role of denial. We will argue that the often-maligned process of denial is natural and often necessary, and that it generally facilitates the process of adaptation to traumatic experiences. Unfortunately, denial has generally been evaluated solely with respect to some external reality and too infrequently in view of the victim's internal reality. First, then, let us consider the nature of this internal world.

RONNIE JANOFF-BULMAN • Department of Psychology, University of Massachusetts, Amherst, MA 01003. CHRISTINE TIMKO • Department of Psychology, Yale University, New Haven, CT 06520.

THE NATURE OF OUR BASIC ASSUMPTIONS

Each of us maintains a personal theory of reality, a coherent set of assumptions developed over time about ourselves and our world, that organizes our experiences and understandings and directs our behavior. Parkes (1971, 1975) labeled such a personal theory one's "assumptive world." This is

> the individual's view of reality as he believes it to be, i.e., a strongly held set of assumptions about the world and the self which is confidently maintained and used as a means of recognizing, planning and acting. . . Assumptions such as these are learned and confirmed by the experiences of many years. (1975, p. 132)

Marris' (1975) "structures of meaning" and Bowlby's (1969) "world models" represent this same conceptual system, our internal reality. Kuhn's (1962) use of "paradigm" represents a parallel conception as well, for Kuhn (1962) regards a paradigm as a set of beliefs (p. 4), a map (p. 108), an organizing principle (p. 120), and a way of seeing (pp. 171–121; see Masterman, 1970). A paradigm provides the framework within which to conduct "normal science," whereas our assumptive world or theory of reality provides the framework within which to conduct normal (i.e., day-to-day) living.

The work of Epstein (1973, 1979, 1980, 1984) is particularly instructive regarding this basic set of assumptions we hold about the world. Epstein's cognitive-experiential self-theory

> assumes that everyone unwittingly develops a personal theory of reality that includes a self-theory and a world-theory. A personal theory of reality does not exist in conscious awareness, but is a preconscious conceptual system that automatically structures a person's experiences and directs his or her behavior. It is not developed for its own sake, but is a conceptual tool for solving life's fundamental problems, which include maintaining a favorable pleasure-pain balance, maintaining a favorable level of self-esteem, and assimilating the data of reality, which requires maintainance of the coherence of the theory. (Epstein, 1984, p. 65)

Epstein's theory of reality is organized into major and minor postulates. The minor postulates represent narrow generalizations derived directly from experience and are, in turn, organized into increasingly major postulates. An example of a low-order postulate might be, "I am a good ping-pong player," a higher-order postulate might be, "I am a good athlete," and a very high-order postulate might be, "I am a worthy person" (Epstein, 1980). Although the consequences are far greater, it is considerably more difficult to invalidate major postulates than minor postulates, for the latter are more readily subjected to the "direct test of experience." Our most basic assumptions about the world represent our most abstract, generalized theories about the nature of the world and ourselves.

THE RELEVANCE OF SCHEMAS TO OUR BASIC ASSUMPTIONS

Although relatively few psychologists have focused specifically on people's assumptive worlds or theories of reality per se, a large and increasing number have devoted attention to the cognitive concept of "schema." A schema is "a cognitive structure that represents organized knowledge about a given concept or type of stimulus" (Fiske & Taylor, 1984, p. 140). In positing schemas, psychologists have implicitly maintained that people actively construct their reality, for schemas serve as preexisting theories that guide what we notice and remember as well as how we interpret new information. As Goleman (1985) writes,

> Perception is interactive, constructed. It is not enough for information to flow through the senses; to make sense of the senses requires a context that organizes the information they convey, that lends it the proper meaning. . . . Schemas embody the rules and categories that order raw experience into coherent meaning. All knowledge and experience is packaged in schemas. Schemas are the ghost in the machine, the intelligence that guides information as it flows through the mind. (p. 75)

The most basic type of schema is generally regarded as that which underlies the use of common categories or concepts, such as dog, cat, rock, or table (see, e.g., Rosch, 1978). The schema concept is also used by researchers in social cognition to explain people's judgments and perceptions of others and themselves. Schemas underlie the process of social categorization (e.g., introvert, extrovert, sophisticate, schizophrenic, sage) just as they do the process of object categorization (Cantor, 1980). There is work demonstrating that we maintain self-schemas for particular attributes, in that we categorize ourselves, too, along particular dimensions (Markus, 1977). In the area of social cognition, it is also generally recognized that we hold schemas for roles; that is, we have mental structures that organize our knowledge about appropriate behaviors and norms associated with particular roles in our society, and it is this type of schema that may provide a cognitive basis for understanding stereotypes (Fiske & Taylor, 1984). We hold schemas for events as well, which are often referred to as "scripts" (Abelson, 1981); these are essentially mental structures of event sequences in well-known situations (e.g., the order of events in a restaurant or at a baseball game). This type of schema makes events readily predictable and comprehensible, in a manner paralleling schemas in the area of social categorization.

The research and theory on schemas has generally been concerned with rules and categories that might be called middle-level abstractions. A schema is always an abstraction, rather than a simple, straightforward accumulation of specific original instances and encounters; a schema goes beyond the data given. Most research in the area has dealt with categories that have relatively clear, identifiable empirical referents. Work on schemas has generally not been concerned with the very basic theories or assumptions people hold about the world (e.g., questions of meaningfulness), the postulates that are most abstract and least subject to the test of reality. Nevertheless, the schema concept is certainly applicable to such levels of analysis, for by its very nature "a schema is like a theory, an assumption about experience and how it works" (Goleman, 1985, p. 76). As Rumelhart (1978) writes,

> Just as theories can be about the grand and the small, so schemas can represent knowledge at all levels—from ideologies and cultural truths to knowledge about the meaning of a particular to knowledge about what patterns of sound are associated with what letters of the alphabet. (quoted in Goleman, 1985, p. 77)

Given the potential of the schema concept for understanding people's basic assumptions and theories about themselves and their world, it is instructive to examine what has been learned about people's reliance upon schemas. Two closely related conclusions can be drawn readily from the empirical research in this area. First, it is clear that we strive for coherence in our schemas, attempting to incorporate and understand the anomalous within the framework of existing schemas. Similarly, we are conservative when it comes to changing schemas, persevering in retaining already existing schemas rather than developing new ones.

There is a great deal of empirical evidence demonstrating that schemas guide our perceptions, memories, and inferences toward schema-relevant and schema-consistent information (Fiske & Taylor, 1984). Not only are we biased towards perceiving consistent information, but it has been shown in the area of person perception that we even incorrectly recognize traits (i.e., misremember) as having been on an earlier stimulus list if they are consistent with our schema for the person described (Cantor & Mischel, 1977). Thus, when shown a videotape of a woman having a birthday dinner with her husband, respondents who were told the woman was a librarian remembered her wearing glasses and owning classical records, whereas those who were told she was a waitress remembered her drinking beer and owning a television. Respondents' memories of the target were shaped by the schemas they held for the two jobs. It has also been demonstrated that presenting a social schema after respondents have processed information about another individual (i.e., labeling the protagonist of a story as a member of a particular social category), results in the reinterpretation of the information so as to make it consistent with the now-relevant schema (Snyder & Uranowitz, 1978). We not only reinterpret information in light of social schemas, but we are very likely to remember schema-consistent information. Thus, for example, it has been shown that people are particularly good at remembering individual behavior when it confirms a group stereotype (Rothbart, Evans, & Fulero, 1979). With regard to our own self-perceptions, there is evidence that we regularly seek and recall information that is consistent with our self-schemas (Swann & Read, 1981a,b). Overall, we see the world through our schematic lenses, and consequently tend to perceive and recall schema-consistent information more than would be deemed justifiable by the data. One implication of this process is that we bend our data to fit our theories far more than we bend our theories to fit the data; that is, we are conservative when it comes to changing our schemas and personal theories. There is much empirical evidence demonstrating that we persevere in maintaining our schemas (see discussions in Fiske & Taylor, 1984, and Nisbett & Ross, 1980). In the most vivid demonstrations of this tendency, Ross and his colleagues (Anderson, Lepper, & Ross, 1980; Ross, Lepper, & Hubbard, 1975) have shown that when people form a theory based on evidence given to them in the research setting, they will persevere in maintaining the theory, even when the evidence is then clearly presented as false. The explanation for this finding has generally been that once the theory is in place, people muster a number of arguments to support the theory, and then the falsification of the specific evidence presented in the research setting removes only one piece of supportive material. To the extent that the theory is simply a reflection of an already existing schema, these studies demonstrate the intractibility of people's schemas and personal theories. To the extent that one could argue a new schema is formed during the experimental session, one can imagine how much more difficult it would be to change older, deeply embedded schemas.

Generally, our personal theories and schemas serve us well. As Nisbett & Ross (1980) write,

> Our schemas and theories similarly stand us in good stead most of the time. Generic knowledge typically is well-founded—in someone else's experience even if not always in our own—and it normally serves as an automatic guide to effective behavior. . . . Heuristics and knowledge structures do sometimes lead people astray when they are overextended or misapplied. Even then, the resulting errors often are inconsequential and are readily forgiven by those with whom we interact. (pp. 154–155)

Philosophers of science have argued in favor of such conservatism in the evaluation of new versus old scientific theories (Popper, 1963). People's rigidity and perseverance in maintaining personal theories is comprehensible, even from a logical, rational perspective, for schemas are abstractions, largely providing information about the general case. It is the general case that allows us to fill in for the specific case (Fiske & Taylor, 1984). As such, schemas are not always directly subject to empirical test; how many specific instances should be sufficient to produce change in the general case? The English sociologist Peter Marris (1975) refers to this fundamental principle of conservatism in discussing what he terms our "structure of meaning." He writes,

> The continuing viability of this structure of meaning, in the face of new kinds of experience, depends on whether we can formulate its principles in terms abstract enough to apply to any event we encounter; or, alternatively, on whether we can ignore or prevent experiences which could not be comprehended in terms of it (experiences where our expectations would be repeatedly and bewilderingly unfulfilled). The first is an extension of learning, the second a constriction of experience: both seek to make life continuously intelligible. (1975, pp. 19–20)

Certainly, in explaining our fundamental conservatism concerning changes in our theories and schemas, one could also point to actual time constraints that preclude the careful search for and integration of all new evidence relevant to a particular belief (Nisbett & Ross, 1980), as well as real limits that may exist in our information-processing capacities. Nevertheless, particularly crucial to an understanding of the phenomenon is our fundamental need for stability and coherence in our conceptual systems (Epstein, 1973, 1980, 1984; Nisbett & Ross, 1980; Sarbin, 1981). Stable knowledge structures provide us with the necessary equilibrium to function in a complex, changing world. It is this stability in one's conceptual system—at the deepest levels of one's personal theories and assumptions—that is dramatically affected by traumatic negative events.

COPING WITH TRAUMA: DENIAL AND THE ASSUMPTIVE WORLD

People's basic assumptions about the world are constructed and solidified over years of experience. They are deeply embedded, coherent, organized structures that generally serve us well in our day-to-day existence. For the most part, they are able to handle anomalies and resist major change, and, as is the case with schemas in general, new information can be understood in terms of already existing structures (see Piaget, 1971, on assimilation). Although perseverance and maintenance of schemas and theories are the norm, it is certainly the case that gradual changes do occur, as repeated instances of new information and anomalies lead to accomodation (Piaget, 1971) in the conceptual system. These are changes that maintain the overall structure of the system and, because they are relatively small and gradual, do not lead to instability or incoherence. As is true in science, awareness of anomalies can lead to changes in the paradigm/schema and need not always lead to crisis. In these noncrisis situations, there is an "additive adjustment of theory" rather than an entire shift in theory, and the anomalous becomes the expected (Kuhn, 1962).

As Epstein (1980) makes clear, adjustments in one's theories are comparatively easy to make when minor postulates are involved. However, the more abstract and generalized the schema or assumption, the less directly tied it is to external reality, and the more difficult and potentially traumatic the adjustment becomes. When the highest-order postulates are violated, an additive adjustment or easy accomodation is no longer viable; rather, a new coherent theory has to be developed to account for the data of one's experience. This is what happens in the case of scientific revolutions. According to Kuhn, anomalies that "call into question explicit and fundamental generalizations of the paradigm" can lead to crises, and the response to a crisis of this sort is a scientific revolution in which a new paradigm is embraced and substituted for the old. The old paradigm had simply been "pushed too far" (Kuhn, 1962). This is also what happens in the case of traumatic negative events; one's conceptual system is threatened with total disruption and instability, as the most basic postulates of the system are severely challenged and often shattered by the experience.

Generally, such fundamental assumptions are outside of awareness (Epstein, 1980, 1984; Parkes, 1971, 1975), yet provide a filter through which we perceive and interpret our daily existence. However, the content of such basic assumptions is made all too apparent as a result of particular crises or events that lead to an objectification and examination of our personal theories (cf. Parkes, 1971, 1975, and his discussion of "psychosocial transitions"). Traumatic negative events, such as serious illness, criminal victimization, severe accidents, and disasters, are such crisis situations. These events are too vivid, too overwhelming, and too deeply experienced to simply ignore. Our conceptual system, built over years of experience, is simply unable to incorporate the "data" of the traumatic experience; the new data do not "fit."

Our work with victimized populations suggests that the traumatic experience threatens the viability of our very basic theories of the world and ourselves, including such primary postulates as an assumption of personal invulnerability (cf. Perloff, 1983, and this volume), an assumption of meaningfulness (i.e., events "make sense" in that they follow accepted social laws or are purposeful), and a belief in one's own self-worth (see Janoff-Bulman, 1985, and Janoff-Bulman & Frieze, 1983, for a review and discussion of these basic assumptions). That these assumptions are threatened by traumatic negative events has been documented in a large body of research on victimization (see, e.g., Bard & Sangrey, 1979; Horowitz, 1980, 1982; Janoff-Bulman, 1985; Janoff-Bulman & Frieze, 1983; Lifton, 1967; Perloff, 1983, this volume; Silver, Boon, & Stones, 1983; Taylor, 1983; Weisman, 1979; Wolfenstein, 1957; Wortman, 1983; Wortman & Dunkel-Schetter, 1979). The anxiety that results from undergoing such negative life experiences is intense and extreme, for such emotions are aroused when there are major threats posed to one's basic assumptions and theories about the world (Epstein, 1980, 1984). Given the very fundamental nature of the threatened assumptions, and given people's very basic tendency to persevere in the maintenance of their theories, the coping task facing the victim of trauma is overwhelming. Victims must revise and rebuild a new assumptive world that is different from the one they have taken for granted all of their lives, without allowing the entire conceptual system to "crash" in the interim. This task is enormous, and yet most victims complete it successfully. Their successful resolution is largely attributable to the often underestimated process of denial.

Denial: Definitions and Background

The term *denial* is a difficult one to define, for there are many ambiguities associated with the concept. In an important way, each of us has a sense of the meaning of the construct, and any discussion of denial relies in part upon this unarticulated understanding. Goldberger (1983) recently presented a good working definition of denial, although as we shall see, others would disagree with particular components of his description:

> Stated succinctly, denial is a term for almost all defensive endeavors which are assumed to be directed against stimuli originating in the outside world, specifically some painful aspect of reality. Perhaps even more succinctly, one might define it as a refusal to recognize the reality of a traumatic perception. Though denial can be direct, because of its unconscious status it is more often than not *inferred* by indirect evidence through behavior that is said to mask, bolster or maintain denial. (p. 85)

The three primary components of this definition are that denial is a defense mechanism, it is a response to an external reality (or the perception of this reality), and it is an unconscious process. Although some researchers and theoreticians disagree with one or more of these definitional components, it appears that they represent the views of the majority of those working in this area.

The description of denial as a defense mechanism originated with Anna Freud (1936). She looked upon denial as a unifying concept for a variety of defenses, in that their common goal is to reduce a threatening portion of reality in order to allow the individual to function under less psychic stress. Earlier, Sigmund Freud (1924) defined denial as a "disavowal" of external reality, and assumed it occurred only in psychosis. Both Anna and Sigmund Freud distinguished denial from repression as being focused on external rather than internal conditions. In psychodynamic theory, denial is viewed as an earlier and more primitive defense than repression; it is used by small children before the mechanism of repression has matured and been perfected.

In its strict psychoanalytic application, denial is a primitive, unconscious defense mechanism that defends against painful stimuli originating in the external world, as contrasted with inner or instinctual demands, the domain of repression. Denial is an elemental component of all outer-directed defenses, such as projection, displacement, and isolation. Generally, psychoanalytic theorists agree that denial is usually succeeded by other modes of coping and by more sophisticated defense mechanisms. In the case of psychosis, however, denial is considered the central defense mechanism (Goldberger, 1983).

Among researchers working in the area of stress and coping, including those who distinguish between defense and coping processes (e.g., Haan, 1977), it is generally accepted that denial is a defense mechanism. In contrast, there is confusion surrounding other components of the psychoanalytic definition and Goldberger's definition (1983). Specifically, there is confusion about the distinction between denial and repression (i.e., the role of internal vs. external reality), and disagreement as to whether denial is a conscious or unconscious process.

Jacobson (1957) extended the psychoanalytic concept of denial to mean a defense against intrapsychic forces (i.e., instinctual fantasies, wishes, impulses). In keeping with this extended definition, Lazarus (1983) defines denial as the negation of a problem or situation in word or act, where the negation can be either of an impulse, feeling, or thought, or of an external demand or reality. Lazarus specifies that denial is an intrapsychic coping mode that is emotion focused rather than problem focused. The broadening of denial to cover internal processes has created inconsistency in whether denial is defined as the negation that a threatening event has or is about to occur, the negation that one has negative feelings about the event, or both. These problems have not been satisfactorily resolved and are part of the continuing uncertainty about how to operationalize and measure the concept (Lazarus, 1983).

In conceptualizing denial, researchers do not agree that denial is necessarily an unconscious process. For example, Weisman and Hackett

(1967) and Kaplan and Kimball (1982) described denial as either an unconscious or conscious phenomenon. Hinton (1984) similarly stated that denial may be unconscious, or "there may be degrees of insight." In contrast, Cameron (1963) viewed denial as operating only at a preconscious or conscious level. Lazarus (1983) distinguished denial from the more conscious process of avoidance, in which the individual deliberately refuses to think or talk about the stressful event, but does not deny its existence. For the most part, however, the psychological literature has tended to ignore the extent to which denial occurs in or out of conscious awareness (Goldberger, 1983).

There are inconsistences and disagreements among psychologists concerning the definition of denial. For purposes of this chapter, we will accept that denial is a defense mechanism that serves to protect the individual, and that it operates outside of people's awareness (in the preconscious or unconscious). In making this assumption, we simply mean that people do not know they are engaged in denial processes; in psychology we are becoming increasingly cognizant of the major role played by processes outside of our awareness (Goleman, 1985). We believe people can deny both external reality as well as internal feelings and thoughts, but the latter are perceptions/emotions related to the occurrence of a painful external event. Of course the question of external reality is philosophically a very sticky one, as are the related issues of truth and accuracy. Rather than maintain that ontology is completely knowable, we would rather argue for a consensual criterion in determining whether an individual is engaging in denial. That is, we could reach a consensus based on shared cultural expectations not only that particular events have occurred, but also that certain types of events (e.g., serious illness with the possibility of imminent death) would be threatening to most people. It is when people disavow that such hypothetically consensually validated events have occurred, or disavow the consensually validated implications of these events, that we would argue we could reasonably maintain that denial is operating.

The Adaptive Role of Denial

Traditionally, denial has been viewed as a maladaptive defense mechanism that interferes with the accurate perception of reality. A longstanding dominant assumption of psychiatry and clinical psychology has been that the accurate perception of reality is a major indicator of mental health. The psychiatric and psychological literatures have tended to point out the beneficial effects of using coping strategies that emphasize accurate reality testing. Traditionally, self-deception has been equated with mental disorder (Lazarus, 1983). Much of the psychiatric writing on denial in particular describes its use by psychotics. Perhaps as a result of such descriptions, behavioral scientists have been apt to regard denial as a signal of serious underlying psychopathology (Eitinger, 1983; Hackett & Cassem, 1974).

This view of denial evaluates the process solely in terms of its relationship to external reality and completely disregards its relationship to the internal reality of the denier. Certainly, from an outsider's perspective, it no doubt looks odd and perhaps even somewhat pathological to deny, for example, that one has a dread disease after being specifically told by one's doctor, or to deny that death is a possibility, even a likely outcome for most people with the disease. Observers essentially match the denier's words and acts against the external facts (i.e., the doctor's words, culturally defined knowledge about the disease). However, the denier's internal reality—the conceptual system that has guided perceptions, memories, inferences, behaviors—is equally "real" to the denier him or herself (Brickman, 1978), although not generally shared. When matched against this inner reality, the words and acts of the denier do not appear odd or pathological. This internal reality has been maintained over the years preceding the traumatic event and has served the individual well. Now, as a result of an overwhelming traumatic experience, this conceptual system must be changed.

The process of change must necessarily be a slow, gradual one, in order to provide sufficient internal stability and coherence to preclude a complete breakdown in the conceptual system and in psychological functioning. From the research on schemas, we know that people are loath to alter their theories; to the extent that change involves the most basic assumptions of one's conceptual system, we would expect all the greater resistance. It is the process of denial that provides for the proper pacing in the revison and rebuilding of one's basic theories and assumptions. Immediately following the traumatic event, one would expect a great deal of denial, for this is when the shock to the conceptual system is apt to be overwhelming, and the consequent emotional reaction is apt to be too intense. A dramatic, unmodulated attack on the primary postulates of one's assumptive world is controlled by the process of denial, which allows the individual to face slowly and gradually the realities of the external world and incorporate them into his or her internal world.

This view is consistent with Epstein's (1967) work on anxiety, in which he maintains that denial

> may be useful in permitting the individual to master certain aspects of a task which by themselves produce all the anxiety he can manage. Thus "abnormal" defenses should not be judged so much by the specific quality of the defense as by whether

they shut off the process of mastery, or simply help pace it. . . . Not until an acute state of arousal has somewhat dissipated can the work of mastery begin, and even then pacing is important, as excessive increments in arousal will tend to reverse the process. (pp. 51–52)

The work of Horowitz (1980, 1982, 1983) is also instructive regarding the adaptive value of denial in pacing the recovery process following trauma. Horowitz, too, recognizes the individual's need to change "inner models or schemata" following serious life events (so that they conform to the new reality), as well as the mind's tendency to maintain one's inner models of the self and the world. He argues that a serious life event will eventually change inner models, but the change is generally slow. Horowitz calls the tendency to integrate reality and schemata the "completion tendency." Until completion occurs, new information (i.e., the negative life event) is stored in active memory. The victim compares ideas related to the stress event with relevant schemata that were in existence prior to the event. The individual finds that there is a discrepancy, and this discrepancy evokes a powerful emotion. With optimal controls to slow down the recognition processes, completion will eventually occur; one's inner models will conform to the new reality. It is denial that provides the "optimal controls" for slowing down the recognition processes. In Horowitz's terms, denial is adaptive because it prevents the individual from being overwhelmed with panic and allows for the processing of tolerable doses of both new information and emotional responses.

Lazarus (1983) also discussed the positive value of denial. He argued that denial may be adaptive during the early stages of coping with a stressful event, when one's resources are insufficient to act more constructively and realistically. Denial buys time to make the recognition of a threatening event gradual and manageable rather than overwhelming. Further, according to Lazarus (1983), when direct action is irrelevant to the outcome of a threatening event, denial can be of value by reducing distress and allowing the individual to get on with other matters (also see Eitinger, 1983).

The view of denial as adaptive and even necessary following traumatic negative events is consistent with recent arguments regarding the positive value of illusions and self-deception for mental health (Greenwald, 1980; Sackeim, 1983; Sarbin, 1981; Snyder, Higgins, & Stucky, 1983; Taylor, 1983). Accuracy is no longer regarded as the hallmark of mental health; rather, "self-deceptive practices may be efficient strategies by which to promote psychological health and, at least in some circumstances, their use may lead to higher levels of functioning than their absence" (Sackeim, 1983, p. 135). In fact, recent empirical work on depression has found that depressives are less likely than nondepressives to use self-deceptive strategies and illusions. It is the depressives, and not the nondepressives, who are most accurate in their perceptions and inferences (e.g., Alloy & Abramson, 1979; Golin, Terrell, Weitz, & Drost, 1979).

Viewed within the framework of the individual's need to alter his or her assumptive world, denial following negative life events is apt to be not only adaptive, but generally necessary in preventing total psychological breakdown. Denial enables an individual to pace his or her recovery following trauma by reducing excessive amounts of anxiety and confusion. One would therefore predict a great deal of denial immediately after a traumatic event, followed by less and less denial over time. To the extent that denial does not decrease over time, and extreme levels remain long after the traumatic event, denial would interfere with mastery of the event and would become maladaptive (Epstein, 1967; Horowitz, 1980, 1982). In such a case, denial would limit the range of information to be used in planning one's present life. Denial that does not decrease over time will prevent the complete processing of the negative event; one's personal theories will fail to be useful guides, for they will not have incorporated the data of the traumatic event.

EMPIRICAL FINDINGS

Based on the previous discussion one would expect the normal coping process following trauma to be characterized by a great deal of denial immediately following the negative event, with less and less denial manifested over time. Paralleling this prediction is the assumption that high levels of denial soon after the event are adaptive, whereas high levels of denial with increasing temporal distance from the event (several months to a year) are maladaptive. What are the empirical findings with regard to denial? What is the natural course of denial, and what evidence is there of its adaptiveness (or lack thereof)?

Psychological defenses such as denial are difficult to measure. Any attempt to measure fright, worry, or anger, for example, in response to threat may yield a negative response either because the individual truly does not experience these affects, or because the person is using psychological defenses that lead to the active negation of the threat (Breznitz, 1983b). In order to investigate whether or not an individual is using denial, Breznitz (1983b) recommends studying reactions to unequivocally stressful events, studying the recall of factual information about the traumatic event, and examining responses on different levels of subjective control, because responses to stress often exhibit a complex dyssynchrony between the cognitive, affective, and behavioral levels.

Two primary operationalizations of denial are generally relied upon in empirical research. Hackett and Cassem's (1974) 31-item denial scale is often used; it is administered by an interviewer, and is based on Anna Freud's (1936) concept that denial is a general psychological goal that can be achieved in many diverse ways. Some of the items express denial explicitly, whereas in others the denial is implicit (e.g., a seriously ill patient minimizes physical symptoms, uses cliches when discussing death, worries about others rather than the self). This measure has been criticized for including a variety of denial-like mechanisms and thereby failing to make clear distinctions between denial and related concepts such as avoidance (Cohen & Lazarus, 1979; Lazarus, 1983; Shaw, Cohen, Doyle, & Palesky, 1985). In the majority of studies, denial is operationalized as the absence of negative affect about the negative life event in question, the assumption being that very traumatic events would ordinarily elicit powerful negative emotions. From an examination of the literature, it becomes very apparent that researchers investigating reactions to negative life events frequently find a great deal of denial, and this denial is generally regarded as a normal part of the coping process.

In their study of the coping strategies employed by parents of children who were fatally ill with neoplastic disease, Chodoff, Friedman, & Hamburg (1964) suggested that the parents' reactions to the child's diagnosis followed a natural course. Initially the parents felt stunned and experienced a sense of unreality. Then, they came to accept intellectually the child's diagnosis and prognosis, but were unable to accept the threat at an emotional level. During the greatest portion of the illness, the parents became increasingly vulnerable to the emotional impact of their child's impending death. Finally, the parents engaged in anticipatory mourning, which was described as a gradual detachment from the child, enabling the death to be accepted more calmly, almost with relief. Denial was reported to be a ubiquitous and pervasive defense among the parents. It enabled them to maintain some optimism, emphasize favorable and minimize unfavorable developments, and continue to live their day-to-day existence. Nevertheless, there appeared to be a negative side of denial as well, for parents who engaged in strong denial were inhibited in their anticipatory mourning such that their reaction to the child's death was more distressed. It was when denial interfered with the latter stage of the coping process (i.e., anticipatory mourning) that it proved maladaptive. Apparently, denial was most effective when it abated gradually so as to allow the paced processing of the extremely traumatic event. For those who did not engage in anticipatory mourning, the denial remained at a high level long after the onset of the traumatic experience (i.e., diagnosis of the child's illness). Lindemann's (1944) work on grieving is consistent with Chodoff *et al.*'s (1964) findings regarding the negative implications of denial that does not decrease over time. Lindemann (1944) discussed the problems associated with continuing to deny trauma long after it has occurred; people who continue to deny the death of a loved one do not complete their "grief work," and as a result do not readjust to an environment in which the deceased is missing (also see Bowlby, 1961).

Hamburg and Adams (1967), in summarizing studies of burn and polio patients, stated that a broad sequence of reactions characterized most of the patients in the months or years following the onset of their severe condition. At first there was extensive denial of the nature of the illness, its seriousness, and its probable consequences. Patients later came to face the actual conditions of the illness by seeking information about their recovery and attempting to assess the long-term implications of their medical problem. As the second phase of acceptance progressed and denial diminished, patients usually showed a temporary increase in depressive symptoms. The transition from denial to recognition was accomplished as a series of approximations through which the patients gradually came to a comprehensive understanding of their situation.

Dudley, Verney, Masuda, Martin, & Holmes, (1969) found that among patients with irreversible diffuse pulmonary syndrome, a condition of chronic lung failure requiring close medical attention, one of the most consistently used defense mechanisms was denial. Similarly, denial has been found to be commonplace among people with a terminal illness (Hackett & Weisman, 1969; Hinton, 1984; Weisman, 1972; Weisman & Hackett, 1967). These researchers have also pointed out that denial is often encouraged by relatives and friends. Weisman (1972) described patients' awareness of their own imminent death as "middle knowledge" because the patients are caught between knowing that their physical symptoms signify eventual death and being told by those around them that they are not going to die.

Research on victims of crime also points to the pervasiveness of denial early in the coping process. Bard and Sangrey (1979) state that some denial is an essential part of the healing process following criminal victimization. For some victims, this denial may take a "hyperactive form," in which they throw themselves into work or some activity unrelated to the crime and appear consistently busy. Many other victims experience "direct denial," in that they describe themselves as emotionally detached and unable to feel anything. "Between these periods of denial, victims begin to deal with their feelings about the crime" (Bard &

Sangrey, 1979, p. 41). Research with rape victims has also found the utilization of denial. Sutherland and Scherl (1970) write of the shock, disbelief, and disruption in the initial "acute reaction" phase of rape victims. Within a few days to a few weeks following the rape, the victim frequently returns to her normal life patterns, but Sutherland and Scherl maintain that this is a period of "pseudoadjustment," for there is a great deal of denial involved in this "outward adjustment" phase. This period is followed by "integration and resolution," in which the event is finally processed and integrated. The fear and anxiety of rape victims is intense, and it could be argued that some denial may be necessary to prevent victims from experiencing a complete psychological breakdown following their trauma (cf. Burgess & Holmstrom, 1974; Notman & Nadelson, 1976).

Eitinger's (1983) personal experience in a concentration camp in Nazi Germany led him to conclude that the pervasiveness of impending death in the camps frequently provoked a serious denial reaction. In the camps the denial reaction helped the inmates to behave as though the most dangerous situations did not exist, allowing some of them to survive. This applied especially to the newcomers to the camps during the first weeks and months of imprisonment. After the initial period, one could psychologically afford to be more aware of the life threatening aspects of the situation. Lifton (1967) stated that many of the survivors of the Hiroshima atomic bombs would undoubtedly have been unable to avoid psychosis were it not for the extremely widespread and effective use of "psychic closing off." This defense mechanism is closely related to denial and involves unconsciously turning off one's emotional reactions despite having a clear sense of what is happening in a traumatic situation.

There have been a number of empirical studies conducted using cardiac patients with the specific intent of investigating the role of denial in the coping process. Patients who have suffered heart attacks are an attractive population for studying denial, because there are assumptions that denial reduces anxiety, and that decreased anxiety immediately following the attack is likely to result in decreased risk of death. Druss and Kornfeld (1967) found that cardiac patients most often used the defense mechanisms of denial and isolation of affect to protect themselves from overwhelming anxiety. On the basis of such findings, Cassem and Hackett (1971) suggested that the emotional reactions of the heart attack patient follows a natural history. Patients are anxious when first admitted to the hospital, but then tend to deny their condition until the 3rd or 4th day of their stay. By then, patients become more cognizant of their condition and so despondency sets in.

Morse and Litin (1969) compared cardiac patients who did or did not experience postoperative delirium, which was defined as disorientation with respect to time, place, or person. Denial of anxiety was found significantly more often among the nondelirious patients (cf. Layne & Yudofsky, 1971). Kennedy and Bakst (1966) classified potential cardiac surgery patients into six groups. The group that was found to have the fewest medical and psychiatric complications entered the hospital with a history of denial of illness. They recognized the risks of surgery and the possibility of death, but used denial to block out any idea of unpleasantness or difficulty that could occur in the operating and recovery rooms. The denying patients also demonstrated a tremendous motivation to become healthy and to live.

Gentry, Foster, & Haney (1972) classified one half of a small sample of heart attack patients as deniers because they said they never felt afraid during the first 5 days of their hospital stay; nondeniers said they had felt afraid at some time. Results showed that deniers were lower on state anxiety than nondeniers. In addition, of the two deaths that occurred in the 6 months after the subjects' initial hospitalization, both were of nondeniers. In Froese et al.'s (1974) study of hospitalized cardiac patients, the group of deniers were defined as scoring relatively high on the Hackett-Cassem Denial Scale compared to the group of nondeniers. Deniers decreased significantly in anxiety by Day 3 or 4 of hospitalization, whereas nondeniers took longer to show a reduction in anxiety level.

Hackett, Cassem, and Wishnie (1968) found that 40% of their sample of heart attack patients were major deniers, in that they stated unequivocally that they did not experience any feelings of fear or apprehension during the hospital stay or earlier in their lives. Partial deniers, composing 52% of the sample, initially denied being frightened, but eventually admitted feeling at least some fear. Only 8% of the sample were minimal deniers who either complained of anxiety or readily admitted being frightened. There were no significant relationships between extent of denial and the patients' mood states. However, of four deaths that occurred during subjects' hospitalization, two were of minimal and two were of partial deniers.

Any relationship between denial and physical outcome in the case of heart disease is comprehensible, for denial is presumed to minimize anxiety, and high levels of anxiety are regarded as dangerous for the heart attack patient. It is little wonder, then, that researchers in the field suggest that denial may reduce risk for coronary patients (Hackett et al., 1968). The potential impact of denial on physical outcome in other diseases, such as cancer, is far more difficult to hypothesize because of our present lack of knowledge about the actual psychological-biological links in this disease. There are a number of studies of cancer patients that assessed emotional responses at the time of diagnosis or surgery and then assessed long-term health outcomes (usually life versus death). In evaluating the role of denial, such studies are problematic, for it is unclear whether initial emotional responses (e.g., denial) are predictive of later emotional responses. For optimal psychological functioning, we would expect high levels of denial immediately following the diagnosis, and less denial (fewer and less extreme episodes) over time; if psychological functioning is predictive of physical outcome, we would maintain that this would be the optimal course for physical health as well. In studies that measure emotional responses only at the time of diagnosis, and health outcome long afterward, the course of the emotional adjustment is unclear (e.g., Was there continued high denial? Did denial decrease and lead to the processing and integration of the event?). As might be expected given the uncertain nature of the psychological-biological links in cancer and the single baseline psychological testing in the studies, the research findings are very mixed, with some finding early denial and the minimization of negative affect associated with fewer instances of death and cancer recurrence, and others finding the opposite (see, e.g., Derogatis, Abeloff, & Meslisaratos, 1979; Greer, Morris, & Pettingale, 1979; Rogentine *et al.,* 1979; Visintainer & Casey, 1984).

In a very different type of study from any reviewed thus far, Suls and Fletcher (1985) conducted a meta-analysis to examine the relative short- and long-term efficacy of attention and avoidance strategies in coping with various stressors. Although they were not specifically interested in denial, denial would be included under the rubric of their avoidance processes. They defined avoidance coping strategies as those that focus attention away from the source of stress or away from one's psychological or somatic reactions; attention strategies focus attention upon the source of stress and/or one's reactions to it.

When all studies were examined together, analyses revealed that avoidance strategies were associated with better adaptation to stress, but that the effect was not very strong. When only short-term outcome studies were considered—those in which the outcome (e.g., distress, pain, temperature) was measured concurrently or immediately after exposure to the stressor (e.g., cold pressor, film, verbal task)—avoidance strategies were again associated with better adaptational outcomes. In the analysis of long-term outcome studies alone—those in which the outcome (e.g., recurrence of illness, use of medications, return to employment) was measured at least several days after stressor onset (e.g., myocardial infarction, pain)—attention strategies were found to be more effective, especially when the outcome measure was taken at least 2 weeks after the onset of the stressor. The authors suggested that avoidance has more positive effects than attention at early stages of a stress experience because the individual's resources are not sufficient to cope actively with stressful circumstances at that time. Avoidance may also be very useful in the case of a stressful life occurrence that is brief and has no serious long-term consequences (Haan, 1977).

Suls and Fletcher's (1985) findings are completely consistent with our view of denial. Using their terms, we would describe denial as an avoidance strategy, for it inhibits attention to a stressor or one's emotional or somatic responses to the stressor by minimizing or eliminating one's conscious awareness of them. The studies reviewed earlier strongly suggest that denial is not an abnormal process, but rather one to be expected, to a greater or lesser extent, in the immediate aftermath of a traumatic life event. The assumption of short-term adaptiveness appears to be fairly well grounded. It is more difficult to find research that provides relevant feedback about the long-term implications of denial; far more longitudinal work is needed on the course and impact of denial. There does appear to be evidence that denial generally decreases over time, and that when it does not, psychological functioning and day-to-day living are apt to be disrupted (see, e.g., Chodoff *et al.*, 1964, on the lack of anticipatory mourning, or Lindemann, 1944, on the failure to complete "grief work"). Only by finally integrating the experience can victims of traumatic negative events reestablish psychological equilibrium and get on with the business of life.

FINAL NOTES: DENIAL VERSUS HOPE

The intense trauma associated with severe, negative life events is largely attributable to the inability of one's assumptive world readily to integrate such events. Our conceptual system is built over years of experience and generally serves us well; the components of the system may not be accurate (i.e., a direct reflection of "reality"), but they are accurate enough and enable us to fulfill our needs for stability and coherence in dealing with our world. All of our perceptions, memories, and inferences are guided by theories (schemata) that tend stubbornly to persevere in the name of stability. When people are struck by traumatic negative events, their assumptive worlds—the very basic theories that have served them so well to that point—are severely threatened, for they are unable to account for and readily assimilate the traumatic experience. One's basic theories about the benevolence and meaningfulness of the world and the invulnerability and worthiness of the self no longer seem adequate, and the individual is threatened by complete psychological disorganization. It is this internal reality of the victim that must be taken into account when evaluating the role of denial. When considered in light of a consensually validated external reality, denial clearly looks odd and pathological; when considered in light of the trauma victim's task—that of rebuilding and reshaping one's cognitive world—denial becomes an adaptive process.

Certainly, people differ in the extent to which they rely on denial in coping. Those whose personal theories are least threatened (i.e., are least subject to invalidation because of their particular content), and who physiologically possess the greatest tolerance for anxiety, would be expected to engage in less denial than others. Nevertheless, some denial is likely to be involved in the coping process of most people, and this denial is likely to be most apparent in the immediate aftermath of the traumatic event. Over time, denial will be used less and less, as the trauma victim paces his or her confrontation with the data derived from the experience: As the conceptual integration process becomes too anxiety provoking, some denial will once again set in, only to be disengaged when the individual can again deal emotionally with the experience (Epstein, 1967; Horowitz, 1983). With the passage of time and the successful accomodation of one's assumptive world, it is unlikely that denial will be manifested any longer, and the trauma survivor (Figley, 1985) will be able to deal directly with the implications of the negative experience and plan activities and behaviors accordingly.

The trauma survivor is sadder but wiser; his or her assumptive world is unlikely to look quite so rigidly rosey. Nevertheless, the achieved ability to confront directly the reality of one's situation carries with it benefits, and not simply pessimism. Apart from the sense of mastery that may come from the integration of the traumatic experience, the individual can utilize hope and maintain some optimism. Breznitz (1983a) has distinguished between denying the negative components of one's circumstances and hope, which involves extracting the positive aspects of information and concentrating on them. For Breznitz, hope and denial are distinct constructs, for hope is an active state, involving awareness.

> By concentrating on certain positive features of a situation, the person tries actively to dwell upon it, to imagine it, to provide lucky scenarios for the eventual outcome, etc. . . . One of the main problems with denying facts of objective reality is that the reality will not go away simply because it is unwanted. Therefore, there will always be the danger that sooner or later the objective facts will be able to pierce through the protective veil of illusion, and the person will be found totally unprepared. . . However, that is not the situation in the case of hope, particularly if the hope is not based on false illusion. (pp. 299–300)

Breznitz argues that the best coping involves hope and no denial, for the denial of a threat precludes consideration of any positive aspects of one's situation, and hope with denial is really "false hope" and involves efforts by the individual to defend continually against contrary information.

We would maintain that as denial recedes in the successful coping process, hope advances. The individual who can now directly confront his or her negative situation is an individual who has largely completed processing the experience. Denial is no longer involved in the coping process; rather, it is replaced by hope in the face of one's actual prospects. One's circumstances are not disavowed, but there is a tendency to focus on possible positive outcomes and positive aspects of one's situation. Surprisingly, perhaps, those who have experienced traumatic negative events frequently report on the benefits they have derived from their experience. They report that although they may not have chosen their circumstances, in many ways they are glad the event happened; this is true even in cases involving permanent disability (Bulman & Wortman, 1977) and diseases such as cancer (Janoff-Bulman & Timko, 1985; Taylor, 1983; Taylor, Wood & Lichtman, 1983). The benefits derived from negative events include a newfound appreciation of life and a recognition of what is really important, as well as a more positive view of one's own possibilities and strengths (Janoff-Bulman & Timko, 1985). For those who have cognitively mastered the negative event by reshaping and rebuilding their assumptive worlds, hope now offers the benefits of focusing on the positive aspects of one's experience and potential positive outcomes in the future. Thankfully, the human condition is characterized by certain protections that serve to shield us from experiencing utter misery and despair. Denial is one of these protections; when its work is completed, hope can take its place.

REFERENCES

Abelson, R. P. (1981). The psychological status of the script concept. *American Psychologist, 36,* 715–729.

Alloy, L. B., & Abramson, L. Y. (1979). Judgment of contingency in depressed and non-depressed students: Sadder but wiser? *Journal of Experimental Psychology: General, 108,* 441–485.

Anderson, C. A., Lepper, M. R., & Ross, L. (1980). Perseverance of social theories: The role of explanation in the persistence of discredited information. *Journal of Personality and Social Psychology, 39,* 1037–1049.

Bard, M., & Sangrey, D. (1979). *The crime victim's book.* New York: Basic Books.

Bowlby, J. (1961). Processes of mourning. *The International Journal of Psycho-analysis, 42,* 317–340.

Bowlby, J. (1969). *Attachment and loss (Vol. 1): Attachment.* London: Hogarth.
Breznitz, S. (1983a). Denial versus hope: Concluding remarks. In S. Breznitz (Ed.), *The denial of stress.* New York: International Universities Press.
Breznitz, S. (1983b). Methodological considerations in research on denial. In S. Breznitz (Ed.), *The denial of stress* (pp. 287–296). New York: International Universities Press.
Brickman, P. (1978). Is it real? In J. H. Harvey, W. Ickes, & R. F. Kidd (Eds.), *New directions in attribution research* (Vol. 2, pp. 5–34). Hillsdale, NJ: Erlbaum.
Bulman, R. J., & Wortman, C. B. (1977). Attributions of blame and coping in the "real world": Severe accident victims react to their lot. *Journal of Personality and Social Psychology, 35,* 351–363.
Burgess, A. W., & Holmstrom, L. L. (1974). Rape trauma syndrome. *American Journal of Psychiatry, 131,* 981–985.
Cameron, N. (1963). *Personality development and psychopathology: A dynamic approach.* Boston, MA: Houghton Mifflin.
Cantor, N. (1980). Perceptions of situations: Situation prototypes and person-situation prototypes. In D. Magnusson (Ed.), *The situation: An interactional perspective.* Hillsdale, NJ: Erlbaum.
Cantor, N., & Mischel, W. (1977). Traits as prototypes: Effects on recognition memory. *Journal of Personality and Social Psychology, 35,* 38–48.
Cassem, N. H., & Hackett, T. P. (1971). Psychiatric consultation in a coronary care unit. *Annals of Internal Medicine, 75,* 9–14.
Chodoff, P., Friedman, S. B., & Hamburg, D. A. (1964). Stress, defenses, and coping behavior: Observations in parents of children with malignant disease. *American Journal of Psychiatry, 120,* 743–749.
Cohen, F., & Lazarus, R. S. (1979). Coping with the stress of illness. In G. C. Stone, F. Cohen, & N. E. Adler (Eds.), *Health psychology* (pp. 217–254). San Francisco: Jossey-Bass.
Derogatis, L. R., Abeloff, M. D., & Melisaratos, N. (1979). Psychological coping mechanisms and survival time in metastatic breast cancer. *Journal of the American Medical Association, 242,* 1504–1508.
Druss, R. G., & Kornfeld, D. S. (1967). The survivors of cardiac arrest. *Journal of the American Medical Association, 201,* 291–296.
Dudley, D. L., Verney, J. W., Masuda, M., Martin, C. J., & Holmes, T. H. (1969). Long-term adjustment, prognosis, and death in irreversible diffuse obstructive pulmonary syndromes. *Psychosomatic Medicine, 31,* 310–325.
Eitinger, L. (1983). Denial in concentration camps: Some personal observations on the positive and negative functions of denial in extreme life situations. In S. Breznitz (Ed.), *The denial of stress* (pp. 199–212). New York: International Universities Press.
Epstein, S. (1967). Toward a unified theory of anxiety. In B. A. Maher (Ed.), *Progress in experimental personality research* (Vol. 4). New York: Academic Press.
Epstein, S. (1973). The self-concept revisited, or a theory of a theory. *American Psychologist, 28,* 404–416.
Epstein, S. (1979). The ecological study of emotions in humans. In P. Pliner, K. R. Blankstein, & I. M. Spigel (Eds.), *Advances in the study of communication and affect* (Vol. 5.): *Perception of emotions in self and others* (pp. 47–83). New York: Plenum Press.
Epstein, S. (1980). The self-concept: A review and the proposal of an integrated theory of personality. In E. Staub (Ed.), *Personality: Basic issues and current research* (pp. 82–132). Englewood Cliffs, NJ: Prentice-Hall.
Epstein, S. (1984). Controversial issues in emotion theory. In P. Shaver (Ed.), *Review of*

personality and social psychology: Emotions, relationships, and health (pp. 64–88). Beverly Hills, CA: Sage.

Figley, C. R. (1985). From victim to survivor: Social responsibility in the wake of catastrophe. In C. R. Figley (Ed.), *Trauma and its wake* (pp. 398–415). New York: Brunner/Mazel.

Fiske, S. T., & Taylor, S. E. (1984). *Social cognition.* Reading, MA: Addison-Wesley.

Freud, A. (1936). *The ego and the mechanisms of defense.* New York: International Universities Press.

Freud, S. (1961). The loss of reality in neurosis and psychosis. *Standard Edition* (Vol. 23, pp. 271–278). London: Hogarth. (Originally published 1924)

Froese, A., Hackett, T. P., Cassem, N. H., & Silverberg, E. (1974). Trajectories of anxiety and depression in denying and nondenying acute myocardial infarction patients during hospitalization. *Journal of Psychosomatic Research, 18,* 413–420.

Gentry, W. D., Foster, S., & Haney, T. (1972). Denial as a determinant of anxiety and perceived health status in the coronary care unit. *Psychosomatic Medicine, 34,* 39–44.

Goldberger, L. (1983). The concept and mechanisms of denial: A selective overview. In S. Breznitz (Ed.), *The denial of stress* (pp. 83–95). New York: International Universities Press.

Goleman, D. (1985). *Vital lies, simple truths: The psychology of self-deception.* NY: Simon & Schuster.

Golin, S., Terrell, T., Weitz, J., & Drost, P. L. (1979). The illusion of control among depressed patients. *Journal of Abnormal Psychology, 88,* 454–457.

Greenwald, A. G. (1980). The totalitarian ego: Fabrication and revision of personal history. *American Psychologist, 35,* 603–618.

Greer, S., Morris, T., & Pettingale, K. W. (1979). Psychological response to breast cancer: Effect on outcome. *The Lancet, 2,* 785–787.

Haan, N. (1977). *Coping and Defending.* New York: Academic Press.

Hackett, T. P., & Cassem, N. H. (1974). Development of a quantitative rating scale to assess denial. *Journal of Psychosomatic Research, 18,* 93–100.

Hackett, T. P., & Weisman, A. D. (1969). Denial as a factor in patients with heart disease and cancer. *Annals New York Academy of Sciences, 164,* 802–811.

Hackett, T. P., Cassem, N. H., & Wishnie, H. A. (1968). The coronary-care unit: An appraisal of its psychologic hazards. *The New England Journal of Medicine, 279,* 1365–1370.

Hamburg, D. A., & Adams, J. E. (1967). A perspective on coping behavior. *Archives of General Psychiatry, 17,* 277–284.

Hinton, J. (1984). Coping with terminal illness. In R. Fitzpatrick, J. Hinton, S. Newman, G. Scambler, & J. Thompson (Eds.), *The experience of illness* (pp. 227–245). New York: Tavistock.

Horowitz, M. J. (1980). Psychological response to serious life events. In V. Hamilton and D. Warburton (Eds.), *Human stress and cognition* (pp. 235–256). New York: Wiley.

Horowitz, M. H. (1982). Stress response syndromes and their treatment. In L. Goldberger & S. Breznitz (Eds.), *Handbook of stress* (pp. 129–159). New York: Free Press.

Horowitz, M. J. (1983). Psychological response to serious life events. In S. Breznitz (Ed.), *The denial of stress.* New York: International Universities Press.

Jacobson, E. (1957). Denial and repression. *Journal of the American Psychoanalytic Association, 5,* 61–92.

Janoff-Bulman, R. (1985). The aftermath of victimization: Rebuilding shattered assumptions. In C. R. Figley (Ed.), *Trauma and its wake* (pp. 15–35). New York: Brunner/Mazel.

Janoff-Bulman, R., & Frieze, I. H. (1983). A theoretical perspective for understanding reactions to victimization. *Journal of Social Issues, 39,* 1–17.

Janoff-Bulman, R., & Timko, C. (1985). Working with victims: Changes in the researcher's assumptive world. In A. Baum & J. Singer (Eds.), *Advances in Environmental Psychology* (Vol. 5, pp. 75–97). Hillsdale, NJ: Erlbaum.

Kaplan, W., & Kimball, C. (1982). The risks and course of coronary artery disease: A biopsycholosocial perspective. In T. Millon, C. Green, & R. Meagher (Eds.), *Handbook of clinical health psychology* (pp. 69–90). New York: Plenum Press.

Kennedy, J. A., & Bakst, H. (1966). The influence of emotions on the outcome of cardiac surgery: A predictive study. *The Bulletin of the New York Academy of Medicine, 42,* 811–845.

Kuhn, T. S. (1962). *The structure of scientific revolutions.* Chicago, IL: The University of Chicago Press.

Layne, O. L., & Yudofsky, S. C. (1971). Postoperative psychosis in cardiotomy patients: The role of organic and psychiatric factors. *The New England Journal of Medicine, 284,* 518–520.

Lazarus, R. S. (1983). The costs and benefits of denial. In S. Breznitz (Ed.), *The denial of stress* (pp. 1–30). New York: International Universities Press.

Lifton, R. J. (1967). *Death in life: Survivors of Hiroshima.* New York: Simon & Schuster.

Lindemann, E. (1944). Symptomatology and management of acute grief. *American Journal of Psychiatry, 101,* 141–148.

Markus, H. (1977). Self-schemata and processing information about the self. *Journal of Personality and Social Psychology, 35,* 63–78.

Marris, P. (1975). *Loss and change.* Garden City, NY: Anchor/Doubleday.

Masterman, M. (1970). The nature of a paradigm. In I. Lakatos, & A. Musgrave (Eds.), *Criticism and the growth of knowledge* (pp. 59–89). Cambridge, England: Cambridge University Press.

Morse, R. M., & Litin, E. M. (1969). Postoperative delirium: A study of etiologic factors. *American Journal of Psychiatry, 126,* 388–395.

Nisbett, R. E., & Ross, L. (1980). *Human inference: Strategies and shortcomings of social judgment.* Englewood Cliffs, NJ: Prentice-Hall.

Notman, M. T., & Nadelson, C. C. (1976). The rape victim: Psychodynamic considerations. *American Journal of Psychiatry, 133,* 408–413.

Parkes, C. M. (1971). Psycho-social transitions: A field for study. *Social Science and Medicine, 5,* 101–115.

Parkes, C. M. (1975). What becomes of redundant world models? A contribution to the study of adaptation to change. *British Journal of Medical Psychology, 48,* 131–137.

Perloff, L. S. (1983). Perceptions of vulnerability to victimization. *Journal of Social Issues, 39,* 41–61.

Piaget, J. (1971). *The construction of reality in the child.* New York: Basic Books.

Popper, K. R. (1963). *Conjectures and refutations: The growth of scientific knowledge.* New York: Harper & Row.

Rogentine, G. N., van Kammen, D. P., Fox, B. H., Docherty, J. P., Rosenblatt, J. E., Boyd, S. C., & Bunney, W. E. (1979). Psychological factors in the prognosis of malignant melanoma: A prospective study. *Psychosomatic Medicine, 41,* 647–655.

Rosch, E. (1978). Principles of categorization. In E. Rosch, & B. B. Lloyd (Eds.), *Cognition and categorization* (pp. 27–48). Hillsdale, NJ: Erlbaum.

Ross, L., Lepper, M. R., & Hubbard, M. (1975). Perseverance in self-perception and social perception: Biased attribution processes in the debriefing paradigm. *Journal of Personality and Social Psychology, 32,* 880–892.

Rothbart, M., Evans, M., & Fulero, S. (1979). Recall for confirming events: Memory processes and the maintenance of social stereotyping. *Journal of Experimental Social Psychology, 15,* 343–355.

Rumelhart, D. (1978). *Schemata: The building blocks of cognition.* San Diego, CA: Center for Human Information Processing, University of California at San Diego.

Sackeim, H. A. (1983). Self-deception, self-esteem, and depression: The adaptive value of lying to oneself. In J. Masling (Ed.), *Empirical studies of psychoanalytical theories* (Vol. 1, pp. 101–157). Hillsdale, NJ: Erlbaum.

Sarbin, T. R. (1981). On self-deception. In T. A. Sebeok, & R. Rosenthal (Eds.), *The Clever Hans phenomenon: Communication with horses, whales, apes, and people.* New York: New York Academy of Sciences.

Shaw, R. E., Cohen, F., Doyle, B., & Palesky, J. (1985). The impact of denial and repressive style on information gain and rehabilitation outcomes in myocardial infarction patients. *Psychosomatic Medicine, 47,* 262–273.

Silver, R. L., Boon, C., & Stones, M. H. (1983). Searching for meaning in misfortune: Making sense of incest. *Journal of Social Issues, 39,* 81–101.

Snyder, C. R., Higgins, R. L., & Stucky, R. J. (1983). *Excuses: Masquerades in search of grace.* New York: Wiley.

Snyder, M., & Uranowitz, S. W. (1978). Reconstructing the past: Some cognitive consequences of person perception. *Journal of Personality and Social Psychology, 36,* 941–950.

Suls, J., & Fletcher, B. (1985). The relative efficacy of avoidant and nonavoidant coping strategies: A meta-analysis. *Health Psychology, 4,* 249–288.

Sutherland, S., & Scherl, D. (1970). Patterns of response among victims of rape. *American Journal of Orthopsychiatry, 40,* 503–511.

Swann, W. B., Jr., & Read, S. J. (1981a). Acquiring self-knowledge: The search for feedback that fits. *Journal of Personality and Social Psychology, 41,* 119–1128.

Swann, W. B., Jr., & Read, S. J. (1981b). Self-verification processes: How we sustain our self-conceptions. *Journal of Experimental Social Psychology, 17,* 351–372.

Taylor, S. E. (1983). Adjustment to threatening events: A theory of cognitive adaptation. *American Psychologist, 38,* 1161–1173.

Taylor, S. E., Wood, J. V., & Lichtman, R. R. (1983). It could be worse: Selective evaluation as a response to victimization. *Journal of Social Issues, 39,* 19–40.

Visintainer, M., & Casey, R. (1984, August). *Adjustment and outcome in melanoma patients.* Paper presented at the American Psychological Association Meeting, Toronto.

Weisman, A. D. (1972). *On dying and denying.* New York: Behavioral Publications.

Weisman, A. D. (1979). *Coping with cancer.* New York: McGraw-Hill.

Weisman, A. D., & Hackett, T. P. (1967). Denial as a social act. In S. Levin, & R. J. Kahana (Eds.), *Psychodynamic studies on aging: Creativity, reminiscing, and dying* (pp. 79–110). New York: International Universities Press.

Wolfenstein, M. (1957). *Disaster: A psychological essay.* Glencoe, IL: Free Press.

Wortman, C. B. (1983). Coping with victimization: Conclusions and implications for future research. *Journal of Social Issues, 39,* 197–223.

Wortman, C. B., & Dunkel-Schetter, C. (1979). Interpersonal relationships and cancer: A theoretical analysis. *Journal of Social Issues, 35,* 120–155.

7

Daily Life Events and Mood

JOHN M. NEALE, JILL M. HOOLEY, LINA JANDORF, and ARTHUR A. STONE

In this chapter we will report the results of a series of studies in which life experiences and mood were recorded daily in prospective investigations. The studies to be described were not originally designed to address a specific set of questions pertaining to events and mood; rather, they were exploring the relationship between daily events and physical symptoms. Nonetheless, the prospective methods used in the data collection and the particular techniques for assessing daily mood gave us a unique opportunity to explore a variety of commonsense questions about mood as well as the psychological stress model of illness. As the reader will see in the forthcoming pages, some of the assumptions lay people and researchers have had about mood were not borne out by the data.

Our work in this area began with the creation of a method for gathering reliable and valid reports of daily experiences. The development of this instrument was stimulated by an interest in stress and illness and by the serious shortcomings in existing life-events inventories and methodologies (see Rabkin & Struening, 1976). Measures of mood were routinely included in our studies for several reasons. First, changes in

JOHN M. NEALE • Department of Psychology, State University of New York, Stony Brook, NY 11784.   **JILL M. HOOLEY** • Department of Psychology and Social Relations, Harvard University, Cambridge, MA 02139.   **LINA JANDORF** • Department of Psychiatry, State University of New York, Stony Brook, NY 11794.   **ARTHUR A. STONE** • Department of Psychiatry, State University of New York, Stony Brook, NY 11794. This research was supported by ONR contract N0004-77-0693 and NSF grant BNS 79-23715.

mood in response to life events had not been carefully examined in any prior longitudinal research. Second, a change in mood could also serve as an indicant of a change in illness vulnerability. That is, only those stressful events that yield clear-cut mood changes may be linked to increased probability of illness onset.

Our presentation first describes in some detail the assessments of both daily events and mood that were used in the studies. The event assessment was entirely new; thus, we present results demonstrating that it performs according to our expectations. Mood was assessed with the short form of the Nowlis Adjective Checklist (MACL: Nowlis, 1965), a well-known mood adjective checklist. But because little was known about how well the MACL performed as a measure of an entire day's mood, we present results showing how ratings of mood for an entire day relate to point assessments of mood throughout the day. The second section of the chapter describes various associations between daily events and mood. In this second section we present synchronous or same-day associations and then describe our efforts to detect lagged effects of daily experiences on mood.

DEVELOPMENT OF THE ADE

Before describing our data on mood changes we will first review Stone and Neale's (1982) development of the Assessment of Daily Experience (ADE).

Because we were devising an instrument to be used on a daily basis over substantial time periods, it was important that the recording task itself not be excessively onerous. Devising a relatively small but representative set of event categories, as opposed to a very lengthy checklist of specific events, was our solution to this problem. To obtain a sample of daily activities, we first had community residents record their experiences in diary format for 14 days. These events were independently reviewed by two research assistants who summarized the content by creating a list of categories arranged in outline form. A final outline list including 66 events and 18 headings and subheadings was produced. The five headings (all capitals) and 13 subheadings are now given. WORK RELATED ACTIVITIES: concerning boss, supervisor, upper management, and so on; general happenings concerning target at work; LEISURE ACTIVITIES: physical; nonphysical; vacation; outings; personal; FINANCIAL ACTIVITIES; FAMILY AND FRIEND ACTIVITIES: concerning target and spouse; concerning children; concerning

relatives; concerning friends and neighbors; family duties; OTHER AC-
TIVITIES AND HAPPENINGS concerning target.

Next, 26 couples completed the event form as well as a symptom
and mood scale for 14 consecutive days. Each event experienced was
rated on the three dimensions derived from Redfield and Stone's (1979)
factor analysis of dimensions that had been used in life-events research;
the derived dimensions were desirability/undesirability, change/stability,
and meaningfulness. In addition, a recording space was provided to
allow subjects to note if an event was anticipated in the near future.
These anticipated events were also rated on the three dimensions. Anticipated events were included in the ratings because of the large literature
demonstrating their powerful effects on both mood and physiological
variables (Ursin, Baade, & Levine, 1978). Husbands recorded events,
symptoms, and moods for themselves and wives completed the same
form, but about their husbands. Thus, we were able to examine husband–wife concordance rates.

An average of 5.3 events and 1.2 anticipated events were reported
per day. One hundred and six events, less than 3% of the total reported,
were written in. Thus, the instrument functioned well in the sense that it
did allow subjects to code their daily experiences, with infrequent use of
the blank spaces for write ins.

Event concordances were computed by calculating daily agreements
divided by the sum of husband-only reports, wife-only reports, and
agreements. Across all event categories the mean concordance was .33
with a range of 0 to .64. Further analyses examined several hypotheses
concerning variations in concordance rates. We expected, for example,
that concordance would increase for highly meaningful events. The correlation between meaningfulness and concordance was .76, supporting
our prediction. Similarly, we expected higher concordances for actual
than for anticipated events. This prediction was also confirmed. In sum,
although the overall concordance figures were modest, a finding that is
rather typical in other work using similar methods (e.g., Nelson, 1977),
the concordance rates did vary in expected ways.

The modest concordance rate demanded that we further explore
the reasons for the disagreements. There were several possibilities: (a)
the items on the form were ambiguous, making it impossible for spouses
to report with a high degree of accuracy; (b) the instructions concerning
how and what to record were not clear or specific enough; or, (c) the
disagreements were not due to any shortcoming of the instrument itself,
but simply to the nature of how people remember their day, namely,
forgetting, minimizing, and so on.

The daily recording form used in the next study was the result of a substantial revision of that used in the previous one. All of the items were reviewed and the wording of several was clarified; the overall content covered by the items, however, remained the same. In addition to the three event-rating dimensions used on the first version, we replaced the anticipation dimension, which was difficult to analyze, with one called "control over the events's occurrence" for the sake of indexing the theoretically interesting quality of perceived control over the environment (see Averill, 1973). Also, all of the instructions printed on the form were greatly expanded; several pages were devoted to how to classify and rate events and report symptoms and mood. A further major procedural change aimed at insuring that participants were adequately familiar with the task of recording daily events was the addition of an at-home interview with the couple prior to the recording period. A research assistant read through the entire form with the couples, had them code the previous 2 days using the form, and answered all questions concerning any aspect of the procedure. We felt these interviews would not only insure proper use of the form, but would also increase our subjects' motivation to use the form correctly.

The purpose of this study was, then, twofold: (a) to obtain an estimate of event concordance with the revised instrument and (b) to obtain information to help us understand why disagreements came about. This second purpose was achieved by assigning our couples to two groups. All couples received a home interview to train them in the use of the instrument. Couples in the "call" group were told that on several evenings during the 2-week recording period they would receive telephone calls from us during which we would speak with both members of the couple simultaneously. It was explained that the purpose of the calls was to understand how event disagreements came about. To do this, we would go over the two forms that had been completed on the day of the call. When disagreements were found, the couples were asked why and their responses recorded. Convenient times, usually in the late evening, were arranged for these calls.

Husband–wife event concordance rates improved somewhat. Eliminating events the wife would be unlikely to observe, concordances were, for the most part, in the 60% to 70% range. From the telephone interviews, we found that disagreements about event occurrence between spouses were largely caused either by the wife (Observer) not knowing about an occurrence reported by the husband (Target), or the husband forgetting an event that occurred but that his wife remembered. Thus, having ratings from both husband and wife, a procedure we have routinely continued, provides an optimal characterization of a day. The third source of discordance stemmed from differences in the way some events were perceived. An example illustrates a typical disagreement: husband was repairing the garage and upon coming into the house, his wife gave him a kiss and praised him for his efforts. He recorded the event as "praise from spouse," whereas she recorded it as "household duties." This last type of discordance is also addressed by the data collection procedure that grew out of the third study. The procedure is as follows. Husbands (Targets) and wives (Observers) first work through the ADE independently, recording the husband's experiences of the day. They then reconvene and go through the event categories together to produce a master list of the husband's experiences that day. With this procedure the husband is forced to confirm events he recorded but were not observed by the wife, the wife can remind him of some experiences, and the couple can discuss and agree upon how experiences are to be classified on the ADE. We have used this recording procedure in most of the studies reported in this paper and believe that it provides an acceptable solution to the problems often inherent in self-monitoring.

THE MEANING OF DAILY MOOD ASSESSMENTS

Before turning to results concerning the effects of life experiences on mood we need to consider how a daily mood assessment should be interpreted. In our research as well as that of other groups who have been studying daily mood (e.g., Grossup & Lewinsohn, 1980; Rehm, 1978), mood was conceptualized as an average of moods throughout the day and subjects were required to report their mood for the entire day. These instructions are not really consistent with our common understanding of the term *mood*. Affective states are generally not thought to be all-day affairs; an individual can only rarely be said to be in one mood for the length of a day. When people are asked to report mood for an entire day, how do they take into account the variability of their moods across the day? Or, more broadly, what does a daily mood report measure? The importance of this question can be illustrated by an enumeration of several possible answers.

1. Mean. A daily mood report may represent the average of all of the mood states experienced during a day. This hypothesis seems to be the one assumed by most researchers. The concept of averaging is a deceptively simple one in this context, however; because subjects would have to account for both intensity and duration of moods in arriving at an average daily rating.

2. Peak. The daily mood report may reflect only the peak, or highest

intensity, moods of the day. One might expect that, in looking back on the mood of an entire day, low-intensity affective experiences would be lost to recall, so that only peak experiences would be recorded.

3. Recency. The daily mood report, because it is completed at the end of the day, could show a recency effect for end-of-day mood; that is, subjects' reports may be biased toward the moods they have experienced closest in time to the report.

Hedges, Jandorf, and Stone (1985) examined the issue of the meaning of daily mood reports by having subjects complete the short form of the MACL for 21 consecutive days. Two types of mood reports were made, momentary and daily. When subjects provided a momentary report, their instructions were to describe their mood at the moment they were being asked. These momentary reports were made at approximately 9 a.m., 1 p.m., 4 p.m., and 7 p.m. on 14 consecutive days of the 21-day period. Mood ratings were collected by telephone, rather than by written report, to reduce the reactivity of making multiple ratings per day. Daily mood reports were taken by asking subjects to rate their mood for the entire day at approximately 10 p.m. for each of the 21 days of the study. The purpose of reporting only daily mood for one week was to provide data with which to assess the possible reactive effect on daily mood of making four momentary reports earlier in the day.

Analyses were conducted on factor scores derived from prior analyses of the MACL (Stone, 1981). The positive mood factor includes feeling playful, elated, energetic, kind, self-centered, and a leisurely mood; the negative mood factor includes feeling sad, concentrating, angry, skeptical, and clutched up. One way to evaluate the alternative hypotheses concerning the best predictor of daily mood is to compare the absolute level of daily mood scores with those of momentary mood scores and indexes derived from the momentary scores. Each subject's four momentary mood reports were averaged to provide a mean of momentary reports. The hypothesis that daily reports represent the peak mood of the day was evaluated by selecting the minimum of the four momentary mood scores (i.e., the most intense mood) for each subject on each day. Figure 1 shows that the level of peak momentary mood provided the best approximation to that of daily mood when the data were examined across all subjects.

A second means of evaluating hypotheses concerning the best predictor of daily mood is to correlate daily mood within subjects with all indexes of momentary mood report, across days of participation. Figure 2 shows averages across subjects of the correlations between these indexes and daily mood. For negative and positive mood, the average of all momentary reports was most highly correlated with daily mood; peak

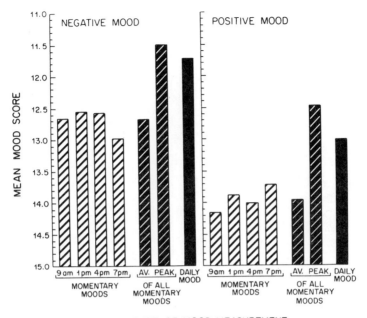

Figure 1. Average Negative and Positive Moods for Time-of-Day measures, Daily Average and Peak measures, and Overall Daily Mood measure. AV = Average. ($N = 21$)

mood was in both cases the next highest correlated. For negative mood the daily-to-average momentary mood coefficient was significantly higher than were the other coefficients. For positive mood, both the daily-to-peak correlation and the daily-to-1-p.m. correlations were not significantly different from the daily-to-averaged momentary mood correlation.

In summary, when the criterion was absolute level of mood report values, daily mood was most representative of the peak mood of the day. Although this finding surprised us, it is understandable if one thinks of an end-of-day, daily mood report as a retrospective event. Researchers tend to use daily reports because such reports hold retrospective biases to a practical minimum. But it is likely that some forgetting takes place in the course of the day, and that the moods least subject to forgetting are those that have been most intense or salient. If this is the case—and support exists for this assumption (e.g., Tversky & Kahnemann, 1974)—then even if subjects try to report daily mood by simply averaging their moods for the day, their reports will be biased toward intense moods

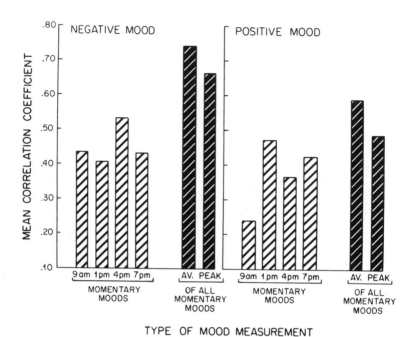

Figure 2. Average Within-Subject Correlations of Negative and Positive Daily Mood with Time-of-Day measures, and Daily Average and Peak measures. AV = Average. (N = 21)

because the data available to recall, on which they reckon that average, will be biased toward intense moods.

On the other hand, if the purpose of collecting daily mood reports is to examine day-to-day fluctuations in mood, then the second, correlational criterion applied to these data indicates that day-to-day fluctuations in daily mood reports best conform to those produced by averaging momentary mood reports. Here, however, the evidence favoring a single best predictor is more equivocal; for both positive and negative mood, peak mood was the second highest correlate of daily mood, and in the case of the positive factor, the peak-to-daily correlation was not significantly lower than the averaged-to-daily correlation.

SYNCHRONOUS EFFECT OF DAILY EXPERIENCE ON MOOD

Most people believe that their moods are determined, at least in part, by their daily experiences. Findings from a multitude of laboratory studies offer some support for this commonsense view; self-reported mood, physiological correlates of emotion, and directly observed behavioral aspects of mood can all be causally linked to manipulations such as failure, frustration, and competition. As we move out of the laboratory, however, the data become less convincing. Lewinsohn and his colleagues, for example, have conducted several studies in which subjects reported their daily experiences and ratings of depressed mood. In one of these investigations (Lewinsohn & Libet, 1972), the number of pleasant events correlated −.37 with depression. Same-day correlations of similar magnitude have also been reported by Rehm (1978) and Stone (1981). In Stone and Neale's study, wherein 50 community residents reported life events and mood for over 80 days, the correlation between undesirable life events and positive and negative mood were −.32 and .39, respectively. Desirable events correlated −.32 with negative mood and .48 with positive mood (Stone, 1981).

From these data it is clear that there is a synchronous association between life events and mood. From the data we have collected we are also able to examine some additional issues concerning this association, specifically: How does mood vary by day of the week? Are events in specific content areas differentially associated with mood? Is there a particular event appraisal that maximizes predictability of mood?

Day-of-the-Week Effects

The expression "blue Monday" reflects a commonly held belief in our culture that Monday is the worst day of the week, representing the low point for affective states. Nevertheless, surprisingly few data have been brought to bear on an evaluation of this belief. Pecjak (1970) directly examined the accuracy of the term "blue Monday" in a cross-cultural study of college students' associations among colors, emotional states, and days of the week. Among the strongest relationships to emerge were those between Monday and the color gray (blue was a possible choice), and between Monday and the emotion anger. These associations, or "verbal synesthesiae," suggest that Monday is viewed grimly. Farber (1953) had 80 college students rank the days of the week according to general preference. The rank order he obtained, in descending order of preference, was Saturday, Friday, Sunday, Thursday, Wednesday, Tuesday, and Monday. In a study by Rossi and Rossi (1977) 67 college women completed a daily mood rating form for 40 consecutive days. In contrast to expectation, positive affect peaked on Friday and was at a low point on Tuesday. Positive mood on Friday, Saturday, and Sunday was higher than on all other days of the week, which did not differ from each other. Though this finding is interesting, its generality is limited because the subjects were all young, undergraduate women.

Increases in dysphoric mood have far-reaching social implications, potentially affecting suicide rates, work productivity, illness and symptom presentation, alcohol abuse, and marital discord. Therefore, attempts to understand the factors that are associated with rises in dysphoric mood would appear to be a worthwhile undertaking. Considering how widely accepted the notion of a blue Monday is, it is surprising that there is no evidence of increased dysphoric mood on Monday from studies with rigorous designs using well-accepted mood assessment measures. Our longitudinal data using the ADE and MACL mood scales provided an opportunity to explore day-of-the-week effects. Data arranged according to day of the week from Stone, Hedges, Neale, & Satin (1985) using several samples of community residents are presented in Figure 3. Husbands' ratings are for their own moods; wives' ratings

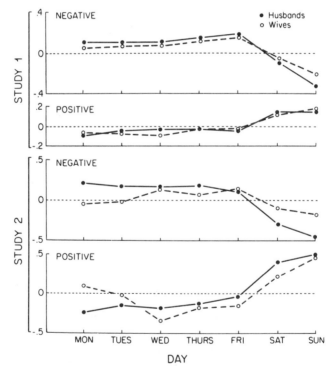

Figure 3. Average Negative and Positive Mood for Husbands and Wives by Day of the Week.

concern their husbands' moods. In both studies a strong day-of-the-week effect was observed. However, this effect is due to the weekends, not to Monday. Mood, both positive and negative, is stable throughout the week. On weekends, however, positive mood increases and negative mood decreases.

Why is there a discrepancy between our subjects' actual mood reports and our cultural beliefs about Monday? One possibility is that our subjects did not really think that Monday was "bluer" than other days. Though their mood reports appeared discrepant with general beliefs, perhaps the reports were not at odds with the subjects' own beliefs. To test this possibility we telephoned subjects in one of the samples after they had completed daily reporting and asked them on which day of the week their mood was worst and on which day it was best. Sixty-five percent chose Monday as the day with the worst mood, 9% Tuesday, 5% Wednesday, 2% Thursday, 4% Friday, 2% Saturday, 5% Sunday; 8% said no day was worst. The distribution of responses to the question "Which day has the best mood?" was 2% Monday, 4% Tuesday, 5% Wednesday, 0% Thursday, 35% Friday, 25% Saturday, and 28% Sunday. Clearly, subjects believed that Monday was the worst day of the week and that Friday and weekends were the best.

We offer two speculative explanations for why subjects' belief in blue Monday was at odds with their mood reports. The first is that people adhere to a blue Monday cultural myth that causes them to choose Monday when asked for the worst day of the week, but does not interfere with their longitudinal reports of their moods in a different (and presumably more accurate) pattern. Daily mood report and summary statements about daily mood must be, in some sense, cognitively distinct. If they were not, we surely would have observed an effect of the blue Monday belief on daily reports.

The second explanation we offer draws on the finding that weekends were less negative and more positive than all weekdays. Perhaps beliefs about mood over days of the week are not simply the reflection of mood experienced on a given day, but are also reactive to the change in mood from one day to the next. Mondays are thought of as most negative because, compared to the relatively good mood reported on Sundays, they represent the largest average decrement in mood throughout the week. Mood reports are not, however, entirely determined by such a contrast effect; if they were, Saturday would have been chosen as the "best" day of the week because the largest increase in positive mood occurs from Friday to Saturday. Preferences for best day of the week, however, were spread across Friday, Saturday, and Sunday. Nonetheless, perception of days may be influenced by this contrast effect to some degree. In the case of Monday, which is very much like the other week-days, this effect is enough to sway subjects' preference data so that they choose it as the worst day of the week.

Event Content

Because there is evidence that events in different categories such as family, work, spouse, etc., may impact differentially on health (Chiriboga & Dean, 1978; Paykel, 1974) it is therefore of interest to examine whether or not the various event categories of the ADE are differentially associated with mood.

Stone (in press) has completed such an analysis using the 11 categories from the ADE and conducting the analyses separately for desirable and undesirable events falling within each category. Desirability ratings were determined by subjects' ratings of events, whereas event content was determined by our outline of categories. Because a given event could be rated as either desirable or undesirable, depending on the rater and circumstances surrounding the event, indexes separately represented desirably rated events and undesirably rated events. Results are presented in Table 1.

Examining the desirable indexes, it is clear that spouse, children,

Table 1. Correlations of Event Category Frequencies with Positive and Negative Mood

Event content	Desirable classification		Undesirable classification	
	Correlations with mood		Correlations with mood	
	Positive	Negative	Positive	Negative
Work	−.11*	.09*	−.19*	.22*
Spouse	.18*	−.11*	−.08*	.15*
Children	.15*	−.09*	−.04*	.07*
Family-leisure	.36*	−.26*	−.01	.05
Family-relatives	.20*	−.09*	−.03	.06*
Social-leisure	.17*	−.09*	−.01	.02
Financial	.01	.01	−.04*	.05*
Personal-leisure	.02	−.03	−.02	.01
Goals	.06*	−.00	−.04*	.09*
Health & Other	.06*	−.04	−.10*	.10*
Household	.08*	−.07	−.02	.02

Note. The desirable classification refers to events rated by subjects on the desirable pole of the desirable–undesirable event rating scale, the undesirable classification refers to those rated as undesirable. Correlations are means of within-subject daily correlations.
*$p < .001$.

family-leisure, friends-relatives, and social-leisure had a significant association with mood, with the strongest relationship being found for family-leisure events. In contrast, desirable work events had a reverse pattern of association with mood, although the magnitude of the correlation is small. The pattern of correlations for the undesirable indexes is different: here we see only three event categories with meaningful associations with mood: work, spouse, and health events.

Like other investigations of event content, Stone (in press) found that various event categories were differentially related to mood. Moreover, the set of desirable events that was most strongly associated with mood (family-leisure) was not the same as the undesirable event with the same characteristic (work). Because certain event contents were more strongly associated with mood than others, perhaps they should be the object of future research attempting to characterize stressful environments.

Event Appraisal

Another perspective on categorizing life events comes from the concept of appraisal. We have already reported data with events categorized by one of our appraisal dimensions—desirability-undesirability—but have routinely collected data on several others. In addition, other findings suggest that dimensional qualities may have considerable influence in understanding an event's impact. Learned helplessness theorists (e.g., Abramson, Seligman, & Teasdale, 1978) suggest that controllability is of great importance; Holmes and Rahe (1967) used change and readjustment as their markers of the stress concept.

Lennox and Stone (1985) examined the relationship between the appraisal dimensions of the ADE, and combinations thereof, and negative mood. Each subject's daily reports were examined for a single 4-day period with a day of high negative mood (target day) preceded by three days of low negative mood. An isolated negative mood day was chosen to permit easier evaluation of the event–mood relationship. Negative mood was identified as high if it was substantially above the individual's mean for his recording period. Low negative mood was defined relative to the target day rather than an absolute standard.

In order to determine which aspects of events were most predictive of mood, all the major weighting schemes reported in the literature were computed. Given the comprehensiveness of our data set with regard to subjects' event appraisals, the additional information available permitted evaluation of other potentially relevant systems as well. A total of 49 event indexes were computed for each of the participants for every day of the 4-day recording period.

It is not possible in the limited space here to describe fully all 49 appraisal classification schemes. Instead, we will briefly mention several of the major classifications and quickly describe the themes of the others. We used the total number of events experienced per day, a procedure equivalent to the unweighted change scores used in major life event studies (Rahe, 1972). The sum of events appraised by subjects as desirable is similar to an event index used by Lewinsohn and Amenson (1978), whereas the sum of undesirable events has been shown to have predictive ability by Lewinsohn and Amenson (1978) and by Mueller, Edwards, and Yarns (1978), among others. Another set of event indexes were formed by summing the desirability ratings and the undesirability ratings to address the magnitude, as well as the frequency of event experience; the method is similar to that used by Lewinsohn and Amenson (1978) and Sarason, Johnson, and Siegal (1978). Likewise, the sum of changingness ratings formed another index, similar in nature to the social readjustment concept used by Holmes and Rahe (1967). Control ratings were also summed because of their presumed relationship to psychological functioning (Abramson *et al.,* 1978; Hammen & Mayol, 1982). More complex indexes were also created to address other concepts, such as the difference between frequency of desirable and undesirable events (a test of the hypothesis that the two types of events cancel each other's effects out, Ross & Mirowsky, 1979) or the ratio of desirable to undesirable events, which has been shown in the major-life-events area to predict symptomatology (Myers, Lindenthal, & Pepper, 1974). Many other indexes were created on theoretical grounds and still others were created to test the effects of new combinations of event experiences (see Table 2).

For every individual, correlations between each event index and positive and negative mood were computed for the 4-day period. Correlations with high values indicate that the event index and mood follow the same pattern (positive correlations) or the opposite pattern (negative correlations). In order to obtain adequate summary measures, the median correlation for each index was computed over all subjecfs (see Table 2).

Whereas some of the more complex schemes (e.g., undesirable × control × meaningfulness × change ratings) yielded substantial correlations (e.g., median Pearson r, negative mood = .83, positive mood = −.39), a simple index (i.e., total number of undesirable events) did very well in predicting mood. The median Pearson r for negative and positive moods, respectively, was .68 and −.56. Even the best overall predictors, defined by the magnitude of combined correlations for negative and positive mood, did not fare considerably better than the simple additive index. In general, higher correlations resulted with indexes based on

Table 2. Median Correlations of Mood and Daily Event Indexes

	Mood	
Index	Negative	Positive
Total # of events	.03	.00
Total # desirable events	−.53	.35
Total # undesirable events	.68	−.56
Summation of ratings		
Desirable ratings	−.57	.49
Undesirable ratings	.71	−.49
Change ratings	.52	−.29
Change ratings desirable events	−.10	.19
Change ratings undesirable events	.74	−.47
Stabilizing ratings	−.22	.09
Stabilizing ratings desirable events	−.22	.23
Stabilizing ratings undesirable events	−.41	−.08
Meaningfulness ratings	−.41	.18
Meaningfulness ratings desirable events	−.47	.37
Meaningfulness ratings undesirable events	.59	−.39
Control ratings	−.01	.10
Control ratings desirable events	−.55	.35
Control ratings I[a] undesirable events	.60	−.40
Control ratings II[b] undesirable events	.57	−.42
Undesirable ratings + desirable ratings	.04	.06
Difference formulas		
Total # undesirable events−total # desirable events	.71	−.62
Undesirable ratings−desirable ratings	.75	−.52
Change ratings−stabilizing ratings	.42	−.33
Change ratings desirable events− stabilizing ratings desirable events	.10	−.07
Change ratings undesirable events− stabilizing ratings undesirable events	.65	−.44
Change ratings undesirable events− change ratings desirable events	.52	−.47
Stabilizing ratings desirable events− change ratings desirable events	−.11	.00
(Change ratings undesirable events− stabilizing ratings undesirable events)− (stabilizing ratings desirable events− change ratings desirable events)	.42	−.26
Ratio schemes		
Total # undesirable events/total # desirable events	.60	−.51
Undesirable ratings/desirable ratings	.77	−.49

(continued)

Table 2. (*Continued*)

Index	Mood	
	Negative	Positive

Multiplicative summaries

Desirable × stabilizing ratings	−.22	.09
Desirable × meaningfulness ratings	−.43	.37
Desirable × control ratings	−.54	.50
Desirable × control × meaningfulness ratings	−.42	.54
Desirable × control × meaningfulness × stabilizing ratings	−.21	.12
Undesirable × control I ratings	.68	−.45
Undesirable × control II ratings	.69	−.34
Undesirable × change ratings	.78	−.53
Undesirable × meaningfulness ratings	.79	−.41
Undesirable × control I × meaningfulness ratings	.77	−.52
Undesirable × control II × meaningfulness ratings	.80	−.32
Undesirable × control I × meaningfulness × change ratings	.83	−.39
Undesirable × control II × meaningfulness × change ratings	.80	−.36

Differences between multiplicative summaries

(Undesirable × control I ratings)− (desirable × control ratings)	.68	−.54
(Undesirable × control II ratings)− (desirable × control ratings)	.57	−.55
(Undesirable × change ratings)− (desirable × stabilizing ratings)	.57	−.57
(Undesirable × control I × meaningfulness ratings)− (desirable × control × meaningfulness ratings)	.44	−.53
(Undesirable × control II × meaningfulness ratings)− (desirable × control × meaningfulness ratings)	.38	−.51
(Undesirable × control I × meaningfulness × change ratings)−(desirable × control × meaningfulness × stabilizing ratings)	.29	−.44
(Undesirable × control II × meaningfulness × change ratings)−(desirable × control × meaningfulness × stabilizing ratings)	.32	−.44

[a]Control ratings I = high value associated with no control for undesirable events.
[b]Control ratings II = low value associated with no control for undesirable events

undesirable events (mean r_{xy} for undesirable event indexes with negative mood = .64; mean r_{xy} for undesirable event indexes with positive mood = −.41; mean r_{xy} for desirable event indexes with negative mood = −.33; mean r_{xy} for desirable event indexes with positive mood = .27) and with negative mood as the criterion (mean absolute value r_{xy} for negative mood with indexes = .49; mean absolute value r_{xy} for positive mood with indexes = .36).

The higher correlations for undesirable event schemes strongly suggest the importance of the desirability dimension. As evidenced in the set of median correlations, aversive event schemes were uniformly better predictors of negative mood and frequently better predictors of positive mood than their desirable event counterparts. As previous investigators have not typically assessed the relative ability of both types of occurrence to predict positive affective states, this finding is informative. That desirable events do not predict negative mood as well as their undesirable counterparts is consistent with previous research (e.g., Lewinsohn & Amenson, 1978; Sarason, Johnson, & Siegal, 1979; Zautra & Reich, 1981).

The finding that a simple additive index predicted as well as others based on much more information of demonstrated relevance is somewhat surprising. That including appraisals of meaningfulness, change, control, and degree of undesirability did not add substantially to predictions based solely on the sum of undesirable events runs counter to expectations (Abramson et al., 1978; Hammen & Mayol, 1982; Mullen, 1980; Redfield & Stone, 1979). Ross and Mirowsky (1979), however, also found that this simple index compared favorably to more complex schemes, though their data set did not include information about subjective perceptions of events. With regard to our investigation, it is possible that the manner in which we selected days to study partly accounts for the findings. As negative mood on Day 4 was markedly different from that on each of Days 1 to 3, we probably maximized the probability that any undesirable event index would predict this variable well. The large correlations for most of the undesirable event predictors attest to this point. Perhaps the appraisal dimensions would reveal an enhanced sensitivity to subtle fluctuations more typically observed in daily mood. Of course, it is also possible that differential predictability would occur with outcomes other than mood.

LAGGED EFFECTS OF DAILY EXPERIENCE ON MOOD

Synchronous correlations between life events and mood cannot, of course, demonstrate a causal relationship, and the directionality problem is particulárly acute here, because it is quite plausible that mood could influence event reporting. Nelson and Craighead (1977) and Clark and Teasdale (1982) have shown, for example, that depressed mood is linked to the likelihood of reporting an event and to the evaluation of the event when reported.

The most convenient way of attempting to gather more persuasive evidence for a causal relationship is a longitudinal study wherein events and mood are reported over a period of many days. In one such study, Rehm (1978) found that lagged correlations between events and next-day mood ratings were nonsignificant. Similarly, Lewinsohn and Libet (1972) failed to find a reliable lagged relationship between events and mood. Both these studies, however, have limitations. For example, Rehm used only a worst ever (0) to best ever (10) scale to assess mood, and Lewinsohn and Libet only assessed depression. Even more important, neither study explicitly selected events that could be anticipated to have enough impact to produce more than a one-day mood shift. We would not necessarily expect all events to produce lasting mood changes and, thus, the analyses reported in previous studies might be obscuring a relationship that was present, but only for the most severe events in their samples.

In order to increase the chances of observing an effect of events on mood, Stone and Neale (1984a) wanted to predict mood from events that would be expected to exert a substantial psychological impact. The event-appraisal questions provided the information necessary to select events that potentially packed a "psychological punch." Ratings on two of the appraisal dimensions were used to define severity: ratings of "quite" or "more undesirable," and "extremely" or "more meaningful."

Another issue that had to be considered was that events could occur on days prior to and subsequent to the index day, that is, the day selected because it had a severe event. If events did exert their presumed effect on mood, then nonindex days with events, unless they were randomly distributed among prior and subsequent days relative to the index day, might confuse our interpretations. There are several indications that both major events and daily events do cluster to some degree (Hurst, 1979; Roghmann & Haggerty, 1973), so this was likely to be a problem.

To assess thoroughly mood prior to and subsequent to the day with the severe event we chose a 21-day period to analyze; 10 days preceded the index day, which was on Day 11, and 10 days followed the index day. The ideal 21-day period should not have any other severe events besides the one on the index day, especially following the index day, as this would tend to support artifactually our hypothesis that events affect subsequent mood. Selection could not be that restrictive, however, and we allowed some other severe events to occur several days before and after the event, but not within 5 days in either direction.

Only 17 (34% of the eligible sample) subjects had events that met our criteria. Twelve different events were represented among the 17 with the following frequencies (in parentheses): "children sick or injured" (2); "death of friend, neighbor, or acquaintance" (2); "argument with spouse" (2); "witnessed something unusual" (2); "major personal problems" (2); "daily routine getting to you" (1); "minor personal problem" (1); "relative sick or death of relative" (1); "disciplining children" (1); "weather getting to you" (1); "not getting along with spouse" (1); and, "emotional interaction with co-worker" (1).

Our major question was whether mood would be affected on the days following the occurrence of an event. Husbands' ratings of their own negative and positive daily moods are presented in Figure 4. The

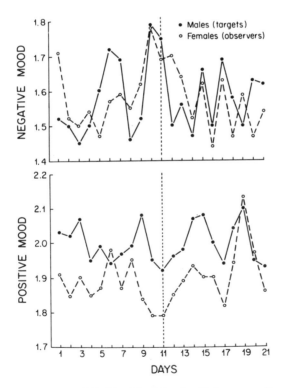

Figure 4. Average Negative and Positive Mood for the 10 days preceding the Index day, For the Index day (Day 11), and for the 10 days following the Index day for Males and Females. ($N = 17$)

index day is labeled as Day 11. The points in the figure were computed by averaging the mood ratings of the 17 subjects. Days prior to the index day are found to the left of Day 11 (Days 1–10) and days subsequent to the index day are found to the right (Days 12–21). There is a peak in negative and a trough in positive mood on Day 10, one day prior to the index day. Surprisingly, there is actually more negative mood on the day prior to the index day than on the index day. Mood scores on Day 12, the day following the index day, are surprising in another way: scores bounce back to pre-index-day levels, indicating no carryover effects from the index day. The wives' view of their husbands' moods are also plotted and the pattern closely replicates that of their husbands, with the exception that wives may view their husband's negative mood as elevated on the day following the severe event. This evidence of a lagged effect does not, however, replicate in the next study.

Because of the nature of this finding further research on the durability of the mood changes in response to such life events was considered necessary. Data from a second sample of community residents were therefore analyzed in an effort to clarify the affective sequelae of severe life events.

As in the study described previously, subjects in this second community sample were also males, whose wives acted as observers of their husband's mood. Severe events were defined subjectively using two appraisal criteria. In order to select events with the greatest potential for negative impact, the appraisal dimensions of undesirability and meaningfulness were both required to be rated as "extreme." Only subjects who experienced an event that was subjectively appraised in this way were included in the analysis, and, in cases where subjects had more than one event meeting these criteria, the target event was randomly selected from those available.

A total of 26 (of 79 potential subjects) individuals experienced an event which was severe, and, in addition, had 10 recording days occurring before it and 10 recording days taking place after it. All events occurred on Day 11 of the 21-day reporting period and no other severe events occurred for any individual at any other time during these 3 weeks.

As can be seen from Figure 5, there was a marked peak in negative mood on the index day. The figure also reveals a corresponding decrease in positive mood on Day 11. However, it is quite apparent that the mood changes that occur on the index day are transient; by Day 12, both positive and negative mood ratings have returned to preevent levels. These findings thus replicate those of the earlier study, and provide further support for the absence of prolonged changes in mood after a severe negative life event.

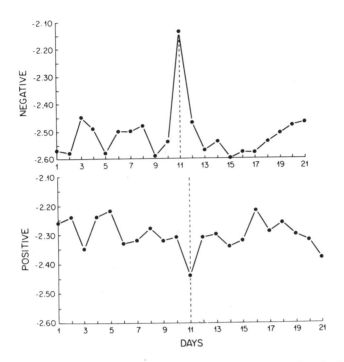

Figure 5. Average Negative and Positive Mood for the 10 days preceding the Index day, for the Index day (Day 11), and for the 10 days following the Index day. ($N = 26$)

Although the results of the analysis conducted on the second sample of community residents converged with those of the initial sample, we were still interested in the possibility that lagged mood effects might occur in some individuals. Because Goplerud and Depue (1985) have suggested that sustained mood changes might be most marked in dysthymics, we decided to reconduct our analyses (a) using the time period of 16 days employed by these investigators, and (b) focusing on those individuals who might be most likely to experience a more durable affective response. A subgroup of individuals scoring high on our dysphoria scale were therefore selected. This scale represents a translation of the DSM-III criteria for dysphoria into a self-report format.[1] Subjects who scored in the upper third of the Dysphoria Scale and who also experi-

---

[1]Some examples of items on our dysphoria scale include: sleeping too much; tearfulness or crying; feeling sad; decreased productivity at work or at home; and not doing many pleasurable activities. The choice of answers was hardly ever, sometimes, often, or all the time.

enced a severe life event on Day 8 of a 16-day reporting period (without experiencing any severe events on any of the remaining 15 days), were thus compared with subjects who also experienced a severe event on Day 8 but who scored only in the lower third of the Dysphoria Scale ($n=11$ vs. $n=14$). Mean negative mood ratings for each of these groups over 16 days are presented in Figure 6. As is clear from this figure, both dysphorics and nondysphorics show an elevation in negative mood on the index day. However, this increase is again only transient, and, mood ratings made after the index day are very similar to the mood ratings made prior to the occurrence of the severe event. Thus, even in a subsample purposely selected to provide the greatest chance of obtaining a positive result, durable mood changes in response to severe events remain elusive.

As we have already mentioned, Goplerud and Depue (1985) have recently reported lagged mood effects in a small sample of subjects. Dysthymics took an average of 7.7 days to recover from a severe event, cyclothymics 3.9 days, and normals 2.3 days. There are many differences

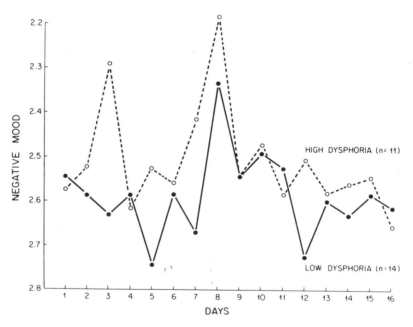

Figure 6. Average Negative Mood for High Dysphoric ($N = 11$) and Low Dysphoric ($N = 14$) groups for 7 days preceding the Index day, for the Index day (Day 8), and for 8 days following the Index day.

between the Goplerud and Depue study and the research we have just reported. Gopelrud and Depue's life events assessment was simply a rating of the degree of pleasantness/unpleasantness of subjects' most important positive and negative experiences of each day. Severe events were defined as those 1.5 standard deviations from the subjects' own mean unpleasantness rating and that were also judged moderately or extremely stressful by a panel of judges. The dependent variable was the Inventory of Behavioral Variation, a 24-item measure covering mood, drug use, sleep, health, and work pressure. Finally, Goplerud and Depue studied college students whereas our research had focussed on older community residents.

Because our life-event assessment is more detailed than Goplerud and Depue's and because there was no reason to suspect that the MACL was less sensitive than the IBV,[2] we decided to conduct a final study with a subject sample comparable to that used by Gopelrud and Depue, namely college students. A daily recording form was developed including the short form of the MACL, a description of the most serious problem of the day (rated on dimensions from the ADE as well as a 10-point stressfulness scale), six of the affect scales from the IBV, and the daily coping assessment we have developed (Stone & Neale, 1984b).[3] The daily recording forms were completed by a sample of 27 undergraduates, recruited from two psychology classes, who agreed to complete life-event and mood ratings each day for a 28-day period. During the course of the study, however, six students either withdrew their participation or failed to complete the recording booklets correctly. The data to be discussed in the following are thus based on a final N of 21 (13 females; 8 males) undergraduates.

In order to be considered as a severe event, the daily events reported by subjects had to be appraised as undesirable, and also given a stressfulness rating which was more than 1.5 standard deviations above each subjects' own 28-day mean on the 10-point stressfulness scale. In cases were subjects had more than one event meeting both of these criteria, a verbatim description of each event was given to a panel of three independent judges who then selected the most objectively severe event. In the one instance where at least two of these three judges could not reach consensus on objective severity, the event in question was selected at random. Of the 21 available subjects, 19 experienced an event

---

[2]Depue (personal communication) had also told us that the IBV results held up when mood items were analyzed separately.

[3]Another reason for searching for lagged mood effects is that they would provide a convenient paradigm in which to study coping efficacy.

during the 4-week rating period that met the severity criteria. The 19 events reported were as follows: "overtired and have to take physical exam for service tomorrow"; "financial problems and worries about finding a job"; "children and fiance (who is also ex-husband) don't want to have anything to do with each other"; "found out someone close had deceived me"; "term paper due—not started it yet"; "trying to study for 3 big tests on 3 consecutive days this week"; "didn't do well on calculus test taken today"; "problems with family and boyfriend"; "remembrance of a previous fight between self and girl down the hall"; "behind in course assignments and in preparation for finals"; "woke up late. One hour late for work"; "Had to take a plane trip—very nervous about it"; "had to tell best friend that I might not be able to attend her bridal shower in 2 weeks because of work pressure"; "did poorly in exam taken today"; "got test back—did 'horribly'"; "realized will 'almost assuredly' fail math"; "went to semi-formal and saw ex-boyfriend very happy with another girl"; "problems deciding what to major in"; and, "difficulties with financial aid application".

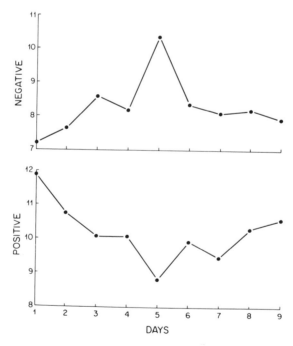

Figure 7. Average Negative and Positive Mood for 4 days preceding the Index day, for the Index day (Day 5), and for 4 days following the Index day ($N = 19$).

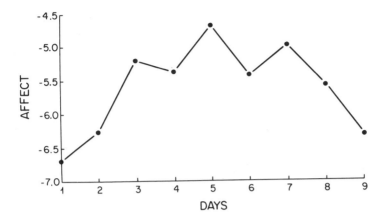

Figure 8. Average Affect for 4 days preceding the Index day, for the Index day (Day 5), and for 4 days following the Index day ($N = 19$).

In keeping with Goplerud and Depue's (1985) earlier study, mood ratings from the 4 days prior to and the 4 days past the severe event day were examined. A rating period of 9 days per subject was therefore analyzed, with the index day occurring on Day 5. Figure 7 shows the mean negative and positive mood ratings during these 9 days. As can be seen, there is a clear peak in negative mood on the day on which the severe event occurs. This elevated level of dysphoria is also accompanied by a corresponding decrease in positive mood on Day 5. However, in neither case are the mood changes occurring on the index day sustained. On Day 6, ratings of both positive and negative mood are back again to preevent (Day 4) levels.

Plots of the data from the affect scales of the IBV reveal a similar picture. When ratings for optimism/pessimism, elation/irritability, energy/fatigue, elation/depression, and anxiety were combined into a composite mood scale, no evidence of any durable affective response to the severe event was again apparent (see Figure 8). In fact, the mood changes that are measured by these 10-point scales are less marked than those obtained using the MACL.

Contrary to our initial expectations, therefore, college students do not constitute a different population from community residents with respect to lagged mood effects. In both types of populations, clear affective sequelae to severe negative life events cannot be demonstrated. Given that the majority (78%) of the subjects in our student population rated their severe event as either having become worse or not changed at all by the end of the index day, the apparent absence of durable mood change is even more surprising.

Why have we been unable to detect lagged effects of severe events on mood? One possibility is that the events we have studied are not severe enough. Examination of individual subjects in our studies, however, shows that even subjects with the most severe events do not show carryover effects. It remains a possibility, however, that only truly catastrophic events, more severe than those studied by us, would yield mood changes of several days duration. Alternatively, it might be argued that we fail to detect lagged mood effects because our mood assessment on the lagged day occurs too late. All the intervening experiences of the lagged day may have an effect on that day's mood which obscures the effect of the severe event from the previous day. Finally, regardless of the foregoing, our data document the resiliency of our subjects. Across varying populations experiencing varied stressful events, people show a remarkable capacity to bounce back from an unpleasant experience.

CONCLUSIONS

This chapter has described our efforts aimed at understanding how daily events and the way that they are experienced relate to self-reported daily mood. This was accomplished using our ADE as the measure of daily experience and the MACL as the mood assessment. We have presented evidence showing that the ADE is an adequate measure of experiences and that daily ratings of mood with the MACL reasonably approximate point assessments of mood throughout a day. These measures, then, combined with the longitudinal designs of the studies reported are a powerful means for exploring events and mood.

Our findings concerning same-day relationships show that mood is related to day of the week in an unexpected manner: Mondays turn out not to be any more negative or any less positive than other days of the week, whereas weekends are less negative and more positive. A contrast effect may be operating when people summarize their feelings about "worst" and "best" days of the week. As for the content of events and their association with mood, we found that events in different life areas were in fact differentially related to mood. Undesirable work events and desirable family-leisure events were moderately related to mood, suggesting increased attention to these content areas in the conceptualization of stressful environments. Our attention to psychological appraisals that subjects gave events were also examined in an effort to determine the best predictors of concurrent mood. Although a wide variety of schemes were produced from the four appraisal dimensions, many of which directly related to the work of other researchers, we were somewhat surprised to find that a simple count of events rated as undesirable was essentially as effective a predictor as any of the more complex appraisal combinations. We do not interpret these results as a refutation of the theories underlying the appraisal combinations; it is, however, curious that appraisal dimensions with considerable face validity, for example, control and meaningfulness, added so little to the prediction of mood.

Our efforts at understanding lagged effects of events and mood focused on the effects of psychologically severe events; the assumption was that these sorts of events would have the highest likelihood of producing lagged mood effects. The events chosen for the analyses were based on subjects' appraisals of the experiences and yielded a set of events that, indeed, for the most part appeared capable of producing a high proportion of lagged effects. Counter to our expectations, we only observed same-day changes in negative and positive moods. This result was replicated in a second study using similar methodology and largely replicated in a college student sample. Extending the analysis to look separately at dysphoric versus nondysphoric subjects, as suggested by other researchers, did not produce a different mood pattern over days. These results call into question the idea that daily events have extended effects, at least on mood measures, and that later physical symptomatology is due to a multiday change in affective state.

REFERENCES

Abramson, L. Y., Seligman, M. E. P., & Teasdale, J. D. (1978). Learned helplessness in humans: Critique and reformulation. *Journal of Abnormal Psychology, 87,* 49–74.

Averill, J. R. (1973). Personal control over aversive stimuli and its relationship to stress. *Psychological Bulletin, 80,* 286–303.

Chiriboga, D. A., & Dean, H. (1978). Dimensions of stress: Perspectives from a longitudinal study. *Journal of Psychosomatic Research, 22,* 47–55.

Clark, D. M., & Teasdale, J. D. (1982). Diurnal variation in clinical depression and accessibility of memories of positive and negative experiences. *Journal of Abnormal Psychology, 91,* 87–95.

Farber, M. L. (1953). Time-perspective and feeling-tone: A study in the perception of the days. *Journal of Psychology, 35,* 253–257.

Goplerud, E., & Depue, R. A. (1985). Behavioral response to naturally occurring stress in cyclothymia and dysthymia. *Journal of Abnormal Psychology, 94,* 128–139.

Grosscup, S., & Lewinsohn, P. M. (1980). Unpleasant and pleasant events and mood. *Journal of Clinical Psychology, 36,* 252–259.

Hammen, C., & Mayol, A. (1982). Depression and cognitive characteristics of stressful life-event types. *Journal of Abnormal Psychology, 91,* 165–174.

Hedges, S. M., Jandorf, L., Stone, A. A. (1985). Meaning of daily mood assessments. *Journal of Personality and Social Psychology, 48,* 428–434.

Holmes, T. H., & Rahe, R. H. (1967). The social readjustment rating scale. *Journal of Psychosomatic Research, 11,* 213–218.

Hurst, M. W. (1979). Life changes and psychiatric symptom development: Issues of content, scoring, and clustering. In J. E. Barrett, R. M. Rose, & G. L. Klerman (Eds.), *Stress and mental disorders* (pp. 17–36). New York: Raven Press.

Lennox, S. S., & Stone, A. A. (1985). *Combinations of daily experiences associated with mood changes.* Manuscript submitted for publication.

Lewinsohn, P. M., & Amenson, C. S. (1978). Some relations between pleasant and unpleasant mood-related events and depression. *Journal of Abnormal Psychology, 87,* 644–654.

Lewinsohn, P. M., & Libet, J. (1972). Pleasant events, activity schedules, and depressions. *Journal of Abnormal Psychology, 79,* 291–295.

Mueller, D. P., Edwards, D. W., & Yarvis, R. M. (1978). Stressful life events and community mental health center patients. *Journal of Nervous and Mental Disease, 166,* 16–24.

Mullen, B. D. (1980, September). *Undesirable, uncontrollable life changes and illness: A prospective study.* Paper presented at the American Psychological Association meeting, Montreal, Canada.

Myers, J. K., Lindenthal, J. J., & Pepper, M. P. (1974). Social class, life events, and psychiatric symptoms: A longitudinal study. In B. S. Dohrenwend & B. P. Dohrenwend (Eds.), *Stressful life events: Their nature and effects* (pp. 191–205). New York: Wiley.

Nelson, R. E., & Craighead, W. E. (1977). Selective recall of positive and negative feedback, self-control behaviors, and depression. *Journal of Abnormal Psychology, 86,* 379–388.

Nelson, R. O. (1977). Methodological issues in assessment via self-monitoring. In J. D. Cone & R. P. Hawkins (Eds.), *Behavioral assessment: New directions in clinical psychology* (pp. 217–240). New York: Brunner-Mazel.

Nowlis, V. (1965). Research with the mood adjective checklist. In S. S. Tompkins & C. E. Izard (Eds.), *Affect, cognition and personality* (pp. 352–389). New York: Springer.

Paykel, E. S. (1974). Life stress and psychiatric disorder: Applications of the clinical approach. In B. S. Dohrenwend & B. P. Dohrenwend (Eds.), *Stressful life events: Their nature and effects* (pp. 135–149). New York: Wiley.

Pecjak, V. (1970). Verbal synesthesiae of colors, emotions, and days of the week. *Journal of Verbal Learning and Verbal Behavior, 9,* 623–626.

Rabkin, J. G., & Struening, E. L. (1976, December 3). Life events, stress, and illness. *Science, 194,* 1013–1020.

Rahe, R. H. (1972). Subjects' recent life changes and their near-future illness reports. *Annals of Clinical Research, 4,* 250–265.

Redfield, J., & Stone, A. A. (1979). Individual viewpoints of stressful life events. *Journal of Consulting and Clinical Psychology, 47,* 147–154.

Rehm, L. P. (1978). Mood, pleasant events, and unpleasant events: Two pilot studies. *Journal of Consulting and Clinical Psychology, 46,* 854–859.

Roghmann, K. J., & Haggerty, R. J. (1973). Daily stress, illness, and use of health services in young families. *Pediatric Research, 7,* 520–526.

Ross, C. E., & Mirowsky, J. (1979). A comparison of life-event weighting schemes: Change, undesirability, and effect-proportional indices. *Journal of Health and Social Behavior, 20,* 166–177.

Rossi, A. S., & Rossi, P. E. (1977). Body time and social time: Mood patterns by menstrual cycle phase and day of the week. *Social Science Research, 6,* 273–308.

Sarason, I. G., Johnson, J. H., & Siegal, I. M. (1978). Assessing the impact of life changes: Development of the Life Experience Survey. *Journal of Consulting and Clinical Psychology, 46,* 932–946.

Stone, A. A. (1981). The association between perceptions of daily experiences and self- and spouse-rated mood. *Journal of Research in Personality, 15,* 520–522.

Stone, A. A. (in press). Event content in a daily survey differentially predicts mood. *Journal of Personality and Social Psychology.*

Stone, A. A., & Neale, J. M. (1982). Development of a methodology for assessing daily experiences. In A. Baum & J. Singer (Eds.), *Environment and Health,* (Vol. IV, pp. 49–83). New York: Erlbaum.

Stone, A. A., & Neale, J. M. (1984a). Effects of severe daily events on mood. *Journal of Personality and Social Psychology, 46,* 137–144.

Stone, A. A., & Neale, J. M. (1984b). A new measure of daily coping: Development and preliminary results. *Journal of Personality and Social Psychology, 46,* 892–906.

Stone, A. A., Hedges, S. M., Neale, J. M., & Satin, M. S. (1985). Prospective and cross-sectional mood reports offer no evidence of a "blue Monday" phenomenon. *Journal of Personality and Social Psychology, 49,* 129–134.

Tversky, A., & Kahnemann, D. (1974). Judgements under uncertainty: Heuristics and biases. *Science, 185,* 1124–1131.

Ursin, H., Baade, E., & Levine, S. (1978). *Psychobiology of stress.* New York: Academic Press.

Zautra, A. J., & Reich, J. W. (1981). Positive events and quality of life. *Evaluation and Program Planning, 4,* 355–361.

8

Coping After a Relationship Ends

SHARON S. BREHM

The most typical form of romantic/sexual relationships in our society today is that of serial monogamy. Though our culture still plays lipservice through the mass media to the idea of one great love, the actual experience of the vast majority of our citizens involves an extended series of greater, or lesser, loves. Dating, for example, now begins at an extremely early age and lasts longer as the average age at first marriage has risen over the last decade Divorce has become commonplace and so has remarriage. Never before in human history have so many people had so many romantic/sexual involvements.

It should be noted that even this radical change in cultural mores continues to be constructed in terms of traditional differences between the genders (Brehm, 1985). What we might call strict serial monogamy is characteristic of females in our society, who regardless of their sexual orientation are only infrequently involved with multiple partners at any one time. Such multiple, nonexclusive involvements remain, by and large, a male preserve. Men's multiple involvements are, however, usually not equivalent in importance, and many males—gay and straight— engage in what can be called loose serial monogamy: a sequence of relatively nonoverlapping, serious involvements that stands out against the background of more casual encounters. Figuratively speaking, a woman's lovelife could be said to resemble a string of beads whereas a

SHARON S. BREHM • Department of Psychology, the University of Kansas, Lawrence, KS 66045.

man's approximates a tune heard above static. What is significant for the present argument is that both have increased in length.

The explanation for this dramatic increase over previous standards in the number of sequential primary partners rests, I believe, on the equally dramatic increase in personal freedom that we have achieved in this country. Some of that freedom is inherent in any technologically modern society; ease of transportation and communication increases all of our options in life, including the romantic ones. But some of this current personal freedom is more politically derived than it is technologically based. Sexual/romantic freedom has always been one of the privileges bestowed by power, and aristocrats and men have always had more sexual/romantic choices available to them than commoners and women. That ordinary people, especially ordinary female people, now have more of these choices than they used to reflects the shifting distribution of power in our society.

In addition to signifying the expansion of power and personal freedom among the members of formerly disadvantaged social groups, the current increase in the number of sequential primary partners has the added virtue of replacing the myth of the one great love with a more realistic view of sexual/emotional attachments between human beings. At most times in most societies, of course, most people experienced no great love at all, but were confined to whatever type of sexual/marital relationships that social norms and economic constraints dictated. When, however, we examine the lives of those who were in a position to have had some choice in the matter, most of them appear to have experienced that one great love more than once.

As important as it is not to romanticize the past history of romance and to recognize the political implications of appeals to return to singular monogamy, it is also necessary to face the problems that serial monogamy has brought in its wake. We need to be aware that serial monogamy involves repeated relational losses as well as repeated relational gains (Weingarten, 1985) and that, for many people, some of these losses can be catastrophic. The practice of serial monogamy may also contribute to a relational style of superficiality and lack of commitment. In the United States, beset as we are with the constant appeals of consumer capitalism to switch and move up to something better, we may be particularly prone to view our partners as disposable commodities we cast off once they are no longer of use to us. Although most of this chapter examines issues involved in coping with the end of a relationship, my concluding remarks will focus on how we may be able to avoid trivializing our existing attachments within the context of serial monogamy.

As we all know from our own personal experiences and/or observations of others, breaking up is rarely easy to do. At the extreme, some people kill themselves in despair, others kill the partner they are about to lose, and some kill the partner as a prelude to their own self-destruction. More generally, there is ample evidence (e.g., Bloom, Asher, & White, 1979; Somers, 1981) that the end of a marital relationship puts the former spouses at high risk for virtually every kind of physiological and psychological disaster imaginable. Although relationships not involving the legal contract of marriage do not leave behind the kind of archival records that allow us to track their effects in the systematic way we can study marriage and divorce, there is no reason to believe that personal devastation is restricted to the end of legally recognized commitments. Instead, we can take it as a basic principle that the end of any sexual/romantic relationship that the individual regards as meaningful in his or her life puts that individual at risk for psychological distress, physiological impairment, and behavioral disturbance. To reduce this risk we need to understand those factors that affect it, and I would suggest that those factors can be divided into three classes: the practical, the psychological, and the social.

THE PRACTICAL CONSEQUENCES OF THE END OF A RELATIONSHIP

The practical losses that an individual can sustain when a relationship ends are often severe. For couples that have pooled their financial resources, the breakup of the relationship often means a hard lesson in the truth of the old adage that two can live more cheaply than one. The financial consequences of a relationship's end are especially traumatic for heterosexual women who are usually dependent on the greater earning capacity of their male partners. Increasingly, "the poor" in our country consist of women and their children who have been divorced or deserted by their men (Ehrenreich, 1983). For all levels of socioeconomic status, divorced and widowed women suffer considerably more financial hardship than their male counterparts (e.g., Albrecht, 1980; Atchley, 1975; Guidubaldi & Cleminshaw, 1985; Mitchell, 1983).

Though financial assets usually constitute the most important practical contribution to a relationship that is lost if the relationship ends, money is only one of a large array of practical contributions partners make to an ongoing relationship. Much of being a couple involves the coordinated management of the daily tasks of life. Berscheid (1983) has called the assistance that one partner gives to the other in everyday endeavors facilitation, and notes that facilitation may become so embedded in a long-term relationship that the partners cease to be aware how much they are dependent on it. It is only when the relationship ends that the partners are faced with the absence of what they had previously taken for granted. Based on her application of Mandler's (1984) theory of emotion, Berscheid hypothesizes that it is the loss of such practical, day-to-day facilitation (e.g., sharing household chores, having someone to talk to, attending social events together) that determines one's emotional reaction after the breakup. The greater the amount of facilitation that has been lost (i.e., the greater the amount of interruption in one's organized behavioral sequences), the greater should be the individual's emotional distress.[1] Berscheid goes on to posit that emotional recovery should depend on "how rapidly (and if) the [person] can find a substitute means of completing these sequences" (p. 146).

Recently, some students and I began to investigate Bercheid's hypotheses. Our initial study (Stevenson, Brehm, & DeFelice, 1986) was, by necessity, a bootstrap operation. We examined only the heterosexual relationships of female college students and were not able in this first study to gather comparative data on gender, sexual orientation, or type of relationship. Moreover, like many who study relationships, we were forced to use a retrospective design, and had to develop many of our own measures, some of which were quite complex. Despite these limitations, the results of this research are not without some interesting implications.

The subjects in this study were 20 female students (all but one were undergraduates) who had broken up with their boyfriends 1 to 15 months previously (90% within the past 6 months); each subject was seen individually. At the first research session, subjects completed a battery of questionnaires (consisting mostly of widely used and well-established measures) assessing their current adjustment (e.g., mood, health, social life). At the second session, subjects were interviewed on either (a) their emotional response immediately after the breakup or (b) the day-to-day assistance their former partner had provided them in 12 multi-item areas of assistance and, for each specific item of assistance, whether they

---

[1]An alternative formulation to Berscheid's notion of facilitation is provided by Stephen (1984) who develops a concept of symbolic interdependence (defined as "a shared view of the world") rather than emphasizing more practical/behavioral kinds of interdependence. In his longitudinal study of undergraduate couples, Stephen found that although symbolic interdependence did not predict which of these couples would breakup during the 6 months period they participated in the research, it was significantly related to postbreakup distress. Those individuals who indicated more symbolic interdependence with their partner when first assessed displayed greater emotional distress after the breakup had occurred.

had found someone else to assist them since the breakup. The third session consisted of whichever interview had not been given at the second session.

To test the predictions based on Berscheid's theoretical proposals, we looked at two major sets of correlations. First, if emotional response immediately after the breakup is determined by loss of facilitation, then there should be a correlation between reported amount of loss in day-to-day assistance from the former partner and recalled emotional response immediately after the relationship ended. Because Berscheid (following Mandler) places particular emphasis on the debilitating effect of unexpected losses (i.e., "interruptions"), this correlation between loss and emotional response should be more likely to occur for those who (at least according to their retrospective accounts) were unprepared for the breakup than for those who saw it coming. Second, a similar set of correlations was examined in regard to subjects' total current coping score. In this case, there should be a correlation between the amount of current loss (i.e., the original loss of assistance in each area corrected for substitutes obtained since the breakup) and overall level of current adjustment; the impact of subjects' expectations about the occurrence of the breakup was also investigated for these variables.

When the total emotional response score was correlated with the 12 areas of immediate loss (education, occupation, transportation, health, leisure activities, friends, emotional sharing, sexual activity, residence, household tasks, future plans made by the couple before the breakup, and past opportunities deferred by the subject in order to maintain the relationship), only one significant correlation was obtained. Among those subjects who were relatively surprised by the relationship's coming to an end, greater immediate loss of sexual activities was associated with a greater degree of negative emotional response, $r(9) = .79, p < .01$. There were no significant correlations between immediate loss and emotional response for those subjects who had expected the relationship to end.

When current coping was correlated with current loss, three marginally significant correlations were obtained. Only one of these was consistent with Berscheid's formulation: greater current loss of sexual activity was associated with poorer current coping for subjects who had not expected the relationship to terminate, $r(9) = -.58, p < .10$. The other two marginally significant correlations found between current loss and current coping were either opposite in direction from the association predicted by Berscheid's model (among low expectation subjects, greater loss of future plans once planned with the partner was associated with better coping, $r(9) = .61, p < .10$) or unique to subjects who had expected the relationship to end (greater current losses in the area of education being associated for these subjects with poorer current coping, $r(11) = -.57, p < .10$).

Thus, out of 12 areas of assistance, only the effects of loss of sexual activity (a measure that examined singularity of sexual involvement with the former partner as well as intensity of sexual activity directly preceding the breakup) were uniform across time (being associated with retrospective reports of immediate emotional response as well as with the index of current coping) and specific to the low expectation group. In these analyses, subjects' expectations were measured in terms of a question concerning how much they had expected the breakup to occur. It is possible, however, to define expectations in terms more directly related to emotional experience. Thus, subjects in this study were also asked how much they had expected to feel the way they did after the breakup had taken place. The correlation between these two questions was nonsignificant.

When the associations between loss and response were examined as a function of subjects' expectations about their postbreakup feelings, significant correlations were obtained for the incongruent group (i.e., those who had not expected to have the feelings they had) in four areas of assistance; all four involved the association between current loss and current coping. Three of these correlations were in the predicted direction, such that greater loss was associated with poorer coping: sexual activities, $r(8) = -.82, p < .01$; emotional sharing, $r(8) = -.70, p < .05$; leisure activities, $r(8) = -.82, p < .01$. The remaining correlation between current loss and current coping for those subjects who had not expected their postbreakup feelings was in the opposite direction from that predicted by Berscheid's model; greater loss of future plans was associated with better coping, $r(8) = .78, p < .05$. Among those subjects who indicated that they had expected to feel the way they did after the relationship ended, there was only one significant correlation between loss and response, with a greater immediate loss of friends being associated with a greater negative emotional reaction immediately after the breakup, $r(12) = .60, p < .05$. There were no significant correlations between immediate loss and emotional response for incongruent-expectations subjects, nor any between current loss and current coping for congruent-expectations subjects.

When the data from the analyses concerning expectations to occur and expectations about feelings are considered together, two basic patterns emerge. First, among the young women participating in this study, the overall relationship between loss of partner assistance (immediately after the breakup or corrected for later substitutes obtained) and personal adjustment was not strong. There were few significant correlations relative to the total number of loss–response associations that were examined. Second, of the five correlations that reached the reasonably robust magnitude of .70 or better, four of them were in the direction and among the expectation groups that would be predicted by Berscheid's model. These two patterns suggest the possibility that different types of losses may differ in importance for different types of relationships. Subjects in the present study had not been married to nor cohabitating with their former partners. For such young women, many areas of practical assistance may have been irrelevant. The areas of loss that were associated here with more problems in coping with the breakup (sexual activities, companionship in leisure activities, having a confidant with whom to share feelings) may, then, simply reflect the reality of the kind of partner assistance that young, unmarried females value highly, and, therefore, the kind of loss that those who were unprepared for the end of their romantic relationship would miss the most.

Whether we conceptualize expectations in terms of expecting the breakup to occur or of becoming aware of the feelings we will have after the relationship has ended, the notion that we suffer most from relationship losses that we have not anticipated is also one of the major conclusions reached by investigators who have studied the widowed (Glick, Weiss, & Parkes, 1974) and the divorced (Spanier & Castro, 1979; Weiss, 1975). In addition, it appears that preparedness and gender may interact so as to influence the time course of an individual's distress during the divorce process. There is some evidence (Chiriboga & Cutler, 1977; Green, 1983; Hagestad & Smyer, 1982; Jacobson, 1982) that for women the worst time is prior to the actual separation/divorce, whereas for men the worst time is afterward. Women may, then, be more fully cognizant of what they will lose as a consequence of divorce and suffer as they weigh these anticipated losses against whatever benefits they believe they could derive from marital dissolution. In contrast, men may be relatively naive about what they will lose if the marriage ends, and the unexpectedness of the losses they do suffer may serve to increase the emotional distress they experience after the separation/divorce.

It seems reasonable to assume that this kind of gender difference in foreseeability and preparedness comes about by means of the division of labor built into the structure of traditional marriage, where the husband's contribution of a paycheck is highly visible to both spouses whereas the wife's contribution of personal services can more easily be taken for granted. In fact, however, any strict division of labor (whether based on gender or personal preference) within a relationship should make both partners more vulnerable to catastrophic loss after the relationship ends. This proposition is perhaps best documented in Chiriboga and

Thurner's (1980) study of the relationship between (retrospectively recalled) marital life-style and personal happiness after marital separation.
These researchers found a general tendency (which differed in its partic-
ulars depending on gender and age) for individuals who reported having
been less dependent on their spouse's skills and interests to be happier
after separation from the spouse than those individuals who reported
having been more dependent on the spouse. Thus, although two halves
may sometimes form a convenient whole, either half is likely to have a
hard time standing alone.

   This consideration of the practical consequences of the end of a
relationship suggests that practical losses cannot be understood outside of
a context that is both psychological and structural. A practical loss that is
anticipated and prepared for may be less of a loss. Some practical losses,
however, result not so much from the personal characteristics of the
individuals involved as from societal structures that allocate different
roles to different groups of people. Moreover, there may be an interaction
between the psychological and the structural such that the impending loss
of the more visible contributions to a relationship is more readily anticipated and prepared for, but such contributions may also be more difficult
to replace. Future research on the effects and correlates of relational
losses might well profit from taking these two factors more explicitly into
account. Was the specific loss itself (as opposed to the overall loss of the
relationship) expected and was the person prepared for his or her emotional reaction to that loss? Has the person tried to obtain a substitute for
that specific loss (by being with another person and/or learning new skills
oneself), and, if so, how difficult has that proved to be? Researchers in the
area of close relationships are now in a position to move beyond conceptualizing loss in general and rather vague terms to an investigation of how
particular losses, embedded in a psychological and structural context,
affect individuals who have lost particular types of relationships.

PERCEIVED RESPONSIBILITY FOR THE BREAKUP

   In addition to pointing out the possible effects of being prepared for
the end of a relationship, researchers interested in psychological factors
that may promote better postrelationship coping have also examined
people's perceptions of responsibility for the breakup. One way in which
responsibility has been assessed is in terms of initiator status—that is,
who left whom. Or, more precisely, what people say about who left
whom, because former partners do not always agree in their accounts
about who initiated the breakup (Hill, Rubin, & Peplau, 1976). Though
earlier studies (e.g., Goode, 1956; Hill et al., 1976; Spanier & Thompson,

1983) had concluded that those who said they left fared better than those who said they were left, more recent work by Pettit and Bloom (1984) has questioned the magnitude and endurance of any such leavetaking advantage.

Subjects in the study by Pettit and Bloom were 144 newly separated men and women who were divided into two categories: initiators, who reported having had primary responsibility for the decision to separate or who perceived the separation as based on a mutual decision (preliminary analyses of the data indicated no significant differences between these two groups on the dependent measures)[2] versus noninitiators, who attributed primary responsibility for the decision to their spouses. Pettit and Bloom administered a large number of measures throughout the course of their longitudinal study; surprisingly, however, few differences were obtained between initiators and noninitiators. At first, initiators did report more positive self-regard than noninitiators, but self-regard did not differ between the two groups at follow-up assessments conducted 6 and 18 months later. Indeed, only two benefits of viewing oneself as an initiator were reasonably stable throughout the study. Initiators (male and female) indicated a more positive attitude toward being divorced than did noninitiators; female initiators perceived more benefits from being divorced than female noninitiators. Thus, the results of this unusually thorough study suggest that "only a small proportion of the variance in adjustment to marital disruption is accounted for by initiator status" (p. 592).

One explanation for why initiator status may not be a particularly powerful predictor of coping after a relationship has ended is that knowing who makes the decision to leave tells us nothing about the process that led up to that decision. One individual may leave a relationship to pursue what he or she believes is a better alternative relationship; another person may feel driven to leave by what he or she considers intolerable behavior by the partner (Kabatznick, 1985). Both leave, but for very different reasons. People's perceptions of the reasons why the relationship ended might, therefore, be more crucial for their later adjustment than their understanding of who left whom.

This was exactly the approach to the matter taken by Newman and Langer (1981). The divorced women who participated in this study were asked to "explain the main reason why they had become divorced."

[2]This commonality between self-initiated and mutually initiated divorces contradicts the finding by Thompson and Spanier (1983) that for the divorced males in their study, mutual initiation was associated with better adjustment (i.e., more acceptance of marital termination) than was either self- or spouse-initiated divorce. Initiator status was not significantly related to the adjustment of their divorced females.

Their responses were then divided by judges into two categories: explanations that emphasized the (negative) characteristics of the spouse (e.g., his selfishness) versus those that emphasized the unsatisfying nature of the interaction between the partners (e.g., lack of closeness). Interestingly, none of these women supplied explanations that emphasized their own characteristics (positive or negative). At three different measurement times (immediately after giving their explanations, 10 days later, and 6 months later), those women who had pointed to their spouse's deficiencies as the main reason for the divorce appeared to be adjusting less well than those who had focused on an unsatisfying marital interaction.

Newman and Langer interpret their results in terms of person as opposed to interactive attributions of responsibility for the failure of a relationship. Their position is that interactive attributions, in which both partners are viewed as sharing the responsibility, foster better coping after the end of a relationship, whereas person attributions, in which negative characteristics of either partner or self are viewed as responsible, interfere with adequate coping. Unfortunately, Newman and Langer could not fully evaluate this proposal in their study because they did not have a group of subjects who cited their own characteristics as the main reason for the divorce.

Moreover, close inspection of the interconnections among the measures employed by Newman and Langer reveals a complicated set of findings not easily accommodated by any single theoretical principle. For example, there seems to be no compelling reason to expect that those women who relied on their husband's negative characteristics to explain why they were divorced would blame themselves for failure in general. Yet when Newman and Langer asked their subjects how much they "blamed themselves rather than outside forces for failures," subjects who made person attributions to the spouse took on greater general self-blame than did subjects who made interactive attributions. Self-blame was also greater among those women who reported that their spouse had initiated the divorce than for those who said they initiated it, and there was some evidence of lower self-esteem among noninitiators who made person attributions. However, though person attributions and non-initiator status were each related to increased self-blame and, conjointly, to decreased self-esteem, the two variables themselves were imperfectly correlated. Indeed, among those women who made person attributions to the husband's negative characteristics, more were initiators than non-initiators.

Some other findings relevant to the effects of perceived responsibility for the breakup come from data collected during the previously described study (Stevenson *et al.*, 1986) of college-age women who had recently experienced the termination of a heterosexual involvement. These young women were asked to allocate responsibility for the break-up among themselves, their former partners, and "other" factors in terms of their perceptions immediately after the breakup and now. Analyses of the effects of attributions to self and partner suggest that perceived responsibility was a relatively weak predictor of either past or present adjustment status. Attributions of responsibility to the self or to the partner, for immediately after the breakup or currently, were not significantly related to either (retrospectively recalled) immediate emotional response or current coping.

Furthermore, changes in attributions of responsibility (i.e., immediately after the breakup to now) for either self or partner failed to correlate significantly with current coping, and there were no significant correlations between immediate attributions to self or partner and immediate loss perceived in the 12 areas of partner assistance examined in this study. There was some evidence, however, that current attributions of responsibility were associated with current loss (i.e., immediate loss corrected for substitutes obtained). Two significant correlations were obtained between current attribution of responsibility to self and current loss (in the areas of transportation assistance and help with education), whereas three were found between current attribution of responsibility to partner and current loss (in the areas of transportation, leisure time companionship, and future plans). This set of correlations indicated that subjects who presently attributed greater responsibility to themselves perceived greater current losses, whereas attributing greater responsibility to the partner was associated in two (transportation, leisure) out of the three instances with the perception of less loss.

Overall, these data fail to support Newman and Langer's contention that attributing responsibility for the breakup to either self or the former partner "may be harmful . . . in the long run" (p. 231). What little evidence there was in the Stevenson *et al.* study that attributions of responsibility were associated with adjustment did suggest that self-attributions may be harmful, because self attributions were associated with greater perceived loss. In contrast, partner attributions in the Stevenson *et al.* study tended to be associated with less perceived loss and, thus, may to some extent constitute a benefit. To add to the empirical confusion, however, it should be noted that Spanier and Thompson (1984) found no such advantage for partner attributions relative to attributions of responsibility to the self. Indeed, among the separated and divorced women in their study, assigning blame to others as opposed to taking at least some of the blame on oneself for the dissolution of the relationship was associated with poorer coping. There was no association between source of blame and postbreakup coping for the men in the study by Spanier and Thompson.

At this point, I presume that the reader is as uncertain as I am about the role of perceived responsibility in adjusting to the end of a relationship. It is extremely difficult to develop any kind of coherent conceptual framework out of the findings described in this section; too many of the bits and pieces do not fit together. It may be, of course, that what we are dealing with is in essence a methodological artifact. For example, two of the studies mentioned here (Newman & Langer, 1981; Stevenson *et al.*, 1986) were conducted with small, volunteer subject samples, which may be unrepresentative of the larger populations of interest. It is also possible, however, that the confusing state of these data reflects the complex state of reality. In particular, it should be noted that the three studies investigating causal accounts used different terms (Newman & Langer: "reason"; Spanier & Thompson: "blame"; Stevenson *et al.*: "responsibility"), and that Pettit and Bloom (1984) did not examine subjects' perceptions of personal/interpersonal causation. Although the lack of methodological and empirical consistency across studies can be lamented, it can also be taken seriously to suggest that perceiving who is responsible for the breakup of a relationship may be a multidimensional psychological process, the components of which we should not expect to fit together in any simple fashion. There may well be actual, crucial differences among one's perceptions of reasons for the breakup of a relationship, one's allocation of responsibility for the breakup, the blame one places for that and other disappointments in life, and the view one has of one's own actions in regard to ending the relationship. Until we have a more adequate conceptual framework for considering these various psychological factors (see Fincham & Jaspars, 1980, for their comments on this issue), we are going to have great difficulty assessing their impact on the way people cope after a relationship is over.

THE ROLE OF SOCIAL SUPPORT

Another factor that may affect the ease or difficulty of the transition into a new postbreakup life-style and the quality of that new life-style once established is social support from people other than the former partner. Though this proposition seems commonsensical in the extreme, cogent evaluation of it is made difficult by the interpretive problems characterizing so much of the empirical research literature on social support. I will not try to review this literature here (see Cohen & Wills,

1985; also Brehm & Smith, 1986), but will point out that the fundamental reason for our now having a massive data base that yields few readily comprehensible views of the social support process itself is that so much previous research on social support proceeded in the complete absence of a conceptual definition of what was being measured. In this chapter, I want to briefly describe two more recent approaches to social support that may help us to generate a more coherent understanding.

Social Networks. Network analysis views every individual as being embedded in a social network and proposes that some kinds of networks will be more beneficial than others as a function of the specific coping requirements of an individual's current situation. Thus, network analysis seeks to determine the fit between various network characteristics and level of adjustment to specific life events. It makes no *a priori* assumptions about any one type of network's being uniformly beneficial and, therefore, avoids the rather mindless optimism of early research on social support that seemed to view all social interaction as necessarily supportive and never, in itself, stressful.

A study by Wilcox (1981) illustrates what network analysis can tell us about adjustment after the end of a relationship. Wilcox assessed the social networks of a group of divorced females, half of whom were evaluated as adjusting well to the divorce and the other half as adjusting poorly. Retrospective accounts of their predivorce social networks indicated no significant differences between the two groups in terms of range (number of members) and density (interconnectedness among members). However, by comparing the predivorce social network members designated by the women in the study with their ex-husbands' reports of their own predivorce social networks, it was found that the women who were having greater difficulty adjusting after the divorce had predivorce networks that overlapped with those of their husbands to a greater extent than did those of women who were adjusting better after the divorce. Poor adjustment was also associated with increased reliance on relatives (as opposed to nonkin) for emotional and tangible support after the divorce and greater turnover in network membership from the pre- to postdivorce periods. These latter findings have been replicated by Spanier and Hanson (1981), who found a slightly negative relationship between reported support from kin and adjustment after divorce, and in a study by Daniels-Mohring and Berger (1984), in which greater change in divorced individuals' social networks was associated with poorer adjustment.

Although Wilcox's results are, in part, retrospective and, in whole, correlational, they suggest the possibility that having one's own friends during the marriage may be a crucial component in promoting better adjustment after the marriage ends. That is, women whose friendships are more shared with their husbands may suffer more friendship losses as a consequence of divorce. This greater loss may then contribute to their turning more toward family members for assistance in coping with the divorce—an assistance that as Kasl and Wells (1985) note may be problematic if "the source of help disapproves of the stressful event (divorce)" (p. 188). Becoming more embedded in kinship networks may also inhibit efforts to establish new social contacts in the wider world.[3]

The Attributional Connection. My own research on social support has been concerned with avoiding the limitations of correlational methods and attempting to document a causal sequence in the social support process. From my perspective (Brehm, 1982; 1984; Hunt & Brehm, 1986), the essence of social support is that it gives you the confidence that there are people out there who will respond positively to you and will, if you need it, help you out. Thus, my emphasis is not on the characteristics of one's social network nor on the number or type of specific acts of good will a person has received in the past, but rather on the person's expectations about what will be available in the future. However, because optimistic expectations must themselves arise from one's past history of social interaction, the theoretical task is to figure out how individuals translate their specific social histories into more general positive expectations about future social events.

As investigators (Major, Carrington, & Carnevale, 1984; Sigall & Michela, 1976) have noted in regard to extremely physically attractive individuals, the psychological benefits we receive from the prosocial actions of others may depend, at least in part, on the causal attributions we make for these actions. For those who are extremely physically attractive, the dilemma arises from trying to differentiate other people's response to physical beauty from their response to the "real person" underneath. For most of the rest of us, the problem is not so much the "Marilyn Monroe syndrome" of discounting love as physical attraction, but of sorting among alternative causal agents such as our own personal characteristics, other people's characteristic response biases, and situational constraints mandating social behavior. In general, it should be the case

---

[3]Chiriboga and Thurner (1980) provide only mixed confirmation of the value of social independence during marriage. In their large sample of individuals who had filed for divorce, retrospective reports of having had separate friends while married were associated with reduced happiness after the separation for women over 40 and men under 40. However, for these same groups, retrospective reports of having had separate social activities while married were associated with greater happiness after the separation. For the two remaining groups (women under 40 and men over 40), neither separateness of friends nor of social activities was significantly correlated with post-separation happiness.

that when we can believe that someone has behaved positively toward us because that person responded to our own desirable, enduring personal characteristics, we should gain both self-esteem and confidence that, in the future, others too will respond positively to us. Furthermore, confidence that people have responded and will continue to respond positively to us because of our enduring personal characteristics[4] should reduce the pressure on us to conform our behavior to social norms, as the belief in one's own personal power to elicit social approval offsets the need to try to ensure that approval through behavioral conventionality. Thus, when we interpret positive actions we receive from others as implying support for the way we are, this kind of social support can set us free.

Initially, I assumed that the connection between various types of causal accounts for prosocial actions received and subsequent personal autonomy vis-à-vis others should be manifest regardless of the current state of the individual involved. This *main effect hypothesis* should be distinguished from what is called the *buffer hypothesis* of social support, which states that social support produces its primary or sole benefit when the individual encounters stressful life events. The buffer hypothesis has been one of the most popular perspectives in the study of social support, though the relevant empirical findings are decidedly mixed (e.g., see reviews by Cohen & Wills, 1985; Thoits, 1982; Wallston, Alagna, De-Vellis, & DeVellis, 1983). None of this previous research, however, examined the role of causal attributions in the social support process.

In the course of pilot work on the present attributional model, repeated difficulties in demonstrating a reliable difference between subjects who were provided a receiver attribution (i.e., led to attribute the apparently spontaneous prosocial behavior of an experimental confederate to the confederate's response to the subject's own desirable personal characteristics) and subjects in various control conditions (e.g., no attribution: the confederate behaved prosocially, but no attribution for this behavior was provided by the experimenter; no prosocial behavior: there was no spontaneous prosocial behavior on the part of the confederate) suggested to us that we should consider the possibility of combining the attributional model with the buffer hypothesis. Perhaps when people are in a relatively good mood and feeling relatively self-confident (as we assume most of our subjects usually are), causal attributions about good

---

[4]The full model (Brehm, 1982) also describes another form of social support called communally-based social support, in distinction to the personally-based social support discussed in this chapter. As an empirical examination of communally-based social support has only just begun, this aspect of the model will not be addressed here.

events are relatively unimportant (Schwarz & Clore, 1983). On the other hand, when people undergo stressful experiences that can damage their self-esteem, causal attributions about previous good events may function to prevent decreases in self-regard.

There is some evidence from research on psychotherapy and behavior change programs that is consistent with this notion that buffering effects may be mediated by causal attributions. Studies of client attributions (see Brehm & Smith, 1986, for a review) have suggested that when clients attribute their therapeutic progress to their own efforts and capabilities (instead of attributing it to, for example, the skills of the therapist or the structure of the program), the prospects for maintaining therapeutic gains are enhanced. What is particularly noteworthy in the present context is that these self attributions do not appear to produce immediate therapeutic benefit, but only affect long-term maintenance. One way to account for such delayed action is to posit that self-confident attributions about the therapeutic endeavor help create a more general self-confidence, which serves to buffer the individual against the stresses of daily life. The need for such a buffer should become most pronounced once the therapeutic relationship has ended and the therapist is no longer available to give assistance and encouragement.

A recently completed study by Hunt & Brehm (1986) examined the possible relationship between causal attributions and reactions to stress in terms of the present model of social support processes. We hypothesized that receiver attribution subjects should maintain self-confident, autonomous social behavior in the face of personal stress, whereas subjects who had not received this attribution should decrease in autonomy as a function of stress. Cross-cutting the four experimental conditions of interest (receiver attribution, no attribution, no prosocial behavior—all described earlier—and a provider attribution condition, in which subjects were led to attribute the confederate's prosocial behavior to the confederate's desirable personal characteristics) with a stress manipulation, we found that subjects conformed more to peer opinions under stress than under no stress conditions except when they had been given a receiver attribution for a prosocial action received prior to, and independently from, the stressful experience. Thus, the receiver attribution acted as a buffer against the usual reduction in attitudinal autonomy produced by stress. This pattern of means (see Table 1) is exactly as had been predicted, yields a significant planned comparison ($df = 1, 88$; $F = 4.27$; $p < .05$), and accounts for 70% of the between-subject variance. However, the effect was not strong enough to produce a significant interaction on the overall 2×4 ANOVA.

We would, of course, have preferred a stronger effect, but I believe

Table 1. Conformity to Peer Opinions

Experimental condition	No stress	Stress
Receiver attribution	1.15	1.09
Provider attribution	1.14	1.28
No attribution	1.02	1.34
No prosocial behavior	1.01	1.19

Note. $n = 12$ per cell; the higher the number, the greater the conformity.

that these results are sufficient to suggest that the process of social support may be far more complicated and delicate than many investigators have assumed. It may not be enough to have helpful, supportive people around when one is confronted with stressful events—whether one benefits from these positive encounters may depend on how one interprets their causal origins. If we discount the importance of our own desirable characteristics in eliciting positive behavior toward us (e.g., "You have to say that, you're my mother/therapist"), then what looks from the outside like ample social support may on the inside produce remarkably little benefit. The kind of social support we need after the end of a relationship may require the presence of individuals who express their positive regard for us and whose loving judgment of us we take to heart.

COPING BETTER AFTER A RELATIONSHIP ENDS

This review of various factors, at least some of which appear to exert some influence on how well individuals cope after the end of a relationship, suggests that life after the breakup is likely to be better if before the breakup the person (a) has an adequate source of income independent of the partner; (b) is reasonably skilled in performing a wide range of the tasks of daily life; and (c) has a nonkin social network that is independent of the partner. In addition to these relatively objective assets, there may be certain states of mind that reduce the stress of adjusting to the end of a relationship, such as (a) having faced the possibility of the dissolution of the relationship and being, to some degree, prepared for how it will feel to be without it; and (b) being able to believe that those who care about us do so because we are worth caring about. Though I have here separated these two sets of tentative prescriptions into the more objective and the more subjective, I suspect that in reality they are closely related. The person who has a life of his or her own should be more prepared (both practically and psychologically) for the end of a relationship and should be less likely to regard the failure of a relationship as proving total failure as a human being. To have a life of one's own, as well as a life with the partner, appears to me to be the best insurance for surviving life without the partner.

It is not, however, the policy most widely subscribed to. Regardless of what people's lives were like during a relationship, the most popular solution to losing one partner is to find another one; among the divorced, for example, it is estimated (Burgess, 1981) that some 80% eventually remarry (with men remarrying more often and more quickly than do women).[5] What is unclear about this process of sequential marriages, and about serial monogamy in general, is how much of it reflects the self-sufficiency of people who do not suffer from excessive dependency on a single partner, and how much of it derives from a lack of self-security sufficient enough for people to be either personally independent or interpersonally committed.

When we think over these alternatives of independence and commitment, we can find ourselves behaving like bewildered philosophers, going back and forth over the various relevant moral precepts. On the one hand, most of us believe independence is a good; we are all, after all, existentially alone and there is some honor in confronting that aloneness. On the other hand, we regard superficiality as an evil; people should not be treated as though they were things to be used and then discarded. Then again, leaving a harmful relationship is considered a mark of strength; however, failing to make an effort to sustain a relationship would be a weakness. But, we note, women have to be especially careful about how they respond to any pronunciamento advocating commitment to others. The historical record is quite clear that it has been men who preached the virtue of self-sacrifice whereas women were required to practice it. And yet, what reasonable person (male or female) would want to endorse the stereotypical masculine modes of aggression ("strong") and fear of intimacy ("silent")?

I have no philosopher's stone to offer to still this debate within our society and within ourselves. I do have, however, a couple of suggestions

---

[5]The extent of the remarrying inclinations of Americans is further demonstrated by Cherlin and McCarthy's (1985) estimate that at present 20% of married households in the U.S. involve at least one individual who has been married (to someone else) before. It should also be noted that second marriages are more at risk for divorce than are first ones: the median length of marriage before divorce is 5 years for a second marriage as compared to 7 years for a first marriage (Cherlin, 1983); the estimated current divorce rate for second marriages runs from around 49% to 61% as compared to an estimated rate of 47% to 49% for first marriages (Furstenberg & Spanier, 1984). Increasingly, it appears that the likelihood of fulfilling the promise "till death us do part" has more to do with the age of the participants than with the intended strength of the commitment.

that might help us get off the horns of this dilemma and get on with building lives that we can, as Mary Gordon (1981) says, "admire [ourselves] for living." First, we must eradicate gender dimorphism: in terms of women's economic and political inferiority, of behavioral competencies that make men and women excessively dependent on the skills of the opposite sex, and of the distribution of attachment and autonomy within heterosexual relationships. This eradication must take place on a societal level, not simply as a personal arrangement. For as long as the society in which we live remains fundamentally sexist in its beliefs and practices, it is delusional to hope for genuinely egalitarian relationships between individual men and women.

Second, we can begin to think about possible variations on the theme of serial monogamy. Here I do not mean the strict and loose versions I mentioned previously, but what we might call discrete and cumulative forms. In the discrete form, each relationship is a separate event in one's life, and so each one is erased when another begins. In the cumulative form, the commitment between the two individuals continues though the nature of their relationship may change (Brehm, 1985; Kelley, 1983). Recognizing that serial monogamy can be cumulative means that we acknowledge that we have a choice: we can choose to discard our former partners or we can choose to keep them with us. Should we be able to develop a capacity to fall in love in anticipation of permanent friendship and to turn former lovers into present friends, we might just be able to change serial monogamy from a history of repeated failure into an evolving, continuous process of caring. We might also be able to create relationships that are mutually affirming rather than either superficial or enslaving.

From this perspective, the real issue is not so much how we can cope better with the end of a relationship, but how we can better construct the relationships we have. The terrible pain and suffering that so many people have experienced as they have been tossed about in the throes of serial monogamy have forced us to begin to question all of our preconceived notions about relationships and, therefore, to take on the arduous task of coming up with some new possibilities. It is this effort, and my faith in its eventual outcome, that leads me to regard at least some of our affliction as a blessing in disguise.

ACKNOWLEDGMENTS

A number of individuals contributed to the two research projects described in this chapter. For their intellectual stimulation, hard work, and good humor despite all the obstacles we encountered along the way, I want to thank Paul Biner, Diane Cade, Dawn Conell, Willard Davis, Judy

DeFelice, Holly Hunt, Jeanne Miranda, Julie Phillips, Cathy Stevenson, and Debbie Taylor. I am also grateful to the General Research Fund of the University of Kansas for its financial assistance in carrying out the research on social support. An earlier version of this chapter was presented at Bucknell University as part of the Central Pennsylvania Lecture Series, March 13, 1985.

REFERENCES

Albrecht, S. L. (1980). Reactions and adjustments to divorce: Differences in the experiences of males and females. *Family Relations, 29,* 59–68.

Atchley, R. C. (1975). Dimensions of widowhood in later life. *Gerontologist, 15,* 176–178.

Berscheid, E. (1983). Emotion. In H. H. Kelley, E. Berscheid, A. Christensen, J. Harvey, T. Huston, G. Leringer, E. McClintock, L. Peplau, & D. Peterson. (Eds.), *Close relationships* (pp. 110–168). New York: W. H. Freeman.

Bloom, B., Asher, S. J., & White, S. W. (1978). Marital disruption as a stressor: A review and analysis. *Psychological Bulletin, 85,* 867–894.

Brehm, S. S. (1982). Social support processes: Theoretical and methodological issues. *Recherches de Psychologie Social, 4,* 25–34.

Brehm, S. S. (1984). Social support processes. In J. C. Masters & K. Yarkin-Levin (Eds.), *Boundary areas in social and developmental psychology* (pp. 107–129). New York: Academic Press.

Brehm, S. S. (1985). *Intimate relationships.* New York: Random House.

Brehm, S. S., & Smith, T. W. (1986). Social psychological approaches to psychotherapy and behavior change. In S. Garfield & A. E. Bergin (Eds.), *Handbook of psychotherapy and behavior change* (pp. 69–115, 3rd Ed.). New York: Wiley.

Burgess, R. L. (1981). Relationships in marriage and the family. In S. Duck & R. Gilmour (Eds.), *Personal relationships 1: Studying personal relationships* (pp. 179–196). New York: Academic Press.

Cherlin, A. (1983). The trends: Marriage, divorce, remarriage. In A. S. Skolnick & J. H. Skolnick (Eds.), *Family in transition* (pp. 128–137, 4th ed.). Boston, MA: Little, Brown.

Cherlin, A., & McCarthy, J. (1985). Remarried couple households: Data from the June 1980 current population survey. *Journal of Marriage and the Family, 47,* 23–30.

Chiriboga, D. A., & Cutler, L. (1977). Stress responses among divorcing men and women. *Journal of Divorce, 1* (Winter), 95–106.

Chiriboga, D. A., & Thurner, M. (1980). Marital lifestyles and adjustment to separation. *Journal of Divorce, 3*(Summer), 379–390.

Cohen, S., & Wills, T. A. (1985). Stress, social support, and the buffering hypothesis. *Psychological Bulletin, 98,* 310–357.

Daniels-Mohring, D., & Berger, M. (1984). Social network changes and the adjustment to divorce. *Journal of Divorce, 8*(Fall), 17–32.

Ehrenreich, B. (1983). *The hearts of men.* Garden City, NY: Anchor Press/Doubleday.

Fincham, F. D., & Jaspars, J. M. F. (1980). Attribution of responsibility: From man the scientist to man as lawyer. In L. Berkowitz (Ed.), *Advances in experimental social psychology* (Vol. 13, pp. 81–138). New York: Academic Press.

Furstenberg, F. F., Jr., & Spanier, G. B. (1984). The risk of dissolution in remarriage: An examination of Cherlin's hypothesis of incomplete institutionalization. *Family Relations, 33,* 433–441.

Glick, I. O., Weiss, R., & Parkes, C. M. (1974). *The first year of bereavement.* New York: Wiley.

Goode, W. J. (1956). *After divorce.* Glencoe, IL: Free Press.

Gordon, M. (1981). *The company of women.* New York: Ballantine Books.

Green, R. G. (1983). The influence of divorce prediction variables on divorce adjustment: An expansion and test of Lewis' and Spanier's theory of marital quality and stability. *Journal of Divorce, 7*(Fall), 67–81.

Guidubaldi, J., & Cleminshaw, H. (1985). Divorce, family health, and child adjustment. *Family Relations, 34,* 35–41.

Hagestad, G. O., & Smyer, M. A. (1982). Dissolving long-term relationships: Patterns of divorcing in middle age. In S. Duck (Ed.), *Personal relationships 4: Dissolving relationships* (pp. 155–188). New York: Academic Press.

Hill, C. T., Rubin Z., & Peplau, L. A. (1976). Breakups before marriage: The end of 103 affairs. *Journal of Social Issues, 32,* 147–168.

Hunt, H. A., & Brehm, S. S. (1986). *Social support processes: Causal attributions, stress, and conformity.* Unpublished paper, University of Kansas.

Jacobson, G. F. (1982). *The multiple crises of marital separation and divorce.* New York: Grune & Stratton.

Kabatznick, R. (1985, September). Parting shots. *Ms.,* p. 45.

Kasl, S. V., & Wells, J. A. (1985). Social support and health in the middle years: Work and the family. In S. Cohen & S. L. Syme (Eds.), *Social support and health* (pp. 175–198). Orlando, FL: Academic Press.

Kelley, H. H. (1983). Love and commitment. In H. H. Kelley, E. Berscheid, A. Christiansen, J. Harvey, T. Huston, G. Levinger, E. McClintock; L. Peplau, & D. Peterson (Eds.), *Close relationships* (pp. 265–314). New York: W. H. Freeman.

Mandler, G. (1984). *Mind and body.* New York: W. W. Norton & Company.

Major, B., Carrington, P. I., & Carnevale, J. D. (1984). Physical attractiveness and self-esteem: Attributions for praise from an other-sex evaluator. *Personality and Social Psychology Bulletin, 10,* 43–50.

Mitchell, D. (1983). The price tag of responsibility: A comparison of divorced and remarried mothers. *Journal of Divorce, 6*(Spring), 33–42.

Newman, H. M., & Langer, E. J. (1981). Post-divorce adaptation and the attribution of responsibility. *Sex Roles, 7,* 223–232.

Pettit, E. J., & Bloom, B. L. (1984). Whose decision was it? The effects of initiator status on adjustment to marital disruption. *Journal of Marriage and the Family, 46,* 587–596.

Schwarz, N. Y., & Clore, G. L. (1983). Mood, misattribution, and judgments of well-being: Informative and directive function of affective states. *Journal of Personality and Social Psychology, 45,* 513–523.

Sigall, H., & Michela, J. (1976). I'll bet you say this to all the girls: Physical attractiveness and reactions to praise. *Journal of Personality, 44,* 611–626.

Somers, A. R. (1981). Marital status, health, and the use of health services: An old relationship revisited. In P. J. Stein (Ed.), *Single life: Unmarried adults in social context* (pp. 178–190). New York: St. Martin's Press.

Spanier, G. B., & Castro, R. F. (1979). Adjustment to separation and divorce: A qualitative analysis. In G. Levinger & O. C. Moles (Eds.), *Divorce and separation* (pp. 211–227). New York: Basic Books.

Spanier, G. B., & Hanson, S. (1981). The role of extended kin in the adjustment to marital separation. *Journal of Divorce, 5*(Fall/Winter), 33–48.

Spanier, G. B., & Thompson, L. (1983). Relief and distress after marital separation. *Journal of Divorce, 7*(Fall), 31–49.

Spanier, G. B., & Thompson, L. (1984). *Parting: The aftermath of separation and divorce.* Beverly Hills, CA: Sage.

Stephen, T. D. (1984). Symbolic interdependence and post-breakup distress: A reformulation of the attachment construct. *Journal of Divorce, 8*(Fall), 1–16.

Stevenson, C. D., Brehm, S. S., & DeFelice, J. (1986). *Coping after a relationship ends: An examination of Berscheid's model of loss and response.* Unpublished paper, University of Kansas.

Thoits, P. A. (1982). Conceptual, methodological, and theoretical problems in studying social support as a buffer against life stress. *Journal of Health and Social Behavior, 23,* 145–159.

Thompson, L., & Spanier, G. B. (1983). The end of marriage and acceptance of marital termination. *Journal of Marriage and the Family, 45,* 103–113.

Wallston, B. S., Alagna, S. W., DeVellis, B. Mc., & DeVellis, R. F. (1983). Social support and physical health. *Health Psychology, 4,* 367–391.

Weingarten, H. R. (1985). Marital status and well-being: A national study comparing first-married, currently divorced, and remarried adults. *Journal of Marriage and the Family, 47,* 653–662.

Weiss, R. S. (1975). *Marital separation.* New York: Basic Books.

Wilcox, B. L. (1981). Social support in adjusting to marital disruption: A network analysis. In B. H. Gottlieb (Ed.), *Social networks and social support* (pp. 97–115). Beverly Hills, CA: Sage.

IV

Social Comparison Perspectives

Imagine for a moment a world without other people. This is a difficult task, because we have never known such an existence. Our earliest memories are filled with other people—first Mom and Dad, and later a string of relatives, friends, co-workers, as well as the multitude of others with whom we share this planet. We obviously have first-hand information about some other people, but for the great majority of others, our sources of information are more indirect (e.g., hearsay, newspapers, and television). Visions of other people, and how we compare with those people, frequently visit our lives. Indeed, this social comparison process is often related to how we perceive negative life events and cope with them.

Recall the "Survivor Case" of Jan described previously in Chapter 1. Jan was talented, worked hard, and believed that only good things would happen to her. This attitude enabled her to take risks and attempt one goal after another. Through her teenage and subsequent college years, she sought one challenge after another. Buoyed by success, and the fact that none of the traumatic events of life seemed to happen to her, Jan was convinced that she was lucky. She found that bad events were happening to friends (e.g., parents dying, divorcing, personal illness, etc.) or acquaintances (e.g., sexual assault, muggings, drug-related accidents), but because these were not happening to her, she viewed them as highly unlikely possibilities; moreover, Jan had difficulty empathizing with those who did encounter such difficulties. In truth, Jan believed that the bad things happened to weak, unlucky, and unprepared people. This latter view was especially illusory because Jan took few precautions to lessen the probability of misfortune happening to her. She walked alone in dangerous parts of the city; she used drugs (e.g., cocaine) without thought of the consequences; she worked long hours and ate poorly; and she drove beyond the speed limit (never having been given a ticket, although she did get a warning once).

It was this latter behavior that precipitated Jan's accident. Returning from her Thanksgiving visit to her parent's house, Jan ignored suggestions that it was too slick to drive. After all, she was a superb driver, and her new front-wheel drive Subaru was excellent in snowy conditions. Driving as usual, in excess of the speed limits, Jan simply could not see the jack-knifed semi-trailer truck in front of her. Given her speed, she initiated a terrifying slide into the truck.

The wreck left Jan with serious injuries, including the amputation of her crushed legs. Not surprisingly, Jan's immediate attitude was "this can't be happening to me." This attitude continued for many days, and Jan was profoundly depressed. Eventually, however, she came to the conclusion that she was lucky to be alive. A major factor in this sentiment appeared to be the state trooper (the one who arrived at the scene of the accident) recounting to her how he could not believe that she survived the wreck. Although Jan suffered enormous physical pain and subsequent limitations because of the amputations, she refused to see herself as disadvantaged. Rather, she emphasized how fortunate she was relative to those who had died or suffered totally debilitating injuries due to wrecks.

This "Survivor" case illustrates the importance of the social comparison processes that are described in the two chapters in the present section. In Chapter 9, Linda Perloff develops the concept of unique invulnerability. Perloff suggests that persons who have not been victims of traumatic life events may preserve illusions of unique invulnerability (i.e., "It won't happen to me") by engaging in downward social comparison or comparing with others who may be more at risk. There are at least three negative repercussions of this unique invulnerability. First, such persons may not understand or empathize with those who have been victimized. Second, this belief is theorized to make a person more likely to encounter life crises because appropriate precautions are not taken. Third, the illusion may make the impact of an actual traumatic event even more severe. On the positive side, this illusion may facilitate some sense of personal control and thereby may free a person from becoming immobilized by fear. In the case of Jan, the sense of unique invulnerability may have fostered a sense of control, but it also may have contributed to her accident through her overzealous driving.

In Chapter 10, Thomas Wills argues that people who have undergone negative life events may invoke downward social comparisons as a coping strategy. By comparing oneself with another person who is even worse off than us, Wills suggests that we preserve our esteem. This may be done through relatively passive means (such as taking advantage of available comparisons), or it may be more active (such as finding less advantaged comparison persons). Returning to the case of Jan, it can be readily seen that her "I'm lucky to be alive" statement implicitly employs a downward social comparison strategy.

Overall, therefore, an understanding of the social comparison processes may help to unravel the factors that contributed to Jan's accident and her coping with it; moreover, social comparison processes may be applied to a variety of other examples in which people perceive and cope with negative life events.

9

Social Comparison and Illusions of Invulnerability to Negative Life Events

LINDA S. PERLOFF

INTRODUCTION

Nonvictims, individuals who have not been victimized by undesirable life events, often underestimate their own personal vulnerability to victimization relative to other people's vulnerability. In other words, nonvictims appear to have an illusion of unique invulnerability, in which they see themselves as less vulnerable to victimization than they see most other people (Perloff, 1983). This biased perception is reflected in the common saying, "It won't happen to me," a statement that generally implies that it will instead happen to others. Although many studies have demonstrated the existence of these illusions, we still know relatively little about the underlying causal mechanisms or the behavioral consequences of harboring these misperceptions. Past evidence suggests that people who feel invulnerable to victimization are less likely to engage in precautionary behaviors than are people who feel vulnerable (Becker, 1974; Haefner & Kirscht, 1970; Tyler, 1980). Thus, illusions of invulnerability may be dangerous insofar as they discourage adequate self-protective, preventive behavior (cf. Weinstein, 1980).

In an attempt to increase our understanding of perceptions of invul-

LINDA S. PERLOFF • Department of Psychology, University of Illinois at Chicago, Chicago, IL 60680.

nerability, the present chapter focuses specifically on the social comparisons nonvictims engage in when appraising their risk. This chapter has two major purposes. One purpose is to explore the role of social comparison processes in nonvictims' perceptions of invulnerability to negative events. The second objective is to examine the potential consequences of these perceptions. Research will be described that demonstrates that people maintain their illusions of unique invulnerability in part by engaging in downward comparisons. I will argue that nonvictims often make inappropriate social comparisons, choosing to compare themselves with someone who is more vulnerable and at risk than they are. Such comparisons enable people to perceive themselves as less susceptible to negative life events than the average person. I will also suggest that nonvictims see themselves as better able to cope with hypothetical victimization than the average person and that this may help to explain nonvictims' negative reactions to victims.

I will begin by reviewing evidence indicating that people often perceive themselves as uniquely invulnerable to future negative events, and I will suggest several mechanisms and motives that may underlie such perceptions. Then I will describe some recent research that examines the ways in which people's perceptions of their own vulnerability differ from their perceptions of others' vulnerability. Finally, I will address the potential adaptive versus maladaptive consequences of nonvictims' illusions of unique invulnerability.

NONVICTIMS' PERCEPTIONS OF INVULNERABILITY

As many theorists have observed, nonvictims tend to underestimate the likelihood or frequency of negative life events. People have been found to underestimate the probability of natural disasters, such as earthquakes and floods (Kunreuther, 1979) as well as the frequency of various causes of death, such as asthma, drowning, and diabetes (Slovic, Fischhoff, & Lichtenstein, 1976). In addition, nonvictims tend to judge themselves as personally invulnerable to negative life events. For example, results from health surveys suggest that whereas people express considerable fear of developing cancer, they greatly underestimate their own chances of contracting and dying from the disease (Knopf, 1976). Thus, individuals may underestimate both the overall frequency of negative events in a population as well as their own personal susceptibility to those events.

What is particularly fascinating about nonvictims, however, is their tendency to underestimate their own personal vulnerability relative to other people's vulnerability. In other words, nonvictims appear to have an illusion of *unique invulnerability*, seeing themselves as less vulnerable to victimization than they see most other people (e.g., "It won't happen to me"). Numerous studies have documented this tendency. For example, people tend to judge themselves as less likely than others to be victims of diseases such as cancer, heart attack, pneumonia, leukemia, alcoholism, and venereal disease (Harris & Guten, 1979; Kirscht, Haefner, Kegeles, & Rosenstock, 1966; Lang, 1980; Perloff, 1982; Weinstein, 1980). A similar tendency was reported by Snyder (1978) who administered "insurance company longevity" data to college students. Although students were told that these data predicted people's age of death, they tended to estimate that *they* would live 10 years longer than the actuarial average. And Los Angeles residents were found to perceive themselves as healthier than the average person and as having fewer illnesses per year (Larwood, 1978). Finally, college students see themselves as less likely than the typical person their age to get divorced or to be unfaithful to their spouse, as more likely to work hard at making their marriage a success (Perloff & Farbisz, 1985), and as easier than average to live with (Schriber, Larwood, & Peterson, 1985).

Similarly, other past research has found that people see themselves as less likely than others to be involved in a serious automobile accident (Robertson, 1977; Weinstein, 1980). Consistent with this finding, Slovic, Fischhoff, and Lichtenstein (1978) reported that from 75% to 90% of drivers interviewed in various countries felt that their driving ability was better than average (see also Svenson, 1981). And in a recent Gallup report (1981), 77% of the nation's drivers said they obeyed the speed limit "all of the time" or "most of the time," and only 13% admitted that they often violated the speed limit. These same drivers, however, estimated that only 42% of other motorists observed the legal limit "most of the time" and that 49% often violated it. Thus, many motorists see themselves as safer and as more skillful than the average driver. People also perceive themselves as less likely than others to be victims of crime (Perloff, 1982; Weinstein, 1980) and they believe that crime is less serious in their neighborhood than elsewhere—regardless of actual crime rates (Hindelang, Gottfredson, & Garofalo, 1978; Skogan & Maxfield, 1981).

MECHANISMS UNDERLYING ILLUSIONS OF INVULNERABILITY

Given the strong evidence demonstrating an illusion of unique invulnerability among nonvictims, what are the determinants of this perception? Several researchers have suggested that perceptions of unique invulnerability may stem from ego-defensive mechanisms (e.g., denial) that serve to reduce nonvictims' anxiety. Weinstein (1977) speculated that such "self-deceptive coping strategies may be employed to reduce anxiety or fear by denying or distorting the existence of the threat" (p. 3). Consistent with an ego-defensive perspective, Kirscht et al. (1966) found that subjects who saw a disease as very serious were most likely to perceive their own chances of contracting the disease as less than average. Similarly, the more stressful and unpleasant college students viewed divorce, the more they saw their own chances of getting divorced as less than average (Perloff & Farbisz, 1985).

Nonvictims' perceptions of unique invulnerability may also reflect a need for personal control. For example, many people harbor an "illusion of control" over random events (Langer, 1975) or an exaggerated belief in their ability to contol chance outcomes. This illusion of control may lead people to overestimate their ability to obtain positive outcomes and to avoid negative outcomes. In addition, the general tendency for people to view themselves as better than average (Myers & Ridl, 1978; Perloff & Brickman, 1982) and as more intelligent than their average peer (Wylie, 1979) may generalize to beliefs about the future and may lead people to believe that they are more capable than the typical person of controlling their lives and avoiding negative outcomes. Consistent with this, college students predicted that, in the future (10 years from now), they would be better off (e.g., happier, more confident, more hardworking, less lonely) than the average person their age (Perloff & Bryant, 1985).

These beliefs in personal control and invulnerability are especially apparent in nonvictims' reactions to victims of misfortune. A substantial body of research has demonstrated that observers often blame innocent victims for their misfortune (e.g., Coates, Wortman, & Abbey, 1979; Lerner, 1980; Lerner & Miller, 1978; Walster, 1966). According to Lerner's just world theory (Lerner, 1980; Lerner & Miller, 1978), individuals are motivated to believe in a fair and orderly world in which people get what they deserve and deserve what they get, a world in which bad things do not happen to good people. By blaming or derogating victims, nonvictims are able to reassure themselves that they will not be vulnerable to a similar plight. Walster (1966) has similarly argued that people blame victims in order to avoid acknowledging the possibility of their own victimization. According to Walster, if people view serious negative outcomes as random happenings, then they are forced to admit that an accident or misfortune could happen to them. If, however, nonvictims can blame the victim and convince themselves that they are somehow different from, and more capable than, the victim, then they can avoid facing the frightening prospect of their own victimization. In both Lerner's and Walster's formulations, blaming victims helps us to preserve our illusions of invulnerability. Perhaps explicitly comparing our own good fortune with victims' bad fortune strengthens our belief that we are better than average, thereby facilitating the perception that we are uniquely invulnerable.

In addition to the need for personal control, egocentric thought processes and a failure to consider other people's precautionary behaviors may contribute to nonvictims' perceptions of unique invulnerability (Weinstein, 1980, 1983; Weinstein & Lachendro, 1982). In one study (Weinstein, 1980), college students were asked to list all of the factors that they thought increased or decreased the probability that a variety of negative events would happen to them. A second group of subjects who read these lists showed weaker perceptions of unique invulnerability. Thus, simply learning other nonvictims' reasons for feeling immune significantly decreased subjects' biased perceptions of risk. Weinstein and Lachendro (1982) found that merely having subjects think about their peers' risk status—without providing any information about these other people—reduced subjects' illusions. This research suggests that nonvictims may only be aware of the factors that reduce their own vulnerability and they may fail to realize that others may have just as many factors in their favor.

Finally, one's choice of comparison others may also contribute to nonvictims' perceptions of unique invulnerability. A basic principle of social comparison theory is that how we feel about ourselves depends in part on whom we compare ourselves to (Festinger, 1954; Wills, 1981). Whether we view ourselves as more or less vulnerable than others to future victimization may depend in part on who those others are. To the extent that we make "downward comparisons" (Wills, 1981), comparing ourselves to others who are less fortunate and more at risk than we are, we may be apt to see ourselves as uniquely invulnerable. Both motivational and cognitive mechanisms may underlie these downward comparisons. From a motivational perspective, downward comparisons with vulnerable others may serve an ego-defensive function by reducing nonvictims' anxiety and enhancing feelings of personal control (cf. Perloff, 1983; Wills, 1981). As Taylor, Wood, and Lichtman (1983) noted, "downward comparisons have the psychological advantage of making one feel good about one's situation relative to the comparison other" (p. 27).

In contrast to this motivational framework, Weinstein (1980) has suggested a cognitive explanation for how downward social comparisons facilitate perceptions of unique invulnerability. He refers to such perceptions as, "unrealistic optimism"—that is, the tendency to see oneself as less likely than others to experience negative events and as more likely than others to experience positive events. According to Weinstein (1980), people are unrealistically optimistic in part because they compare themselves with an inappropriate standard, "an unrealistic stereotype of a person who does nothing to improve his or her chances or even engages in counter-productive activity" (p. 819). Weinstein has speculated that such inappropriate comparisons stem from people's reliance on a "representativeness" heuristic (Kahneman & Tversky, 1973). Use of the representativeness heuristic involves assigning an individual to a particular category on the basis of whether his or her attributes resemble the characteristic features of this category. According to Weinstein,

> For many events—contracting lung cancer or becoming an alcoholic, for example—people may have a stereotyped conception of the kind of person to whom this event happens. If they do not see themselves as fitting the stereotype, the representativeness heuristic suggests that people will conclude that the event will not happen to them, overlooking the possibility that few of the people who experience the event may actually fit the stereotype (1980, p. 808).

In a study reporting results consistent with this reasoning, college students who had a clear image in their minds of a particular type of person to whom a negative event was likely to happen saw their chances of experiencing the event as less than average (Weinstein, 1980, Study 1).

To summarize, numerous studies have documented that nonvictims have illusions of unique invulnerability to negative life events, and several underlying mechanisms or processes have been offered to explain these illusions. In the next section, I will describe some recent research that specifically focuses on the conditions under which people's judgments of their own risk differ from their judgments of others' risk.

JUDGMENTS OF OWN VERSUS OTHERS' RISK

One unaddressed question concerns the specific conditions under which people engage in downward social comparisons when judging their susceptibility to negative events. In past studies of perceived risk, subjects have usually been asked to compare their chances of experiencing a particular negative event with the chances of the "average" or "typical" person (e.g., Harris & Guten, 1979; Lang, 1980; Larwood, 1978; Perloff, 1982; Robertson, 1977; Svenson, 1981; Weinstein, 1980, 1983, 1984). Insofar as people tend to view themselves as better than average (Myers & Ridl, 1979) and as more intelligent than their average peer (Wylie, 1979), the "average person" may be seen as someone who is, almost by definition, less advantaged, less intelligent, and generally worse off than oneself. Consequently, it is perhaps not surprising that subjects believe they are more immune to negative events than the average person.

Whereas most previous research on perceived vulnerability has focused on the average person as the target for social comparison, the commonly observed illusion of unique invulnerability may not occur with other comparison targets. More specifically, although people tend to see themselves as less vulnerable to undesirable life events than the average person, it is not clear whether they also see themselves as less vulnerable than their friends or relatives. There are two reasons to expect subjects to see themselves and their friends or relatives as *equally* vulnerable, while seeing themselves as *less* vulnerable than the average person. First, we might expect people to resist acknowledging the susceptibility of their friends or family for the same reasons that they resist acknowledging their own personal risk—to reduce anxiety and fear. Indeed, other researchers have found that self-serving biases extend to include perceptions of one's close friends and loved ones (e.g., Burger, 1981; Schlenker & Miller, 1977). Second, the "average person" may be a sufficiently vague and ambiguous target that it leads people to visualize an abstract stereotype or "prototype" (Cantor & Mischel, 1977) of a person at risk. Having this prototype in mind may make it easier to construe the average person as the kind of person who is particularly vulnerable to victimization. In contrast, when the target is a concrete, specific individual, it may be more difficult either to manufacture a hypothetical other who is highly vulnerable or to distort the risk-relevant characteristics of the specific target.

In a recent study, Perloff and Fetzer (1986) examined the conditions under which nonvictims rate others as more vulnerable than they rate themselves. Specifically, we wondered whether people would see themselves as uniquely invulnerable, regardless of the specific comparison other, or whether this bias would emerge only when subjects made judgments about relatively impersonal, vague comparison targets, such as the "average person" or the "average college student." Based on the preceding discussion, we hypothesized that subjects' ratings of their own vulnerability would be lower than their ratings of the "average person's" vulnerability (i.e., subjects would show perceptions of unique invulnerability). In contrast, we also hypothesized that subjects would rate themselves and a close friend or family member as equally invulnerable.

To test these hypotheses, we asked introductory psychology students to estimate both their own vulnerability and another person's vulnerability to ten negative life events: cancer, heart attack, hypertension, drinking problem, venereal disease, diabetes, injury in a car accident, nervous breakdown, mugging, and divorce. Estimates of personal vulnerability were obtained by asking subjects how likely they thought it was that they would experience the particular event sometime during their life. Subjects also rated the vulnerability of one of several different comparison targets: (a) "the average person of your sex," (b) "the average college student of your sex at the University of Illinois at Chicago," (c) "your closest friend," (d) "the sibling closest to you in age," or (e) "one of your parents." In the latter condition, females were instructed to think about their mother, and males were instructed to think about their father. Estimates of the comparison target's vulnerability were assessed by asking subjects how likely they thought it was that the comparison other would experience the event sometime during his or her life. Responses were made on 7-point Likert scales, ranging from 1 (not at all likely) to 7 (extremely likely).

Because we were primarily interested in comparing subjects' judgments of their own and others' relative vulnerability, rather than their absolute self and other estimates, a vulnerability difference score was calculated for each event. This difference score was calculated for each event by subtracting each subject's estimate of the other's vulnerability from their estimate of their own vulnerability to that particular event. Negative scores signified perceptions of relative invulnerability (perceiving oneself as *less* vulnerable than the comparison other), positive scores signified perceptions of relative vulnerability (perceiving oneself as *more* vulnerable than the comparison other), and scores near zero signified perceptions of relative consensus (seeing oneself and the other as equally vulnerable or invulnerable).

A general pattern emerged in which difference scores in the two average target groups were significantly larger than difference scores in the friend, parent, and sibling groups. In other words, difference scores in the friend, parent, and sibling conditions were significantly closer to zero than the difference scores in the two average target conditions. This overall pattern suggested that subjects perceived differences between their own risk and the average targets' risk, but not between their own risk and the risk of their friends and relatives.

Additional analysis revealed that, relative to themselves, subjects perceived the average person as significantly more vulnerable to 7 out of 10 events and saw the average student as significantly more vulnerable to 8 out of 10 events. In marked contrast, subjects (a) saw their closest friend as significantly more vulnerable than themselves to only one event (divorce), (b) saw their sibling as significantly more vulnerable than themselves to only three events (drinking problem, venereal disease, and divorce), and (c) did not see their parent as significantly more vulnerable to any of the events. (In fact, subjects saw themselves, perhaps accurately, as more vulnerable than their parent to venereal disease and divorce). Thus, illusions of unique invulnerability were primarily observed when subjects rated themselves and the average person or the average college student. When subjects were asked to compare themselves with their friends or family, on the other hand, these illusions essentially disappeared. Consistent with this, positive difference scores (reflecting a tendency to rate oneself as more vulnerable than the comparison other) were found only in the three "close target" groups (i.e., friend, parent, sibling); all difference scores in the two average target groups were negative.

The main finding of our study was that individuals do not uniformly view all other people as more vulnerable than themselves to victimization. As predicted, illusions of unique invulnerability commonly reported in past research were observed here only when subjects rated an "average" target. When the comparison other was an actual, specific person whom the subject knew, these illusions essentially disappeared. The findings demonstrate that people appraise various targets' risk status differently and that they see themselves and close others as less vulnerable than they see average others.

One explanation for the pattern of results obtained in this study is that when people are given a vague comparison target, such as the "average person" or the "average student," they are able to engage in downward comparisons, thereby comparing themselves with someone who is worse off and more at risk (cf. Wills, 1981). In contrast, such downward comparisons were more difficult to make when the comparison other was a specific, fixed entity (i.e., one's parent, sibling, or closest friend) whose vulnerability is not so easily distorted. We observed anecdotal evidence for this interpretation in a pilot test we had conducted. Specifically, in an initial pilot study, we asked subjects in the "friend" condition simply to estimate the vulnerability of "one of your friends." During debriefing, many subjects indicated that they had chosen a different friend for each of the 10 events. When asked what governed their choice of a friend, many of these subjects reported selecting a friend who seemed especially vulnerable to that particular event. Because we wanted subjects in the friend condition to keep the same friend in mind for all 10 events (just as we wanted other subjects to keep the same parent or sibling in mind for all events), we altered the instructions for the actual study and asked subjects to think about their "closest friend." However, we remained intrigued by the possibility that when given the opportunity, people may actively make downward comparisons by selecting others who are particularly vulnerable (cf. Taylor, Wood, & Lichtman, 1983), and that this may occur even when these others are friends. A second study was conducted that further explores this idea.

In this second study (Perloff & Fetzer, 1986, Study 2), we asked subjects to estimate the vulnerability of one of three comparison targets: the "average college student," "one of your friends," or "your closest friend." To the extent that people find it easier to make downward comparisons when the target is vague and abstract, we predicted that subjects would construe both the average college student and "one of their friends" as more vulnerable than themselves, but that they would perceive their closest friend as equally invulnerable as themselves. In addition to asking subjects to estimate vulnerability, we also asked subjects in the "one of your friends" condition to explain what made them think of the particular friend they had in mind for each event. Consistent with the anecdotal evidence from the Study 1 pilot test, we predicted that subjects would report selecting a friend who seemed vulnerable to the particular event. In sum, we hypothesized that subjects would make downward comparisons whenever the target allowed them to do so. The vagueness of a target may make it easier for subjects to imagine a real or hypothetical individual who resembles the typical victim, even when the vague target happens to be a friend.

To test this hypothesis, we asked introductory psychology students to estimate their own personal vulnerability and the target's vulnerability to each of two events. Data was gathered from two separate groups of subjects. Group A consisted of 41 men and 42 women who estimated vulnerability to a heart attack and to a drinking problem. Group B consisted of 50 men and 57 women who estimated vulnerability to cancer and to divorce. In addition to estimating vulnerability to each event, subjects were asked to describe their standing on a list of risk factors for each event, as well as the target's standing on these same risk factors. For each event, we selected five risk factors that are commonly thought to influence one's chances of experiencing the event (cf. Weinstein, 1983). For example, the risk factors for heart attack were: amount of cholesterol in the person's diet; number of eggs eaten per week; number of meals per week at which red meat is eaten; amount of exercise per week; and how health-conscious the person is. The risk factors for drinking problem were: how often the person drinks beer, wine, or liquor; number of drinks or glasses of an alcoholic beverage consumed on a typical occasion; number of times per month the person drinks alone; number of times per month the person "gets drunk"; and how often the person uses alcohol to reduce stress and anxiety (see Perloff & Fetzer, 1986, for a description of the cancer and divorce items).

Subjects were told that they would first be asked to estimate how likely it was that each of several different events would happen to them. After estimating their personal vulnerability to the event on a 7-point scale (ranging from "not at all likely" to "extremely likely"), subjects described their standing on each of the five risk factors for that event. The two events always appeared in the same order: (a) having a heart attack and (b) developing a drinking problem (Group A); or (a) contracting cancer and (b) getting a divorce (Group B).

After describing themselves on both events, subjects were asked to describe another individual on the same events. Subjects were randomly assigned to answer questions about either (a) "the average college student of your sex at the University of Illinois at Chicago"; (b) "your closest friend"; or (c) "one of your friends." In the "closest friend" condition, subjects were asked to "keep the same person in mind as you answer all of the following questions." In the "one of your friends" condition, subjects were asked to "think of a different person for each event." Subjects in all three conditions estimated the target's vulnerability to the given event and then estimated the target's standing on the five risk factors for that event. Because the major issue of interest was again subjects' comparative self–other judgments, all analyses were performed on difference scores that were computed for each item by subtracting ratings of the target from ratings of the self.

A similar pattern of results emerged for all events. As predicted, subjects perceived both the average college student and one of their friends to be more vulnerable than themselves to the negative event, but they perceived their closest friend and themselves to be equally invulnerable. For example, subjects saw themselves, relative to the average student or one of their friends, as significantly less vulnerable to heart attack; as more health-conscious; and as eating fewer eggs, less red meat, and less cholesterol. In contrast, subjects believed that their closest friend was just as likely as they were to have a heart attack, and they saw their closest friend as being equally health-conscious as themselves and as having similarly healthy (e.g., low cholesterol) diets. Analysis of the physical exercise item was not significant, although the mean difference scores followed a similar pattern.

This same predicted pattern also emerged for the drinking problem items. Relative to both the average student and one of their friends, subjects viewed themselves as significantly less likely to develop a drinking problem, as drinking less often, as drinking smaller amounts of alcohol on a typical occasion, as drinking alone less often, as getting drunk less often, and as being less likely to use alcohol to reduce stress in their lives. In contrast, subjects perceived no differences between themselves and their closest friend on these same dimensions. This same pattern was obtained for the cancer and divorce items. Again, relative to the average student and to one of their friends, subjects viewed themselves as significantly less vulnerable to cancer and to divorce, but they perceived no differences between themselves and their closest friend on the same dimensions.

In formulating predictions for Study 2, we had hypothesized that for vague targets (i.e., the "average student" or "one of your friends"), subjects would choose a person who fit their stereotype of someone to whom the given event typically happens. To examine this idea, we asked subjects in the "one of your friends" condition to explain in their own words what made them think of the particular friend they had in mind for each event. We were primarily interested in whether these subjects would spontaneously report that they had selected a friend who seemed especially likely to experience the given event. Therefore, we categorized responses according to whether subjects in this condition stated that they (a) chose a friend who seemed vulnerable to the event; (b) chose a friend who seemed invulnerable; (c) chose a friend who was vulnerable on some dimensions but invulnerable on others; or (d) chose a friend for reasons unrelated to the friend's risk status. Each open-ended response was coded by three independent judges into one of these four categories.

We then used chi-squares to test the hypothesis that subjects would be more likely to describe a vulnerable friend than to describe a friend who fell in any of the remaining three categories. Supporting this prediction, in Group A, most subjects in the "one of your friends" condition selected a vulnerable friend. When asked to estimate one of their friend's vulnerability to a heart attack, 68% of these subjects (19 out of 28) reported choosing a friend who seemed especially likely to have a future heart attack ($\chi^2 = 24.9$, $df = 3$, $p < .001$). When asked to estimate a friend's vulnerability to a drinking problem, 61% of these same subjects (17 out of 28) reported choosing another friend who seemed especially likely to develop a future drinking problem ($\chi^2 = 21.7$, $df = 3$, $p < .001$). In Group B, when estimating "one of their friend's" vulnerability to cancer, 62.5% of the subjects in this condition (26 out of 40) reported choosing a vulnerable friend ($\chi^2 = 32.4$, $df = 3$, $p < .001$); and when estimating a friend's vulnerability to divorce, 52.5% of these same subjects (21 out of 40) reported selecting a vulnerable friend ($\chi^2 = 25.0$, $df = 3$, $p < .001$). These subjects in the "one of your friends" condition tended to mention behaviors, personality traits, life-styles, family backgrounds, or hereditary factors that increased their friend's chances of experiencing the given event.

For example, subjects offered the following explanations for why they thought of a particular friend when responding to the heart attack items:

His life-style is so crazy and he is so hyper that he comes to mind when I think about the question of heart attack.

He has weight problems, so of all the people I know, I would think that he would be the most likely candidate.

Her mother has been in and out of hospitals for heart problems and her grandmother died of a heart attack.

My friend smokes too much, worries too much, and doesn't take care of her body.

Subjects gave similar reasons for choosing a particular friend when responding to the drinking items:

He is always drinking at all hours of the day, so he was the first to come to mind.

I chose this person because he is on the road to a drinking problem right now. He has a lot of free time on his hands, so he drinks.

Her mother drinks occasionally and her grandfather was an alcoholic.

Thus, as these statements illustrate, the majority of subjects in the "one of your friends" condition reported that they selected a friend who seemed vulnerable to the given event.

The results of Study 2 indicated that, when subjects were given a vague, ambiguous comparison target, they chose to think about a hypothetical college student (in the "average college student" condition) or an actual friend (in the "one of your friends" condition) who was more vulnerable to a particular negative outcome than they themselves were. In contrast, when subjects were instructed to think about a specific other, namely their closest friend, they perceived virtually no differences between their own vulnerability and risk status and that of their closest friend. Consistent with this finding, most subjects in the "one of your friends" condition reported choosing a friend who seemed especially likely to experience the particular event. Considered together, the results of our first and second studies suggest that, when the vagueness of the target allowed people to exercise choice in their selection of a real or hypothetical other, they made downward comparisons, seeing themselves as relatively less vulnerable. However, self–other differences in perceived risk disappeared when subjects were forced to think about a specific person (i.e., their closest friend, sibling, or same-sex parent).

One cognitive explanation for these findings draws on Kahneman and Tversky's (1973) representativeness heuristic. As mentioned earlier, when people think about a particular negative outcome, they may invoke a stereotyped image or an abstract prototype of the kind of person who seems particularly likely to be victimized by that outcome (cf. Weinstein, 1980). When subjects are given a specific target such as their closest friend, they may then use a feature-matching strategy (Tversky, 1977) to compare their friend's risk-relevant attributes (e.g., behaviors, lifestyle, family background) to those of the prototypical victim. Because the prototypical victim by definition possesses many risk-increasing attributes, a specific target may be seen as less vulnerable by comparison. Subjects may use a similar feature-matching strategy to appraise their own personal risk.

In contrast to specific targets, vague targets' vulnerability may be evaluated differently. When subjects are presented with a vague target, they must first select a real or hypothetical person who fits the vague category (e.g., "one of your friends"). Because the prototypical victim is already salient in their minds, they may visualize or choose a member of the vague category who resembles this prototype of the person at risk. Supporting this idea, roughly two thirds of the subjects in the "one of your friends" condition reported selecting a friend who seemed likely to be victimized (i.e., a friend who fit their stereotype of the typical victim). Because the person from the vague category has been selected to match the typical victim, subjects are apt to see themselves as less vulnerable relative to the vague target.

A related explanation is that negative events, such as a heart attack, serve as cues or primes that make the prototypical victim salient. This is known as a priming effect (Higgins, Rholes, & Jones, 1977) in which recently activated schemata or categories are more accessible than schemata that have not been activated. The words that were presented to subjects in the present studies (e.g., heart attack, drinking problem) may have primed or made accessible various category-related terms, including people who appeared to belong to the category.

In contrast to these cognitive explanations, there are several plausible alternative explanations that are motivational in nature. One motivational interpretation is that the closer one is emotionally to a comparison target, the more one wishes to see the target as invulnerable. Specifically, we may be more motivated to protect those closest to us (cf. Burger, 1981; Schlenker & Miller, 1977). In addition, because close friends are likely to be relatively similar to us, the prospect of their victimization may drive home the possibility of our own victimization. In Study 2, the friend chosen in the "closest friend" condition may in fact have been closer to subjects than the friend or acquaintance chosen in the "one of your friends" condition. Consequently, subjects may have been more invested in viewing their closest friends as invulnerable than they were in viewing one of their acquaintances as invulnerable.

A second motivational explanation is that people have to confront the fact that negative events do occur, and this prospect produces anxiety. One way people can reduce this anxiety is to focus selectively on someone they know who is more at risk than they are. In this way, people acknowledge the occurrence of unpleasant events but preserve a belief in their own personal immunity by focusing on a real or hypothetical other who is particularly vulnerable. In other words, people may be motivated to make ego-defensive downward comparisons (cf. Wills, 1981) and will do so whenever the opportunity arises. In contrast to specific targets whose vulnerability may not be so easily distorted, vague targets allow people to construe themselves as relatively better off. The research reported earlier does not allow us to rule out these two motivational explanations, and future research is clearly needed to specify the exact role of motivational factors in people's choice of comparison others.

At any rate, these two studies suggest that when people are allowed to select any comparison target (e.g., one of their friends or peers), they appear to exercise this freedom to its fullest by choosing especially vulnerable others. This is theoretically important because it represents an extension of downward comparison phenomena. Whereas much of the past work in this area (see Wills, 1981) has demonstrated downward comparisons with targets who were not familiar to subjects (e.g., unknown members of lower-status minority groups), the present research observed downward comparison processes not only for targets who were strangers but also for targets who were identified as friends of the subjects.

Perloff and Fetzer's (1986) findings support Wills' (1981) statement that "downward comparison can occur on a passive basis in which persons take advantage of available opportunities for comparison with a less fortunate other" (p. 246). The favorable comparison that results enables a person to increase his or her subjective well-being. Wills further hypothesizes that subjective well-being can also be "achieved through comparison with an equally unfortunate other" (p. 245). In some circumstances, it may be difficult to make downward comparisons (e.g., when a person already feels disadvantaged). In such cases, it may be easier for people to preserve self-esteem by viewing others as equally disadvantaged and unfortunate. Support for this latter notion comes from a survey (Perloff, 1982) of college students' perceptions of vulnerability to one of two negative events—an illness outcome (getting cancer) or a crime outcome (being mugged).

In this survey, Perloff (1982) found that subjects who felt highly invulnerable (to getting cancer or to being mugged) saw themselves as less likely than the typical person to be victimized ($M = 1.94$ and 2.97, respectively, on 7-point scales). In contrast, subjects who felt personally vulnerable to the event did not view the typical person as being even more vulnerable than themselves, but instead judged their own likelihood and the typical person's likelihood as equal ($M = 3.54$ and 3.68, respectively). In addition, invulnerable subjects judged their own chances of victimization as lower than others' chances ($M = 10.5\%$ and 23.6%, respectively). Vulnerable subjects, in contrast, judged their own chances and others' chances as equal (34.7% and 33.7%, respectively). Thus, when nonvictims do in fact feel vulnerable, they may seek to comfort themselves by construing others as equally vulnerable and at risk.

A similar result was obtained by Suls and Becker (1980) who found that the more fearful a female student felt about certain objects or situations (e.g., snakes, spiders, injury, failing a test), the more she perceived the typical female undergraduate as fearful of these same objects. That is, high-fear subjects tended to see others as more similar to themselves than did either low-fear or moderate-fear subjects. Both Perloff (1982) and Suls and Becker (1980) concluded that subjects who felt most vulnerable or fearful had the strongest need to be ego defensive and therefore were more motivated to perceive consensus than were subjects who felt less vulnerable.

This is consistent with Schachter's (1959) work on affiliation, which suggests that people prefer to interact with others who are equally vulnerable as themselves. In a series of experiments, Schachter repeatedly found that subjects who expected to receive painful shocks preferred to wait with others who shared their unpleasant fate rather than waiting alone or with others who were not to be shocked. According to Schachter, people anticipating frightening outcomes seek out similarly afflicted others in order to interpret the ambiguous internal states they are experiencing, to determine how appropriate their feelings and reactions are, and to reduce their anxiety (see also Cottrell & Epley, 1977; Darley & Aronson, 1966; Zimbardo & Formica, 1963). This work on affiliation suggests that people who perceive themselves as vulnerable to future victimization may derive comfort from the presence or knowledge of equally vulnerable others and may thus be motivated to see themselves and others as being "in the same boat" (cf. Coates & Winston, 1983).

NONVICTIMS' BELIEFS ABOUT COPING WITH VICTIMIZATION

The research described in the preceding sections indicates that many people underestimate their vulnerability to negative life events and that they engage in downward comparisons when appraising their risk. This research suggests that people have an illusion of primary control in which they exaggerate their ability to avoid negative outcomes. Rothbaum, Weisz, and Snyder (1982) distinguish between *primary control* (people's attempts to control or change actual events) and *secondary control* (attempts to control or change one's feelings in response to events). A similar distinction may be relevant in the present context. Just as nonvictims have illusions of primary control over negative life events, they may also have illusions of secondary control over their reactions to these events. To examine this idea, Perloff, Bryant, and Davidson (1986) asked college students to imagine that they had recently experienced one of two negative events (a heart attack or a divorce). Subjects were then asked to make predictions about their own recovery from the event and the average person's recovery from the same event. Subjects estimated that they would require less time than the average person to recover emotionally from the event, that they would work harder than the average person to recover, and that overall they would cope better with the event than the average person.

Several theorists (e.g., Coates & Wortman, 1980; Wortman & Dunkel-Schetter, 1979) have observed that nonvictims often become impatient and frustrated with victims' coping attempts. Nonvictims may have misconceptions about coping with stressful life experiences that may lead to erroneous expectations about victims' ability to adjust to or overcome their misfortune. For example, according to Silver and Wortman (1980), people may believe that victims should recover relatively quickly from life crises. Perloff, Bryant, and Davidson's results indicate that people believe that they would recover more quickly than the average person from a stressful life experience such as a heart attack or a divorce. This suggests that nonvictims' impatience and frustration with victims may reflect in part nonvictims' beliefs in their own superior coping abilities. Thus, not only may nonvictims feel protected from victimization because they believe they would behave differently (e.g., more intelligently) than victims (Lerner, 1980; Walster, 1966), but they may also believe that, should misfortune actually occur, they will cope better than the average person. In other words, nonvictims may have illusions of primary control over negative events and illusions of secondary control over their anticipated reactions to those events. Future research is needed to determine whether beliefs about one's own ability to cope with hypothetical victimization contribute to derogation of individuals who have already been victimized.

Thus far, I have presented evidence that nonvictims hold illusions of unique invulnerability to undesirable life events, and I have considered a variety of different explanations for such perceptions, including ego-defensive motives and the need for personal control. In particular, I have focused specifically on the downward comparisons people make to preserve their illusions of invulnerability. Given that these illusions exist, what are their consequences? Are they ultimately adaptive or maladaptive? The following section addresses these questions.

PERCEIVED INVULNERABILITY: ADAPTIVE OR MALADAPTIVE?

As I have discussed elsewhere (see Perloff, 1983), illusions of invulnerability may have both beneficial and harmful consequences. Perceiving oneself as less likely than average to be victimized may benefit nonvictims by (a) reducing their feelings of anxiety, (b) enhancing feelings of personal control, and (c) allowing them to carry out everyday activities without being hypervigilant and eternally on guard. Perceived vulnerability often creates symptoms of emotional distress such as acute anxiety, depression, helplessness, and excessive fear (see Janoff-Bulman & Lang-Gunn, in press; Perloff, 1983). Thus, to the extent that perceptions of invulnerability mitigate psychological distress, they may be adaptive for the individual. Indeed, several theorists (e.g., Kirscht et al., 1966; Weinstein, 1977) have suggested that people are motivated to see themselves as invulnerable in order to reduce anxiety.

Literature on downward comparison processes is also consistent with the idea that perceptions of unique invulnerability may reduce nonvictims' negative affect. According to Wills (1981), people are most likely to make downward comparisons when they feel threatened. The function of such comparisons is to preserve or restore the threatened person's self-esteem. Because illusions of unique invulnerability appear to involve some form of downward comparisons (Perloff & Fetzer, 1986), they may thus enhance nonvictims' self-esteem and subjective well-being.

In addition to reducing anxiety and enhancing well-being, illusions of unique invulnerability may also be adaptive because they promote feelings of personal control. Learned helplessness theorists (Seligman, 1975) argue that enhancing one's feelings of personal control over the environment is valuable and beneficial. As Langer (1975) has contended, individuals are motivated to "avoid the negative consequences that accompany the perception of having no control" (p. 323). Such negative consequences include feelings of helplessness, passivity, pessimism, apathy, and low self-esteem (see, e.g., Abramson, Seligman, & Teasdale,

1978). Perceived lack of control may also be a central precipitating factor in depression (Abramson *et al.*, 1978; Seligman, 1975). Thus, perceived vulnerability may be maladaptive and debilitating to the extent that it fosters helplessness and passivity. Perceived invulnerability, in contrast, may be adaptive to the extent that it is associated with feelings of personal control over one's environment.

Finally, illusions of invulnerability may be adaptive because they allow people to go about the business of everyday life without being completely immobilized by fear. In their study of crime victims, LeJeune and Alex (1973) write that

> assumptions of invulnerability and trust make it possible for urban citizens to carry out their everyday essential activities with relative psychological ease. To "live with fear" . . . turns the most elementary activities of urban living . . . into major "hassles". (p. 263)

Thus, feelings of invulnerability may help provide people with a basic sense of security and trust in their environment necessary for everyday survival. In addition, such perceptions of personal invulnerability may enhance people's beliefs that their world is orderly and predictable (see also Janoff-Bulman & Lang-Gunn, in press).

Whereas the preceding discussion suggests that illusions of invulnerability may be adaptive, there are also several reasons why such perceptions may have maladaptive consequences. First, such perceptions might ultimately increase an individual's objective vulnerability by lulling the nonvictim into a false sense of security. Specifically, such perceptions might lead the nonvictim to think that precautionary behaviors are unnecessary. A number of researchers have suggested that nonvictims who feel vulnerable to misfortune are more likely than those who feel invulnerable to engage in self-protective, preventive behaviors. For example, perceived susceptibility to illness has been shown to predict compliance with treatments prescribed during preventive dental instruction, cancer screening, and heart disease (e.g., Becker, 1974; Fink, Shapiro, & Roester, 1972; Haefner & Kirscht, 1970; Kegeles, 1963). And people who are afraid of crime are more likely to adopt crime prevention behaviors, such as installing burglar alarms and special locks or avoiding walking alone at night, than are people who are not afraid of crime (e.g., Dubow, McCabe, & Kaplan, 1978; Ennis, 1967; Tyler, 1980).

Moreover, some theorists have suggested that individuals who feel uniquely invulnerable may take the fewest precautions. For example, Snyder (1978) suggested that an illusion of uniqueness may help to explain smokers' reluctance to quit smoking. Similarly, Slovic, Fischhoff, & Lichtenstein (1978) speculated that the widespread failure to use seat belts may partly stem from drivers' beliefs that their driving skills are better than average. Public campaigns and media attempts to increase seat belt usage and discourage drinking while driving are notoriously ineffective (see, e.g., Robertson, 1977), perhaps because perceiving oneself as more skillful than others encourages greater risk taking. As Svenson (1981) notes, "Why should we pay much attention to information directed towards drivers in general if we are safer and more skillful than they are?" (p. 147). In sum, to the extent that nonvictims' beliefs in their unique invulnerability discourage them from taking adequate precautions, such beliefs may, ironically, ultimately increase their chances of being victimized.

A second potentially maladaptive consequence of perceived unique invulnerability concerns people's ability to cope after they have actually been victimized. Several bodies of literature suggest that people who underestimate their own personal susceptibility to life crises may have more difficulty adjusting to such crises should they occur. In general, unexpected, unforeseen, or unpredictable events are more difficult to cope with than expected, foreseen, or predictable ones (see, e.g., Janis, 1958; Johnson & Leventhal, 1974; Schulz, 1976). For example, Glass and Singer (1972) found that subjects exposed to unpredictable noise experienced higher levels of frustration and performed more poorly on a subsequent task than did subjects exposed to predictable noise. As Wortman (1976) has suggested, "people with exaggerated notions of personal control, or with considerable past experience at controlling the important events in their lives, may find uncontrollable outcomes all the more difficult to accept when they occur" (p. 45). Wortman and Brehm (1975) have argued that exaggerating one's ability to control or alter outcomes may sometimes be maladaptive, and when an outcome is truly uncontrollable or unavoidable, the most adaptive response may be to give up and accept the situation. In a similar vein, Janoff-Bulman and Brickman (1982) stress the importance of being able to distinguish between situations in which one has control and situations in which one does not, and they warn of the potential dangers of mistakenly assuming that one has control.

In support of this general argument, Wolfenstein (1957) stated that although denial may reduce an individual's anxiety before a disaster, it may make the individual feel more overwhelmed later.

> There is likely to be more emotional disturbance following the event on the part of those who beforehand warded off all anxiety, and denied the reality of the threat, than on the part of those who were able to tolerate some anticipatory alarm and to acknowledge that the disaster could happen. (Wolfenstein, 1957, pp. 25–26)

Similarly, in a study of rape victims, Scheppele and Bart (1983) observed that many women rely on "rules of rape avoidance" (p. 77), such as not walking alone at night or not dressing provocatively, which guide their behavior and which they believe will protect them from rape. Scheppele and Bart found that those women who "followed the rules" and who were nevertheless raped (i.e., were raped in a situation which they had believed was safe) had the most difficult time recovering from the rape. Specifically, these women were more likely to feel distrustful of other people, to experience pervasive feelings of fear, and to perceive the world as a dangerous place than were women who had suspected that their attack situation was unsafe. This finding suggests that rape victims who cope the worst may be those who initially felt safest (i.e., least vulnerable). Similarly, women who had been using contraception and got pregnant anyway were more depressed and less likely to believe they had control over their lives than women who had not taken any steps to avoid pregnancy (Janoff-Bulman & Golden, 1984). More generally, people who are victimized despite the fact that they took precautions and avoided risky situations may feel especially distressed because their assumptions of trust and safety were so drastically violated (see also Wortman, 1983).

Research on reactions to illness and hospitalization also points to the potential maladaptiveness of illusions of invulnerability. For example, Janoff-Bulman and Marshall (1982) found that the elderly residents who coped least well with living in a nursing home were those who felt they had had a great deal of control over their lives before entering the home. Similarly, in a study by Felton and Kahana (1974), institutionalized elderly who persisted in making internal attributions for daily problems over which they actually had little control appeared less well-adjusted than those elderly individuals who made more external attributions for daily problems. And Kubler-Ross (1969) suggested that among terminally ill patients, those who have lived active, controlling, high-pressured lives have more difficulty adjusting to the prospect of death than do more simple, passive people. Finally, Taylor's (1979) distinction between "good patients" and "bad patients" is relevant in the present context. Unlike "good patients" who comply with physicians and staff, "bad patients" question staff behavior, resist recommendations and medications, and are typically unwilling to give up control. Taylor suggests that individuals who have been most accustomed to controlling and managing their environment in the past may have the most difficulty coping with hospitalization and may be most likely to exhibit bad patient behavior. Such resistive behavior is potentially dangerous and may create health risks for bad patients by motivating staff to ignore them, treat their complaints as less serious than those of other patients, overmedicate them, refer them to psychiatrists for treatment, or even discharge them prematurely (Taylor, 1979).

In sum, this body of research suggests that victims who have the most difficulty adjusting to a life crisis may be precisely those individuals who felt least vulnerable before being victimized. Thus, one's previctimization beliefs about risk may determine in part how one copes with actual misfortune. As I have discussed elsewhere (Perloff, 1983), there is evidence that victimization itself tends to shatter a person's illusions of invulnerability, creating a new and unfamiliar sense of vulnerability. Although most victims must contend with this sudden transformation, it may be especially jarring and distressing to those individuals who felt least vulnerable prior to the misfortune.

CONCLUDING REMARKS

A recurring theme throughout this chapter has been the idea that nonvictims preserve their illusions of invulnerability by engaging in downward comparisons and comparing themselves with someone who is more at risk than they themselves are. Not only do nonvictims see themselves as less vulnerable to victimization than many others, but they also estimate that, if they were to be victimized by a particular negative event, they would cope better and recover more quickly than the average person. Such perceptions have important implications for nonvictims' ability to cope with misfortune should it occur and for their reactions to others who have already been victimized. First, as discussed earlier, people's illusions of invulnerability prior to victimization may make an actual life crisis all the more traumatic. Furthermore, if nonvictims believe that they could cope relatively easily with victimization, any difficulties that later arise may be unexpected and therefore all the harder to overcome. Finally, illusions of primary and secondary control may make it difficult for nonvictims to understand, tolerate, and sympathize with individuals experiencing misfortune.

Several important questions remain to be answered about the processes underlying nonvictims' choice of comparison targets and the implications of such choices for precautionary behavior. For example, under what conditions will individuals make upward comparisons, choosing to compare themselves with invulnerable, low-risk others? When will people choose an actual, specific other who is especially vulnerable to a particular negative event (e.g., one of their friends, a well-known celebrity, a specific victim reported in the media), and when will they manufacture a hypothetical target or conjure up images of the prototypical or stereotypical victim? Finally, if downward comparisons foster distorted perceptions of invulnerability, how can people be taught to make adaptive social comparisons?

Encouraging adaptive social comparison strategies is important for several reasons (see Perloff, 1983). First, illusions of unique invulnerability may stem from inappropriate comparison choices (Perloff & Fetzer, 1986; Weinstein, 1980). Second, Weinstein (1980, 1982, 1984) has further speculated that people may only be aware of the factors that reduce their own vulnerability and they may fail to realize that others may have just as many factors in their favor. Indeed, simply learning other nonvictims' reasons for feeling immune significantly decreased subjects' illusions of unique invulnerability (Weinstein, 1980). Because people who feel invulnerable to victimization are less likely to engage in precautionary behaviors than are people who feel vulnerable (Becker, 1974; Haefner & Kirscht, 1970; Tyler, 1980), it is important to continue to explore the role of social comparison in perceptions of risk. Any strategy or intervention that encourages nonvictims to consider a wider range of comparison others, instead of only high-risk targets, may be adaptive in the long run.

REFERENCES

Abramson, L. Y., Seligman, M. E. P., & Teasdale, J. D. (1978). Learned helplessness in humans: Critique and reformulation. *Journal of Abnormal Psychology, 87*, 49–74.
Becker, M. H. (Ed.). (1974). *The Health Belief Model and personal health behavior*. Thorofare, NJ: Charles B. Slack.
Burger, J. M. (1981). Motivational biases in the attribution of responsibility for an accident: A meta-analysis of the defensive-attribution hypothesis. *Psychological Bulletin, 90*, 496–512.
Cantor, N., & Mischel, W. (1977). Traits as prototypes: Effects on recognition memory. *Journal of Personality and Social Psychology, 35*, 38–48.
Coates, D., & Winston, W. (1983). Counteracting the deviance of depression: Peer support groups for victims. *Journal of Social Issues, 39(2)*, 171–196.
Coates, D., & Wortman, C. B. (1980). Depression maintenance and interpersonal control. In A. Baum & J. E. Singer (Eds.), *Advances in environmental psychology: Applications of personal control* (Vol. 2, pp. 149–182). Hillsdale, NJ: Erlbaum.
Coates, D., Wortman, C. B., & Abbey, A. (1979). Reactions to victims. In I. H. Frieze, D. Bar-Tal, & J. S. Carroll (Eds.), *New approaches to social problems* (pp. 21–52). San Francisco, CA: Jossey-Bass.
Cottrell, N. B., & Epley, S. W. (1977). Affiliation, social comparison, and socially mediated stress reduction. In J. M. Suls & R. L. Miller (Eds.), *Social comparison processes* (pp. 43–68). Washington, DC: Hemisphere.
Darley, J. M., & Aronson, E. (1966). Self-evaluation vs. direct anxiety reduction as determinants of the fear-affiliation relationship. *Journal of Experimental Social Psychology, Supplement 1*, 66–79.
Dubow, F., McCabe, E., & Kaplan, G. (1978). *Reactions to crime: A critical review of the literature*. Unpublished manuscript, Center for Urban Affairs, Northwestern University.

Ennis, P. H. (1967). *Criminal victimization in the United States: A report of a national survey.* Washington, DC: U.S. Government Printing Office.

Felton, B., & Kahana, E. (1974). Adjustment and situationally-bound locus of control among institutionalized aged. *Journal of Gerontology, 29,* 295–301.

Festinger, L. (1954). A theory of social comparison processes. *Human Relations, 7,* 117–140.

Fink, R., Shapiro, S., & Roester, R. (1972). Impact of efforts to increase participation in repetitive screenings for early breast cancer detection. *American Journal of Public Health, 62,* 328–336.

Gallup Report, (1981; March). "Most favor 55 mph limit but few obey." Report No. 186.

Glass, D. C., & Singer, J. E. (1972). *Urban stress.* New York: Academic Press.

Haefner, D., & Kirscht, J. P. (1970). Motivational and behavioral effects of modifying health beliefs. *Public Health Reports, 85,* 478–484.

Harris, D. M., & Guten, S. (1979). Health-protective behavior: An exploratory study. *Journal of Health and Social Behavior, 20,* 17–29.

Higgins, E. T., Rholes, W. S., & Jones, C. R. (1977). Category accessibility and impression formation. *Journal of Experimental Social Psychology, 13,* 141–154.

Hindelang, M. J., Gottfredson, M. R., & Garofalo, J. (1978). *Victims of personal crime.* Cambridge, MA: Ballinger.

Janis, I. L. (1958). *Psychological stress.* New York: Wiley.

Janoff-Bulman, R., & Brickman, P. (1982). Expectations and what people learn from failure. In N. T. Feather (Ed.), *Expectations and actions* (pp. 207–237). Hillsdale, NJ: Erlbaum.

Janoff-Bulman, R., & Golden, D. (1984). *Attributions and adjustment to abortion.* Paper presented at the annual meeting of the American Psychological Association, Toronto.

Janoff-Bulman, R., & Lang-Gunn, L. (in press). Coping with disease and accidents: The role of self-blame attributions. In L. Y. Abramson (Ed.), *Social-personal inference in clinical psychology.* New York: Guilford.

Janoff-Bulman, R., & Marshall, G. (1982). Mortality, well-being, and control: A study of an aged population of institutionalized elderly. *Personality and Social Psychology Bulletin, 8,* 691–698.

Johnson, J., & Leventhal, H. (1974). Effects of accurate expectations and behavioral instructions on reactions during a noxious medical examination. *Journal of Personality and Social Psychology, 29,* 710–718.

Kahneman, D., & Tversky, A. (1973). On the psychology of prediction. *Psychological Review, 80,* 237–251.

Kegeles, S. S. (1963). Some motives for seeking preventive dental care. *Journal of the American Dental Association, 67,* 90–98.

Kirscht, J. F., Haefner, D. P., Kegeles, S. S., & Rosenstock, I. M. (1966). A national study of health beliefs. *Journal of Health and Human Behavior, 7,* 248–254.

Knopf, A. (1976). Changes in women's opinions about cancer. *Social Science and Medicine, 10,* 191–195.

Kubler-Ross, E. (1969). *On death and dying.* New York: Macmillan.

Kunreuther, H. (1979). The changing societal consequences of risks from natural hazards. *The Annals of the American Academy of Political and Social Science, 443,* 104–116.

Lang, L. (1980). *Sickness as sin: Observers' perceptions of the physically ill.* Unpublished manuscript, University of Massachusetts, Amherst.

Langer, E. (1975). The illusion of control. *Journal of Personality and Social Psychology, 32,* 311–328.

Larwood, L. (1978). Swine flu: A field study of self-serving biases. *Journal of Applied Social Psychology, 18,* 283–289.

LeJeune, R., & Alex, N. (1973). On being mugged: The event and its aftermath. *Urban Life and Culture, 2*, 259–287.

Lerner, M. J. (1980). *The belief in a just world: A fundamental delusion.* New York: Plenum Press.

Lerner, M. J., & Miller, D. T. (1978). Just world research and the attribution process: Looking back and ahead. *Psychological Bulletin, 85*, 1030–1051.

Myers, D. G., & Ridl, J. (1979). Can we all be better than average? *Psychology Today, 13*, 89–98.

Perloff, L. S. (1982). *Nonvictims' judgments of unique and universal vulnerability to future misfortune.* Unpublished doctoral dissertation, Northwestern University, Evanston, IL.

Perloff, L. S. (1983). Perceptions of vulnerability to victimization, *Journal of Social Issues, 39*, 41–61.

Perloff, L. S., & Brickman, P. (1982). False consensus and false uniqueness: Biases in perceptions of similarity. *Academic Psychology Bulletin, 4*, 475–494.

Perloff, L. S., & Bryant, F. B. (1985, August). *Effects of temporal perspective on false consensus and false uniqueness.* Paper presented at the American Psychological Association meeting, Los Angeles, CA.

Perloff, L. S., & Farbisz, R. (1985, May). *Perceptions of uniqueness and illusions of invulnerability to divorce.* Paper presented at the Midwestern Psychological Association meeting, Chicago, IL.

Perloff, L. S., & Fetzer, B. K. (1986). Self-other judgments and perceived vulnerability to victimization. *Journal of Personality and Social Psychology, 50*, 502–510.

Perloff, L. S., Bryant, F. B., & Davidson, L. (1986, August). *Nonvictims' beliefs about coping with victimization.* Paper presented at the American Psychological Association meeting, Washington, DC.

Robertson, L. S. (1977). Car crashes: Perceived vulnerability and willingness to pay for crash protection. *Journal of Community Health, 3*, 136–141.

Rothbaum, F., Weisz, J. R., & Snyder, S. S. (1982). Changing the world and changing the self: A two-process model of perceived control. *Journal of Personality and Social Psychology, 42*, 5–37.

Schachter, S. (1959). *The psychology of affiliation.* Palo Alto, CA: Stanford University Press.

Scheppele, K. L., & Bart, P. B. (1983). Through women's eyes: Defining danger in the wake of sexual assault. *Journal of Social Issues, 39(2)*, 63–81.

Schlenker, B. R., & Miller, R. S. (1977). Egocentrism in groups: Self-serving biases or logical information processing? *Journal of Personality and Social Psychology, 35*, 755–764.

Schriber, J. B., Larwood, L., & Peterson, J. L. (1985). Bias in the attribution of marital conflict. *Journal of Marriage and the Family, 47*, 1–5.

Schulz, R. (1976). Effects of control and predictability on the physical and psychological well-being of the institutionalized aged. *Journal of Personality and Social Psychology, 33*, 563–573.

Seligman, M. E. P. (1975). *Helplessness: On depression, development, and death.* San Francisco, CA: Freeman.

Silver, R. L., & Wortman, C. B. (1980). Coping with undesirable life events. In J. Garber and M. E. P. Seligman (Eds.), *Human helplessness: Theory and application* (279–340). New York: Academic Press.

Skogan, W. G. & Maxfield, M. G. (1981). *Coping with crime.* Beverly Hills, CA: Sage.

Slovic, P., Fischhoff, B., & Lichtenstein, S. (1976). Cognitive processes and societal risk taking. In J. S. Carroll & J. W. Payne (Eds.), *Cognition and social behavior* (pp. 165–184). Hillsdale, NJ: Erlbaum.

Slovic, P., Fischhoff, B., & Lichtenstein, S. (1978). Accident probabilities and seat belt usage: A psychological perspective. *Accident Analysis and Prevention, 10*, 281–285.

Snyder, C. R. (1978). The "illusion" of uniqueness. *Journal of Humanistic Psychology, 18,* 33–41.

Suls, J., & Becker, M. (1980). *False consensus and the perceptions of others' fears: "I'm afraid, you're afraid."* Unpublished manuscript, State University of New York at Albany.

Svenson, O. (1981). Are we all less risky and more skillful than our fellow drivers? *Acta Psychologica, 47,* 143–148.

Taylor, S. E. (1979). Hospital patient behavior: Reactance, helplessness, or control? *Journal of Social Issues, 35,* 156–184.

Taylor, S. E., Wood, J. V., & Lichtman, R. R. (1983). It could be worse: Selective evaluation as a response to victimization. *Journal of Social Issues, 39,* 19–40.

Tversky, A. (1977). Features of similarity. *Psychological Review, 84,* 327–352.

Tyler, T. R. (1980). Impact of directly and indirectly experienced events: The origin of crime-related judgments and behaviors. *Journal of Personality and Social Psychology, 39,* 13–28.

Walster, E. (1966). Assignment of responsibility for an accident. *Journal of Personality and Social Psychology, 3,* 73–79.

Weinstein, N. D. (1977, August). *Coping with environmental hazards: Reactions to the threat of crime.* Paper presented at the American Psychological Association Convention, San Francisco.

Weinstein, N. D. (1980). Unrealistic optimism about future life events. *Journal of Personality and Social Psychology, 39,* 806–820.

Weinstein, N. D. (1982). Unrealistic optimism about susceptibility to health problems. *Journal of Behavioral Medicine, 5,* 441–460.

Weinstein, N. D. (1983). Reducing unrealistic optimism about illness susceptibility. *Health Psychology, 2,* 11–20.

Weinstein, N. D. (1984). Why it won't happen to me: Perceptions of risk factors and susceptibility. *Health Psychology, 3,* 431–457.

Weinstein, N. D., & Lachendro, E. (1982). Egocentrism as a source of unrealistic optimism. *Personality and Social Psychology Bulletin, 8,* 195–200.

Wills, T. A. (1981). Downward comparison principles in social psychology. *Psychological Bulletin, 90,* 245–271.

Wolfenstein, M. (1957). *Disaster: A psychological essay.* Glencoe, IL: The Free Press.

Wortman, C. B. (1976). Causal attributions and personal control. In J. H. Harvey, W. J. Ickes, & R. F. Kidd (Eds.), *New directions in attribution research* (Vol. 1). Hillsdale, NJ: Erlbaum.

Wortman, C. B. (1983). Coping with victimization: Conclusions and implications for future research. *Journal of Social Issues, 39,* 195–221.

Wortman, C. B., & Brehm, J. W. (1975). Responses to uncontrollable outcomes: An integration of reactance theory and the learned helplessness model. In L. Berkowitz (Ed.), *Advances in experimental social psychology* (Vol. 8, pp. 277–334). New York: Academic Press.

Wortman, C. B., & Dunkel-Schetter, C. (1979). Interpersonal relationships and cancer: A theoretical analysis. *Journal of Social Issues, 35,* 120–155.

Wylie, R. C. (1979). *The self-concept: Theory and research on selected topics.* (Vol. 2). Lincoln, NB: University of Nebraska Press.

Zimbardo, P., & Formica, R. (1963). Emotional comparison and self-esteem as determinants of affiliation. *Journal of Personality, 31,* 141–162.

10

Downward Comparison as a Coping Mechanism

THOMAS ASHBY WILLS

This chapter discusses the use of downward comparison as a means of reducing the psychological impact of negative life events. I focus on how social comparison processes can be used by distressed persons to maintain or enhance their subjective well-being. The essence of downward comparison as a coping mechanism is to arrange comparison with other persons so that the outcome of the comparison is favorable to the self. Through this process, the self is perceived to be better off (in some sense) than the comparison target; the favorable outcome of the comparison process thus produces an enhancement of the person's psychological state. In the following sections I outline the theoretical basis for downward comparison as a coping mechanism, summarize the current empirical support for downward comparison processes, and discuss a number of empirical issues for further research on coping through social comparison.

THE THEORY OF DOWNWARD COMPARISON

The fundamental proposition of social comparison theory is that many psychological characteristics, such as abilities, opinions, and feel-

THOMAS ASHBY WILLS • Departments of Psychology and Epidemiology, Ferkauf Graduate School of Psychology and Albert Einstein College of Medicine, 1300 Morris Park Avenue, Bronx, NY 10461.

ings, are not easily evaluated by reference to some absolute standard. As a consequence of this psychological fact, comparison theory posits that people may approach the understanding of their psychological characteristics by comparing themselves with other persons on some relevant dimension (Festinger, 1954). Through comparison with others in the social environment, it is postulated, persons arrive at self-appraisals that are clearer or perhaps more confidently held than would have been the case in the absence of social comparison. Whether the self-appraisal is actually more accurate in an objective sense is an important issue that is discussed in following sections.

From the outset it was realized that there is a potential conflict between self-evaluation and self-enhancement in social comparison. In theory, social comparison could be pursued in such a way as to obtain the most accurate evaluation of the self (self-evaluation) or in such a way as to obtain the most favorable evaluation of the self (self-enhancement). These two aspects of social comparison may pose a dilemma for a person, particularly when the available comparisons are not entirely favorable to the self. At the theoretical level, comparison theories have addressed these issues separately. Festinger's (1954) social comparison theory focused on the evaluation of abilities and delineated the principles of self-evaluative comparison, usually known as upward comparison because laboratory studies showed that persons seeking to evaluate their abilities typically compare with better-off others (Gruder, 1977). Downward comparison theory (Wills, 1981) addressed the issue of self-enhancing comparison by persons who are stressed or threatened; this theory focuses on how people may compare downward, that is, with worse-off others, in order to achieve self-enhancement.

Balance between Self-Evaluation and Self-Enhancement

In considering a general model of human functioning, one recognizes that there must be some kind of balance between self-evaluation and self-enhancement. If self-evaluation were discarded entirely, actions would become divorced from objective environmental contingencies, removing a crucial link that is necessary for adequate coping and maintained feelings of efficacious functioning (Bandura, 1977). On the other hand, when challenges to self-esteem are present, such as when performances are criticized (Snyder, Higgins, & Stucky, 1983), then focusing on comparisons that are adverse to the self will have negative psychological consequences, which increase to the extent that unfavorable comparisons are pursued. Under such conditions, self-enhancing comparisons should be more conducive to subjective well-being.

The theory of downward comparison as a coping mechanism (Wills, 1983) posits that behavioral patterns under naturalistic conditions represent a mixture of self-evaluative and self-enhancing comparisons. At the most general level, self-enhancing comparison is predicted to increase as the level of psychological distress increases. Under everyday conditions self-evaluative comparison should be the prevailing type, whereas for persons currently experiencing a high level of negative life events, downward comparisons should increase in probability.[1] At a more specific level an individual's behavioral repertoire is based on a number of ability and interest dimensions that undoubtedly vary in current level of positive evaluation from the social environment and in their centrality for individual definitions of self-esteem (cf. Fisher, Nadler, & Whitcher-Alagna, 1982; McGuire, 1984; Tesser & Campbell, 1983). Thus within an individual's life space there should be some dimensions where self-evaluative comparison is dominant, and some where self-enhancing comparison may be dominant. Pure self-evaluation and self-enhancement are posited to represent the end points of a comparison continuum, and it is presumed that at a given point in time an individual is concurrently pursuing comparison processes that represent various points on this dimension.

The theory of comparison-oriented coping depends crucially on a theory of the impact of life events. Although there has been a large amount of research on the cumulative impact of life events (e.g., Dohrenwend & Dohrenwend, 1981), there has been relatively little attention to the specific coping requirements evoked by particular types of events (Cohen & Wills, 1985). In the present context I would note that negative events produce disruption and distress, and that coping through social comparison is primarily relevant to the reduction of distress. Coping through cognitive mechanisms may be pursued primarily when coping through instrumental action is difficult or impractical (Wills, 1981).

It is possible to note some propositions about life-event impact that will be the basis for the subsequent discussion. First is the proposition that a crucial element in the impact of negative events is threat to self-esteem; although events may also create disruption of established behavior patterns, many types of events present severe threats to self-esteem, especially those involving interpersonal conflict and rejection (e.g., Bloom, Asher, & White, 1978; Wills & Langner, 1980). It is this element

---

[1]It is recognized that psychological distress may also be internally created, for example by depressive tendencies (Lewinsohn, Hoberman, Teri, & Hautzinger, 1985), personality factors such as self-consciousness (Pyszczynski & Greenberg, Chap. 4, this volume), or other factors. The focus here, though, is on reactions to objective negative events.

of threat of self-esteem that is presumed to be the primary focus of comparison-oriented coping. Second, there are several variables that may relate to the impact of life events, such as controllability versus uncontrollability and discrete versus enduring nature (see Pearlin & Schooler, 1978; Stone & Neale, 1984). A straightforward prediction is that comparison-oriented coping will be more probable for events that are uncontrollable. Whether this type of coping will be more prevalent for enduring strains such as marital or job dissatisfaction rather than for discrete events is difficult to predict, but I incline to the latter prediction.

Mechanisms of Coping through Downward Comparison

Given that a central element of self-esteem has been threatened because of a negative event, downward comparison theory posits that subjective well-being can be enhanced or restored by pursuing comparisons that produce a relatively favorable outcome for the self. Downward comparison theory makes a distinction between passive comparisons, in which individuals take advantage of an available opportunity (not of their own making) for a self-enhancing comparison, and active comparisons, in which persons engage in a cognitive or behavioral action that produces a downward comparison (Wills, 1981). Downward comparison as pursued in natural settings probably comprises a group of related processes, perhaps used for different problems or by different types of persons. Following are specific mechanisms that can be used to achieve downward comparisons; they are listed roughly in order from passive to active.

Conceivable Worse Alternatives. Given that an adverse event has occurred, it is possible for a person to imagine more adverse versions of the same event, and thus to cope with the actual event by feeling relatively well-off in comparison with the hypothetical worse event. This may be termed the "could have been worse" strategy. Strictly speaking this is not a social comparison mechanism because the comparison is not with other persons, but rather with the self under different circumstances, making it close to a branch of temporal comparison theory (Albert, 1977). It is, nonetheless, a coping mechanism based on comparison.

Coincidental Occurrence of Comparison Target. Various sources may present examples of persons worse off than the self, who can then be used as targets for downward comparison if self-enhancement motivation is operative. Probably the best example is media presentations: TV shows, newspapers, and magazines daily present examples of persons who have been victims of negative events (e.g., crime, accident, natural disaster, personal problems). Individuals in the audience can, if they are so inclined, employ such presentations as targets for downward comparison. In principle such instances of comparison could occur totally by accident, merely involving the coincidental viewing of an appropriate target at an appropriate time. The suspicion, however, is that there is some element of self-selection in downward comparison through media presentations, because persons choose which TV shows to watch and which newspaper to buy. There is a considerable range in the typical level of negative-events reporting across different newspapers, for example, and the high prevalence of disaster and misfortune displayed daily in certain newspapers may, purposively or inadvertantly, be based on the provision of downward comparison for a proportion of the audience.

Selective Abstraction of Positive Attributes. Various information-processing strategies or heuristics may be employed to arrive at a perception of the self that is relatively favorable, based on the available information. Given that some negative element of the self is acknowledged, for example, individuals may make assumptions about population base rates so that the negative element is assumed to be common in the population; alternatively, persons can make probabilistic assumptions suggesting that their known positive attributes are relatively rare in the population. Differential memory for attributes of the self is another possible cognitive mechanism, which could work to produce underrecall of one's negative attributes or overrecall of one's positive attributes in comparison with available information about population base rates for those attributes.[2]

Selective Focus. Concerning mechanisms that involve more active use of comparison, downward comparison theory posits that persons may purposively select a target in such a way as to provide a favorable comparison for the self. There are at least two ways in which this can be achieved. The first is to choose a target who is generally at the same level of adjustment or distress as the self, but is worse off on a particular dimension. The focusing of the comparison process on this dimension thus produces a downward comparison for the index person. Using this mechanism, persons may select comparison others who have the same type of problem as the self, but are coping less well with some aspect of the problem (Wills, 1983; Wood, Taylor, & Lichtman, 1985). This may be termed comparison with an equally unfortunate other.

Selective Target Choice. By actively selecting a comparison target who is worse off than the self on several dimensions, one can achieve the

---

[2]Note that accurate knowledge about population base rates is often quite difficult to obtain, either in practice or in principle (Rothbart, 1981). Thus cognitive heuristics have considerable flexibility in determining self-perceptions.

widest disparity in social comparison. From the range of figures available in the social milieu, a target can be chosen who is worse off than the focal person with respect to psychological functioning, health, economic circumstances, or any other dimension that may be salient for the subject. In theory, this type of comparison may be somewhat more restrictive than the selective-focus mechanism, which is less restrictive with regard to targets. Conceivably the disadvantage from the standpoint of target availability could be offset by the greater advantage in comparison favorability.

Derogation of Others. By actively derogating the ability or personality attributes of others, persons may increase the psychological distance between the self and the other, and thus achieve a type of active downward comparison. Coping with an ego-threat by attributing negative traits to others, or actively devaluing others' personality attributes, is a process that has been termed projection, scapegoating, or displaced aggression.[3]

EMPIRICAL SUPPORT FOR DOWNWARD COMPARISON

In the following sections I summarize the current empirical support for downward comparison theory. The presentation concentrates on evidence derived from situations in which persons' well-being has been decreased, as in ego-threat manipulations, psychological distress, or physical illness. The discussion focuses on showing how downward comparison has been demonstrated across a variety of situations that involve coping with negative affect.

Laboratory Studies of Self-Esteem Threat

The basic prediction of downward comparison theory is that persons experiencing a threat to their self-esteem will shift toward comparison with worse-off others. This proposition is supported by a variety of studies that manipulated variables relevant to downward comparison. In the original Hakmiller (1966) study, ego threat was manipulated by informing subjects that they had undesirable personality traits, and subjects were then allowed to select information about potential comparison targets from a group of six persons. Hakmiller found that in the high-threat condition, 95% of comparison choices were directed at worse-off

---

[3]In downward comparison theory, direct physical aggression is also construed as an active comparison mechanism (Wills, 1981).

others, a substantial shift from the pattern of choices shown by subjects in a low-threat condition. Similarly, the pattern of results from studies testing what was termed the fear-affiliation effect were consistent with a downward comparison formulation, showing that threatened subjects consistently choose affiliates who are worse off than the self (see Wills, 1981). Other studies have indicated that subjects low in self-esteem are more likely to make downward comparisons (Friend & Gilbert, 1973; Wilson & Benner, 1971). In two laboratory studies, Gibbons (1986) found that a mood-lowering manipulation caused a preference for information about negative occurrences to other persons; this downward comparison effect was specific to a group of subjects previously classified as depressed, and did not obtain for a group of nondepressed subjects.

Recent laboratory studies using cognitive psychology paradigms have also shown evidence of downward comparison mechanisms among subjects who are threatened or distressed. For example, Sherman, Presson, & Chassin (1984) gave subjects success or failure feedback on an experimental task and then asked them to make estimates of the typical performance of other persons. Two studies showed that a specific effect of the failure condition was to alter (downward) subjects' estimates of the level of successful performance in the population. An analogous study of attributions (Pyszczynski, Greenberg, & LaPrelle, 1985) indicated that subjects in a failure condition requested more information about other persons when they expected it to reveal that most persons performed poorly. These studies represent instances where probabilistic judgment or information selection is altered in such a way as to create a more favorable comparison for the threatened subject. Amabile and Glazebrook (1982) verged into a study of projection by inducing a relatively low status for subjects and then allowing them to make evaluative ratings of others. Several studies showed that when subjects' status was experimentally lowered their evaluations of other persons shifted in a negative direction, thereby producing a greater comparison discrepancy.

Projection and Scapegoating

A specific prediction from downward comparison theory is that persons whose self-esteem is threatened will make more negative evaluations of target persons so as to alter the social comparison situation between the self and the other. A body of literature dealing with what traditionally has been construed as "scapegoating" or "displaced aggression" provides evidence for this phenomenon: across a wide variety of threat manipulations and targets (usually, but not always, racial minorities), it is found that threat produces more negative evaluations of others (see Wills, 1981). Traditional field studies of social prejudice are also consistent with this formulation, indicating prejudice to be strongest among persons whose self-esteem is low or whose social status is either low or declining (Brewer & Campbell, 1976; Ehrlich, 1973; Stephan & Rosenfield, 1978; Taylor, Sheatsley, & Greeley, 1978).

Research based on the psychoanalytic concept of projection has also been construed in downward comparison terms because the experimental designs employed in studies of projection are essentially identical to those used in studies of scapegoating. Indeed, the typical finding in projection studies is that threatened subjects make more negative evaluations of target persons (see Holmes, 1978; Wills, 1981). Recent studies of attributive projection continue to show evidence for self-enhancing comparison. For example, Campbell (1986) asked subjects to make estimates of the extent to which their own abilities and their own opinions were shared by others in the population. It was found that compared with population base rates, subjects underestimated the prevalence of their own abilities (thus making themselves appear relatively advantaged) and overestimated the prevalence of their own opinions (thus making themselves appear more socially normative). Moreover, this study showed that the underestimation of consensus for abilities varied directly with the centrality of the ability for the subject's self-esteem, providing direct evidence of a self-enhancement basis for this projection process.

Effect of Comparison on Subjective Well-Being

A major issue for laboratory studies is determining whether comparison processes produce changes in subjective well-being, as predicted by downward comparison theory. Because this issue has not been specifically delineated in previous research, investigations of actual changes in well-being were not systematic; but evidence from several areas has shown changes on relevant measures.

In studies of fear-affiliation, for example, it has been found that subjects given an opportunity to affiliate with worse-off others show decreases in self-rated anxiety and in physiological measures of stress (see Wills, 1981). In studies of social comparison choice, decreases in self-rated distress have been noted in conditions where threatened subjects compare with worse-off others (Hakmiller, 1966). Studies of projection have produced erratic results, probably because of methodological difficulties with the types of comparison targets provided, but several studies have shown evidence of stress reduction when threatened subjects are allowed to attribute negative personality traits to target persons (Bennett & Holmes, 1975; Burish & Houston, 1979). More recently a direct test was conducted by Crocker and Gallo (1985) in a laboratory study where subjects were induced either to compare upward by referring to self-defined desirable social groups (of which the subject was not a member) or to compare downward by referring to self-defined undesirable social groups (of which the subject was not a member). Results showed that subjects in the downward comparison condition showed decreased anxiety and depressive mood, and increased life satisfaction. From several types of analyses the authors concluded that the results derived from a specific effect of downward comparison's increasing well-being, not one of well-being's decreasing through upward comparison. Similarly, Gibbons (1986) found that a downward comparison opportunity improved mood states among a group of subjects previously classified as depressed; for nondepressed subjects, the downward comparison opportunity had no effect on mood states.

Studies of Social Comparison in Children

Research on social comparison in children has focused on descriptive studies of comparison in school settings and studies of how comparison changes with age (see Levine, 1983; Suls & Mullen, 1982). A number of studies have shown that children as early as kindergarten do perceive and utilize social comparison information (e.g., Ruble, Boggiano, Feldman, & Loebl, 1980). Although studies of children have traditionally concentrated on self-evaluation, there have been some recent investigations of downward comparison processes in child populations. For example, a study by Levine and Green (1984) placed children in a laboratory setting where their performance (as indicated by experimental feedback) either improved or deteriorated; subjects were then provided with an opportunity to select information about the performance of other children. Results showed that when children perceived their performance was getting worse they more frequently chose information about the scores of inferior others, and the preference for downward comparison information increased over trials. This study provides a clear demonstration of downward comparison among relatively young children.

Laboratory evidence is complemented by field studies conducted by Tesser and colleagues (see Tesser, 1984). In a school sample of 270 fifth and sixth graders, the investigators had children rate their own performance on both personally relevant and irrelevant activities, and then to rate the performances of other children who were either close (friends) or distant (nonfriends). The results (Tesser, Campbell, & Smith, 1984) showed that children rated themselves as superior to close others on personally relevant dimensions, whereas they rated themselves as inferior to close others on low-relevant dimensions, a pattern that the investigators interpreted as allowing children to maintain self-enhancing comparison while also maintaining interpersonal relationships with other children. Other field studies have examined social comparison processes among samples of children with adjustment difficulties, since some paradoxical observations indicated that mentally retarded children often rated their own competence as equal to that of regular classroom pupils (Gibbons, 1985a; Renick & Harter, 1984). Measurements of comparison indicated that these effects were based on a selective comparison process; retarded children often compared themselves with retarded peers who were even less competent, thus producing relatively favorable evaluations for the self (Gibbons, 1985a; Silon & Harter, 1985). The investigators suggested that the selective comparison process was used by these children in the attempt to cope with the self-esteem consequences of their disadvantaged status (Gibbons, 1985b; Harter, 1985).

Field Studies of Social Comparison

Laboratory evidence on downward comparison has been extended in several field studies that have examined how comparison processes are employed by threatened persons in natural settings. These studies have investigated crime fear, physical illness, psychological distress, and general well-being.

Fear of Crime. A telephone survey by Heath (1984) was based on the prediction that residents' fear of crime in their own area would be reduced through comparison with other areas where the crime level was worse. This was tested by obtaining ratings of crime-fear perception from samples of residents in 36 localities and relating this variable to codings of crime reports published in the newspaper for that locality. Results confirmed the prediction, indicating that there was a lower level of crime fear among residents whose local newspaper contained a high level of reports of crime in other cities.

Physical Illness. Coping with physical illness was investigated by Wood, Taylor, and Lichtman (1985) in a sample of 78 private-practice patients undergoing treatment for breast cancer. Respondents were questioned about whether they had sought information about their illness from media sources, and about the types of comparisons they had made with other patients. The results showed primarily downward comparisons. Seventy-eight percent of the respondents indicated that they felt they were coping better with their illness, compared with other cancer patients. Data on specific comparisons showed that the respondents made comparisons with other patients in such a way as to emphasize dimensions on which they were more favorably situated, or coping better with the illness, compared with the target persons. The investigators interpreted these data as indicating that the respondents used downward comparison mechanisms to reduce the threat produced by their illness. Somewhat similar results were found by Gerrard, Gibbons, and Sharp (1985) in a study of self-help groups for bulimic clients. Explicit measures of comparison choices were obtained for group members blocked on level of current depression. Results showed that all subjects preferred comparison with a person who had a fairly severe case of bulimia. The high-depression subjects, however, showed a clear preference for comparison with a person who was not coping well with her problem. This preference was not found among low-depression subjects, who preferred comparison with someone having a fairly severe case of bulimia and who was coping well.

Physical Disability. Mixed results were obtained in a study of 100 middle-aged persons disabled through spinal cord injury, interviewed an average of 20 years after the disability had occurred (Schulz & Decker, 1985). The interview schedule included questions about intrapersonal comparisons (before vs. after the injury) and social comparisons (current life situation compared with other disabled or nondisabled persons). The results were complex in that respondents rated their life situation as worse after the disability (compared with before) but at the same time they rated their own life situation in relatively favorable terms compared with that of nondisabled persons. The authors reported that this result occurred because respondents emphasized what they felt to be unique positive characteristics on which they were relatively advantaged, such as intellectual accomplishment, interpersonal relationships, and sensitivity to others' needs. In this study, however, the measures of social comparison were not related to measures of current psychological distress.

Psychological Distress. In an epidemiological study of a community sample of 2,300 adults in the Chicago metropolitan area, Pearlin and Schooler (1978) defined a coping mechanism that they termed Positive Comparison. This measure was based on factorial items indicating that a respondent coped with problems by comparing their own situation favorably with that of other persons and appreciating their own situation more after seeing what others' situations were like. This coping mechanism was related to reduced psychological symptomatology on a concurrent basis (Pearlin & Schooler, 1978) and was shown to be related to reduced distress and problem levels on a prospective basis over a 4-year interval (Menaghan, 1982).[4]

---

[4]There is, however, some ambiguity with the comparison measure used in this study. For marital coping, the items in the Positive Comparison factor were "How would you com-

General Well-Being. Studies of overall well-being and life satisfaction in general populations typically have not been designed with respect to social comparison theory, but they include a number of variables that are relevant to social comparison propositions. Diener (1984) discussed this literature from a multitheoretical perspective and concluded that among several alternative models, social comparison theory was quite consistent with the evidence on subjective well-being, particularly so because of the common finding that objective measures of life circumstances (e.g., grades, income) do not correlate well with subjective perceptions of well-being. A study by Emmons and Diener (1985) tested this proposition in a sample of 149 college students. It was found that measures of objective life conditions did not account for much variance in subjective well-being, whereas a measure of social comparison, indexing the perception that the person was doing better in comparison with others, was the best predictor of subjective well-being.

To summarize, the work previously discussed indicates that downward comparison is used as a mechanism for coping with distress and negative affect in several different types of situations. Demonstrations of downward comparison processes have been obtained with both adults and children, and confirmations of downward comparison have occurred in both laboratory and field settings. This research has suggested several cognitive and perceptual mechanisms through which persons may increase their subjective well-being through comparison with selected targets. Together, the cumulative results from these various areas of research provide grounds for considering that downward comparison may be a prevalent mechanism for coping with negative life events.

RESEARCH ISSUES FOR COPING AND SOCIAL COMPARISON

In the following section I discuss some theoretical and methodological issues that are of importance for research on downward comparison as a coping mechanism. I consider some issues that are currently

---

pare your marriage with that of other people," "With time, does your marriage get better," and "How often do you appreciate your own marriage more after seeing what other marriages are like." Of these three items the first appears to be more an outcome measure (i.e., marital satisfaction), the second is ambiguous, possibly indexing either coping or outcome, and only the third appears on face value to clearly index social comparison. Of the three items, the social comparison item had the lowest loading on the factor. Thus there is considerable ambiguity in the measure, and there may be a confounding of coping with outcome.

controversial in social comparison research, some issues that are relatively unexplored, and some issues that are not being examined in current research.

Studies of Social Comparison in Natural Settings

A pervasive issue in social-psychological research is the complementary relationship between laboratory studies and field studies. Laboratory paradigms used in human research have the advantage of strong demonstration of causality, but are open to doubt concerning the external validity of the results. Field studies present complementary characteristics, in that results obtained with a reasonably large sample in field settings are quite strong from the standpoint of external validity; interpretation of causal relationships, however, may be ambiguous when cross-sectional correlations are the only data. Prospective analyses of longitudinal data sets are a reasonable solution to causality issues, but are relatively rare (see Cohen & Syme, 1985; Wills, 1986).

One fruitful approach to dealing with this issue is research that alternates between laboratory and field studies, generating hypotheses about stress and coping on the basis of laboratory research and then testing such hypotheses in field settings (e.g., Cohen, Evans, Krantz, & Stokols, 1980; Wood, Taylor, & Lichtman, 1985). The experience from this research is that some laboratory results are confirmed in the field, and some are not, or are supported in rather different ways than would have been expected from laboratory models. The results from Wood *et al.* (1985), for example, provided general confirmation of downward comparison predictions but indicated that respondents pursued comparison by focusing on particular dimensions on which they were relatively advantaged in comparison to the target, a process that had not generally been studied in laboratory research.

For field studies of social comparison there are two issues that are crucial from a theoretical standpoint: similarity and target selection. Theories of social comparison have focused on propositions about comparison with similar versus dissimilar others, and because the construct of similarity was well-defined in the original Festinger (1954) social comparison theory and in the related-attributes formulation (Goethals & Darley, 1977), for laboratory studies of social comparison the design issues were straightforward. For studies of downward comparison, however, there is no theoretical requirement that comparison occur on a specified dimension, because downward comparison in principle may be pursued by comparison on any of a variety of dimensions. Analogously, with regard to target selection the upward comparison theory is quite restrictive, whereas downward comparison theory emphasizes the flexibility that persons may have in selection of targets for self-enhancing comparison. In theory the self-enhancement value of downward comparison is posited to be greatest when it is possible to compare with a person who has a similar problem but is worse off than the self, either because of less adequate coping on the problem dimension or because of less favorable status on other dimensions (Wills, 1981). The implication for research design in field settings is that the investigator should consider a wide range of potential comparison targets. Optimally, a study would examine comparison targets with a similar problem as the index subject, targets with a current problem but a dissimilar one, and targets with no current problems. Additionally, it would be desirable to include comparison targets with different social status from the index subjects, because fate similarity and status similarity have often been confounded in previous research.

Effectiveness of Downward Comparison

A related issue for research on coping is determining the consequences of comparisons in natural settings. Although laboratory research has shown short-term changes in affect as a result of downward comparison, the long-term consequences of comparison-oriented coping are largely unknown. The consequences are not easily predictable from theory. It could be argued that if downward comparison in the face of acute threats to self-esteem produces changes in affect, then it could lead to better adjustment over the long run. However, there is a possibility that a pattern of focusing on negative aspects of other persons on a continued basis would lead to a generally negative view of others, with adverse effects on interpersonal relationships. It could also be surmised that an overreliance on cognitive coping mechanisms might decrease the use of active, problem-solving types of coping, with possibly detrimental effects on long-term adjustment. Current findings on the relative effectiveness of cognitive versus behavioral coping mechanisms in different settings are complex (cf. Billings & Moos, 1981; Felton, Revenson, & Hinrichsen, 1983; Folkman & Lazarus, 1980; Wills, 1986) and do not provide any clear guidance for asserting that cognitive approaches to coping are necessarily either beneficial or harmful.

Several methodological points are relevant for tests of the effectiveness of coping mechanisms. One is that the coping mechanisms must be defined and measured in a way that does not confound the process of coping with the outcome of coping (Moos & Billings, 1982). For some coping mechanisms this is neither a trivial nor an easy measurement problem, and measures of social comparison are not immune to this issue (see Footnote 4). In addition, a reasonable test of coping effectiveness almost necessarily requires longitudinal data, because cross-sectional correlations among stressors, coping measures, and outcome measures may be quite ambiguous from the standpoint of causality (cf. Dooley, 1985; Wills, 1986): In many cases it is equally plausible to interpret the coping as causing the outcome, or the reverse. Prospective analyses, predicting Time 2 outcomes from Time 1 coping with control for Time 1 symptomatology, are a preferred solution (Cohen & Wills, 1985), with two-stage least-squares analysis being an alternative procedure (Dooley, 1985). Prospective designs are not, however, a royal road to guaranteed results; the time course of the coping–outcome relationship and the stability of the predictor and outcome measures must be carefully considered so that the design will have the greatest likelihood of showing significant prospective effects (see Cohen & Syme, 1985).

Another important issue for coping research is the generality of coping–outcome relationships. This issue applies particularly to research on coping with physical illness, because processes that are effective for coping with one type of illness (e.g., arthritis) may be less effective for coping with another type of disease, such as cancer (see Felton *et al.*, 1983). At a more basic level, it is important to determine whether comparison-oriented coping is effective for reducing the generalized distress created by any stressor (Dohrenwend, Shrout, Egri, & Mendelsohn, 1981) or whether the comparison process has particular relevance for certain components of the threat evoked by negative events (e.g., ego threat, uncontrollability, unpredictability). Because of these issues the ideal study of coping through comparison would include one group of psychologically distressed persons, at least one group of medically distressed respondents, and one group of matched neighborhood controls so that there could be some determination of whether the coping–outcome process was differentially relevant for various groups. Multidimensional outcome measures would also help to clarify which dimension(s) of psychological distress is reduced through particular coping processes.

Finally, it would be informative to study coping at different stages of the disease process. In principle, coping through comparison could be highly effective at one stage of a disease (e.g., reducing acute distress during the diagnosis or onset phase) but less effective during other phases of the disease, such as adjustment, remission, or long-term maintenance. A plausible hypothesis is that downward comparison may be strongly related to psychological symptomatology during early stages of adaptation to a negative event (Bulman & Wortman, 1977; Brickman,

Coates, & Janoff-Bulman, 1978) but less relevant for adjustment after long-term adaptation to the event has been accomplished (Schulz & Decker, 1985). Thus it would be highly desirable to study coping-outcome relationships during at least two stages of the disease process.

Measurement of Comparison

The other issue for research on comparison as a coping mechanism is how best to measure comparison. In field studies this is not necessarily a trivial matter, because the independent variable (making a relevant comparison with another person or persons) is not an overt behavior and typically has occurred at some time before the point of measurement. Forcing subjects to make narrowly defined contemporaneous comparisons may miss important aspects of long-term comparison processes. On the other hand, when retrospective questions about past comparisons are employed, there is a danger of confounding of past coping and past adjustment. Current investigators have had to choose carefully to steer between these two shoals.

Several measurement approaches are possible in field settings. One is to ask subjects about what types of comparisons they have made. This has possible disadvantages including retrospective error or symptomatology bias, plus the fact that persons may be ambivalent about the social desirability of downward comparisons (Brickman, 1975; Wills, 1981). An example of this approach was used by Schulz and Decker (1985), who presented respondents with an interview question asking subjects with whom they compared themselves to decide how good their life situation was. These investigators found that respondents had difficulty with the question, typically stating that they did not compare themselves with other people; eventual responses to repeated prompting produced data indicating that 59% of respondents did not compare with any particular group of persons. Alternatively, the investigator can present subjects with a range of defined comparison targets and ask them to indicate which comparisons they have made at some time; or the interview protocol can include many prompts about possible comparisons and the free responses made during the interview can subsequently be coded for type of comparison (Wood et al., 1985). The free-response approach has the advantage of reducing the social-desirability component in social comparison questions, but interview questions and probes must be carefully structured so that there is a high probability of eliciting relevant content from a large proportion of respondents.

Procedures employed with child populations are more dependent on the physical situation of the classroom setting but may sometimes be adaptable to research in other settings. Social comparison responses can sometimes be directly recorded by observers (e.g., Frey & Ruble, 1985) in situations where comparison responses are overt and obvious to third parties. In some cases automated devices may be used to record subjects' selection of particular types of social information that may be utilized for social comparison (Levine & Green, 1984).

Whatever approach is chosen, the primary goal in the design phase is determining the probable validity of the comparison measure in relation to the probable nature of the coping–outcome process. Given the type of distress experienced by the subject population, what type(s) of downward comparison could they potentially make? Which comparisons are likely to be more salient or available for this population? Which comparisons would most likely produce changes in subjective well-being for this population? Does the outcome measure provide a pure index of the coping process itself, not confounded with outcome? If these questions are reasonably answered, then the measure will likely be useful.

Self-Esteem and Downward Comparison

An unresolved theoretical and empirical issue for comparison research concerns the relationship between self-esteem and social comparison. The original statement of downward comparison theory postulated that self-enhancing comparison would be more prevalent among persons with low self-esteem (Wills, 1981); this was based on the assumption that these persons have a greater need for self-enhancement and hence should be more likely to pursue self-enhancing (i.e., downward) comparisons. Alternatively, it is possible to derive from formulations such as cognitive consistency theory (Jones, 1973) the prediction that low self-esteem persons will not show self-enhancement processes because negative evaluation is consistent with their self-concept. The current evidence regarding this issue is mixed, possibly because empirical investigations have posed and examined the question in quite different ways.

As noted previously, laboratory studies providing a direct test of the relationship between self-esteem and social comparison choices (Friend & Gilbert, 1973; Wilson & Benner, 1971) did show downward comparison to be more prevalent in the low self-esteem groups. The studies by Tesser and colleagues with school children produced complex results. A significant interaction for actual friendship choices showed self-enhancing choices (i.e., choosing friends whose performance was somewhat inferior on a personally relevant dimension) to be more prevalent among children with low self-esteem. However, a marginal interaction for self-rated performance suggested that the tendency to favorably distort one's perceived performance on a personally relevant dimension was more characteristic of high self-esteem students. The authors tried to resolve these findings by suggesting that persons with high self-esteem were more likely to distort perceived performance differentials whereas persons low in self-esteem may perceive actual performance differentials and direct their efforts at self-enhancement toward actively choosing appropriate comparison persons as friends.

An alternate body of research, based on concepts of depressive realism (e.g., Lewinsohn, Mischel, Chaplin, & Barton, 1980), provides information on how ratings of self and others relate to measures of depression. Tabachnik, Crocker, and Alloy (1983) studied a sample of 40 university undergraduates drawn from dormitory residences, using cut points of Beck Depression Index scores as the indicator of depression. Subjects made ratings of self and others ("average college student") on both positive, negative, and neutral personality traits. There was a strong main effect for depression, with depressive subjects rating others more negatively on negative traits and less positively on positive traits; depressive and nondepressive subjects did not differ on ratings of neutral personality traits, indicating that the effect for depression did not represent a simple rating bias. Because depressives also rated themselves in generally negative terms, their ratings of self and of others did not differ significantly, producing what the investigators termed an "evenhandedness" in ratings. Comparison of subjects' ratings of "average college student" with self-ratings by an independent sample of students indicated a general self-enhancement tendency, with all subjects tending to overestimate negative attributes and underestimate positive attributes compared with self-descriptions by the independent sample. A strong interaction of depression × item type indicated that this self-enhancement effect was significantly stronger among depressive subjects, compared with nondepressives. These data, then, suggest that self-enhancement tendencies are stronger among persons higher in depression (cf. Gibbons, 1986), and correspondingly lower in self-esteem.

Another line of research has examined the relationship between self-esteem and prejudice. Crocker and Schwartz (1985) used a laboratory paradigm where social ingroups and outgroups were arbitrarily designated, and subjects then made ratings of ingroup and outgroup members on positive and negative personality traits. Subjects were blocked into tertiles on the basis of scores on the Rosenberg Self-esteem Scale, and ratings of ingroup/outgroup members were analyzed in relation to self-esteem. In this paradigm there was a main effect for self-esteem, with subjects in the low-esteem group making generally less favorable ratings of targets, compared with the high-esteem group. These data showed no interaction between self-esteem and target group, that is, low-esteem subjects made less favorable ratings of targets but this effect was comparable for ratings of ingroup and outgroup on most trait ratings.

In a related study, Crocker and McGraw (1985) obtained ratings of ingroups and outgroups from members of campus sororities that were either low or high in social status. These results indicated that in high-status sororities, low self-esteem persons showed greater derogation of outgroups. In low-status sororities, however, it was individuals with higher self-esteem who showed greater derogation of outgroups. These findings were interpreted as indicating that downward comparisons may be greater among low self-esteem individuals in the absence of situational threat, but may be greater among high self-esteem persons when a specific situational threat to self-esteem is operative.

It is perhaps premature to try to integrate this set of diverse findings, but the diversity suggests that this is an area where further research will be informative, particularly because of the clinical implications of the issues. The current research suggests that the relation between self-esteem and comparison processes may depend on the way in which comparison is pursued (cognitive changes vs. behavioral choices), and whether a current threat to self-esteem is present. It remains to be investigated whether there is an essential difference between the consequences of chronic depressive tendencies (where there may be a loss of self-esteem maintenance) and the reactions of nondepressive individuals to self-esteem threats. Investigation of comparison processes in general-population samples, where variation in stress, self-esteem, and symptomatology is much greater, would provide greater statistical power for tests of hypotheses and would help to determine whether laboratory findings are representative of comparison processes as they occur under prevailing naturalistic conditions. Using multiple measures in a single study, so that relationships for self-esteem, self-efficacy, and depression could be compared, would also be informative. Such studies would help to determine whether self-enhancement processes are more or less prevalent among persons at higher levels of distress, and might shed some light on how social comparisons are related to help-seeking (Wills, 1983).

Downward Comparison in Relation to Other Coping Mechanisms

A final methodological issue concerns how downward comparison is related to other coping mechanisms. The discussion so far has considered social comparison as a process in isolation; but in naturalistic settings it is probable that several types of coping are pursued either concurrently or successively. This perspective raises a number of questions of different forms. For example, although it may be unlikely that individuals can be characterized in terms of a global coping style (Moos & Billings, 1982), it can be surmized that comparison-oriented coping may be correlated with use of other cognitive coping mechanisms (e.g., minimization, cognitive restructuring, distraction). Because of the distinctions between cognitive and behavioral coping found in various studies (see Wills, Chap. 2, this volume), it is plausible to investigate whether individuals differ in their tendency to use cognitive mechanisms for coping with negative events (cf. Stone & Neale, 1984).

Another issue is whether there is any natural sequence of coping processes that occurs as a stressor is perceived, defined, and coped with. It is conceivable that either cognitive or behavioral coping predominates at different stages of coping with a stressor. Empirical investigation would help to clarify current theoretical structures, which have no clear postulates for predicting how coping processes will change over the time course of the coping process. Additionally, one can question whether cognitive and behavioral coping are typically pursued concurrently, or whether comparison processes are pursued primarily in cases where behavioral coping is restricted (because of severe or uncontrollable stressors) or impoverished (because of a limited repertoire of coping responses).

One can also consider how downward comparison is related to personality factors. Because of the strong component of aggressiveness and hostility in the Type A syndrome, for example, there is a straightforward prediction that derogatory types of downward comparison will be more prevalent among Type A individuals (cf. Holmes & Will, 1985). Relationships with locus of control may also be interesting, if individuals with external locus tend to favor cognitive coping mechanisms more than individuals with internal locus of control (cf. Fleishman, 1984). Finally, there is the issue of sex differences. Some studies have found comparison-oriented coping to be more pronounced among males (Jones, Sansone, & Helm, 1983; Rosen et al.; with mixed results in Tesser et al., 1984); others have noted no difference between males and females (Amabile & Glazebrook, 1982; Marks, 1984; Tabachnik et al., 1983); and a number of studies have not analyzed for sex differences. In view of these differing results it would be informative to examine what types of experimental threat inductions are most salient for males and females, and whether there are any notable differences in the types of social comparisons that males and females make when under stress.

WHAT ARE COPING AND ADAPTATION WHEN VIEWED FROM THIS PERSPECTIVE?

Downward comparison theory may help to understand better how people use cognitive mechanisms for coping with stressful circumstances. It could provide a theoretical basis for delineating how people utilize the potential advantages of cognitive mechanisms for dealing with adverse life conditions. Downward comparison is at the same time a cognitive process and a social process; it emphasizes how persons may employ social information to bolster their own self-esteem when it is threatened, and how they may arrive at more positive evaluation of their own life situation through comparison with other actual or potential situations. The theory posits that at some point in the stress-coping process, distressed individuals commence a search for comparison information that will enable them to feel better about their own situation; that their choice of comparison targets may be guided by some relatively simple principles that will produce a favorable comparison; and that the outcome of the comparison process may be determined by some basic variables such as problem comparability, relative status differential, and fate similarity. Whether comparison-oriented coping is used more for dealing with acute situational demands, or for enduring life strains, is not currently known and deserves further investigation. Whether coping through downward comparison is ultimately beneficial or harmful from a psychological standpoint also is not well established at present, and is a central issue for further research on social comparison.

No discussion of social comparison processes would be complete without recognizing the ambivalence that people feel about social comparison in general and downward comparison in particular (Brickman, 1975; Wills, 1981). Downward comparison may be pursued through a variety of approaches ranging from some that seem relatively benign and constructive (e.g., appreciating one's own situation more through comparison with hypothetical worse outcomes) to some that from a societal standpoint are undesirable (e.g., derogation of outgroups). At the individual level people may themselves respond to this ambivalance, being aware not only of the potentially self-favorable consequences that accrue from making downward comparisons, but also of the hazards of frequently doing so. Persons who are under stress may still use their capacity to respond empathically to observation of other persons experiencing negative states. How this ambivalence is weighed and resolved is not currently understood. How do people deal with the fundamental issues of self-evaluation, self-enhancement, and social empathy? How does a person's resolution of this conflict change as he or she experiences negative life events or failure in initial attempts at coping? These are issues that may help to understand the conflicts that people experience in the stress and coping process.

The concept of downward comparison as a coping mechanism may represent an area where the constructs and methodological tools of social psychology, cognitive psychology, and clinical psychology can be utilized together to work toward a more complete understanding of the stress-coping process. Principles from cognitive psychology, such as the judgmental heuristics of representativeness and availability, may have a bearing on how people perceive and select targets for comparison. Laboratory paradigms for investigating how negative affect influences information processing and memory (e.g., Isen, Shalker, Clark, & Carp, 1978; Natale & Hantas, 1982; Teasdale & Fogarty, 1978) may be useful in investigating cognitive coping at the micro level. Constructs from social psychological theories of attribution and hierarchical organization may help to explicate how particular types of comparisons are used and how they relate to self-esteem enhancement. Finally, constructs from downward comparison theory may be useful to clinical formulations of help-seeking, neurotic conflict and defense, and personality processes of self-organization; many phenomena observed in clinical settings may derive from the efforts of distressed persons to maintain their self-esteem in the face of challenges from the environment. Together these constructs and approaches may help to understand how people use their cognitive resources to resolve and overcome adversity.

REFERENCES

Albert, S. (1977). Temporal comparison theory. *Psychological Review, 84,* 485–503.
Amabile, T. M., & Glazebrook, A. H. (1982). A negativity bias in interpersonal evaluation. *Journal of Experimental Social Psychology, 18,* 1–22.
Bandura, A. (1977). Self-efficacy: Toward a unifying theory of behavioral change. *Psychological Review, 84,* 191–215.
Bennett, D. H., & Holmes, D. S. (1975). Influence of denial and projection on anxiety associated with threat to self-esteem. *Journal of Personality and Social Psychology, 32,* 915–921.
Billings, A. G., & Moos, R. H. (1981). The role of coping responses and social resources in attenuating the stress of life events. *Journal of Behavioral Medicine, 4,* 139–157.
Bloom, B. L., Asher, S. J., & White, S. W. (1978). Marital disruption as a stressor. *Psychological Bulletin, 85,* 867–894.
Brewer, M. B., & Campbell, D. T. (1976). *Ethnocentrism and intergroup attitudes: East African evidence.* New York: Halstead.
Brickman, P. (1975). Adaptation level determinants of satisfaction with equal and unequal outcome distributions in skill and chance situations. *Journal of Personality and Social Psychology, 32,* 191–198.

Brickman, P., Coates, D., & Janoff-Bulman, R. (1978). Lottery winners and accident victims: Is happiness relative? *Journal of Personality and Social Psychology, 36,* 917–927.

Bulman, R. J., & Wortman, C. B. (1977). Attributions of blame and coping in the "real world": Severe accident victims react to their lot. *Journal of Personality and Social Psychology, 35,* 351–363.

Burish, T. G., & Houston, B. K. (1979). Causal projection, similarity projection, and coping with threat to self-esteem. *Journal of Personality, 47,* 57–70.

Campbell, J. D. (1986). Similarity and uniqueness: The effects of attribute type, relevance, and individual differences in self-esteem and depression. *Journal of Personality and Social Psychology, 50,* 281–294.

Cohen, S., & Syme, S. L. (1985). Issues in the study and application of social support. In S. Cohen & S. L. Syme (Eds.), *Social support and health* (pp. 3–22). Orlando: Academic Press.

Cohen, S., & Wills, T. A. (1985). Stress, social support, and the buffering hypothesis. *Psychological Bulletin, 98,* 310–357.

Cohen, S., Evans, G. W., Krantz, D. S., & Stokols, D. (1980). Physiological, motivational, and cognitive effects of aircraft noise on children: Moving from the laboratory to the field. *American Psychologist, 35,* 231–243.

Crocker, J., & Gallo, L. (1985, August). Self-enhancing effects of downward comparison: An experimental test. In T. A. Wills (Chair), *Self-esteem maintenance: Theory and evidence.* Symposium presented at the meeting of the American Psychological Association, Los Angeles, CA.

Crocker, J., & McGraw, K. M. (1985). *Prejudice in campus sororities: Effects of self-esteem and ingroup status.* Manuscript submitted for publication.

Crocker, J., & Schwartz, I. (1985). Prejudice and ingroup favoritism in a minimal intergroup situation: Effects of self-esteem. *Personality and Social Psychology Bulletin, 11,* 379–386.

Diener, E. (1984). Subjective well-being. *Psychological Bulletin, 95,* 542–575.

Dohrenwend, B. S., & Dohrenwend, B. P. (Eds.). (1981). *Stressful life events and their contexts.* New York: Prodist.

Dohrenwend, B. P., Shrout, P. E., Egri, G., & Mendelsohn, F. S. (1980). Nonspecific psychological distress and other dimensions of psychopathology: Measures for use in the general population. *Archives of General Psychiatry, 37,* 1229–1236.

Dooley, D. (1985). Causal inference in the study of social support. In S. Cohen & S. L. Syme (Eds.), *Social support and health* (pp. 109–125). Orlando: Academic Press.

Ehrlich, H. J. (1973). *The social psychology of prejudice.* New York: Wiley.

Emmons, R. A., & Diener, E. (1985). Factors predicting satisfaction judgments: A comparative examination. *Social Indicators Research, 16,* 157–167.

Felton, B. J., Revenson, T. A., & Hinrichsen, G. A. (1984). Stress and coping in the explanation of psychological adjustment among chronically ill adults. *Social Science and Medicine, 18,* 889–898.

Festinger, L. (1954). A theory of social comparison processes. *Human Relations, 7,* 117–140.

Fisher, J. D., Nadler, A., & Whitcher-Alagna, S. (1982). Recipient reactions to aid. *Psychological Bulletin, 91,* 27–54.

Fleishman, J. A. (1984). Personality characteristics and coping patterns. *Journal of Health and Social Behavior, 25,* 229–244.

Folkman, S., & Lazarus, R. S. (1980). An analysis of coping in a middle-aged community sample. *Journal of Health and Social Behavior, 21,* 219–239.

Friend, R. M., & Gilbert, J. (1973). Threat and fear of negative evaluation as determinants of locus of social comparison. *Journal of Personality, 41,* 328–340.

Frey, K.S., & Ruble, D. N. (1985). Conflicting goals in social comparison in the classroom. *Journal of Personality and Social Psychology, 48,* 550–562.

Gerrard, M., Gibbons, F. X., & Sharp, J. (1985). *Social comparison in a self-help group for bulimics.* Paper presented at the meeting of the American Psychological Association, Los Angeles, CA.

Gibbons, F. X. (1985a). Social stigma perception: Social comparison among mentally retarded persons. *American Journal of Mental Deficiency, 90,* 98–106.

Gibbons, F. X. (1985b). A social-psychological perspective on developmental disabilities. *Journal of Social and Clinical Psychology, 3,* 391–404.

Gibbons, F. X. (1986). Social comparison and depression: Company's effect on misery. *Journal of Personality and Social Psychology, 51,* 140–148.

Goethals, G., & Darley, J. (1977). Social comparison theory: An attributional approach. In J. M. Suls & R. L. Miller (Eds.), *Social comparison processes: Theoretical and empirical perspectives* (pp. 259–278). Washington, DC: Hemisphere.

Goethals, G. R., Arrowood, A. J., Suls, J., Wheeler, L., & Wills, T. A. (1986). Social comparison theory: Psychology from the lost and found. *Personality and Social Psychology Bulletin, 12,* 261–299.

Gruder, C. L. (1977). Choice of comparison persons in evaluating oneself. In J. M. Suls & R. L. Miller (Eds.), *Social comparison processes: Theoretical and empirical perspectives* (pp. 21–41). Washington, DC: Hemisphere.

Hakmiller, K. L. (1966). Threat as a determinant of downward comparison. *Journal of Experimental Social Psychology, 1966, 2* (Supplement 1), 32–39.

Harter, S. (1985). Developmental perspective in understanding child and adolescent disorders. *Journal of Social and Clinical Psychology, 3,* 484–499.

Heath, L. (1984). Impact of newspaper crime reports on fear of crime. *Journal of Personality and Social Psychology, 47,* 263–276.

Holmes, D. S. (1978). Projection as a defense mechanism. *Psychological Bulletin, 85,* 677–688.

Holmes, D. S., & Will, M. J. (1985). Expression of interpersonal aggression by angered and nonangered persons with the Type A and Type B behavior patterns. *Journal of Personality and Social Psychology, 48,* 723–727.

Isen, A. M., Shalker, T. E., Clark, M., & Karp, L. (1978). Affect, accessibility of material in memory, and behavior. *Journal of Personality and Social Psychology, 36,* 1–12.

Jones, S. C. (1973). Self- and interpersonal evaluations: Esteem theories versus consistency theories. *Psychological Bulletin, 79,* 185–199.

Jones, W. H., Sansone, C., & Helm, B. (1983). Loneliness and interpersonal judgments. *Personality and Social Psychology Bulletin, 9,* 437–441.

Levine, J. M. (1983). Social comparison and education. In J. M. Levine & M. C. Wang (Eds.), *Teacher and student perceptions* (pp. 29–55). Hillsdale, NJ: Erlbaum.

Levine, J. M., & Green, S. M. (1984). Acquisition of relative performance information: The roles of intrapersonal and interpersonal comparison. *Personality and Social Psychology Bulletin, 10,* 385–393.

Lewinsohn, P. M., Hoberman, H., Teri, L., & Hautzinger, M. (1985). An integrative theory of depression. In S. Reiss & R. Bootzin (Eds.), *Theoretical issues in behavior therapy* (pp. 331–359). New York: Academic Press.

Lewinsohn, P. M., Mischel, W., Chaplin, W., & Barton, R. (1980). Social competence and depression: The role of illusory self-perceptions. *Journal of Abnormal Psychology, 89,* 203–212.

Marks, G. (1984). Thinking one's abilities are unique and one's opinions are common. *Personality and Social Psychology Bulletin, 10,* 203–208.

McGuire, W. J. (1984). Search for the self: Going beyond self-esteem and the reactive self. In R. A. Zucker, J. Aronoff, & A. I. Rabin (Eds.), *Personality and the prediction of behavior* (pp. 73–120). New York: Academic Press.

Menaghan, E. (1982). Measuring coping effectiveness: A panel analysis of marital problems and coping efforts. *Journal of Health and Social Behavior, 23,* 220–234.

Moos, R. H., & Billings, A. G. (1982). Conceptualizing and measuring coping resources and processes. In L. Goldberger & S. Breznitz (Eds.), *Handbook of stress* (pp. 212–230). New York: MacMillan.

Natale, M., & Hantas, M. (1982). Effect of temporary mood states on selective memory about the self. *Journal of Personality and Social Psychology, 42,* 927–934.

Pearlin, L. I., & Schooler, C. (1978). The structure of coping. *Journal of Health and Social Behavior, 19,* 2–21.

Pyszczynski, T., Greenberg, J., & LaPrelle, J. (1985). Social comparison after success and failure: Biased search for information consistent with a self-serving conclusion. *Journal of Experimental Social Psychology, 21,* 195–211.

Renick, M. J., & Harter, S. (1984). *Role of social comparison in the self-concept structure of learning-disabled children.* Unpublished manuscript, University of Denver.

Rosen, S., Tomarelli, M. M., Kidda, M. L., Jr., & Medvin, N. (1986). Effects of motive for helping, recipient's inability to reciprocate, and sex on devaluation of the recipient's competence. *Journal of Personality and Social Psychology, 50,* 729–736.

Rothbart, M. (1981). Memory processes and social beliefs. In D. L. Hamilton (Ed.), *Cognitive processes in stereotyping and intergroup behavior* (pp. 145–181). Hillsdale, NJ: Erlbaum.

Rothbart, M., & John, O. P. (1985). Social categorization and behavioral episodes: A cognitive analysis. *Journal of Social Issues, 41*(3), 81–104.

Ruble, D. N., Boggiano, A. K., Feldman, N. S., & Loebl, J. H. (1980). Developmental analysis of the role of social comparison in self-evaluation. *Developmental Psychology, 16,* 105–115.

Schulz, R., & Decker, S. (1985). Long-term adjustment to physical disability: The role of social support, perceived control, and self-blame. *Journal of Personality and Social Psychology, 48,* 1162–1172.

Sherman, S. J., Presson, C. C., & Chassin, L. (1984). Mechanisms underlying the false consensus effect: The special role of threats to the self. *Personality and Social Psychology Bulletin, 10,* 127–138.

Silon, E., & Harter, S. (1985). Assessment of perceived competence and anxiety in segregated and mainstreamed educable mentally retarded children. *Journal of Educational Psychology, 77,* 217–230.

Snyder, C. R., Higgins, R. L., & Stucky, R. J. (1983). *Excuses: Masquerades in search of grace.* New York: Wiley.

Stephan, W. G., & Rosenfield, D. (1978). Effects of desegregation on racial attitudes. *Journal of Personality and Social Psychology, 36,* 795–804.

Stone, A. A., & Neale, J. M. (1984). A new measure of daily coping: Development and preliminary results. *Journal of Personality and Social Psychology, 46,* 892–906.

Suls, J., & Mullen, B. (1982). Comparison and self-evaluation across the life span. In J. Suls (Ed.), *Psychological perspectives on the self* (Vol. 1, pp. 97–125). Hillsdale, NJ: Erlbaum.

Tabachnik, N., Crocker, J., & Alloy, L. B. (1983). Depression, social comparison, and the false-consensus effect. *Journal of Personality and Social Psychology, 45,* 688–699.

Taylor, D. G., Sheatsley, P. B., & Greeley, A. M. (1978). Attitudes toward racial integration. *Scientific American, 238*(6), 42–49.

Teasdale, J. D., & Fogarty, S. J. (1979). Differential effects of induced mood on retrieval of pleasant and unpleasant events from episodic memory. *Journal of Abnormal Psychology, 88,* 248–257.

Tesser, A. (1984). Self-evaluation maintenance processes: Implications for relationships and for development. In J. Masters & K. Yarkin (Eds.), *Boundary areas in social and developmental psychology* (pp. 271–299). New York: Academic Press.

Tesser, A., & Campbell, J. (1983). Self-definition and self-evaluation maintenance. In J. Suls & A. Greenwald (Eds.), *Social psychological perspectives on the self* (Vol. 2, pp. 1–31). Hillsdale, NJ: Erlbaum.

Tesser, A., Campbell, J., & Smith, M. (1984). Friendship choice and performance: Self-evaluation maintenance in children. *Journal of Personality and Social Psychology, 46,* 561–574.

Wills, T. A. (1981). Downward comparison principles in social psychology. *Psychological Bulletin, 90,* 245–271.

Wills, T. A. (1983). Social comparison in coping and help-seeking. In B. M. DePaulo, A. Nadler, & J. D. Fisher (Eds.), *New directions in helping (Vol. 2): Help-seeking* (pp. 109–141). New York: Academic Press.

Wills, T. A. (1985). Stress, coping, and substance use in early adolescence. In S. Shiffman & T. A. Wills (Eds.), *Coping and substance use* (pp. 67–94). New York: Academic Press.

Wills, T. A. (1986). *Coping processes and psychological outcomes: Prospective analyses in two cohorts of urban adolescents.* Manuscript submitted for publication.

Wills, T. A., & Langner, T. S. (1980). Socioeconomic status and stress. In I. L. Kutash & L. B. Schlesinger (Eds.), *Handbook on stress and anxiety* (pp. 159–173). San Francisco: Jossey-Bass.

Wilson, S. R., & Benner, L. A. (1971). Effects of self-esteem and situation on comparison choices during ability evaluation. *Sociometry, 34,* 381–397.

Wood, J. V., Taylor, S. E., & Lichtman, R. R. (1985). Social comparison in adjustment to breast cancer. *Journal of Personality and Social Psychology, 49,* 1169–1183.

V

Image Maintenance Perspectives

The entertainer Sammy Davis, Jr. has offered the following insight about himself: "As soon as I go out of the door of my house in the morning I'm on, Daddy, I'm on!" (cited in Burns, 1973, p. 37). This is not a new perspective (recall Shakespeare's "All the world's a stage, and all the men and women merely players," *As You Like It,* Act II), but the idea that people are "acting" as they go about their daily affairs is viewed negatively by laypeople. After all, is not acting a way of pretending? Is it not purposefully misleading other people? Surely, people must be more spontaneous than this; moreover, people must have other more noble, respectable motives that drive their behavior. In psychology, however, the notion that people are motivated to establish and maintain a positive image of themselves has a long list of distinguished proponents including William James, Alfred Adler, Karen Horney, Harry Stack Sullivan, Gordon Allport, Abraham Maslow, Fritz Heider, and others. In recent years, moreover, there has been a rekindling of interest in this motive among psychologists. Whether it is called impression management or self-presentation, the central idea here is that people are motivated to preserve a positive image.

Returning to the "Booze Held Me Back" case described earlier in Chapter 1, it may be recalled the the middle-aged salesman longed for some respect. The promotions that were routinely occurring for other territorial sales representatives seemed to elude Ray. The yearly regional and national conventions were especially difficult for him. He tried to be an outgoing, fun-loving fellow, and even took a brief course in dressing for success. Although he rarely focused on the insight that he was painfully shy and uncomfortable around people, he continually faced this dilemma in calling upon customers. "Sell, sell, sell" was like a broken record in Ray's head. Shake another hand; wait for 10, 20, 30 or more minutes for the buyer; push the latest "deal" when he finally was allowed time to make his presentation. "You have to sell yourself before you sell the product" were the words of Ray's boss. The pressure was excrutiating for Ray.

Ray's father was a cold, aloof man, who was rarely satisifed with Ray as a boy. It was hard to please the "old man" and Ray hungered for his approval. Dad's major advice to Ray was some variant of "Be a man . . . go out there and prove yourself." Easier said than done in Ray's life.

Ray's drinking began in his teenage years. He found that it relieved his worries; it gave him time out from all the demands that he perceived. The progression of preferred drinks went from beer to rum and coke, to various other mixed drinks; eventually, he settled on drinking straight gin, or "gin neat" as it was called. Fortified with a few drinks from the bottle in the glove compartment of his company car, Ray could confront the stress of the repeated sales pitches. To hear Ray talk about it, however, the previous causality was all wrong. If he admitted to any problem at all, it was his drinking that was the real villain, not the stress and discomfort associated with selling. He would be successful in his work if the booze did not hamper him. It was not that he lacked talent, it was just that "temporary" drinking problem.

This case study obviously highlights the role that image maintenance may play in the coping process. The authors in this section utilize this motive in building their theoretical frameworks. In Chapter 11, for example, Barry Schlenker develops a model in which the central proposition is that people want to establish and maintain desired identity dimensions. When people encounter impediments to their desired identity images, Schlenker hypothesizes that three resistance processes may be activated simultaneously. First, the person engages in an intensified examination of information about the self, situation, or audience. Second, the person generates explanations bearing on the predicament. Third, the individual can initiate activities to cope with the impediment; included here are counterattacks against the problem, strengthening the identity by compensation, and gathering social support. According to Schlenker, the aforementioned resistance processes are mediated by a self-identification outcome expectation, which reflects the perceived probability that the desired identity images can be held in spite of the impediment. The lower the perceived self-identification outcome expectation in relation to the impediment, the greater the degree of perceived stress; moreover, persons with low perceived self-identification outcome expectations tend to have a self-protective (rather than self-assertive) stance, and are characterized by withdrawal from the situation. Lacking the possibility of avoidance, they merely lock into a counterproductive cycle. Further, they are depicted as being anxious and insecure. In the case of Ray, for instance, it appears that a low self-identification outcome expectation was operative in that he continually experienced the "presentational" demands of sales to be difficult. Ray's coping strategy, in this context, centered on a rather self-defeating dependence on alcohol as an explanation or excuse.

In Chapter 12, Ann Baumgardner and Robert Arkin also assume that people are motivated to see themselves in a positive light. Building on this motive, these authors develop a framework for understanding how differences in self-confidence (e.g., positive or negative self-concept) may be related to a passive or active coping style for avoiding social disapproval. The passive style includes the various strategies that are aimed at managing social disapproval after it has happened. Included here are self-deceptive maneuvers in which the person denies the existence of disapproval cues, or denies the relevance of negative feedback. Baumgardner and Arkin conclude that these passive (denial/self-deception) strategies are employed more frequently by persons with a strong positive self-concept. In contrast, persons with a less positive self-concept are thought to use more active strategies in which there are attempts to alter or avoid the sense of impending disapproval. Included in these more active strategies are (a) engaging in downward social comparison; (b) manufacturing lower normative standards; (c) directing attention to strengths; and (d) excuse-making and self-handicapping. In this latter vein, it may be that the protagonist in "The Booze Held Me Back" case history was employing his drinking in a strategic excuse-making fashion. By maintaining the drinking problem, Ray may have been attempting to preserve an image (perhaps for himself and others) that he really was a talented salesman and could be a success if it were not for the liquor.

In Chapter 13, C. R. Snyder and Robert Harris also employ an image maintenance perspective in positing a model of excuse-making. In particular, these authors suggest that excuses are driven by the fact that people are motivated to preserve a positive image for both oneself and others. In the process of making excuses in anticipation of or after ego-threatening situations, people are portrayed as calling on three types of similarity/difference information. Borrowing from Harold Kelley's covariance principles, Snyder and Harris argue that consensus, consistency, and distinctiveness information implicitly appears in excuses. First, in regard to consensus, it is reasoned that the similarity/difference dynamic involves the excuse maker comparing himself or herself in a given situation with other people in the same situation. By raising consensus, therefore, the excuse-giving person implicitly suggests that the situation is causing the poor performance. Unlike consensus raising wherein the excuse functions by comparing the person with other people (i.e., a between-subject comparison), in consistency lowering and distinctiveness raising excuses the person is employing within-subject comparisons. In consistency-lowering excuses, the person suggests that the negative event is unusual for that person for the particular situation; in distinctiveness-raising excuses, the person suggests that the negative event is unusual (for that person) relative to other arenas in his or her life. Returning to the case history again, it may be recalled that Ray suggested that once his temporary drinking problem was conquered, he would be a success. This sounds like a consistency-lowering excuse.

Overall, it can be seen that a concern for one's image plays an important role in understanding the case history of how Ray confronted the negative events in his life. These same image maintenance perspectives, however, obviously can be applied to other instances in which people cope with the traumatic events in their lives.

REFERENCE

Burns, E. (1973). *Theatricality: A study of convention in the theatre and in social life.* New York: Harper & Row.

11

Threats to Identity
Self-Identification and Social Stress

BARRY R. SCHLENKER

In the physical sciences, stress is a relative concept that reflects the pressure or force on a body to deform its shape versus the strength or resistance of the body to hold its shape. When external force exceeds internal resistance, the body bends and ultimately breaks, losing its integrity. If internal resistance is greater than external force, the integrity of the entity survives.

The psychological concept of stress is derived from its physical counterpart. Stress reflects pressure on a person to change shape versus the person's capacity to resist the pressure. In this case, the person's "shape" is his or her identity, or definition and integrity as a structured, functioning entity. Pressure is an event of environmental origin that could conceivably change identity in a manner that is undesired by the individual. That is, it is a potential threat to identity that arises from events that jeopardize desired identity images. Resistance is the personal and environmental resources of the person that can counteract the threat, either because of the threat's weakness or the person's resourcefulness.

This chapter will apply a self-identification approach to the analysis of stress. The approach is transactional, in that it regards the phenomenon in terms of a dynamic interplay, or transaction, between people and the environmental forces that might change them (see Folkman,

BARRY R. SCHLENKER • Department of Psychology, University of Florida, Gainesville, FL 32611.

1984; Laux, 1986; Lazarus & Launier, 1978). Accordingly, stress is not found in the person or the environment, and neither is it merely a stimulus or a response. Rather, it represents the reciprocal interaction of the environment and the person's handling of it. Stress is rooted in the battle between the forces that attack and the forces that resist attacks to identity. When the former emerge victorious, as in the cases of anxiety (where a threat exists and resistance is weak), depression (where a loss has occurred), or even catatonia (where unconditional surrender occurs), psychological problems ensue. When the latter win, the victory is normally a satisfying one. Yet, there are occasions where victory is purchased through illegitimate means, as when people's coping mechanisms build a wall between them and the reality that is perceived by most other people. An extreme example is paranoia, where threats are dissipated by elevating one's identity to the realm of the sacrosanct and blaming problems on conspiratorial attacks by jealous mortals. Coping has a ground rule: people must keep in touch with reality as it is perceived by the members of their social groups. When people violate the rule of consensual validation, they risk preserving a solipsistic identity at the expense of their standing in the social community.

At the core of the approach is the proposition that people strive to construct and maintain *desired identity images* (Schlenker, 1980, 1982, 1984, 1985, in press; Schlenker & Leary, 1982a, 1985). These images are neither idealistically glorifying nor faithful to the fine nuances of evidence as might be seen by an omniscient observer. Rather, desirable identity images represent a compromise between one's wishes—the *personal beneficiality* component, or the extent to which the image serves the holder's values and goals—and reality—the *believability* component, or the extent to which the image is perceived to be an accurate, defensible interpretation of the evidence (Schlenker, 1980, 1984, 1985, in press; a formula for assessing desirability has been proffered by Schlenker, 1980, 1981). These images represent what people believe they both should and can be on particular occasions, being reality edited yet somewhat glorified images of self. People have a stake in the construction and preservation of these images, both privately and publicly, and are threatened when they might be damaged by events. When threats arise, people take action to defuse them. They cope as best they can, given their resources, and change their desired identities only reluctantly, when the threat overpowers their efforts.

Impediments to the construction and maintenance of desired identity images generate resistance that takes three generic forms. First, problems produce a more *intensified examination of information* about the self, situation, and audience than would otherwise occur. Actors become focused on information that is relevant to the problem and the means of dealing with the difficulty. For example, a man who lost his job ruminates about his personal standing on job-related attributes, about his past failures and accomplishments, about his relationship to his employer, and about the employer's perceived personal characteristics (e.g., Is he intelligent or stupid, fair or spiteful, persuasible or dogmatic?). Second, problems generate *explanations* that bear on the causes of the difficulty and have implications for the self (e.g., "Did I lose my job because of my incompetence or because of the stupidity and mean-spiritedness of my employer?"). These explanations define the nature of the problem. Third, problems generate *strategic activities* designed to overcome the difficulty. These activities include (a) direct counterattacks against the problem (e.g., trying to persuade the employer that he was wrong and should reverse his decision), (b) attempts to strengthen desired identity images (e.g., compensating for a failure by working harder and getting an even better job with another company), and (c) attempts to obtain support from other people to reaffirm desired images (e.g., seeking confirmation of one's desired attributes from family and friends, who agree that the job loss was unfair). These activities can take place in our imaginations as well as through our overt behavior.

It is proposed that the three categories are interrelated in a parallel fashion, and are not sequentially ordered. Phrased differently, the categories are linked such that the course or outcome of the activities in one category influences what transpires in the others. For example, after being fired, the social support a man seeks and receives from his wife makes him more likely to contemplate self-reaffirming information, less likely to experience self-doubts, and more likely to blame the employer's unfairness and mean-spiritedness for losing his job. Together, the three types of resistance comprise an appraisal of the problem and means of coping with it. Even the examination of information can serve to cope with the problem as well as appraise it. For example, an actor who fails a test may search out and find information (in memory and in the environment) that validates desired identity images (e.g., recalling similar past successes); basking in these past glories can overwhelm the failure with contradictory information and facilitate the explanation that the test was invalid.

It is proposed that the course of resistance is mediated by the actor's *self-identification outcome expectation,* which is the perceived likelihood that the desired images can be constructed and maintained despite the impediment. This expectation is generated by an initial assessment of the impediment and possible resistance to it. The lower this expectation is, and the greater the perceived damage to identity that may occur, the more stressful the experience will be. Low expectations are associated with the self-disparaging examination of information, the construction of self-derogatory explanations that internalize blame, and defensive strategic activities that are unlikely to overcome the problem. High expectations, in contrast, are associated with self-reaffirming ruminations, explanations, and activities. Expectations are not static, of course, and can be altered over time as efforts to deal with the problem modify the situation. Nonetheless, at any point in time, self-identification outcome expectations mediate the amount of stress that is experienced and stress-reducing activities.

The remainder of the chapter will elaborate this overview of the model. We will first examine the nature of impediments to desired identities. The concept of social stress will be considered in this context. We will then turn to a more detailed analysis of each of the three categories of resistance and their impact on social stress.

SELF-IDENTIFICATION AND IDENTITY IMPEDIMENTS

Identity and Self-Identification

Identity is a theory of self (or self-schema) that is formed and maintained through actual or imagined interpersonal agreement about what the self is like (see Schlenker, 1985, in press, for further discussion). It organizes the contents of our experiences and it influences our thoughts, feelings, and actions (Epstein, 1973; Greenwald & Pratkanis, 1984; Schlenker, 1985, in press). Further, like a theory in science, it is subject to the process of consensual agreement by significant others to provide validation by the appropriate, judging community (Erikson, 1959; Harré, 1983; Schlenker, 1980, 1985, in press).

Self-identification is the process, means, or result of showing oneself to be a particular type of person, thereby defining identity (Schlenker, 1984, 1985, in press). It is accomplished privately, through contemplation of oneself, and publicly, through self-disclosure, self-presentation, and other activities (e.g., dress, task performance) that symbolically communicate one's identity to others. Self-identification (a) is a goal-directed activity that specifies the properties of the self, (b) *always* occurs in a particular context consisting of a *social situation* and one or more salient *audiences* for the activity (the self, other people, and/or reference others), and (c) involves standards for goal-completion (i.e., satisfactorily constructing the desired identity images) that people attempt to satisfy through their cognitive and behavioral activities (see Schlenker, 1985, in

press, for further discussion). Self-identification is a necessary component of any dealings with the environment, because a definition of one's
identity is essential if one is to relate to others or to decide how to act.
On any given occasion, an initial assessment of the situation, the
audience, and the self generates a goal (or set of goals) that can be
satisfied, a script or plan for goal achievement, and a set of desired
identity images that will be projected (Schlenker, 1985). These desired
identity images represent what the actor would like to be and believes he
or she can be given the context. Unless problems develop along the way,
the occasion proceeds rather routinely, as people follow their plans in
the pursuit of their goals (James, 1890; Langer, 1978; Schlenker, 1980,
1984, 1985). Their desired identity images are projected and (usually)
validated by events, and goal achievement occurs.

Impediments to Desired Identity Images

On some occasions, however, problems develop or are anticipated
during the self-identification process. *Impediments* to self-identifying activities indicate that something may go wrong (or has gone wrong) and
people's desired identity images may not be satisfactorily constructed or
maintained. Perceived or anticipated impediments can arise because of
events created by people's own behaviors (e.g., failures, ineptness, accidents, transgressions), by events in the environment (e.g., desired identity images are challenged by others; a person loses a job because of the
bankruptcy of the company or loses a spouse through death), or by a
combination of personal and environmental events (e.g., a person says
something that other people misinterpret in an undesired manner; a
person loses a job because of personal incompetence or is divorced because of mental or physical cruelty to the spouse).

An impediment represents a blocking or interruption of planned
activities that has potential implications for people's goals and identity.
When impediments arise, people's cognitive and behavioral activities
become focused and mobilized in order to deal with the potential problem. People then engage in a more in-depth assessment of self, situation,
and audience than they otherwise might, and a process of resistance is
engaged that is designed to eliminate or control the problem (Schlenker,
1984, 1985, in press; Schlenker & Leary, 1982a).

Self-Identification and Social Stress

An impediment is not, in and of itself, a threat to identity. Whether
it is perceived as a threat depends on the actor's expectation that it can be

successfully handled. The assessment process (triggered by the impediment) produces an expectation of the likelihood that the actor's goals will be achieved and relevant identity images will be constructed and maintained (Carver, 1979; Carver & Scheier, 1981; Schlenker, 1984, 1985; Schlenker & Leary, 1982a). These self-identification outcome expectations reflect the extent to which potential problems are likely to be rectified given the nature of the audience, the situation, and the actor's attributes and personal resources (e.g., perceived social skills, supportive friends). As discussed elsewhere (Schlenker & Leary, 1982a), these expectations will be lower when (a) audiences are perceived to be more demanding, less supportive, and more evaluative (e.g., powerful, attractive, or expert others who are perceived to be critical), (b) the situation is more demanding, difficult, evaluative, or ambiguous (e.g., tasks on which past failures have occurred; novel or ambiguous situations that produce uncertainty about how to proceed effectively; "test" rather than "game" situations; publicly identifiable performances in which one is the center of others' attention, as opposed to situations in which one is anonymous or can share responsibility with co-performers), and (c) the actor's perceived skills and resources relevant to the task are lower (e.g., low self-regard, poor social or communication skills, high social anxiety) and he or she is especially concerned about the evaluative implications of the performance (e.g., high need for approval, high fear of failure, high self-consciousness). Lower self-identification outcome expectations generate greater social stress.

Given low expectations, the magnitude of the potential damage to identity, and the amount of the resulting stress, is a function of (a) the importance of the relevant identity images that are jeopardized, and (b) the size of the perceived discrepancy between the identity that will result and the standards that are associated with the desired identity. Desired identity images are more important when (a) they are associated with more significant needs and values (e.g., being intelligent is a more important identity image for a college professor than is being a good cook), (b) they are more central to an actor's identity (e.g., the image of intelligence subsumes numerous, more specific skills), and (c) the actor has invested more of his or her resources in them to the exclusion of alternative images (e.g., the football player whose life has been targeted for a professional career and who is not prepared to face alternative possibilities). When goals and their associated identity images are more important, a failure to neutralize relevant problems has greater repercussions for identity.

The problem also is greater when larger discrepancies are perceived or anticipated between the identity images that are created and the relevant personal or social standards that are applied. All goal-oriented activities imply the existence of standards for goal accomplishment, and desired identity images contain standards that people attempt to fulfill (Schlenker, 1984, 1985). Desired images are jeopardized when people fall short (or expect to fall short) of these standards, either quantitatively (e.g., having to claim less of the image than is dictated by one's standards, as when a person appears to be somewhat intelligent but desires to be extremely intelligent) or qualitatively (e.g., when people are forced to abandon an identity image and claim alternative, less desired ones, as when a husband is discovered to have a mistress, his claims of fidelity become untenable, and his marriage is threatened).

Even when people appear to be maintaining a "good" identity, as judged by outside observers, they may still be failing to perform as well as their lofty standards prescribe. As Bandura (1969) observed,

> many of the people who seek treatment [for anxiety] are neither incompetent nor anxiously inhibited, but they experience a great deal of personal distress stemming from excessively high standards for self-evaluation, often supported by unfavorable comparisons with models noted for their extraordinary achievements. (p. 69)

Horney's (1945) analysis of neuroticism and anxiety emphasized the role played by unrealistically high standards. She argued that in the face of unfavorable childhood experiences, neurotics attempt to place themselves above others by developing an idealized image of self, thereby affirming their significance and worth. Unfortunately, this idealized image contains standards that are too high, prompting neurotics to feel driven to perform at unrealistic levels, to be indiscriminate in their attempts to be liked and admired, not just by some people but by everyone, and to become excessively anxious, panicky, and depressed when confronted with the portent of failure. Indeed, Gough, Fioravanti, and Lazzari (1983) found that people with larger discrepancies between the real self and the ideal self on particular traits were prone to anxiety and self-doubt and also lacked interpersonal skills. Those with smaller discrepancies were characterized as being more socially poised, confident, and adept in their dealings with the problems of everyday life. The study by Gough et al. is based on correlational data, however, and does not permit us to assess causal relationships or to determine if the patterns were due to exceptionally high standards contained in the self-concept, excessively low actual self-images, or some combination of these.

The experience of social stress is thereby a direct function of two factors: (a) the perceived likelihood of damage to identity, that is, holding lower self-identification outcome expectations, and (b) the perceived amount of damage to identity, that is, the importance of the images that are jeopardized and the extent to which the actor falls short of the relevant standards. More broadly, these factors determine the phenomenological concerns that people experience when they confront impediments (Schlenker, 1984; Schlenker & Leary, 1982a, 1985). People are *indifferent* when impediments are trivial because they strike at unimportant goals or identity images. People are *confident* when they have especially high self-identification outcome expectations, because they are then certain that either no problem exists or they will surely handle the problem. People are *challenged* when the impediment strikes at important goals and images yet they have moderate to high outcome expectations; in other words, a potential problem may exist, but it can be dealt with given the situation, audience, and personal resources. Indeed, it provides an opportunity for displaying effectiveness and mastery. People are *threatened* when the impediment strikes at important goals and images but they have low outcome expectations; a potential problem is perceived, but significant doubts exist about whether it can be handled. Finally, people are *damaged* when important goals and images are attacked and a loss is perceived that cannot be rectified or restored (e.g., loss of a job with no prospects for a new one). The first two experiences, indifference and confidence, represent states where stress does not occur. The latter three involve varying degrees of stress, with threat and damage having the potential for devasting effects.

This analysis of social stress was derived from the self-identification approach, but it bears a resemblance to the cognitive theory of stress developed by Lazarus and his associates (e.g., Coyne & Lazarus, 1980; Folkman, Schaefer, & Lazarus, 1979; Lazarus, 1966, 1981; Lazarus & Launier, 1978). They proposed that cognitive appraisal is generated when potentially difficult situations are encountered. The appraisal process is subdivided into two facets: primary appraisal, in which people evaluate a transaction in terms of its implications for their well being, and secondary appraisal, in which people evaluate their coping resources and options. Primary appraisal produces an assessment of whether the situation involves challenge (an opportunity for mastery or gain), threat (potential harm or loss), or harm/loss (injury or damage that has already been done). Given this appraisal, alternative means of coping are considered and coping activities are employed either to deal with problem (instrumental, or problem-focused coping, as when actions are taken to resolve the problem) or to deal with the dysfunctional emotions that accompany it (palliative, or emotion-focused coping, as when people take comfort in the belief that the loss of a loved one was God's will).

According to the self-identification approach, people attempt to construct and maintain desired identity images. Impediments to doing so generate resistance and a more intensified assessment of and response to the situation than would otherwise occur. The resistance occurs both mentally (e.g., contemplating strategic activities) and in the environment (e.g., carrying out those activities). The magnitude of the problem, and hence the amount of stress that is generated, depends on the perceived relationship between the impediment and the actor's resistance to it. When the probability of damage (i.e., low outcome expectations) and the magnitude of damage (i.e., importance of the images and size of the discrepancy from standards) are high, greater social stress occurs. The remainder of the chapter will analyze the nature and implications of the three generic categories of resistance noted earlier: (a) the examination of impediment-relevant information about the self, situation, and audience, (b) the construction of an explanation for the impediment, and (c) strategic activities that attempt to counterattack against the impediment.

EXAMINING INFORMATION

Impediments trigger an intensified assessment of aspects of the self, situation, and audience that may pertain to the problem. The assessment involves (a) a search for, processing and recall of, and sensitivity to pertinent information, and (b) an increased salience of relevant personal or social standards against which actors compare their performance. By gathering and examining relevant information, a rich data base becomes available in the attempt to counteract the impediment.

Supporting Desired Identity Images

At the outset of assessment, people conduct a search for information that is likely to support their desired identity images. Snyder (1984) has documented people's selective tendency to seek and obtain confirmation for their hypotheses. Hypotheses (beliefs) about the self exhibit the same selective tendency, as people attempt to verify their self-beliefs (M. Snyder, 1984; Swann, 1983, 1985). When impediments to desired self-identifications occur, the preference for supportive information appears to be heightened, motivating people to seek additional self-validating documentation. A variety of research suggests a selective search, both in our memories and in the environment, when problems are encountered. To illustrate, Frey (1981) has shown that when people's identities are threatened by their purported poor performance on an intelligence test, they tend to seek out information that will derogate the validity of the test and thereby dispel the problem. Pyszczynski, Greenberg, and LaPrelle (1985) found that after failure, people most prefer to examine social comparison information when they believe others did poorly on the test rather than well.

People process information more thoroughly and recall it better when it pertains to the self than when it is irrelevant to self (e.g., Greenwald, 1980; Greenwald & Breckler, 1985; Greenwald & Pratkanis, 1984). This pervasive egocentric sensitivity to information is enhanced in the face of impediments. When difficulties arise during self-identification, the demand for an extensive processing of information is magnified over what it would otherwise be, because a more adequate analysis and recall of relevant information can facilitate effective counteraction. It is therefore proposed that impediments to self-identification generate more intensified processing of information than would otherwise occur.

Research supports the proposition and indicates that information processing can be facilitated when people confront problems. To illustrate, Wyer and Frey (1983) found that people display better recall of self-threatening than nonthreatening information, implying that the former has been more thoroughly processed. They suggested that this more in-depth processing is used in people's attempts to counterargue and refute the implications of the information, thereby preserving desired identity images. In a similar vein, Swann and Hill (1982) found that subjects who had received self-discrepant feedback from others made subsequent self-descriptive judgments faster than those who had received self-confirmatory feedback or no feedback. These results suggest that threats to identity increase the accessibility of the relevant identity images in memory, making them more likely to guide the actor's later judgments and actions (Schlenker, in press). Indeed, Swann and Read (1981) and Swann and Hill (1982) found that subjects who received self-disconfirmatory feedback from audiences, as compared to those who received self-confirmatory feedback, were subsequently most likely to try to reaffirm these images by acting in a self-confirmatory manner. Their self-confirmatory actions appeared to be designed to change the opinion of the evaluator and thereby eliminate the threat.

Identity Polarization from Impediments

An interesting implication of intensified information processing is that life's impediments may actually strengthen people's desired identity images. When people's prior self-images are important, strong, and well defined, a large supply of image-supporting information is potentially available in memory. In addition, when people are surrounded by supportive families and friends, they are likely to be comforted during times of trouble with identity-bolstering information. Impediments activate this information and engage the assistance of interpersonal support networks. High self-identification outcome expectations are likely to result, counterarguing occurs to refute the implications of the problem, and desired identity images are reaffirmed. The result is a strengthening (i.e., greater subsequent accessibility in memory and greater resistance to change) or even polarization of desired identity images (see Schlenker, in press).

Spivak and Schlenker (1986) found that impediments to desired identity images can produce the polarization of self-beliefs. In their study, subjects were induced by the experimenter to present themselves positively or negatively to an interviewer on an important trait dimension. The experimenter's instructions emphasized that the self-presentation could be regarded as representative of self (i.e., you can exaggerate your qualities but remain generally truthful) or as unrepresentative of self (i.e., create the impression even if you have to lie, but do not be outrageous in your statements). A negative self-presentation creates a greater impediment to people's desired self-view when it could be regarded as representative rather than unrepresentative of self, whereas a positive self-presentation creates an impediment when it could be seen as unrepresentative rather than representative. When an impediment exists, greater self-assessment and counterarguing should occur. In support of this reasoning, it was found that subjects later increased their self-ratings on the dimension (as compared to control subjects) when situational cues suggested that the negative self-presentation had been representative of self or the positive self-presentation had been unrepresentative of self. No change in self-ratings occurred when the negative self-presentation appeared to be unrepresentative or the positive self-presentation appeared to be representative. These effects, interestingly, are opposite what one would expect on the basis of self-perception theory (Bem, 1972), which would predict that subjects would shift their self-appraisals in the direction of their behavior when cues indicate the behavior is representative of self, thereby bringing their attitudes in line with self-referencing actions.

Threatened and Damaged Identity Images

The intensified search, processing, and recall of pertinent information can facilitate an effective response to impediments if high self-identification outcome expectations result. However, even a biased search is not guaranteed to produce the preferred results, because it may confront an undesired but compelling set of data and an unsupportive context for their evaluation. When the preponderance of the salient evidence is unsupportive, intensified processing will magnify the problem, making it seem worse than it might actually be.

The search for information is more likely to be unsupportive when desired identity images are unrealistic and conflict with salient data. People with low self-esteem provide an example of the problem. Their self-doubts and perceived liabilities make them susceptible to events that suggest they have weaknesses; they are more likely to interpret ambiguous events in a self-negative fashion, are less able to refute any undesired information, and are more likely to accept the pejorative implications (Ickes & Layden, 1978; Wells & Marwell, 1976). The focused attention produced by assessment will magnify weaknesses in identity, and result in a low expectation of being able to deal with the difficulty. Similarly, high self-consciousness—the tendency to focus attention on the self and compare performance against requisite standards—has been associated with an intensified sensitivity and reaction to undesired events (Carver, 1979; Carver & Scheier, 1981). For example, Fenigstein (1979) found that heightened self-attention, either in the form of dispositional high self-consciousness or situationally induced self-awareness, made people more sensitive to negative cues and prompted them to react more negatively to rejection and unfavorable feedback from others.

To the extent that the situation and audience are less supportive, these problems are further magnified. Unsupportive contexts include ones where the impediment has clear diagnostic implications for identity (e.g., failing a valid test with established norms and predictive ability); where upcoming tests are anticipated that will provide additional diagnostic information and are of sufficient difficulty to create concerns about performance (e.g., failing a test and expecting a series of additional tests that could provide further negative information); where audiences are unsupportive or even hostile (e.g., other people appear to attribute the failure to the incompetence of the actor); and where the situation focuses attention on the evaluative, diagnostic implications of the performance (e.g., a public rather than private performance in a test rather than game context) (see Schlenker & Leary, 1982a).

Assessment is an activity whose outcome is a function of the interaction of self, audience, and situation. It is not singly determined by any one of these factors. For example, different aspects of identity (different sets of self-images) will be cued in memory by different combinations of audiences and situations, causing these aspects of self to become salient on the occasion and to guide subsequent activities (see Schlenker, in press). These different self-images provide different combinations of data that are accessed during assessment and that will influence the outcome of the search (e.g., imagine the memories and expectations of a person who interacts with a supportive other in whose company he has experienced numerous pleasant, identity-boosting experiences, as compared to when he interacts with a critical other who has been associated with failures and frustrations). Accordingly, even people with chronic high self-esteem will still experience low self-identification outcome expectations in some contexts (e.g., a difficult task performed before a critical and powerful audience), whereas even whose with chronic low self-esteem will still experience high expectations in some contexts (e.g., easy tasks performed before supportive others).

According to the self-identification approach, the crucial consequence of assessment is whether it produces high or low self-identification outcome expectations. When high expectations result, even people who might otherwise be prone to focus on their liabilities during assessment (e.g., people with low self-esteem or high anxiety) will experience beneficial effects (Schlenker & Leary, 1982a). This hypothesis contrasts with what has often been expected in the literature: that heightening self-attention in chronically anxious people increases their self-preoccupation and debilitates their task performance (e.g., Wine, 1971). Yet, research has shown that people who are chronically anxious and generally fear failure in test situations will improve their performance if (a) their self-attention is increased, and (b) situational conditions are arranged so that they have favorable outcome expectancies (Carver, 1979, p. 1266). The improvement in performance appears to arise because of the combination of assessment and high outcome expectations (Carver, 1979; Schlenker & Leary, 1982a). Given positive expectations of performance, the assessment process focuses attention on relevant information that might otherwise be overlooked, makes standards for performance more salient, and produces greater behavior–standard matching (i.e., monitoring and controlling one's behavior in an attempt to meet the standards) than would otherwise occur. By activating the assessment process, the impediment improves performance over what it might have been if a thorough examination of information had not occurred. Analogously, a professor's lecture is likely to be improved if she or he does not take the class for granted, but instead anticipates possible questions or disruptions and prepares more thoroughly.

In contrast, when assessment produces low outcome expectations, the result is the debilitating effect of stress that is associated with threat or damage to identity. Research has shown that people who have low expectations of achieving a goal will attempt to withdraw from the task in the face of impediments, experience negative affect, and become trapped in obsessive self-appraisals if escape from the situation is impractical (Bandura, 1977; Carver, 1979; Carver & Scheier, 1985). Comparably, low self-identification outcome expectations produce (a) tendencies to withdraw, physically or psychologically, from the stressful situation, (b) negative affect, and (c) intensified assessment in which actors are trapped in the evaluation of self, situation, and audience, obsessively replaying in their minds the problems they confront and their personal liabilities (Schlenker & Leary, 1982a).

Withdrawal tendencies as a result of threats to identity have been widely noted in the literature. Social anxiety has been found to produce the avoidance of and premature withdrawal from identity-threatening situations (Brown, 1970; Buss, 1980; Cheek & Buss, 1981; Sarnoff & Zimbardo, 1961; Sattler, 1965; Schlenker, 1980; Schlenker & Leary, 1982a; Teichman, 1978; Zimbardo, 1977). When physical escape is not practical, cognitive withdrawal becomes likely. People who fail to meet performance standards attempt to minimize self-attention (Carver & Scheier, 1981; Duval & Wicklund, 1972; Wicklund, 1975). They try to take their minds off their problems, embracing opportunities to distract attention from the self. They may read a book, watch television, or go to a movie. The use of alcohol is a classic means of temporarily escaping from the negative cognitive implications of stress, because it minimizes self-consciousness (Hull, Levenson, Young, & Sher, 1983) and provides a temporary artificial boost in self-esteem (Page, 1975). Indeed, people who are chronically self-conscious and experience failures are especially likely to turn to alcohol as an escape (Hull & Young, 1983).

When self-identification outcome expectations are low, people experience negative affect and become trapped in self-assessment, which further buttresses the negative implications for identity. Anxiety and depression are classic clinical examples. People who are highly anxious have been described as self-focused. They concentrate on their own imperfections and inadequacies in an obsessive fashion (Sarason, 1976, 1978; Wine, 1971). People who are high as compared to low in social anxiety are especially likely to experience the cognitive excess of concern about social evaluation (Smith, Ingram, & Brehm, 1983), and they have below-average self-regard (Clark & Arkowitz, 1975; Rehm & Marston, 1968). For people who are socially anxious, the combination of the importance of creating a good impression on others and a focus on information that describes a history of failure will increase the odds of low self-identification outcome expectations; they then become locked into a debilitating process of self-assessment that intensifies their weaknesses (Schlenker & Leary, 1982a). Similarly, depressives are especially likely to perceive themselves negatively (Lewinsohn, Mischel, Chaplin, & Barton,

1980; Pietromonaco & Markus, 1985), contemplate their failures but not their successes (Pyszczynski & Greenberg, 1985), recall more negative and less positive information about themselves (Derry & Kuiper, 1981; Pietromonaco & Markus, 1985), and become self-focused after negative outcomes while avoiding self-focus after positive outcomes (Pyszczynski & Greenberg, 1985). The combination of low outcome expectations and a negative self-focus produces pronounced performance deficits (Strack, Blaney, Ganellen, & Coyne, 1985). The intensified processing of negative information experienced by people who are socially anxious (Arkin, Kolditz, & Kolditz, 1983) or depressed (Peterson, Schwartz, & Seligman, 1981) results in an increased likelihood that they will internalize the cause of problematic events and blame the failure on their character rather than alternative, more self-supporting causes.

Anxiety and depression are similar in their antecedents and consequences. It has been suggested that the major difference between them is that anxiety reflects *threats* to identity, whereas depression reflects an *acknowledged loss* for identity (Oatley & Bolton, 1985). In the case of the former, there is still hope that desired identity images can be maintained, even though substantial doubts exist; in the latter, hope has been abandoned. Indeed, reactions to stress produced by threats and losses are similar in their focus on self-doubt and self-derogation, but differ in the hope that remains. McCrae (1984) found that threats and losses are associated with reactions that emphasize faith (e.g., putting oneself in the hands of God or other people) and fatalism (e.g., believing that nothing can be done, the event was unavoidable, and waiting to see what happens). Threats and losses differ, however, in that threats produce more wishful thinking (e.g., hoping for a miracle, wishing the past could be changed or the situation would go away) whereas losses produce greater expression of feelings that are largely negative (e.g., letting feelings out, talking about feelings). In contrast, reactions to challenges (which, in the present analysis, involve higher self-identification outcome expectations), include more vigorous, assertive activities that are "examples of more mature or non-neurotic coping" (McCrae, p. 927), such as positive thinking, perseverance, rational action, restraint, and drawing strength from adversity.

EXPLAINING IMPEDIMENTS

Impediments must be explained, because by their nature, they represent unwanted, often unanticipated events that have the potential for jeopardizing desired identity images. An explanation provides an interpretation or meaning for an event when its meaning is unclear or might be misinterpreted or misconstrued by audiences (Schlenker, 1982). Impediments trigger explanations that define the potential problem and specify its implications for identity. Once an explanation has been generated, it influences the actor's subsequent cognitions, affect, and behaviors; and it can provide a means of coping with stress. *People attempt to explain events in ways that validate desired identity images and repudiate undesired images* (Schlenker, 1980, 1982). To the extent that this can be accomplished, threats and damage to identity are minimized, the affective consequences are more positive (or less negative), and people can continue to work toward their goals with reasonable expectations of success.

Accounts and Acclamations

Desired identity images are validated and protected through the use of accounts and acclamations, which provide self-serving explanations of events. The concept of an account has a venerable history in psychology, sociology, and philosophy (Austin, 1961; Backman, 1985; D'Arcy, 1963; Goffman, 1971; Mills, 1940; Schlenker, 1980, 1982; Scott & Lyman, 1968; Snyder, 1985; Snyder, Higgins, & Stucky, 1983; Tedeschi & Riess, 1981). An account has traditionally been regarded as an attempt to place a more desirable (or less undesirable) interpretation on conduct that might otherwise appear to be untoward, unexpected, or unacceptable to audiences. More generally, an *account* is a self-serving explanation that attempts to reconcile an undesired event with the personal and social standards that appear to have been violated (Schlenker, 1982). The term has usually been used in the protective sense of avoiding damage to identity following threats, and has rarely been used in the assertive sense of building desired identity images when impediments occur. For the latter purpose, I have used the term *acclamation,* which is an explanation that attempts to show why personal or social standards have been met or exceeded when doubts about the event might otherwise occur (Schlenker, 1978, 1980, 1982). The difference between accounts and acclamations reflects the difference between explanations that interpret a possible identity-threatening failure (e.g., why the loss of our job was not our fault) versus a possible identity-boosting success (e.g., why our promotion was merited and not, as some co-workers seem to insinuate, a matter of politics or luck).

Accounts and acclamations attempt to validate and protect desired identity images by self-servingly interpreting (a) personal responsibility for an event, and (b) the consequences of an event. People use excuses in

order to minimize their personal responsibility for potentially threatening events. Examples include blaming a failure on the situation, fate, or
unstable factors (e.g., an unfair or invalid test, distractions, lack of sleep,
bad luck, God's will, a devil's intrusion) or explaining that a negative
interpersonal evaluation was the result of the evaluator's unperceptiveness or ill will. In a complementary fashion, people use entitlements
in order to maximize their personal responsibility for potentially validating events. Examples include attributing potentially ambiguous successes
or laudatory behavior to one's ability, effort, or worthy motives, or explaining that a desired interpersonal evaluation reflects the perceptiveness of a fair evaluator. People also construct self-serving explanations through their judicious interpretation of the consequences of
events. People use justifications to reduce the undesirability of a threatening event by minimizing its potentially damaging consequences (e.g.,
"I didn't really hurt him in the fight, he just wants to sue me"; or "It was
only a 'white lie'") and maximizing its desirable consequences (e.g., "I
will be stronger for the failure"; or "As a soldier, I killed in order to
preserve the values of our country"). Finally, people use enhancements
to increase the desirability of a potentially validating event by maximizing its desirable consequences and minimizing its undesirable consequences ("My occupation is extremely gratifying, and even though the
pay is poor and others might not think much of it, I make a significant
contribution to society").

Using Accounts and Acclamations

The tendency to use accounts and acclamations has been well documented in the literature and a review is beyond the scope of this paper.
Instead, some general categories of research will be mentioned to illustrate self-serving predilictions.

1. People tend to attribute their successes to their personal attributes whereas they attribute failures to external or unstable factors
(Snyder, Stephan, & Rosenfield, 1978; Tetlock, 1985; Tetlock & Levi,
1982; Weary Bradley, 1978).

2. People explain the loss of loved ones as due to God's will or
explain why they will become stronger because of their failures (Folkman, 1984; Lazarus & Launier, 1978).

3. People derogate the validity of tests on which they do poorly
(Schlenker & Miller, 1977; C. R. Snyder & Clair, 1977; Steiner, 1968)
and derogate the perceptiveness of evaluators who deliver negative interpersonal evaluations (Jones, 1973; Metee & Aronson, 1974).

4. After seeming to be responsible for behaving in ways that harm

others, people shift their attitudes to make them more consistent with the behavior, thereby justifying the conduct (e.g., Collins & Hoyt, 1972; Schlenker, 1982); misperceive the behavior by regarding it as less discrepant from their prior attitudes (Scheier & Carver, 1980); cite a feeling of obligation to perform the behavior (Verhaeghe, 1976); or derogate the individuals who are harmed by the act, making them appear to deserve to be harmed (Verhaeghe, 1976).

5. People describe their own motives for an action as "better" than the motives of others who perform the same act (Schlenker, Hallam, & McCown, 1983).

These tendencies appear to represent identity-assisting preferences for how events are interpreted rather than unbiased deductions from the evidence (Greenwald, 1980; Schlenker, 1980, 1982; C. R. Snyder et al., 1983; Tetlock, 1985). The preference for identity protecting and enhancing information is illustrated in a study by Sicoly and Ross (1977). They found that subjects who believed they had performed poorly on an important test (a) took low personal responsibility for their performance, and (b) derogated others who assigned them higher personal responsibility. In addition, subjects who believed they had performed well on the test (a) took high personal responsibility for their performance, and (b) derogated others who assigned them less responsibility than they had taken. These patterns suggest a tendency to shun failure and embrace success. More generally, however, they suggest a tendency to interpret events in ways that support and protect desired identity images.

People's explanations for the problems they confront not only define the "truth" of the event for themselves and others, but also influence their subsequent cognitions, affect, and behavior. When identity-supporting explanations can be constructed, both privately and publicly, people's goals and plans are preserved, they can maintain beliefs in their relevant skills, they can preserve reasonably high outcome expectations, and they can continue their activities and relationships without significant disruption or alteration. For example, to the extent that people can attribute their difficulties to aspects of the situation (e.g., a hostile or prejudiced instructor), to a temporary internal state (e.g., a cold, being tired), or to an internal deficit that can be overcome with practice, effort, or the passage of time (e.g., working hard to "hone" skills, waiting until one is more mature), their subsequent outcome expectancies are likely to be high when they confront similar difficult situations. In support, Anderson (1983) demonstrated that people who are induced to attribute interpersonal failures to an inappropriate strategy or inadequate effort (unstable, changeable aspects of the self) performed better at an interpersonal task than those who were induced to attribute their failures to their own character or traits. Indeed, explanations that blame difficulties on one's enduring character appear to decrease self-efficacy expectations, produce poorer subsequent task performance, and lead to self-punishment (Bandura, 1977, 1982).

People's explanations also have an impact on their affective experiences. McFarland and Ross (1982) found that people who succeed on a task experience greater positive affect when they attribute their performance to internal causes, whereas people who fail on a task experience less negative affect when they attribute their performance to external causes. Similarly, Mehlman and Snyder (1985) found that people who failed on an important task experienced less negative emotion when they had the opportunity to construct excuses for their performance under conditions of low evaluation by others. Those who were denied the opportunity to proffer excuses, and those who offered excuses under conditions of high evaluation and possible challenge by others, felt more anxious.

Constraints on Explanations

Self-serving explanations are not always viable. Explanations must be fitted to the salient evidence and to the perceived or anticipated beliefs of significant others (real or imagined) who provide consensual information (Backman, 1985; Schlenker, 1980, 1982; Tetlock, 1985). Explanations can be contradicted by facts that are known about the situation (e.g., the loss of a job cannot be blamed on the company's financial problems if they show a profit and only you were fired), facts known about the actor (e.g., prior to the job loss, there was a history of reprimands for incompetence and absenteeism), or the consensus of opinion of significant others (e.g., respected co-workers and neighbors regard the supervisor as a fair person who does not allow personal prejudices to cloud decisions about employees, and they also know of the actor's bad reputation). Conditions that make the situation, the actor's known characteristics, and the opinions of others less ambiguous by eliminating alternative possibilities constrain the explanations people can believably and defensibly construct. The result is a limited selection of viable explanations that vary only in how self-threatening they are.

An explanation is successfully self-serving to the extent that it can be defended to oneself or others. Prior and expected failures constrain the claims people make about themselves, especially when performances are public (e.g., Baumeister & Jones, 1978; Dutton, 1972; Frey, 1978; Schlenker, 1975, 1980, 1982; Schlenker & Leary, 1982b; C. R. Snyder *et al.*, 1983; M. L. Snyder *et al.*, 1978; Tetlock & Levi, 1982; Weary Bradley,

1978; Wortman, Costanzo, & Witt, 1973). Given that the explanations people construct must be fitted to the perceived knowledge and values of the audience in order to be effective, people's explanations take into account the anticipation of how others may react. Often, explanations are jointly constructed and negotiated with others to arrive at a consensually agreed upon version of the truth (Backman, 1985; Schlenker, 1980, 1984; Scott & Lyman, 1968), as when people suggest possibilities and wait for a response (e.g., "You know, I didn't get much sleep last night worrying about the test; do you think that may have hurt my score?").

Although other people, especially friends and family, can help validate desired identity images by assisting with the construction of supportive explanations (see ahead), there are times when people anticipate that others will challenge or debate their preferred interpretations. Even though people may believe their explanation is valid, the anticipation of such challenge can still arouse concern. Indeed, Mehlman and Snyder (1985) found that people whose excuses for a poor performance were assessed in the evaluative context of an all-knowing audience (who supposedly had access to their private states via a bogus pipeline) experienced more negative emotions than those whose excuses were less likely to be evaluated.

Problematic Explanations: Losing Consensual Validation

To cope adequately with stress, explanations of the problem must be believable to audiences who matter, while at the same time accomplishing the self-serving function of preserving desired identity images. Difficulties with either aspect creates problems.

When explanations stray too far from the evidence, they generate rejection from others and lead to negative imputations about identity (e.g., the actor is egotistical, defensive, flawed, incompetent, out of touch with reality) (Schlenker & Leary, 1982b). The extreme clinical case is paranoia. Classic descriptions of the paranoid personality report exaggerated feelings of self-importance and the explanation of personal shortcomings and failures by blaming them on external causes, especially the hostile, persecuting actions of other people (Page, 1975; Shaver *et al.*, 1984).

According to Lemert (1962), the social genesis of paranoia arises from problems that represent an actual or threatened identity loss for the individual, such as the death of a family member, a divorce, the loss of a job, the failure to receive a desired promotion, or bodily mutilations. These changes are perceived to be enduring and intolerable, as in the case of a 50-year-old man who believes he will have an impossible time starting over after the death of his wife. To combat the losses for identity, the paranoid compensates with increased feelings of self-worth that are not substantiated by the data as they are perceived by other members of the community.

The resulting claims about identity create difficulties between the individual and other people (e.g., family, neighbors, co-workers, or superiors). Others regard his assertions as outlandish and begin to raise questions, which produce assertive rebuttals and often result in arguments. Instead of negotiating a mutually acceptable explanation for the problem, the paranoid steadfastly insists that he is right and others are wrong, and constructs explanations for the lack of consensual validation that focus on the imperceptiveness, ill will, and ulterior motives of those others who refuse to accept the "truth" as he sees it. He develops a reputation for being argumentative, discourteous, and difficult to get along with. As a consequence, others begin to avoid and to exclude him from everyday confidences and activities. In order to receive any meaningful feedback from others, he learns that he must provoke them with accusations and insults (Lemert, 1962). The mistrust and conspiratorial nature of the paranoid's exclusion become fact as he is systematically segregated from other members of the community. Initially, the paranoid's extreme behavior is isolated, with arrogance, self-aggrandizement, and the derogation of others occurring primarily in relation to specific identity-threatening situations. Over time, the pattern spreads throughout the paranoid's relationships as his reputation becomes known and discussed.

The paranoid's reaction represents an assertive counterattack against what most people would perceive as a threat and loss for identity. Clinical descriptions suggest that the paranoid is convinced of his interpretation and appears to hold high self-identification outcome expectations in the face of disagreement from the community. By rejecting the consensus of the social community and explaining the disagreements about reality by blaming their ill will, the paranoid is able to maintain his aggrandizing view of self. The extreme, assertive reaction to stress evidenced by the paranoid will be discussed further ahead. We will now examine the more common reaction of self-protection and withdrawal.

Problematic Explanations: Expecting the Worst

The progressive problems created by the paranoid personality illustrate what can happen when self-aggrandizing claims lack community validation. Problems also ensue, however, when people expect the worst and construct explanations that internalize threatening information, blaming the difficulty on the inadequacies of the self. Blaming difficulties on one's enduring character is associated with low self-esteem (Ickes & Layden, 1978; M. L. Snyder *et al.*, 1978), anxiety (Arkin *et al.*, 1983), and depression (Peterson *et al.*, 1981).

People who are chronically anxious are more likely than the average person to perceive constraints on their self-identifications and react by internalizing problems. First, they are more likely to perceive impediments to their self-identifications. They are sensitized to cues that imply difficulties with their performance, focus them on evaluations of self by audiences, and suggest internal arousal in evaluative situations (Schlenker & Leary, 1982a). Second, the examination of self triggered by perceived impediments is likely to generate negative information. High anxiety is associated with lower self-esteem, lower confidence in interpersonal skills that might be used to create a preferred impression on others, and a tendency to regard the self as having a reputation for unsatisfactory performance (see Leary, 1983; Schlenker & Leary, 1982a, 1985). The tendency to perceive and recall negative information about the self is illustrated by findings that subjects who are high in social anxiety, as opposed to those who are not, remember more negative incidents about past interactions (O'Banion & Arkowitz, 1977), rate negative feedback from others as being more negative and more personally upsetting (Smith & Sarason, 1975), and rate favorable evaluations from others as less perceptive and accurate (Lake & Arkin, 1985). Third, the intensified focus on negative information about the self increases the likelihood that the chronically anxious person will hold low self-identification outcome expectations. These low expectations are then likely to intensify their negative self-focus. This is not to suggest that chronically anxious people will always display self-effacing attributions, because they will display self-serving patterns when they have high self-identification outcome expectations. However, they are more likely to be sensitized to cues that imply constraints and to display self-effacing attributions across a wider variety of situations than will the average person.

It follows that anxiety is generally associated with internalizing blame for failure. For example, Arkin *et al.* (1983) found that unsuccessful, test anxious subjects blamed their character, as opposed to the environment or their behavioral tactics, for their failures in a college course. Despite this general tendency, the nature of the situation and audience can modify the extent to which self-effacing patterns emerge. Arkin, Appelman, and Burger (1980) examined context effects on the attributional patterns of subjects who were high and low in chronic social anxiety. Subjects high but not low in social anxiety were found to be more self-effacing in their performance attributions, taking responsibility for failure and rejecting it for success, when a committee of high prestige others would evaluate their behavior as compared to when such an evaluation would not occur. When the threat of evaluation did not exist, socially anxious subjects presented themselves in a more flattering fashion, taking greater responsibility for success than failure. In a second study, Arkin *et al.* replicated the tendency for anxious subjects to take more responsibility for failure than success, and found it was more pronounced when attributions were assessed via the bogus pipeline procedure, in which they believed their private reactions to success and failure could be detected. These findings illustrate the sensitivity of anxious individuals to constraints on their explanations.

The consequences of impediments are similar, though seemingly more pronounced and pervasive, for people who are depressed. Depressives display self-derogating patterns of attribution (e.g., Brewin, 1985; Kuiper, 1978; Rizley, 1978; Seligman, Abramson, Semmell, & Von Baeyer, 1979). Further, they do not merely accept responsibility for failure, but blame it on their character, as opposed to their behavior or other unstable, more modifiable elements (Peterson *et al.*, 1981). The chance that they will hold low self-identification outcome expectations is significantly increased by the depressive's (a) low self-esteem and self-criticism (Tabachnik, Crocker, & Alloy, 1983), (b) generalized negative self-schema (Kuiper, Derry, & MacDonald, 1982; Pietromonaco & Markus, 1985), (c) large discrepancies between the real and ideal self (Nadich, Gargan, & Michael, 1975), (d) history of rejection from others (Hammen & Peters, 1978; Howes & Hokanson, 1979), (e) inappropriate response patterns to others (Hokanson, Sacco, Blumberg, & Landrum, 1980), and (f) tendency to be less comforted by others, feeling less pleasure and more discomfort in social settings (Youngren & Lewinsohn, 1980). The negativity of the identity-relevant information that is salient during assessment acts as a constraint on the types of explanations the depressive can believably accept, resulting in self-blame and self-derogation when difficulties are perceived. By blaming failure on deficits in important identity images, depressives become further locked into the assessment mode, perpetuating their preoccupation with their liabilities and their negative affect.

A chronic tendency to construct self-effacing explanations may even produce a change in how actors come to regard self-serving explanations. People who usually internalize failure and externalize success may justify these self-diminishing activities by regarding them as more insightful, less self-centered and pompous, and therefore less negative than self-enhancing behaviors. Just as people tend to overvalue the at-

tributes they believe they have and undervalue attributes they believe
they lack (e.g., Rosenberg, 1979), they may also overvalue the attributional style they use and undervalue the opposite style. Ickes and Layden
(1978) documented the tendency for people with low as compared to
high self-esteem to display self-effacing patterns of attributions. Further,
in support of the earlier suggestion, they also reported that subjects who
are low in self-esteem regarded their own attributional style (i.e., internalizing failure and externalizing success) as more "appropriate" and
"modest," whereas they regarded the opposite style (i.e., externalizing
failure and internalizing success) as more "immodest" and "egotistical."
These relationships do not tell us whether people with low self-esteem
display a self-effacing style because they regard self-enhancement negatively, regard self-enhancement negatively because they tend to use a
self-effacing style, or both. Nonetheless, it is reasonable to propose that
people will justify their behavior by coming to overvalue their own style
as compared to how it might be perceived by other people. This perception probably provides one of the few consolations available after chronic
self-derogation. However, this minimal solace may serve to perpetuate
the view that the world is a cold habitat occupied by conceited people.
The thought is unlikely to generate much hope for those who are
depressed.

Anticipatory Explanations and Self-Handicapping

The assessment process is triggered when impediments occur *or are
anticipated.* Anticipating a difficulty with self-identification generates an
examination of possible explanations that could support desired identity
images. As examples, people may confront a situation in which failure is
probable and consider the excuses they could use to limit the potential
damage, or contemplate an action that might elicit disapproval from
others and think about how they might explain the behavior in a way
that minimizes rejection.

People's future actions are determined in part by the anticipatory
explanations they can construct (Backman, 1985; Mills, 1940; Schlenker,
1980, 1982; Schlenker *et al.,* 1983; C. R. Snyder *et al.,* 1983; Tetlock,
1985). If identity-preserving explanations can be found, actors are more
likely to go forward with the contemplated behavior. If they cannot, they
are likely to avoid the anticipated problem if doing so is possible, such as
by avoiding difficult tasks or refraining from behaving in a questionable
way. The controlling influence of anticipated explanations is illustrated
in a study by M. L. Snyder, Kleck, Strenta, and Mentzer (1979). They
found that subjects would shun a handicapped person if they could
attribute their discriminatory behavior to a socially acceptable reason

(i.e., preferring to see a movie that is different from the one the handicapped person chose to see). Only when an acceptable explanation for their discrimination was unavailable did subjects choose to associate with the handicapped person.

If actors anticipate an acceptable explanation for potential problems, they will be more likely to engage in activities they might otherwise avoid and feel more comfortable during the performance. Leary (1986) provided support for this hypothesis. He had subjects who previously scored high or low in social anxiety interact with a stranger of the opposite sex while "party noise" was played in the background. Some of the subjects were told that the noise would be loud and distracting, whereas others were told it would be only minimally troublesome and would permit them to get to know one another (the actual loudness of the noise was the same in both conditions). From a self-identification standpoint, subjects who thought the noise would interfere with their ability to interact (a) should assume that their partner would be unlikely to form a confident impression of them, and (b) had a salient excuse for a possible failure to procure a desired evaluation (i.e., the noise, not their skills, was to blame). As predicted, when subjects believed the noise would interfere, high and low social anxious subjects did not differ in the positivity of their self-presentations. However, when the noise supposedly would not interfere, socially anxious subjects presented themselves less positively than did nonanxious subjects. These findings extend those of Brodt and Zimbardo (1981), who found that when subjects could misattribute their arousal during an interaction to the effects of distracting noise, their performance was more effective than when they could not do so.

Self-handicapping is a type of anticipatory account that paradoxically preserves identity by giving the appearance of increasing the likelihood of failure. Self-handicapping involves seeming to place obstacles in one's path so that diagnostic information about identity is minimized, thereby fogging the attributions that can be made about the self. Jones and Berglas (1978) proposed that people construct handicaps to their possible achievements in order to preserve self-esteem. A classic example is alcoholism (at least in some cases). If an alcoholic subsequently fails, the bottle and not his or her (lack of) talent can be faulted; fantasies of glorified achievements, if and when the alcoholic stops drinking, thereby can be maintained. If one succeeds, one must truly be talented, because how else could the obstacle have been overcome?

People display remarkable ingenuity in the handicaps they construct. In a study involving reports of past handicaps, DeGree and Snyder (1985) found that subjects emphasized the adversity of their past life experiences when an uncertain evaluation was expected and the traumatic experiences could serve as an excuse for poor performance. Feelings of anxiety, which would typically debilitate performance on tasks, can also be regarded as a handicap (Greenberg, Pyszczynski, & Paisley, 1984; Leary & Schlenker, 1981; Schlenker & Leary, 1982a; Smith, Snyder, & Handelsman, 1982; C. R. Snyder & Smith, 1982). Smith *et al.* (1982) found that anxiety was used as an excuse for a potentially poor performance by chronically anxious subjects only when anxiety could serve as a viable account for failure on a valid test. If evaluative pressures were low (i.e., the task was described as new and not necessarily valid) or if anxiety had been described as irrelevant to performance on the particular task, even subjects who were chronically anxious did not report high anxiety. Interestingly, subjects who were told that anxiety was irrelevant to task performance reported reduced effort on the task, thereby offering an alternative excuse for their potentially poor performance ("If I didn't try hard, my talents are not diagnosed by a failure").

Self-handicapping appears to occur primarily when (a) a performance is important, (b) actors anticipate a reasonable likelihood that their performance may threaten their identities, (c) less threatening accounts for the performance are unavailable, and (d) actors are uncertain about their standing on the dimension(s) that would be diagnosed by the performance (Jones & Berglas, 1978; Schlenker & Leary, 1982a; C. R. Snyder & Smith, 1982). If the importance of a performance is trivial or if people anticipate success, there is no reason to employ a handicap. Handicaps are useful only when importance is high and failure is feared. However, handicaps usually have negative connotations for identity; alcoholics and the chronically anxious are generally regarded as weak and are rarely admired. Even children regard anxious others as less likeable and strong than nonanxious others (Darby & Schlenker, in press). The negative connotations associated with handicaps make them unattractive unless alternative accounts for potential failures are unavailable. Finally, people who are certain about their (high or low) standing on the attribute have no reason to employ a handicap. If an image is well defined and clearly documented on the dimension, a single isolated performance will have little impact. It is only when pretensions exist but documentation is scarce that it is worth preserving the possibility for claiming desired but uncertain images (Harris & Snyder, 1985).

STRATEGIC ACTIVITIES

Dealing with impediments frequently requires going beyond the examination of information and the construction of explanations. It demands more direct action to deal with the problem. The resulting (cognitive and behavioral) activities can be regarded as strategic in the sense that they attempt to preserve and reaffirm desired identity images, to both ourselves and to others. These activities include (a) counterattacks that attempt to neutralize problematic environmental conditions, (b) actions that attempt to strengthen identity from current and future threats, and (c) the pursuit of support from other people that reaffirms desired identity images. These strategies are illustrated by the actions that occur when identity is threatened by serious illness or disease. As long as hope exists (i.e., expectations that identity can be preserved), people (a) go to great lengths to find a cure for the disease, trying a variety of drugs or procedures to destroy it (e.g., traveling from one institute or shrine to another in their quests), (b) attempt to strengthen their resistance to the disease (e.g., through doses of vitamins, herbs, ointments), and (c) seek out people who affirm hopes for recovery (e.g., seeking physicians who claim that the disease can and will be beaten). Social threats to identity generate comparable strategic activities.

Counterattacks

Counterattacks involve the attempt to alter (in imagination or in the real world) potentially harmful environmental conditions. Five tactics predominate. (a) People can attempt to change the opinions of others who regard them in an undesired manner (e.g., attempting to convince a co-worker that his or her opinions of us are incorrect; altering the co-worker's opinion by demonstrating one's skills on relevant tasks). (b) People can attempt to alter existing relationships with others to provide better opportunities for validating desired identity images (e.g., firing an employee who does not maintain the proper respect; getting a divorce from a critical spouse; trying to change the identity of a spouse so that his or her roles provide a better fit for one's own). (c) People can try to seek out situations in which the probability of success is greater and avoid ones that are potentially threatening (e.g., changing jobs or occupations; seeking out people or tasks that are unlikely to arouse anxiety). (d) People can try to change the nature of the tasks they have to confront in order to reduce the probability of undesired outcomes (e.g., trying to alter job-related responsibilities so as to perform primarily "good" tasks and not "bad" ones on which failure is likely). (e) Finally, people can try to change the applicable rules or standards in ways that better accommodate their desired identity images (e.g., attempting to change laws in society that are disadvantageous to members of one's social group; trying to change the standards or requirements for an "A" grade in a college course such that one's probability of success is increased). If successful, these activities provide "cures" for the difficulty, either retroactively or at least for future problems. At the extreme, counterattacks can involve the forceful removal of the social threat, as in the case of the paranoid who decides he has had enough and kills the person(s) he holds responsible for his problems.

Research by Swann and his associates illustrates the process of counterattack in cases where identity is threatened by undesired evaluations from others. Swann and Hill (1982) had subjects play a game with a confederate in which each alternately took the role of a dominant leader or a submissive assistant. Later, in the context of choosing dominant or submissive roles for a subsequent set of games, the confederate remarked that the subject appeared either to be a dominant, forceful type of person or not to be such a person. If the feedback was congruent with subjects' desired identity images as assessed prior to the session (i.e., dominant subjects received dominant feedback or submissive subjects received nondominant feedback), their subsequent behaviors were largely unaffected and they seemed to accept the confederate's appraisal. However, if the feedback posed a threat to their desired images (i.e., a dominant subject received nondominant feedback or a submissive subject received dominant feedback), they attempted to reaffirm the image through their subsequent behavior. Dominant subjects behaved in an even more dominant fashion, whereas submissive subjects behaved even more submissively. In addition, judges rated the subjects as being more resistant to the discrepant feedback. These behaviors seemed designed to alter the confederate's judgment and to provide unequivocal evidence for their desired identities during the interaction. Interestingly, these results occurred only when subjects had the opportunity to interact further with the confederate and alter his or her undesired opinion. If subjects did not have that opportunity, they polarized their self-appraisals on the dimension, thereby reaffirming desired identity images to themselves and anyone who might view their self-evaluations.

As noted earlier, impediments that result in reasonably high self-identification outcome expectations can improve performance by making standards salient and increasing self-monitoring and control in the attempt to match those standards through performance. Consistent with this reasoning, Swann and Read (1981) found that subjects behaved in ways that elicited desired appraisals of their identities from an interaction partner, and this tendency was most pronounced when they had earlier been led to suspect that their partner might disagree with a desired identity image.

The opinions of others can also be altered by influencing their expectations and standards. On many occasions, people's identities are jeopardized not because their performance is poor but because the applicable social standards are too high (Schlenker & Leary, 1985). In such cases, actors experience anxiety and usually try to reject the standards by showing that they should not be applied to them. Being overpraised provides an example. High praise carries with it high standards and may create expectations of continued superior performance, which can portend failure. Indeed, discomfort is produced by being overpraised in public (Buss, 1980), and subjects who receive inordinate rather than mild praise engage in greater self-criticism (Davis & Brock, 1972). Kanouse and Pullan (described in Kanouse, Gumpert, & Canavan-Gumpert, 1981) demonstrated the rejection of praise that carries future behavioral implications. After performing a task, subjects were praised ("Very good . . . Lot's of people haven't done so well") in a way that either did ("You should do well on the rest of these") or did not ("Let's see what you can do with the next one") have implications for future performance. When performance on related tasks was later assessed, it was found that subjects who received the praise that carried expectations of continued high performance, as compared to those who received no praise or praise that carried no future implications, said they did less well and actually did less well on the tasks, attributed their performance more to luck, and reported greater anxiety. The implications of praise were soundly rejected by these subjects in their apparent attempt to modify the social standards under which they would be judged.

A similar rejection of overly high social standards appears to be involved in the frequently poor task performances of people with low self-esteem. Maracek and Mettee (1972) found that subjects who were low in self-esteem engaged in a concerted effort to lower expectations about their performance. They took low personal responsibility after a sudden increase in performance and subsequently performed less well on subsequent related tasks; however, the effect occurred only when subjects believed they would undergo further evaluation. Thus, when the expectations of audiences hold undesired evaluative implications for identity, subjects act to alter those expectations and construct a social context that is more conducive to the creation of an identity they can preserve (cf. Mettee, 1971).

Strengthening Identity

When the body is attacked by disease, people strengthen their resistance by buttressing its defenses (e.g., by taking vitamins, herbs, and other supposed strengthening agents). Analogously, when social problems occur or are anticipated, people attempt to strengthen their resistance by reaffirming and strengthening desired identity images. The notion of strengthening desired identity images resembles the psychoanalytic concept of compensation. According to Adler (1939), social feelings of inferiority produce compensatory strivings for superiority. Threats to self generated by insecurities and weaknesses are presumed to drive us to actions designed to bolster and improve the self. This bolstering can occur either on the threatened dimension (e.g., the puny weakling whose physique has been the object of ridicule becomes a body builder and ultimately emerges as Mr. Universe) or on unrelated but personally important dimensions (e.g., the puny weakling studies hard and becomes a reknowned scientist). It can also occur immediately in the face of perceived or anticipated threats (e.g., a failure prompts the person to compensate by doing a good deed or by working on a task at which that person has superior talent) or it can result in long-term actions designed to strengthen identity (e.g., the adolescent endures the discomfort and embarrassment of wearing braces in order to achieve an eventual gain in physical attractiveness). The general phenomenon of strengthening identity by rectifying areas of potential weakness is illustrated by the popularity of self-improvement aids (e.g., improving one's social skills by taking dancing lessons or a course in how to win friends and influence people).

Several lines of research provide evidence for identity bolstering. Studies of prosocial behavior have found that laudatory actions frequently occur in order to reaffirm a positive, moral image of self. People who have violated personal or social standards for conduct (e.g., lying, cheating) are more likely to engage in prosocial actions later and thereby increase private and public self-worth (see Tedeschi & Riordan, 1981, for a review).

In a related vein, Schlenker (Schlenker, 1980; Schlenker & Goldman, 1982; Schlenker & Reiss, 1979; Schlenker & Schlenker, 1975) proposed that impediments to desired identity images produce counterattacks that include reaffirming one's standing on the dimension by polarizing relevant attitudes and actions. For example, subjects are more likely to polarize their attitudes when situational cues imply they are not responsible for related behaviors that symbolize important, desired identity images (Schlenker & Goldman, 1982; Schlenker & Riess, 1979; Schlenker & Schlenker, 1975). By polarizing their relevant attitudes, subjects reaffirm desired images that might otherwise be jeopardized.

Additional evidence for compensation has been obtained in studies that have found inflated self-ratings following impediments to desired identity images. In their analysis of symbolic self-completion, Wicklund and Gollwitzer (1981, 1982, 1983; Gollwitzer & Wicklund, 1985; Gollwitzer, Wicklund, & Hilton, 1982) proposed that people who are committed to a particular goal for self (e.g., being a scientist, athlete, musician) strive toward completeness of the self-definition. They accumulate the symbolic evidence of such completeness (e.g., diplomas, trophies) and engage in activities that symbolize the self-definition. When they experience a shortcoming in the self-definition, they attempt to counter it with activities designed to enhance or demonstrate completeness.

Wicklund and Gollwitzer conducted several studies that found compensation for shortcomings. They reasoned that people with weaker as opposed to stronger educational backgrounds in an interest area to which they had committed themselves would be more likely to attempt to provide evidence that supports their self-definition. Consistent with this reasoning, they found that subjects with weaker educational backgrounds expressed a willingness to teach more students about their interest area (Wicklund & Gollwitzer, 1981) and were less willing to admit failure and self-derogate following negative feedback about their performance on an interest-related test (Gollwitzer et al., 1982).

Extending these results, Gollwitzer and Wicklund (1985) gave feedback to college students indicating that their responses on a short, bipolar adjective checklist either were or were not similar to those of successful professional people in the students' aspired interest area. The "similar" feedback supports desired identity images, whereas the "dissimilar" feedback creates an impediment. It was found that subjects who were confronted with an impediment: (a) were more dominant in an interpersonal competition to express positive self-descriptions that were related to their aspired professional career (Experiment 1), and (b) were more self-aggrandizing in self-descriptions that were relevant to their interest areas, even when an attractive member of the opposite sex indicated a preference for more modest, self-deprecating people (Experiment 2). The impediment mobilized subjects activities in the service of reaffirming desired identity images.

Compensation can also occur on dimensions that are unrelated to an identity impediment. Baumeister and Jones (1978) gave subjects either a positive or negative personal evaluation based on the supposed results of a personality test, and also informed them that an interaction partner was or was not aware of the feedback. Subjects then had the opportunity to present themselves to their partner on a variety of dimensions, some of which had been included in the earlier profile and some of which had not been included. Compensation, evidenced by inflated self-ratings, was found only when the threatening negative feedback was publicly known. Further, compensation occurred *only* on dimensions that had not been included in the supposedly valid profile. On the dimensions that were contained in the profile, subjects presented themselves consistently with the publicly known, negative feedback (cf. Schlenker, 1975). Greenberg and Pyszczynski (1985) replicated these findings, showing compensation to occur after a public but not a private failure. Because their study involved anonymous self-ratings, it appears that compensation occurs for both the self-as-audience as well as other people as audiences.

Although failures that occurred privately did not produce compensation in the latter study, this result does not imply that compensatory behavior is limited exclusively to public failings. First, public threats usually have more profound consequences for identity, because they jeopardize our reputations across a wider range of audiences and situations (Goffman, 1959; Kiesler, 1971; Schlenker, 1975, 1980, in press; Wicklund & Gollwitzer, 1982). This is not to say, however, that privately perceived failings are never regarded as serious. Second, private behavior may provide a different set of possibilities for dealing with threats. In most situations private behavior is easier to trivialize, dismiss, or forget if we are so inclined. In private, people are not constrained by the critical gaze of others who may have their own preferences for how important a performance is, how diagnostic it is of particular traits, and how it may be best explained. Such public knowledge limits the ways people can deal with threats by prompting them to avoid self-protective strategies that are expected to be discredited or distrusted by others. Indeed, people adjust their self-presentations and their explanations of events to take into account public beliefs about them (Schlenker, 1975, 1980, 1982; Schlenker & Leary, 1982b; Schlenker; Miller, & Leary, 1983). In public, people may be constrained to regard a failure as important and diagnostic, and cope with it by compensating. In private, the same failure may be seen as unimportant or invalid, thus making compensation unnecessary, or produce attempts to bolster the problematic dimension through self-reaffirmation or self-improvement.

There has been little empirical guidance to indicate when the self will be bolstered on dimensions that are relevant versus irrelevant to a threat. It is reasonable to propose that people (a) prefer to bolster and reaffirm the identity images that are threatened rather than to compensate on irrelevant dimensions, and (b) will experience greater satisfaction and more positive affect if they can do so on the same dimension than on different dimensions. The more important the image is and more committed the person is to it, the greater this preference will be. The preference for strengthening relevant images can be counteracted, however, by (a) the vulnerability of self-beliefs on the dimension (e.g., the identity images are difficult to defend in the face of attack), and (b) the potency of the threat (e.g., a failure is public and is perceived by audiences to be valid and diagnostic). Combining these elements, it is hypothesized that compensation will occur on relevant dimensions when the threatened images are important and less vulnerable, and the threat is not highly potent (see Schlenker, in press, for a more detailed rationale). In contrast, when threats are potent and pertain to vulnerable images, compensation will occur on irrelevant dimensions.

The available evidence is consistent with these hypotheses, at least on the current post hoc basis. The studies by Wicklund and Gollwitzer, which found compensation on the relevant dimension, employed images that were high in personal importance (i.e., subjects' self-designated areas of high interest) and used weak threats (e.g., feedback on a brief, 10-item scale of suspect validity). Similarly, Spivak and Schlenker (1986) found that subjects polarized their self-ratings on an important dimension under conditions of a weak attack (e.g., a comment by the experimenter suggesting that a negative self-presentation might be representative of self). In contrast, the study by Baumeister and Jones (1978), which found compensation on irrelevant dimensions, employed a more potent threat (i.e., feedback from a supposedly valid test battery) that would be more likely to block contradictory claims, at least in public (the importance to subjects of the dimensions that were threatened was not assessed).

Acquiring Support

Maintaining the integrity of desired identity images involves maintaining a support system of others who provide validating and bolstering information. People gravitate toward others who provide support for their desired identity images, being more likely to choose them as friends and partners (Backman, 1983; Schlenker, 1980, 1984, 1985; Secord & Backman, 1965; Swann, 1983, 1985). Further, people are more satisfied in relationships to the extent that their desired identity images are elicited, supported, and enhanced by others (Schlenker, 1984).

Successfully coping with threats to identity is facilitated by the assistance of family and friends. Supportive others can help an individual explain away and cope with his failures (e.g., suggesting an account or coping strategy he may not have considered), can validate a person's strategies and thereby increase his or her confidence they will work (e.g., agreeing that his account of a threat is accurate or that a particular tactic will successfully handle the problem), and can assist in bolstering desired identity images (e.g., reminding one of past accomplishments one may have overlooked, asserting that one's identity is desirable, and trivializing threats such that they seem irrelevant to identity). The greater the inter-personal support people elicit or receive, the easier it is for them to cope.

Support goes beyond the assistance that people receive *after* threats have occurred. Friends and family can help people to avoid events that might jeopardize their desired identity images and also can help to strengthen their identities so that they are more resistant to the inevitable frustrations of life (Schlenker, 1984). (Of course, others may also do the reverse, making it more difficult to maintain desired identity images.) To illustrate, others can influence the symbols of one's identity through gifts or encouragements to wear, display, and purchase items that symbolize desired identity images (e.g., a wife who receives sexy lingerie or expensive perfumes from her husband is likely to feel and respond differently than one who receives long woolen nighties and kitchen appliances). They can influence the jobs or tasks that one undertakes, including the choice of occupation and hobbies (e.g., encouraging one to take or leave a particular job or encouraging or discouraging certain joint activities that might help or hinder one's desired images). They can influence the people with whom one associates, thereby affecting the outcomes and appraisals one receives from those others (e.g., encouraging or discouraging associations with certain other people who may bolster or undermine one's desired identity images). Through their words and deeds, family and friends can provide support for (or repudiation of) one's desired identity images and thereby reduce or exacerbate the stress one experiences.

Swann and Predmore (1985) demonstrated the importance of support when threats to identity arise. Subjects received identity-discrepant feedback after taking a test. They then had the opportunity to interact with a stranger, or a person with whom they were involved in an intimate relationship and who either agreed or disagreed with the subjects' self-conceptions. When subjects' self-ratings were later assessed, it was found that those who interacted with a congruent intimate (i.e., one who agreed with the subjects' self-conception) displayed no change in self-ratings. The intimate had apparently insulated the subjects' against the threat. In contrast, subjects who interacted with either a stranger or a noncongruent intimate shifted their self-ratings in the direction of the feedback.

As these findings indicate, when social support for identity is unavailable, problems ensue. Failure to receive self-validation is stressful in and of itself. People who exhibit the greatest amounts of stress in their interpersonal relations are those who have the greatest discrepancies between their views of self and the perceived or actual appraisals of themselves by others (Lundgren, 1978). Support is especially important in established relationships. Supportive communications contribute to marital happiness, whereas nagging and voicing complaints about one another are related to poor marital adjustment (Goode, 1956; Levinger, 1976; Markham, 1979). Much of the time, nagging appears to be related to dissatisfaction with the identity of one's partner and the attempt to force a change in his or her behavior, as when a husband nags his wife to be something that she does not want to be (Schlenker, 1984).

The lack of supportive relationships, including the loss of prior support or the inability to develop support, is related to social anxiety and depression. People who are socially anxious fear rejection and end up avoiding relationships that might help them bolster their self-view (Cheek & Busch, 1981; Leary, 1983; Schlenker, 1984). Depressives similarly seem to lack stable role relationships that would permit them to cope with stress (Oatley & Bolton, 1985).

The loss of a loved, supportive spouse through death is an especially traumatic experience and ranks as the most stressful of life events. One of the reasons for the trauma (and this is not to minimize the loss of love, shared experiences, and mutual rewards) is the disruption to identity that is created. Over time in a relationship, thought and behavior patterns develop that are intrinsic and unique to it. Based on the identities that have evolved in the relationship, the parties can anticipate how each will interpret situations, the evaluations and outcomes preferred by the other, and the actions the other will proffer. The closer the relationship, the greater the extent to which the evaluation of experiences and outcomes shifts from individual to joint criteria, the interests and needs of the other weigh more heavily as the actor experiences vicarious rewards and costs, and the behavioral plans that exist for a wide variety of situations are based on coordinated team performances, not solitary, individual acts. In especially close relationships, the other becomes an extension of one's own identity, as people come to define themselves partially in terms of their roles in the relationship and their associations with the other. If these interconnections and established patterns are destroyed by separation, divorce, or death, a partial disintegration of identity results (Levinger & Moles, 1979; Weiss, 1975). The interconnectedness is typified by the common lament of those whose long-time spouse has died, "I'm lost without him (her)." In addition to the ripping asunder of parts of one's own identity, the primary support that was available for desired identity images is lost. No longer is a significant other able to aid in coping with the stresses of life, including the most dramatic stress of the partner's own loss.

SELF-PROTECTIVE AND SELF-ASSERTIVE MODES OF COPING

The prior sections describe three major categories of activities that permit people to assess and cope with attacks on their identities: examining information, constructing explanations for the problem, and employing strategic activities. As noted at the outset, feedback loops are presumed to link the categories. Phrased differently, the activities that occur in one of the areas are influenced by the activities in the other areas (e.g., finding a supportive audience increases the likelihood that self-reaffirming information and explanations will result). The evaluative implications for the self in one category appear to carry over to the others. A major link between the categories is presumed to be the self-identification outcome expectations that result from the initial resistance. Higher self-identification outcome expectations generate little or no stress and activities (in all categories) that reaffirm desired identity images. Lower self-identification outcome expectations generate greater stress and activities that are less likely to reaffirm desired identity images (e.g., preoccupation with self-liabilities, internalizing blame, retreating from others and losing the possibility of support). These interrelated activities may even be described heuristically in terms of general modes or styles of coping, in which people act either assertively (fight) or protectively (freeze or flight) to attacks on their identitites.

Assertive versus protective styles of interaction have been noted by several theorists. Thibaut and Kelley (1959) distinguished between people who are oriented toward reward achievement versus those who are oriented toward cost avoidance. More recently, self-acquisitive versus self-protective presentational styles have been discussed by Arkin (1981), and assertive versus defensive self-presentational strategies have been examined by Tedeschi and Norman (1985). People with an acquisitive or assertive style focus on opportunities for self-affirmation and ways to enhance the self, whereas those with a protective or defensive style are sensitized to potential damage to identity and avoid risks that could jeopardize the self.

It is proposed here that when resistance produces moderate to high self-identification outcome expectations, people advance strategically against the problem. The mode of coping is an assertive one that promotes identity and resists the impediment. Further, the tendency for self-assertion is stronger to the extent that the potential gains are more salient relative to the potential losses. In contrast, when assessment produces low self-identification outcome expectations, people freeze or retreat strategically from the threat. Instead of mounting an offense, they are on the defense and engage in behaviors that allow them to protect their identity as best they can given the perceived difficulty (Schlenker & Leary, 1982a, 1985). Their counterattacks are weak or nonexistent, they lower their self-evaluations in response to the threat, and they withdraw from social interactions in which their desired identity images might be rejected by others. The tendency for self-protection is stronger to the extent that the potential losses are more salient relative to the potential gains. These patterns can be situationally induced and they also appear to represent generalized styles of interaction on which individual differences can be observed.

The Self-Protective Style

As a personality constellation, the self-protective style is exemplified by people who are chronically high in social anxiety or depression. The self-identification approach suggests that the behaviors associated with high social anxiety and depression are the ultimate consequence of low self-identification outcome expectations. Low expectations generate negative affect and attempts to withdraw from the difficult situation. If the situation cannot be avoided, people become locked in assessments of self, situation, audience, and the problem. Their minds race with thoughts about the unreachable goal and their problems in attaining it; they become self-focused, continually reexamining their limitations. The combination of cognitive withdrawal and self-preoccupation produces distraction and interferes with social performance. Information processing declines in effectiveness, reducing sensitivity to ongoing events, and self-monitoring and self-control weaken, allowing undesired behaviors (e.g., signs of nervousness, speech errors) to leak through their guard (see Schlenker & Leary, 1982a, for elaboration of the above points). Indeed, high social anxiety is associated with signs of nervousness and lessened self-control, including fidgeting, self-manipulation (playing with one's hair, clothes, etc.), perspiring, and the appearance of tension (Cheek & Buss, 1981; Leary, 1983; Pilkonis, 1977; Schlenker & Leary, 1982a; Slivken & Buss, 1984; Zimbardo, 1977). In addition, people who are socially anxious avoid situations that portend self-presentational difficulties and prematurely leave such situations when they are encountered (Brown, 1970; Brown & Garland, 1971; Cheek & Buss, 1981; Pilkonis, 1977; Twentyman & McFall, 1975; Zimbardo, 1977).

Under these stressful social conditions, people make the best of a difficult situation by entering a protective self-presentational mode that is designed not to achieve major gains but to avoid blatant losses for identity (see Schlenker & Leary, 1985). They limit their participation and present themselves as innocuously but pleasantly as possible. One of the most obvious indications that a person feels socially anxious is that he or she does not participate fully in the interaction. People who are highly anxious in interpersonal settings are less likely to initiate conversations with others, speak less often, talk for a lower percentage of the time, take longer to respond, and are less likely to break silences in conversations (Arkowitz, Lichtenstein, McGovern, & Hines, 1975; Borkovek, Fleischmann, & Caputo, 1973; Cheek & Buss, 1981; Glasgow & Arkowitz, 1975; Leary, Knight, & Johnson, in press; Murray, 1971; Pilkonis, 1977; Slivken & Buss, 1984). Further, the content of their limited participation becomes altered. They respond in ways that permit them to remain engaged in conversation while contributing as little substantive information as possible, such as by asking questions and using contentless utterances that acknowledge having received information, and by avoiding factual topics that might reveal their ignorance (Leary *et al.*, in press). They disclose minimal information about the self, present the self more cautiously and less positively, and are less likely to assert unique qualities that draw attention to the self (Leary, Barnes, & Grieble, 1985; Post, Wittmaier, & Radin, 1978). And, they engage in a passive yet pleasant interaction style that avoids disagreement, such as by smiling pleasantly, seeming to listen attentively, and agreeing with others (Natale, Entin, & Jaffe, 1979; Pilkonis, 1977; Slivken & Buss, 1984). In combination, these activities place few demands on their diminished social capacities and minimize the likelihood of major losses for identity. At the clinical extreme, the self-protective style may result in trying to shut off all external stimulation and stress through extreme withdrawal, as in the case of catatonia.

The Self-Assertive Style

In contrast to the self-protective style, the self-assertive style is characterized by higher self-identification outcome expectations and a focus on rewarding opportunities. Although there is less research on the self-assertive style than on its opposite, it is reasonable to suggest that it is associated with dispositional variables that (a) promote self-positivity and beliefs of high self-efficacy, such as high self-esteem, internal control, and perhaps needs for achievement; (b) reduce sensitivity to possible failure, such as low fear of failure and low fear of negative evaluation; and (c) place a more balanced perspective on one's performances, such that any particular performance is regarded as only one element in an on-going series rather than an event of crucial diagnostic importance for identity (e.g., lower needs for approval would partially fall into this category, although no existing personality variables seem to describe the dimension directly).

The self-assertive style will normally increase the chances of successfully coping with impediments to identity. Problematic events are more likely to be regarded as challenges rather than threats, counterattacks will be mounted, activities designed to strengthen identity will occur, and support will be sought and probably received from family and friends.

When carried to the extreme, however, even the self-assertive style can lose effectiveness and create interpersonal problems for one's identity. The clinical extreme of an abnormally assertive style seems to be the paranoid personality. Paranoids are typically male, older (median age of 50), from higher educational and socioeconomic backgrounds, from families that are more authoritarian and prone to stress superiority, and, as children, were described as more aloof, seclusive, mistrustful, stubborn, and resentful of authority (Coleman, 1964). These patterns increase the likelihood that the paranoid will have developed high standards for achievement, a desire to view the self as superior and to construct an overly inflated set of identity images, seeking support and consolation from imagined audiences and those who agree with his opinions and are willing to affirm his importance. By middle age, the inevitable frustrations of life mount as he finds the aspirations of youth unmatched by actual achievements. A major loss for identity, such as a failure to receive an expected promotion or the actual loss of his job, can trigger a crisis.

The response is a counterattack and the attempt to strengthen and assert his desired identity. Inflated self-appraisals and high needs for achievement appear to contribute to his regarding the problem as something that can and will be overcome, as he continues to hold reasonably high self-identification outcome expectations in the face of problems that raise questions in the mind of the community at large. Given his tendencies toward aloofness, mistrust, and stubbornness, he becomes belligerent, argumentative, and intransigent when others do not seem to show the proper deference to his assertions. The lack of consensual validation is readily blamed on their unperceptiveness, lack of intelligence, or ulterior motives. A rift is produced between him and others, as he gains a reputation for being hostile and odd, and begins to be excluded from conversations and confidences. The systematic exclusion serves to confirm his suspicions that others are conspiring against him, and they become ready targets to blame for his troubles. The perceived conspiracy also serves as evidence of his prominence, because only an important person could marshall the concerted efforts of so many foes.

He seeks out others he believes he can impress with his delusions of self-importance, such as those in low-status positions, while building a wall between himself and the rest of the community. Events are systematically interpreted in ways that support his interpretations, making even innocuous incidents appear to validate his identity. For example, if he wakes up in the morning with a slight headache, he may report being the target of a grandiose scheme against him in which sophisticated laser rays were being shot at his bed while he slept. Often, the paranoid is merely regarded by others as the crotchety, weird old guy who should be avoided. Occasionally, however, his counterattacks may erupt into headlines as he finally decides to terminate his problems by disposing of the conspirators.

SUMMARY

The self-identification approach proposes that people attempt to construct and maintain desired identity images, in both their own minds and in their social environments. Impediments to the construction or maintenance of desired images produce a process of resistance that engages (a) an examination of relevant information about the self, situation, and audience, (b) the construction of an explanation of the difficulty that defines the problem, and (c) strategic activities to deal with the problem, including strategies that attempt to counterattack against the problem, to strengthen identity through compensation, and to gain support for self from others. These activities serve to assess and to cope with the impediment.

The process of resistance to attack generates a self-identification outcome expectation, which is the perceived likelihood that desired identity images can be preserved despite the impediment. These expectations influence the course of subsequent resistance. Higher expectations result in a self-reaffirming examination of information, self-serving explanations of the problem, and more effective strategic activities. These self-assertive activities make it likely that the self will emerge victoriously from the attack. Indeed, it is argued that impediments will often strengthen desired images, making them more accessible in memory and more resistant to subsequent attack.

In contrast, lower expectations result in a self-demeaning examination of information, the internalization of blame for problems, and less effective strategic activities. Self-protective activities are engaged that, at best, try to minimize the damage to identity. It is proposed that social stress is the consequence of lower self-identification outcome expectations. Further, the magnitude of the stress is a direct function of (a) lower self-identification outcome expectations (i.e., a greater perceived probability of damage to identity), and (b) perceptions of greater potential damage, based on the importance of the jeopardized images and the extent to which personal or social standards are not met. Stress thus represents the interplay between events that may damage identity and the actor's perceived resources (personal and environmental) in warding off the attack.

ACKNOWLEDGMENTS

Thanks are extended to C. R. Snyder for his insightful comments on an earlier version of this chapter.

REFERENCES

Adler, A. (1939). *Social interest.* New York: Putnam.
Anderson, C. A. (1983). Motivational and performance deficits in interpersonal settings: The effect of attributional style. *Journal of Personality and Social Psychology, 45,* 1136–1147.
Arkin, R. M. (1981). Self-presentational styles. In J. T. Tedeschi (Ed.), *Impression management theory and social psychological research* (pp. 311–333). New York: Academic Press.
Arkin, R. M., Appelman, A. J., & Burger, J. M. (1980). Social anxiety, self-presentation, and the self-serving bias in causal attribution. *Journal of Personality and Social Psychology, 38,* 23–35.
Arkin, R. M., Kolditz, T. A., & Kolditz, K. K. (1983). Attributions of the test-anxious student: Self-assessments in the classroom. *Personality and Social Psychology Bulletin, 9,* 271–280.
Arkowitz, H., Lichtenstein, E., McGovern, K., & Hines, P. (1975). The behavioral assessment of social competence in males. *Behavior Therapy, 6,* 3–13.
Austin, J. L. (1961). *Philosophical papers.* New York: Oxford University Press.
Backman, C. W. (1983). Towards an interdisciplinary social psychology. In L. Berkowitz (Ed.), *Advances in experimental social psychology* (Vol. 16, pp. 219–261). New York: Academic Press.
Backman, C. W. (1985). Identity, self-presentation, and the resolution of moral dilemmas: Towards a social psychological theory of moral behavior. In B. R. Schlenker (Ed.), *The self and social life* (pp. 261–289). New York: McGraw-Hill.
Bandura, A. (1969). *Principles of behavior modification.* New York: Holt, Rinehart, & Winston.
Bandura, A. (1977). Self-efficacy: Toward a unifying theory of behavioral change. *Psychological Review, 84,* 191–215.
Bandura, A. (1982). The self and mechanisms of agency. In J. Suls (Ed.), *Psychological perspectives on the self* (Vol. 1). Hillsdale, NJ: Erlbaum.
Baumeister, R. F., & Jones, E. E. (1978). When self-presentation is constrained by the target's prior knowledge: Consistency and compensation. *Journal of Personality and Social Psychology, 36,* 608–618.

Bem, D. J. (1972). Self-perception theory. In L. Berkowitz (Ed.), *Advances in experimental social psychology* (Vol. 6). New York: Academic Press.

Borkovec, T. D., Fleischmann, D. J., & Caputo, J. A. (1973). The measurement of anxiety in an analogue social situation. *Journal of Consulting and Clinical Psychology, 44,* 157–161.

Brewin, C. B. (1985). Depression and causal attributions: What is their relation? *Psychological Bulletin, 98,* 297–309.

Brodt, S. E., & Zimbardo, P. G. (1981). Modifying shyness-related social behavior through symptom misattribution. *Journal of Personality and Social Psychology, 41,* 437–449.

Brown, B. R. (1970). Face-saving following experimentally induced embarrassment. *Journal of Experimental Social Psychology, 6,* 255–271.

Brown, B. R., & Garland, H. (1971). The effects of incompetency, audience acquaintanceship, and anticipated valuative feedback on face-saving behavior. *Journal of Experimental Social Psychology, 7,* 490–502.

Buss, A. H. (1980). *Self-consciousness and social anxiety.* San Francisco: Freeman.

Carver, C. S. (1979). A cybernetic model of self-attention processes. *Journal of Personality and Social Psychology, 37,* 1251–1281.

Carver, C. S., & Scheier, M. F. (1981). *Attention and self-regulation: A control-theory approach to human behavior.* New York: Springer-Verlag.

Carver, C. S., & Scheier, M. F. (1985). Aspects of self and the control of behavior. In B. R. Schlenker (Ed.), *The self and social life* (pp. 146–174). New York: McGraw-Hill.

Cheek, J. M., & Busch, C. M. (1981). The influence of shyness on loneliness in a new situation. *Personality and Social Psychology Bulletin, 7,* 572–577.

Cheek, J. M., & Buss, A. H. (1981). Shyness and sociability. *Journal of Personality and Social Psychology, 41,* 330–339.

Clark, J. V., & Arkowitz, H. (1975). Social anxiety and self-evaluation of interpersonal performance. *Psychological Reports, 36,* 211–221.

Coleman, J. C. (1964). *Abnormal psychology and modern life* (3rd ed.). Glenview, IL: Scott & Foresman.

Collins, B. E., & Hoyt, M. F. (1972). Personal responsibility-for-consequences: An integration and extension of the "forced compliance" literature. *Journal of Experimental Social Psychology, 8,* 558–593.

Coyne, J. C., & Lazarus, R. S. (1980). Cognitive style, stress perception, and coping. In I. L. Kutash & L. B. Schlesinger (Eds.), *Handbook of stress and anxiety: Contemporary knowledge, theory, and treatment* (pp. 144–158). San Francisco: Jossey-Bass.

Darby, B. W., & Schlenker, B. R. (in press). Children's understanding of social anxiety. *Developmental Psychology.*

D'Arcy, E. (1963). *Human acts.* New York: Oxford University Press.

Davis, D., & Brock, T. C. (1972). Paradoxical instigation of self-criticism by inordinate praise. *Proceedings of the 80th Annual Convention of the American Psychological Association,* 191–192.

DeGree, C. E., & Snyder, C. R. (1985). Adler's psychology (of use) today: Personal history of traumatic life events as a self-handicapping strategy. *Journal of Personality and Social Psychology, 48,* 1512–1519.

Derry, P. A., & Kuiper, N. A. (1981). Schematic processing and self-reference in clinical depression. *Journal of Abnormal Psychology, 49,* 286–297.

Dutton, D. G. (1972). Effect of feedback parameters on congruency versus positivity effects in reactions to personal evaluations. *Journal of Personality and Social Psychology, 24,* 366–371.

Duval, S., & Wicklund, R. A. (1972). *A theory of objective self-awareness.* New York: Academic Press.

Epstein, S. (1973). The self-concept revisited: Or a theory of a theory. *American Psychologist, 28,* 404–416.

Erikson, E. H. (1959). Identity and the life cycle. In G. S. Klein (Ed.), *Psychological issues* (pp. 1–171). New York: International Universities Press.

Fenigstein, A. (1979). Self-consciousness, self-attention, and social interaction. *Journal of Personality and Social Psychology, 37,* 75–86.

Fenigstein, A., Scheier, M. F., & Buss, A. H. (1975). Public and private self-consciousness: Assessment and theory. *Journal of Consulting and Clinical Psychology, 43,* 522–527.

Folkman, S. (1984). Personal control and stress and coping processes: A theoretical analysis. *Journal of Personality and Social Psychology, 46,* 839–852.

Folkman, S., Shaefer, C., & Lazarus, R. S. (1979). Cognitive processes as mediators of stress and coping. In V. Hamilton & D. M. Warburton (Eds.), *Human stress and cognition: An information-processing approach.* London: Wiley.

Frey, D. (1978). Reactions to success and failure in public and private situations. *Journal of Experimental Social Psychology, 14,* 172–179.

Frey, D. (1981). The effect of negative feedback about oneself and cost of information on preference for information about the source of this feedback. *Journal of Experimental Social Psychology, 17,* 42–50.

Glasgow, R., & Arkowitz, H. (1975). The behavioral assessment of male and female social competence in dyadic heterosexual interactions. *Behavior Therapy, 6,* 488–498.

Goffman, E. (1959). *The presentation of self in everyday life.* New York: Doubleday.

Goffman, E. (1971). *Relations in public.* New York: Basic Books.

Gollwitzer, P. M., & Wicklund, R. A. (1985). Self-symbolizing and the neglect of others' perspectives. *Journal of Personality and Social Psychology, 48,* 702–715.

Gollwitzer, P. M., Wicklund, R. A., & Hilton, J. L. (1982). Admission of failure and symbolic self-completion: Extending Lewinian theory. *Journal of Personality and Social Psychology, 43,* 358–371.

Goode, W. J. (1956). *After divorce.* Glencoe, IL: Free Press.

Gough, H. G., Fioravanti, M., & Lazzari, R. (1983). Some implications of self versus ideal-self congruence on the revised adjective check list. *Journal of Personality and Social Psychology, 44,* 1214–1220.

Greenberg, J., & Pyszczynski, T. (1985). Compensatory self-inflation: A response to the threat of self-regard of failure. *Journal of Personality and Social Psychology, 49,* 273–280.

Greenberg, J., Pyszczynski, T., & Paisley, C. (1984). Effect of extrinsic incentives on use of test anxiety as an anticipatory attributional defense: Playing it cool when the stakes are high. *Journal of Personality and Social Psychology, 47,* 1136–1145.

Greenwald, A. G. (1980). The totalitarian ego: Fabrication and revision of personal history. *American Psychologist, 35,* 603–618.

Greenwald, A. G., & Breckler, S. J. (1985). To whom is the self presented? In B. R. Schlenker (Ed.), *The self and social life* (pp. 126–145). New York: McGraw-Hill.

Greenwald, A. G., & Pratkanis, A. R. (1984). The self. In R. S. Wyer & T. K. Srull (Eds.), *Handbook of social cognition* (Vol. 3, pp. 129–178). Hillsdale, NJ: Erlbaum.

Hammen, C. L., & Peters, S. D. (1978). Interpersonal consequences of depression: Responses to men and women enacting a depressed role. *Journal of Abnormal Psychology, 87,* 322–332.

Harré, R. (1983). Identity projects. In G. M. Breakwell (Ed.), *Threatened identities* (pp. 31–51). New York: Wiley.

Harris, R. N., & Snyder, C. R. (1985). *The role of uncertain self-esteem in self-handicapping.* Mimeographed manuscript, University of Kansas.

Hokanson, J. E., Sacco, W. P., Blumberg, S. R., & Landrum, G. D. (1980). Interpersonal behavior of depressive individuals in a mixed-motive game. *Journal of Abnormal Psychology, 89,* 320–332.

Horney, K. (1945). *Our inner conflicts.* New York: Norton.

Howes, M. J., & Hokanson, J. E. (1979). Conversational and social responses to depressive interpersonal behavior. *Journal of Abnormal Psychology, 88,* 625–634.

Hull, J. G., Levenson, R. W., Young, R. D., & Sher, K. J. (1983). The self-awareness-reducing effects of alcohol consumption. *Journal of Personality and Social Psychology, 44,* 461–473.

Hull, J. G., & Young, R. D. (1983). Self-consciousness, self-esteem, and success-failure as determinants of alcohol consumption in male social drinkers. *Journal of Personality and Social Psychology, 44,* 1097–1109.

Ickes, W., & Layden, M. A. (1978). Attributional styles. In J. H. Harvey, W. Ickes, & R. F. Kidd (Eds.), *New directions in attribution research* (Vol. 2). Hillsdale, NJ: Erlbaum.

James, W. (1890). *The principles of psychology.* New York: Holt.

Jones, E. E., & Berglas, S. (1978). Control of attributions about the self through self-handicapping strategies: The appeal of alcohol and the role of underachievement. *Personality and Social Psychology Bulletin, 4,* 200–206.

Jones, S. C. (1973). Self- and interpersonal evaluations: Esteem theories versus consistency theories. *Psychological Bulletin, 79,* 185–199.

Kanouse, D. E., Gumpert, P., & Canavan-Gumpert, D. (1981). The semantics of praise. In J. H. Harvey, W. Ickes, & R. F. Kidd (Eds.), *New directions in attribution research* (Vol. 3, pp. 97–115). Hillsdale, NJ: Erlbaum.

Kiesler, C. A. (1971). *The psychology of commitment.* New York: Academic Press.

Kuiper, N. A. (1978). Depression and causal attributions for success and failure. *Journal of Personality and Social Psychology, 36,* 236–246.

Kuiper, N. A., Derry, P. A., & MacDonald, M. R. (1982). Self-reference and person perception in depression: A social cognition perspective. In G. Weary & H. Mirels (Eds.), *Integrations of clinical and social psychology* (pp. 79–103). New York: Oxford University Press.

Lake, E. A., & Arkin, R. M. (1985). Reactions to objective and subjective interpersonal evaluation: The influence of social anxiety. *Journal of Social and Clinical Psychology, 3,* 143–160.

Langer, E. J. (1978). Rethinking the role of thought in social interaction. In J. H. Harvey, W. Ickes, & R. F. Kidd (Eds.), *New directions in attribution research* (Vol. 2, pp. 35–58). Hillsdale, NJ: Erlbaum.

Laux, L. (1986). A self-presentational view of coping with stress. In M. H. Appley & R. Trumbull (Eds.), *Dynamics of stress.* New York: Plenum Press.

Lazarus, R. S. (1966). *Psychological stress and the coping process.* New York: McGraw-Hill.

Lazarus, R. S. (1981). The stress and coping paradigm. In C. Eisdorfer, D. Cohen, A. Kleinman, & P. Maxim (Eds.), *Models for clinical psychopathology* (pp. 177–214). New York: Spectrum.

Lazarus, R. S., & Launier, R. (1978). Stress-related transactions between person and environment. In L. A. Pervin & M. Lewis (Eds.), *Perspectives in interactional psychology* (pp. 287–327). New York: Plenum.

Leary, M. R. (1983). *Understanding social anxiety: Social, personality, and clinical perspectives.* Beverly Hills, Sage.

Leary, M. R. (1986). The impact of interactional impediments on social anxiety and self-presentation. *Journal of Experimental Social Psychology, 22,* 122–135.

Leary, M. R., Barnes, B. D., & Grieble, C. (1985, September). *Threats to social- and self-esteem, anxiety and self-presentation.* Paper presented at the meetings of the American Psychological Association, Los Angeles.

Leary, M. R., Knight, P. D., & Johnson, K. A. (in press). Social anxiety and dyadic conversation: A verbal response analysis. *Journal of Social and Clinical Psychology.*

Leary, M. R., & Schlenker, B. R. (1981). The social psychology of shyness. In J. T. Tedeschi (Ed.), *Impression management theory and social psychological research* (pp. 335–358). New York: Academic Press.

Lemert, E. M. (1962). Paranoia and the dynamics of exclusion. *Sociometry, 25,* 2–20.

Levinger, G. (1976). A social psychological perspective on marital dissolution. *Journal of Social Issues, 32,* 21–47.

Levinger, G., & Moles, O. C. (Eds.). (1979). *Divorce and separation: Context, causes and consequences.* New York: Basic Books.

Lewinsohn, P. M., Mischel, W., Chaplin, W., & Barton, R. (1980). Social competence and depression: The role of illusory self-perceptions. *Journal of Abnormal Psychology, 89,* 203–212.

Lundgren, D. C. (1978). Public esteem, self-esteem, and interpersonal stress. *Social Psychology, 41,* 68–73.

Maracek, J., & Mettee, D. R. (1972). Avoidance of continued success as a function of self-esteem, level of esteem certainty and responsibility for success. *Journal of Personality and Social Psychology, 22,* 98–107.

Markham, H. J. (1979). Application of a behavioral model of marriage in predicting relationship satisfaction of couples planning marriage. *Journal of Consulting and Clinical Psychology, 47,* 743–749.

McCrae, R. R. (1984). Situational determinants of coping responses: Loss, threat, and challenge. *Journal of Personality and Social Psychology, 46,* 919–928.

McFarland, C., & Ross, M. (1982). Impact of causal attributions on affective reactions to success and failure. *Journal of Personality and Social Psychology, 43,* 937–946.

Mehlman, R. C., & Snyder, C. R. (1985). Excuse theory: A test of the self-protective role of attributions. *Journal of Personality and Social Psychology, 49,* 994–1001.

Mettee, D. R. (1971). Rejection of unexpected success as a function of the negative consequences of accepting success. *Journal of Personality and Social Psychology, 17,* 287–304.

Mettee, D. R., & Aronson, E. (1974). Affective reactions to appraisals from others. In T. L. Huston (Ed.), *Foundations of interpersonal attraction* (pp. 235–283). New York: Academic Press.

Mills, C. W. (1940). Situated actions and vocabularies of motives. *American Sociological Review, 5,* 904–913.

Murray, D. C. (1971). Talk, silence, and anxiety. *Psychological Bulletin, 75,* 244–260.

Nadich, M., Gargan, M., & Michael, L. (1975). Denial, anxiety, locus of control, and the discrepancy between aspirations and achievements as components of depression. *Journal of Abnormal Psychology, 84,* 1–9.

Natale, M., Entin, E., & Jaffe, J. (1979). Vocal interruptions in dyadic communication as a function of speech and social anxiety. *Journal of Personality and Social Psychology, 37,* 865–878.

Oatley, K., & Bolton, W. (1985). A social-cognitive theory of depression in reaction to life events. *Psychological Review, 92,* 372–388.

O'Banion, K., & Arkowitz, H. (1977). Social anxiety and selective memory for affective information about the self. *Social Behavior and Personality, 5,* 321–328.

Page, J. D. (1975). *Psychopathology: The science of understanding deviance* (2nd ed.). Chicago, IL: Aldine.

Peterson, C., Schwartz, S. M., & Seligman, M. E. P. (1981). Self-blame and depressive symptoms. *Journal of Personality and Social Psychology, 41,* 253–259.

Pietromonaco, P. R., & Markus, H. (1985). The nature of negative thoughts in depression. *Journal of Personality and Social Psychology, 48,* 799–807.

Pilkonis, P. A. (1977). The behavioral consequences of shyness. *Journal of Personality, 45,* 596–611.

Post, A. L., Wittmaier, B. C., & Radin, M. E. (1978). Self-disclosure as a function of state and trait anxiety. *Journal of Clinical and Counseling Psychology, 46,* 12–19.

Pyszczynski, T., & Greenberg, J. (1985). Depression and preference for self-focusing stimuli after success and failure. *Journal of Personality and Social Psychology, 49,* 1066–1075.

Pyszczynski, T., Greenberg, J., & LaPrelle, J. (1985). Social comparison after success and failure: Biased search for information consistent with a self-serving conclusion. *Journal of Experimental Social Psychology, 21,* 195–211.

Rehm, L. P., & Marston, A. R. (1968). Reduction of social anxiety through modification of self-reinforcement. *Journal of Consulting and Clinical Psychology, 32,* 565–574.

Rizley, R. (1978). Depression and distortion in the attribution of causality. *Journal of Abnormal Psychology, 87,* 32–48.

Rosenberg, M. (1979). *Conceiving the self.* New York: Basic Books.

Sarason, I. G. (1976). Anxiety and self-preoccupation. In I. G. Sarason & C. D. Spielberger (Eds.), *Stress and anxiety* (Vol. 2). Washington, DC: Hemisphere.

Sarson, I. G. (1978). The test anxiety scale: Concept and research. In C. D. Spielberger & I. G. Sara9son (Eds.), *Stress and anxiety* (Vol. 5, pp. 193–216). New York: Wiley.

Sarnoff, I., & Zimbardo, P. G. (1961). Anxiety, fear, and social affiliation. *Journal of Abnormal and Social Psychology, 62,* 356–363.

Sattler, J. M. (1965). A theoretical, developmental, and clinical investigation of embarrassment. *Genetic Psychology Monographs, 71,* 19–59.

Scheier, M. R., & Carver, C. S. (1980). Private and public self-attention, resistance to change, and dissonance reduction. *Journal of Personality and Social Psychology, 39,* 390–405.

Schlenker, B. R. (1975). Self-presentation: Managing the impression of consistency when reality interferes with self-enhancement. *Journal of Personality and Social Psychology, 32,* 1030–1037.

Schlenker, B. R. (1978). Attitudes as actions: Social identity theory and consumer research. In K. Hunt (Ed.), *Advances in consumer research* (Vol. 5). Chicago, IL: Association for Consumer Research.

Schlenker, B. R. (1980). *Impression management. The self-concept, social identity, and interpersonal relations.* Monterey, CA: Brooks/Cole (Distributed by Krieger Publishers, Melbourne, FL).

Schlenker, B. R. (1981, August). *Self-presentation: A conceptualization and model.* Paper presented at the 89th Annual Meetings of the American Psychological Association, Los Angeles, CA.

Schlenker, B. R. (1982). Translating actions into attitudes: An identity-analytic approach to the explanation of social conduct. In L. Berkowitz (Ed.), *Advances in experimental social psychology* (Vol. 15, pp. 193–247). New York: Academic Press.

Schlenker, B. R. (1984). Identities, identifications, and relationships. In V. Derlega (Ed.), *Communication, intimacy and close relationships* (pp. 71–104). New York: Academic Press.

Schlenker, B. R. (1985). Identity and self-identification. In B. R. Schlenker (Ed.), *The self and social life* (pp. 65–99). New York: McGraw-Hill.

Schlenker, B. R. (in press). Self-identification: Towards an integration of the private and public self. In R. Baumeister (Ed.), *Public self and private self.* New York: Springer-Verlag.

Schlenker, B. R., & Goldman, H. J. (1982). Attitude change as a self-presentation tactic following attitude-consistent behavior: Effects of choice and role. *Social Psychology Quarterly, 45,* 92–99.

Schlenker, B. R., Hallam, J. R., & McCown, N. E. (1983). Motives and social evaluation: Actor-observer differences in the delineation of motives for a beneficial act. *Journal of Experimental Social Psychology, 19,* 254–273.

Schlenker, B. R., & Leary, M. R. (1982a). Social anxiety and self-presentation: A conceptualization and model. *Psychological Bulletin, 92,* 641–669.

Schlenker, B. R., & Leary, M. R. (1982b). Audiences' reactions to self-enhancing, self-denigrating, and accurate self-presentations. *Journal of Experimental Social Psychology, 18,* 89–104.

Schlenker, B. R., & Leary, M. R. (1985). Social anxiety and communication about the self. *Journal of Language and Social Psychology, 4,* 171–192.

Schlenker, B. R., & Miller, R. S. (1977). Egocentrism in groups: Self-serving biases or logical information processing? *Journal of Personality and Social Psychology, 35,* 755–764.

Schlenker, B. R., Miller, R. S., & Leary, M. R. (1983). Self-presentation as a function of the validity and quality of past performance. *Representative Research in Social Psychology, 13,* 2–14.

Schlenker, B. R., & Riess, M. (1979). Self-presentation of attitudes following commitment to proattitudinal behavior. *Human Communication Research, 5,* 325–334.

Schlenker, B. R., & Schlenker, P. A. (1975). Reactions following counterattitudinal behavior which produces positive consequences. *Journal of Personality and Social Psychology, 31,* 962–971.

Scott, M. B., & Lyman, S. M. (1968). Accounts. *American Sociological Review, 33,* 46–62.

Secord, P. F., & Backman, C. W. (1965). Interpersonal approach to personality. In B. H. Maher, (Ed.), *Progress in experimental personality research* (Vol. 2, pp. 91–125). New York: Academic Press.

Seligman, M. E. P., Abramson, L. Y., Semmel, A., & von Baeyer, C. (1979). Depressive attributional style. *Journal of Abnormal Psychology, 88,* 242–247.

Shaver, K. G., Payne, M. R., Bloch, R. M., Burch, M. C., Davis, M. S., & Shean, G. D. (1984). Logic in distortion: Attributions of causality and responsibility among schizophrenics. *Journal of Social and Clinical Psychology, 2,* 193–214.

Sicoly, F., & Ross, M. (1977). Facilitation of ego-biased attributions by means of self-serving observer feedback. *Journal of Personality and Social Psychology, 35,* 734–741.

Slivken, K. E., & Buss, A. H. (1984). Misattribution and speech anxiety. *Journal of Personality and Social Psychology, 47,* 396–402.

Smith, R. E., & Sarason, I. G. (1975). Social anxiety and the evaluation of negative interpersonal feedback. *Journal of Consulting and Clinical Psychology, 43,* 429.

Smith, T. W., Ingram, R. E., & Brehm, S. S. (1983). Social anxiety, anxious self-preoccupation, and recall of self-relevant information. *Journal of Personality and Social Psychology, 44,* 1276–1283.

Smith, T. W., Snyder, C. R., & Handelsman, M. M. (1982). On the self-serving function of an academic wooden leg: Test anxiety as a self-handicapping strategy. *Journal of Personality and Social Psychology, 42,* 314–321.

Snyder, C. R. (1985). The excuse: An amazing grace? In B. R. Schlenker (Ed.), *The self and social life* (pp. 235–260). New York: McGraw-Hill.

Snyder, C. R., & Clair, M. S. (1977). Does insecurity breed acceptance?: Effects of trait and situational insecurity on acceptance of positive and negative diagnostic feedback. *Journal of Consulting and Clinical Psychology, 45,* 843–850.

Snyder, C. R., Higgins, R. L., & Stucky, R. J. (1983). *Excuses: Masquerades in search of grace.* New York: Wiley-Interscience.

Snyder, C. R., & Smith, T. W. (1982). Symptoms as self-handicapping stratgies: The virtues of old wine in a new bottle. In G. Weary & H. L. Mirels (Eds.), *Integrations of clinical and social psychology* (pp. 104–127). New York: Oxford University Press.

Snyder, M. (1984). When belief creates reality. In L. Berkowitz (Ed.), *Advances in experimental social psychology* (Vol. 18, pp. 247–305). New York: Academic Press.

Snyder, M. L., Kleck, R. E., Strenta, A., & Mentzer, S. J. (1979). Avoidance of the handicapped: An attributional ambiguity analysis. *Journal of Personality and Social Psychology, 37,* 2297–2307.

Snyder, M. L., Stephan, W. G., & Rosenfield, D. (1978). Attributional egotism. In J. H. Harvey, W. Ickes, & R. F. Kidd (Eds.), *New directions in attribution research* (Vol. 2). Hillsdale, NJ: Erlbaum.

Spivak, R., & Schlenker, B. R. (1986). *The impact of self-presentations on self-appraisals: Self-inference or self-affirmation?* Mimeographed manuscript, University of Florida (Gainesville).

Steiner, I. D. (1968). Reactions to adverse and favorable evaluations of oneself. *Journal of Personality, 36,* 553–564.

Strack, S., Blaney, P. H., Ganellen, R. J., & Coyne, J. C. (1985). Pessimistic self-preoccupation, performance deficits, and depression. *Journal of Personality and Social Psychology, 49,* 1076–1085.

Swann, W. B., Jr. (1983). Self-verification: Bringing social reality into harmony with the self. In J. Suls & A. G. Greenwald (Eds.), *Psychological perspectives on the self* (Vol. 2). Hillsdale, NJ: Erlbaum.

Swann, W. B., Jr. (1985). The self as architect of social reality. In B. R. Schlenker (Ed.), *The self and social life.* New York: McGraw-Hill.

Swann, W. B., Jr., & Hill, C. A. (1982). When our identities are mistaken: Reaffirming self-conceptions through social interaction. *Journal of Personality and Social Psychology, 43,* 59–66.

Swann, W. B., Jr., & Predmore, S. C. (1985). Intimates as agents of social support: Sources of consolation or despair? *Journal of Personality and Social Psychology, 49,* 1609–1617.

Swann, W. B., Jr., & Read, S. J. (1981). Self-verification processes: How we sustain our self-conceptions. *Journal of Experimental Social Psychology, 17,* 351–372.

Tabachnik, N., Crocker, J., & Alloy, L. B. (1983). Depression, social comparison, and the false consensus effect. *Journal of Personality and Social Psychology, 45,* 688–699.

Tedeschi, J. T., & Norman, N. (1985). Social power, self-presentation, and the self. In B. R. Schlenker (Ed.), *The self and social life* (pp. 293–322). New York: McGraw-Hill.

Tedeschi, J. T., & Riess, M. (1981). Predicaments and impression management. In C. Antaki (Ed.), *Ordinary explanations of social behavior.* London: Academic Press.

Tedeschi, J. T., & Riordan, C. A. (1981). In J. T. Tedeschi (Ed.), *Impression management theory and social psychological research* (pp. 223–244). New York: Academic Press.

Teichman, Y. (1978). Affiliative reaction in different kinds of threat situations. In C. D. Spielberger & I. G. Sarason (Eds.), *Stress and anxiety* (Vol. 5). New York: Wiley.

Tetlock, P. E. (1985). Toward an intuitive politician model of attribution processes. In B. R. Schlenker (Ed.), *The self and social life* (pp. 203–234). New York: McGraw-Hill.

Tetlock, P. E., & Levi, A. (1982). Attribution bias: On the inconclusiveness of the cognition-motivation debate. *Journal of Experimental Social Psychology, 18,* 68–88.

Thibaut, J. W., & Kelley, H. H. (1959). *The social psychology of groups.* New York: Wiley.

Twentyman, C. T., & McFall, R. M. (1975). Behavioral training of social skills in shy males. *Journal of Consulting and Clinical Psychology, 43,* 384–395.

Verhaeghe, H. (1976). Mistreating other persons through simple discrepant role playing: Dissonance arousal or response contagion. *Journal of Personality and Social Psychology, 34,* 125–137.

Weary Bradley, C. G. (1978). Self-serving biases in the attribution process: A reexamination of the fact or fiction question. *Journal of Personality and Social Psychology, 36,* 56–71.

Weiss, R. S. (1975). *Marital separation.* New York: Basic Books.

Wells, L. E., & Marwell, G. (1976). *Self-esteem: Its conceptualization and measurement.* Beverly Hills, CA: Sage Publications.

Wicklund, R. A. (1975). Objective self-awareness. In L. Berkowitz (Ed.), *Advances in experimental social psychology* (Vol. 8, pp. 233–275). New York: Academic Press.

Wicklund, R. A., & Gollwitzer, P. M. (1981). Symbolic self-completion, attempted influence, and self-deprecation. *Basic and Applied Social Psychology, 2,* 89–114.

Wicklund, R. A., & Gollwitzer, P. M. (1982). *Symbolic self-completion.* Hillsdale, NJ: Erlbaum.

Wicklund, R. A., & Gollwitzer, P. M. (1983). A motivational factor in self-report validity. In J. Suls & A. G. Greenwald (Eds.), *Psychological perspectives on the self* (Vol. 2). Hillsdale, NJ: Erlbaum.

Wine, J. D. (1971). Test anxiety and direction of attention. *Psychological Bulletin, 76,* 92–104.

Wortman, C. B., Costanzo, P. R., & Witt, T. R. (1973). Effects of anticipated performance on the attributions of causality to self and others. *Journal of Personality and Social Psychology, 27,* 372–381.

Wyer, R. S., Jr., & Frey, D. (1983). The effects of feedback about self and others on the recall and judgments of feedback-relevant information. *Journal of Experimental Social Psychology, 19,* 540–559.

Youngren, M. A., & Lewinsohn, P. M. (1980). The functional relation between depression and problematic interpersonal behavior. *Journal of Abnormal Psychology, 89,* 333–341.

Zimbardo, P. G. (1977). *Shyness: What it is and what to do about it.* New York: Jove.

12

Coping with the Prospect of Social Disapproval
Strategies and Sequelae

ANN H. BAUMGARDNER and ROBERT M. ARKIN

Man is the only animal that blushes. Or needs to.

Mark Twain,
Pudd'nhead Wilson's New Calendar, Chapter 20

Samuel Clemens's observation about the human condition is both insightful and amusing. Embarrassment is an all too familiar human emotion, and one that reveals a great deal about the nature of social relations. This chapter is not about embarrassment. Yet the fact that it exists, and can run so deep, does set the stage for the present analysis of the role of disapproval in social exchange.

The motive to avoid social disapproval permeats the literature in social and clinical phenomena. The work on loneliness (Peplau & Perlman, 1982), social reticence (Phillips, 1968), shyness (Jones, Cheek, & Buss, 1986), communication apprehension (Daly & McCrosky, 1984), social anxiety (Leary, 1983), fear of failure (Birney, Burdick, & Teevan, 1969), excuses (Snyder, Higgins, & Stucky, 1983) and other topics share, at least implicitly, a focus on the human need to avoid disapproval.

ANN H. BAUMGARDNER • Department of Psychology, Virginia Polytechnic Institute and State University, Blacksburg, VA, 24061.   ROBERT M. ARKIN • Department of Psychology, 210 McAlester Hall, University of Missouri-Columbia, Columbia, MO 65211.

The purpose of the present chapter is to suggest that concerns over engendering disapproval produce some distinctive styles of coping. Moreover we suggest that individuals adopt a more active or a more passive sort of coping style largely as a function of their confidence in self.

We organize coping tactics into two general and sometimes overlapping categories of responses. In the first section of the chapter, we focus on maneuvers intended to *manage* disapproval once it has occurred. These coping strategies may be viewed as rather passive and reactive in that the individual must deal with disapproval that has already occurred or is ongoing. In the second section, we turn our attention to behavioral strategies, which are more proactive in that these strategies are intended to *alter the course* of evaluation. By manipulating various features of the context in this manner, so that disapproval seems less likely to occur, individuals may circumvent the painful consequences of social rejection.

The distinction drawn between coping strategies here is not new. It approximates earlier distinctions (cf. Rothbaum, Weisz, & Snyder, 1982) such as the one drawn between primary and secondary control (cf. Arkin & Baumgardner, 1986). The first cluster includes attempts to adapt to threatening circumstances; often these maneuvers are cognitive rather than overtly behavioral (e.g., denial of disapproval, denying the personal relevance of disapproval, degrading the source of disapproval). The second cluster includes attempts to manipulate circumstances in an attempt to avert negative feedback altogether; these actions are decidedly more behavioral. Naturally, the distinction between the two categories of responses is slippery and is drawn here more as a heuristic device than as a strict dichotomy.

MANAGING THE IMPACT OF DISAPPROVAL

Most people are motivated to perceive themselves in the most favorable light possible, and will go to some lengths to convince themselves and others that this is an accurate self-conception (Arkin & Baumgardner, 1986). Individuals can accomplish this, in part, by simply denying unfavorable self-relevant information (Arkin, Cooper, & Kolditz, 1981; Bradley, 1978; Zuckerman, 1979). In this section, we address the processes by which individuals attempt to lessen the impact of social disapproval. Specifically, we focus on various ways in which individuals selectively attend to and distort the meaning of social feedback that presents potentially damaging implications for their self-conception.

Our perusal of the literature reveals three response domains clearly related to managing the impact of social disapproval. First, and perhaps on a most basic level, one can simply deny the potential of social disapproval. Here the individual attempts to regulate the salience of social disapproval by suppressing attention to information indicating the imminence of it. However, once social disapproval is clearly imminent, the individual may shift fields to deny the personal relevance or importance of potential disapproval. Finally, an attempt to discredit or degrade the source of social rejection would likely be turned to last.

These denial processes represent rather loose and overlapping categories. Nevertheless, the hierarchy seems sensible. For instance, merely denying the likelihood of social disapproval requires the least effort (cf. Breznitz, 1983). When the likelihood of social disapproval cannot be ignored, however, the individual may proceed to the second and third strategies (i.e., attempt to decrease the legitimacy of social disapproval by claiming it is unimportant and/or that the sources are not credible).

Self-Deception: Denying the Existence of Disapproval Cues

The literature on self-esteem reveals a pervasive theme: individuals are frequently quite optimistic, indeed overly optimistic, about their state in life (e.g., Myers & Ridl, 1979). For instance, people tend to assume more personal responsibility for successful than for failing performances (Bradley, 1978; Zuckerman, 1979), and also tend to overestimate past successes and underestimate past failures (e.g., Lewinsohn, Mischel, Chaplin, & Barton, 1980). In a similar way, people are overly optimistic about their future performances. They deny the prospect of negative events in the future in an apparent preference to view their prospects as rosier than warranted (e.g., Langer & Roth, 1975; Ross, Green, & House, 1977).

Predicting the Future. Weinstein (1980) found that college students were highly optimistic about a variety of potential life events. They overestimated the probability of personally experiencing a variety of positive life events (e.g., "your work recognized with award") and underestimated the probability of personally experiencing a variety of negative ones (e.g., "being fired from a job"). Snyder and Fromkin (1980) argue that when confronted with the prospect of negative information, people generally tend to view it as less applicable to themselves than to others. This illusion of uniqueness allows individuals to believe that they possess a more positive future than their "average" brethren (see also Snyder, 1978).

In a related investigation, Quattrone and Tversky (1984) found that individuals may also attempt to deceive themselves in order to maintain a heightened illusion of personal control over future threats. They had subjects immerse their arms in a chest of circulating ice cold water before and after they engaged in physical exercise. Subjects who had learned in between trials that a long life expectancy was associated with greater tolerance increased their length of immersion. There was also evidence that subjects were unaware of the self-deceptive nature of their attempt to foster a diagnosis of longevity.

Research on denial, tangentially related to such tacit self-deception, stems from health psychology. In particular, researchers have found that individuals confronted with traumatic life events may engage in self-deceptive cognitive maneuvers. Taylor and her colleagues (Taylor, 1983; Taylor Lichtman, & Wood, 1984; Wood, Taylor, & Lichtman, 1985) investigated coping processes of cancer victims. They found that women underestimate the probability of their cancer recurring and, at the same time, seem to believe they have a greater control over the progress of the disease than might be logically justifiable. In sum, an illusion of personal control (where relatively little realistically exists) seems to go hand-in-hand with denial of future negative events.

Avoiding Self-Focus. Under some circumstances, individuals may also deny or minimize the existence of the potential of social disapproval and other negative life events. Several writers in psychology (Erdelyi, 1974; Martin, 1985; Sackeim, 1983) as well as philosophy (Demos, 1960; Finagrette, 1967) have suggested that such denial or self-deception presents a logical paradox. The question posed by these theoreticians has been: "How can an individual lie to him or herself without knowing the truth on some level?" This logical inconsistency may be extended to virtually any concept of denial. In order to deny the existence of a threat, the individual must know that it is there at the outset. It appears that individuals may engage in a dual process in which they are simultaneously aware of threatening information, and paradoxically, able to reject the existence of such information (Sackeim, 1983).

Sackeim and Gur (Gur & Sackeim, 1979; Sackeim, 1983; Sackeim & Gur, 1979) have provided some intriguing empirical demonstrations of such self-deception. In a demonstrative study, they found that individuals who, for various reasons, find their own voices aversive, identified their voices as belonging to another individual (Gur & Sackeim, 1979). Yet it appeared subjects were actually aware of the presence of their voice on some level: they showed an increase in GSR when confronted with their own voice even when they were reportedly unable to identify it. Sackeim and Gur (1979) argued that individuals low in self-esteem were denying the presence of their own voices. Presumably they were attempting to eliminate, through self-deception, the presence of a personal threat, in this case manifest in their own voice!

Sackeim and Gur's findings are controversial (Douglas & Gibbins, 1983; Roth, Snyder, & Pace, 1986). Yet their findings suggest that individuals are motivated to obviate reminders that they are less than competent. Thus, the individual who wishes not to be reminded of his or her shortcomings may attempt to ignore self-relevant information. Avoiding a reminder such as the tone or content of his or her verbal behavior may allow the individual to avoid negative self-relevant thoughts in general.

Finally, individuals selectively attend to self-relevant information by ignoring what is either negative or incongruent with their own self-perceptions (Mischel, Ebbesen, & Zeiss, 1973, 1976; Shrauger, 1975, 1982). Mischel *et al.* (1973) found that subjects who had succeeded on an abilities test avoided examining information describing their liabilities to a greater extent than those who had failed or were uninformed of the outcome. In a similar vein, several studies have found that nondepressed persons avoid focusing on themselves and find such self-focus more aversive following failure than following success (Pyszczynski & Greenberg, in press). As mentioned before, well-adjusted persons seem to avoid focusing on information that discredits them.

Interestingly, these findings do not support the notion that individuals are most likely to engage in denial when threatened with probable failure. Those who should have been least threatened with likely failure (i.e., those who had received success feedback or those who were presumably more confident about their probabilities of succeeding), were most likely to avoid focusing on the prospect of a negative event. Perhaps these individuals felt they had something to lose, such as the glow of recent success, and were therefore most motivated to retain their recent gain. And perhaps nondepressed persons, who are more confident in the likelihood of succeeding in the future, find the loss of success particularly aversive and deceive themselves about the probability of such a loss, as a result.

Denying the Personal Relevance of and Degrading the Source of Evaluation

People are less accepting of negative than of positive information. They will therefore go to some lengths to discredit it (Shrauger, 1982; Snyder, Shenkel, & Lowery, 1977). When social disapproval is inevitable, a variety of cognitive maneuvers to discredit that information come into play. Such maneuvers reflect more activity and intentionality than denial and self-deception discussed in the previous section.

To discredit social disapproval, an individual may attempt to deny the importance of the disapproval itself (e.g., "Trivial Pursuit is only a game. It doesn't indicate anything important about one's general competence."). By denying the importance or legitimacy of the performance domain, the individual may escape the negative implications of a poor performance (Snyder *et al.*, 1983, pp. 87–88).

In addition, an individual may attempt to degrade the source of potential negative feedback. For instance, he or she may attempt to do this by claiming that the source is incompetent or is not subject to the facts in making an ability judgment (Baumgardner & Levy, 1987).

Several investigators have addressed receptivity to negative evaluation. In general, it has been found that individuals who have a solid and certain self-concept tend to view negative (relative to positive) feedback as less personally relevant (e.g., Lake & Arkin, 1985; Shrauger, 1975, 1982; Shrauger & Shoeneman, 1979) and seem less accepting of evaluations from others in general (Snyder & Clair, 1977). For instance, Lake and Arkin (1985) found that nonanxious subjects viewed negative feedback as less credible than their high social anxiety counterparts. The reverse was true for positive feedback; high anxiety subjects viewed it as less credible than low anxiety subjects viewed it to be. This patterns holds for high versus low esteem persons also (Baumgardner & Levy, 1986; Shrauger, 1975; 1982; Shrauger & Shoeneman, 1979).

In a recent study, Arkin & Baumgardner (1985c) found quite different reactions to the source of negative versus positive feedback for high-versus low-anxiety subjects. In this study, high and low social anxiety subjects participated in dyadic conversations where they received either approval or disapproval from a partner that was either extreme or moderate in valence. Low-anxiety subjects reacted to negative information by degrading their partner (the source of that feedback). High-anxiety subjects also reacted to negative information by degrading their partner, but only when the disapproval was extreme in valence. Thus individuals who are most confident are quite willing to reject the source of potential disapproval. In this way, they mitigate the impact of such feedback. However, less confident persons must seemingly be confronted with particularly threatening disapproval before they venture to diminish the source of such disapproval. Therefore, less confident persons may incorporate a greater percentage of the negative feedback they receive, underlining their sense of uncertainty about their self-worth.

Low confidence persons also seem most likely to question the credibility of positive feedback. Paradoxically there is some indication that they are also the most likely to experience very positive affective reactions to such feedback. Lake and Arkin (1985) found that high-anxiety subjects experienced the most positive affect in reaction to praise, even though they were also most likely to doubt the credibility of that praise. This suggests a dilemma for the low confidence individual. Although favorable evaluations may be most gratifying for these persons, they may at the same time be least likely to believe them. In this sense, these persons deprive themselves of a sense of self-worth and efficacy that a belief in favorable self-judgments might afford them.

Effectiveness of these Strategies

Thus far we have described a variety of cognitive maneuvers individuals might engage in in an effort to lessen the impact of potential disapproval. At first blush, one might argue that these sorts of denials are maladaptive. Most psychotherapeutic techniques attempt to counteract denial and self-deception. Psychoanalytic theory, for instance, explicitly ties accuracy of representations to psychological health. Phenomenological theories (e.g., Rogers, 1959) view psychopathology as a consequence of the individual's misunderstanding of his or her "actual" organismic experience. The same is true of contemporary theory. For instance, Beck (1967, 1976) and his colleagues have argued that individuals who distort their experiences, or engage in "faulty thinking," are maladjusted. Psychotherapy should therefore be aimed toward correcting such misrepresentations and toward teaching clients to represent reality accurately. Denial, according to this view, is the hallmark of psychological maladjustment.

Recently, Sackeim (1983) provided a convincing critique of this conceptualization of psychological health. In particular, he has pointed out that depressed persons fail to use cognitive biases and self-deceptive strategies that characterize normals. Depressed persons are actually more accurate in recalling their past performances relative to their "well-adjusted" depression-free counterparts, who tend to view their past through rose-tinted glasses (e.g., Lewinsohn et al., 1980; Nelson & Craighead, 1977). Moreover, individuals who engage in denial of future negative events do, up to a point, seem to cope more effectively with present misfortunes (Taylor, 1983).

Individuals low in social anxiety and high in self-esteem seem most ready to deny the existence and relevance of social disapproval and view skeptically others who evaluate them unfavorably (Arkin & Baumgardner, 1985c). More important to the present analysis, these individuals may be "blissfully unaware" of potential social disapproval, and that denial seems to serve them well, at least up to a point.

What sort of function do these denial strategies serve? Why do they seemingly allow persons to carry on with social life so blissfully? We would like to suggest that such a deception allows individuals two benefits. First, this sort of self-deception allows individuals to maintain and foster a sense of personal control over future outcomes. More specifical-ly, by deceiving the self regarding his or her capabilities, the individual is able to sustain a sense of possibility of control in the future. As we have asserted elsewhere (Arkin & Baumgardner, 1986), individuals engage in such interpretive control (cf. Rothbaum *et al.*, 1982) in order to sustain a belief, however illusory that belief might be, in their power to exert influence over future events. In this way, the individual who engages in such denial processes is able to sustain an "illusion of control" (Langer & Roth, 1975) and the possibility of primary control in future circum-stances. By disregarding the signals of disapproval, the individual may relax and hold on to the belief that all is well. In this sense, it may help an individual delude himself by simply not knowing that he lacks control over future events.

In addition, such self-deception may simply be reinforcing. That is, individuals experience more positive affect and esteem when they can believe that they are competent and that the source of negative evalua-tion is at fault. As an illustration, Baumgardner and Levy (1986) found that subjects who met with disapproval from another and who were subsequently able to degrade that person, showed more positive affect and esteem than those not given such an opportunity. Thus, being able to reject negative information outright allows individuals to sustain a sense of esteem and well-being.

All of this seems to suggest that self-deception and denial are bene-ficial to the psychological well-being of the individual who uses them. Yet a word of caution does seem in order. Denial may be adaptive but it has its limits. Take for instance a graduate student who is convinced that others think well of him and that he is approved of immensely by his superiors. He may do well at the outset of social discourse, whereas he will ignore any later signs of disapproval. These signs might be regarded as irrelevant of as coming from an inferior source. Although his engag-ing in such a denial process may serve short-term esteem needs well, his long-term needs may not be met by such a strategy. By ignoring such signals, the blissfully unaware person fails to use the criticism as a means to improve and regulate his social behavior. After this prolonged but denied social disapproval, the clarity of rejection may culminate in a sudden and perhaps jarring disconfirmation of esteem. For instance, when final orals are viewed as only mediocre or when the job market yields sparse results, the blissfully unaware student may sink into re-morse, and resign himself to an "unjustifiably" mediocre career.

Traditionally, researchers interested in individual differences in self-esteem and related constructs have found that people who perceive themselves in a favorable light are also the most well-adapted. Indeed, healthy self-esteem may often be considered almost synonymous with psychological adjustment. However, this may only hold true of individuals who do not fall at the extreme end of the positive self-conception continuum (Cohen, 1959). These extremely confident persons, as the previous example suggests, may do quite poorly in social interactions but just not know it. By denying negative feedback, even when it is not extreme (e.g., Arkin & Baumgardner, 1985c), these individuals may barge ahead in social interactions, insensitive to cues that they might be looked upon unfavorably. They also might be the sort of persons who are prone to delusional thought patterns, when confronted with a massive dose of rejection (cf. Sackeim, 1983). There may indeed be a fine line between a healthy dose of self-deception and more severe delusions that are disadvantageous to healthy functioning.

In a related way, Taylor (1983) has argued that self-deception in the form of an illusion of control facilitates coping for those faced with terminal illness. However, she adds that the adaptiveness of self-deception may have considerable limits. When an individual believes erroneously that he or she has control over the recurrence of an illness, where such control does not actually exist, disconfirmation of that control may be particularly devastating. Indeed, Taylor uncovered evidence suggesting that women who most actively believed they had control over the recurrence of breast cancer reacted most negatively to an actual recurrence. Believing one has no control at the outset may, under such circumstances, actually be more adaptive than possessing the illusion of control that is disconfirmed at a later time (Wortman & Dunkel-Schetter, 1979).

To summarize then, it seems that the adaptive value of self-deception is clear, yet must be qualified. Some self-deception may facilitate the maintenance of a robust self-concept and allow the individual to maintain a sense, however illusory, of personal control. However, extreme measures (e.g., disregarding any and all disapproval from others; ignoring any and all information that success is not guaranteed) may, over time, have detrimental consequences for the self-concept, subsequent well-being, and actual control over future outcomes.

DECREASING THE PROBABILITY OF DISAPPROVAL IN THE FUTURE

To this point, the focus has been on strategies that might be used when an individual is faced with seemingly inevitable disapproval. In this section, attention is turned to more primary and active attempts individuals may employ in attempting to *alter the course* of disapproval. Because of the imminence of disapproval, the coping mechanisms discussed thus far are characteristically retroactive and may be viewed as attempts to maintain secondary control (Rothbaum *et al.*, 1982).

When feasible, attempts to cope with the prospect of disapproval center on avoiding the negative evaluation itself. The ideal and most obvious of these strategies is to try more and with greater resolve, thereby increasing the likelihood of success. Yet when this does not seem feasible, people may attempt to alter the circumstances of evaluation so that poor performance is not as threatening. There are at least three main response domains that reflect such active attempts. First, when threatened with unfavorable evaluations, people attempt to create circumstances to facilitate comparison to less able others (e.g., Wills, 1981). Second, individuals may attempt to redirect the focus of attention to other behaviors they believe are positive (e.g., Baumeister & Jones, 1978). Finally, people can create or claim impediments to effective performances (i.e., self-handicap), so that attributions to incompetence are not tenable. Surely, there are other strategies that may complement this list; however, for the present purposes, these serve as suitable illustrations.

Downward Social Comparison and Affiliation with Less Fortunate Others

Wills (1981) proposed an analysis of downward social comparison integrating research findings from a range of topical areas within social psychology (e.g., affiliation, aggression, social comparison choice). In brief, he asserts that individuals increase their subjective well-being through comparison with less fortunate others. They are motivated to seek such a downward comparison when they experience a temporary decrease in subjective well-being or if they suffer more or less chronically from uncertainty about their well-being (i.e., they are low in self-esteem). There is some evidence supporting this thesis, although, as Wills notes in Chapter 10, this volume, the evidence is not entirely conclusive at this time.

First, individuals faced with a threat to their esteem prefer to affiliate with and be evaluated in comparison to others less competent than average (Brickman & Bulman, 1977; Cottrell & Epley, 1977; Gruder, 1977). For instance, in an early study, Hakmiller (1966) found that esteem-threatened subjects were more likely to compare with the person worst off in their discussion group. This is consistent with the notion that downward comparison is prompted by desire to restore well-being.

Two studies suggest that low self-esteem persons prefer to compare with less fortunate others when the prospect of disapproval seems likely (Friend & Gilbert, 1973; Wilson & Benner, 1971). For instance, Friend and Gilbert (1973) found that when threatened with likely failure, subjects high in fear of negative evaluation chose to compare themselves to the worst off individual in their group. In contrast, subjects low in fear of negative evaluation seemed relatively unaffected by the threat of failure. Wills (see Chapter 10, this volume) notes that whereas those high in esteem tend to distort differences between themselves and others in a self-enhancing manner, those low in esteem do not. Consequently, low-esteem persons must direct their efforts toward the more active social comparison choice efforts. This is, of course, consistent with the main thrust of this chapter.

In addition to choosing to compare themselves to less fortunate others, individuals may also attempt to criticize other individuals with whom they are compared, and construe them as less competent than they really are (Bers & Rodin, 1984; Salovey & Rodin, 1984). This strategy elevates the individual and decreases a subjective sense of a failing performance.

Interestingly, the empirical thread running throughout downward comparison choice literature suggests a very different picture from strategies discussed in the first section. Recall that it may be the self-confident individual who is most prone to engage in denial of social disapproval. In contrast, it may be the counterpart of these individuals, the person lacking confidence, who is most prone to engage in the more active strategy of downward social comparison. Yet as Wills in Chapter 10, this volume, points out, the relationship between self-esteem and social comparison is not a resolved issue at this time.

Manufacturing Lower Normative Standards

Downward social comparison may be viewed as an attempt to seek an environment where others are likely to measure the individual against the standard of a less competent other. Subjectively, this allows a person to decrease the probability of a failing performance.

Yet performance standards are not always set by external social comparison standards. People judge performance sometimes by social and sometimes by preset, competency-based standards (Nicholls, 1984). Judging one's performance relative to "mastery, understanding or knowledge" (Nicholls, 1984, p. 329) may also come into play in attempts to restructure evaluative standards. Specifically, any given performance sets the stage for future evaluation. A successful performance may result in more stringent future evaluation standards. To the extent a successful performance is threatening in this way, it is advantageous to the individual to create low standards.

For instance, the straight-A student is expected to maintain his or her academic image. When he or she ventures to make a B, this otherwise acceptable performance may be taken as failure. Likewise, envision the reputedly great actor or actress who is expected to be highly entertaining; if only marginally so, the individual and others are disappointed and may dub the performance a failure. Ironically, one's appearing competent may present a unique dilemma. While enjoying the accolades of success, there is also a continuing pressure to perform well. Such a dilemma is likely to be particularly acute for the person who doubts his or her ability to sustain a particular level of performance. When successful, a new, higher level of expectations for the individual emerges. With each success, the probability of success, in a subjective sense, diminishes; success comes to be redefined according to a new, more stringent standard.

A cost associated with being competent, then, is the pressure to continue the success. In order to do this, the individual must exceed (or at least match) the expectations of the audience. The individual is, at least in part, in control of such expectations.

How might the individual orchestrate the environment such that standards remain comfortably low? First, it seems easiest simply to tell others that one is not particularly able. The individual who is uncertain about his or her ability to maintain a string of successful performances may claim personal responsibility for a failing performance or deny personal responsibility for a successful one (cf. Aronson & Carlsmith, 1962). Indeed, several studies have focused precisely on this point (cf., Bradley, 1978). For instance, Wortman, Costanzo, & Witt (1973) found that subjects who believed they would be evaluated at a later time showed an attenuation of the self-serving bias: they denied responsibility for a previous success and claimed responsibility for a previous failure. This finding has usually been interpreted in traditional self-presentational terms: wishing not to embarrass themselves, subjects appeared to be avoiding a failure that would disconfirm immediately an ability they had just asserted. This self-presentational behavior may also be interpreted as serving the function of creating lower evaluation standards. By denying responsibility for success or asserting responsibility for failure, others' expectations for future performances should remain comfortably low. In the traditional view, subjects are characterized as engaging in a protective attempt to avoid embarrassment. In the second view, proposed here, they may be characterized as setting the stage to avoid embarrassment as well as to attempt to exceed the performance standard and regard themselves subjectively as successful.

A second avenue to lowering evaluation standards is rather more dramatic and certainly more effortful. This avenue entails the individual's active attempts to fail as a means to regulate the expectations held for that person's performances. In particular, the individual who is uncertain about his or her ability to maintain a series of smooth performances may perform poorly during initial stages of performance as a way of lowering performance standards that others might apply.

In a test of this strategy, Baumgardner (1985) led subjects to believe that an interviewer expected them to do quite well or expected them to do quite poorly. Further, subjects were led to feel doubtful or confident about their ability to perform in the future. This was done by telling subjects that their past performance was due to either a prodigious amount of effort or to little effort exertion. Subjects high and low in social anxiety were included in the experiment.

Doubtful subjects who believed that an interviewer held high expectations for their future performance were most inclined to fail strategically. This was particularly true when they were high in social anxiety. These are precisely the people and just the conditions under which the most doubt about ability to meet performance standards in the future should be present.

Notably, this literature hinges at a parallel to the social comparison literature. The evidence indicates that individuals low in self-esteem or those who fear negative evaluation are most likely to seek less able comparison others. Likewise, it seems that the same individuals under comparable conditions engage in strategic failure in an apparent attempt to alter and lower evaluation standards. In short, less confident people seem most prone to engage in these sorts of active and behavioral strategies in their attempts to avoid disapproval.

Redirecting the Focus of Evaluation

Of course, not all threatening situations actually provide a means for actively altering the evaluative standards constituting success. When faced with actual disapproval, and the likely prospect of continuing disapproval, a self-presentational dilemma arises. People like to be liked, particularly when that liking is contingent upon valued attributes. How can a person restore his public persona when it has been undermined directly by disapproval?

Baumeister and Jones (1978) created such a dilemma. They had subjects take a personality test and then showed them either bogus favorable or bogus unfavorable results. Subjects were also either informed that their results would be given to a fellow subject with whom they would interact later, or that the other subject would not receive such information.

They found that subjects who shared unfavorable personality test results with another compensated for this negative presentation of self by describing themselves more favorably on other dimensions—ones unrelated to the personality test. They called this *compensatory self-enhancement,* and argued that it serves to alter the focus of evaluation by calling attention to other, potentially more positive attributes.

Similarly, Tesser (1980; Tesser & Paulhus, 1984) has argued that individuals who compare unfavorably to another will view the dimension of evaluation as less relevant and view other dimensions as increasingly important. Tesser argues that such diversionary tactics are part of an effort to maintain a sense of confidence in self.

Whether individuals low in self-esteem are more likely to engage in such redirection efforts is not entirely clear at this time. However, other research has shown that low self-esteem individuals are more receptive to negative feedback than those high in self-esteem, perhaps because they find such information believable (Shrauger, 1982). It seems likely as well that those lacking confidence would be less certain of their ability to "pull off" such a redirection effort (i.e., why redirect evaluation to still another dimension where one is no less doubtful?). Hence they may well be less inclined to use this redirection strategy.

Excuse-Making and Self-Handicapping

A more subtle strategy, also designed to alter the course of social evaluation, is to attempt to influence the attributional logic surrounding a particular performance. For instance, an individual may claim an excuse for poor performance prior to entering into the evaluative situation or handicap their performance in some way so as to have a ready excuse for failure (Arkin & Baumgardner, 1985a). Or, in the self-serving bias, people may view past successes as due to their own abilities and view past failures as attributable to other factors.

As this suggests, attributional tactics may occur prior to a performance (i.e., be proactive as in self-handicapping) or following a performance (i.e., be retroactive as in the self-serving bias). Our focus here is on these more active, behavioral attempts to create excuses for poor performance. In particular, our focus is on self-handicapping behaviors.

Self-handicapping appears to possess all the necessary features of an effective disapproval avoidance strategy. More specifically, the term *self-handicapping* refers to an individual's attempt to reduce a threat to esteem by actively creating inhibitory factors that interfere with performance and thus provide a persuasive causal explanation for potential failure. The introduction of extraneous causal factors may obviate low ability inferences in the case of potential failure (Arkin & Baumgardner, 1985a; Berglas & Jones, 1978).

Conditions that engender self-handicapping coincide with those that promote concerns with disapproval. For instance, individuals who lack confidence in their future performances are more likely to handicap themselves (Baumgardner, Lake, & Arkin, 1985; Berglas & Jones, 1978; Kolditz & Arkin, 1982; Rhodewalt & Davison, 1984). In the initial demonstration of the phenomenon, Berglas and Jones (1978) gave subjects who had previously succeeded at a task the opportunity to choose to protect themselves on a future performance by ingesting a debilitating drug. By taking the drug, subjects were able to manipulate the situation because the impending failure, if it occurred, would be seen as attributable to the debilitating drug. Only those subjects who were led to believe their initial success would not be repeated (i.e., the initial success was not contingent upon their efforts) chose to handicap themselves.

Kolditz and Arkin (1982) later found evidence that subjects handicapped themselves primarily for social reasons. Only those subjects who believed that the handicap would be known to the experimenter chose the debilitating drug. Again, this suggests that self-handicapping served as a means to circumvent social disapproval.

Finally, several researchers (e.g., Arkin & Baumgardner, 1985a; Harris & Snyder, 1986; Leary, 1983; Smith, Snyder, & Handelsman, 1982; Smith, Snyder, & Perkins, 1983; Snyder & Smith, 1982) have suggested that individuals who chronically doubt their ability to obtain approval are most likely candidates for self-handicapping. Individuals who lack esteem or who are anxious about their abilities therefore appear to be most likely to self-handicap. For instance, Smith et al. (1982) examined the self-report of test anxiety as a handicapping strategy. Prior to a test, high and low test anxiety subjects were either informed that anxiety inhibits performance on the test, does not inhibit performance on the test, or were given no instructions. They found that anxious subjects (who are also most inclined to be low in self-regard) claimed test anxiety as a handicap, but only when anxiety was portrayed as a useful handicap. This finding has been replicated with socially anxious (Snyder, Smith, Augelli, & Ingram, 1985) and hypochondriacal (Smith et al., 1983) populations, both of which may be viewed as subsets of individuals lacking confidence.

Harris and Snyder (1986) have shown that self-handicapping serves an important function in social relations for less confident individuals. In this study, they found that males who were uncertain about their ability practiced less for an upcoming task, relative to those who were certain of themselves. Moreover, they found that those subjects who practiced less, and therefore had a feasible handicap, showed a correspondingly lower anxiety than those who practiced more. This suggests that individuals may handicap their performances in order to avoid an aversive state of anxiety.

Effectiveness of these Strategies

Until recently, there was no direct evidence bearing on the impact or effectiveness of active attempts to decrease the probability of disapproval (cf. Arkin & Baumgardner, 1985a). Yet some progress in overcoming this lack of clarity, particularly in the study of self-handicapping, has been made. At this point, we can address three interrelated questions about the impact of self-handicapping. First, is self-handicapping an effective coping strategy on a personal or private level, as Harris and Snyder (1986) suggest?; second, is it effective socially (i.e., do others believe it)?; and third, do self-handicappers receive such information (i.e., feedback) from relevant others?

Arkin & Baumgardner (1985d) addressed the second question in an investigation of audience reactions to self-handicapping targets. Subjects were presented with written scenarios. These described an individual who, prior to an important examination, handicapped of his own volition, was forcibly handicapped by unfortunate circumstances, or was handicap free. In addition, subjects learned that the target had performed well, average, or poorly on the examination. Following this, subjects were asked to infer several traits, most notably ability, and to make causal attributions concerning ability or lack of ability.

When only causal attributions are considered for examination performance, self-handicapping was seemingly quite effective: subjects' causal attributions indicated that they attributed success more to ability and failure more to extraneous factors when the handicap was present. This occurred even when the handicap was set in place by the individual as well as by unfortunate circumstances.

However, the results of the study were not encouraging for the avid self-handicapper in a more important respect. Trait attributions to ability were quite discrepant from causal attributions to ability. Specifically, subjects inferred that the target was less competent in general when he handicapped intentionally than when he did not handicap. This suggests self-handicapping may not be nearly as effective as intended or common sense might lead one to assume.

Although self-handicapping may not be an effective impression management strategy in the long run, there is reason to believe that it may still serve as an effective coping mechanism on a personal level. In particular, handicapping may provide a misattribution for a poor impression and as such, allow uncertain persons to relax in otherwise threatening situations. Individuals who lack confidence or are socially anxious may be most inclined to benefit from self-handicaps. A poor impression may be readily attributed to a handicap. Apparently for this reason the presence of a persuasive handicap has quite a salutary effect on a number of indexes of acute social anxiety (Brodt & Zimbardo, 1981; Harris & Snyder, in press; Leary, 1984).

Along similar lines, Arkin and Baumgardner (1985b) had subjects high and low in social anxiety participate in a 10-minute personal encounter. All subjects listened to background white noise during their conversations. The crucial manipulation was whether subjects, in the presence of their partners, were led to believe the noise would handicap their social performance. Half the subjects were told the background noise would interfere with their ability to present themselves favorably; the remaining subjects received no such instructions.

As predicted, subjects high in social anxiety were quite receptive to the presence of the handicap, as indicated by several measures. They rated their conversations more enjoyable and said they were more relaxed than their high anxiety counterparts who had no handicap. Moreover, they actually outperformed their counterparts (i.e., their partners rated them more positively overall). It is important to note, however, that in this study, subjects' partners had been informed that the subjects did not choose to handicap themselves. Had they believed the subject had chosen the handicap, they may not have been so generous in their assessments (as demonstrated in the Arkin & Baumgardner, 1985b, study).

There is a paradox in the findings of these two studies. Handicapping seems to forestall disapproval by facilitating performance among less confident people (Arkin & Baumgardner, 1985b). However, others who may learn of a chosen handicap disapprove of the handicapper. Yet surely handicappers intend their impediments to convince their audiences (cf. Kolditz & Arkin, 1982). Is it the case that they are fooling themselves and believing erroneously that they are presenting the desired impression?

Indeed, this may very well be the case. As Arkin & Baumgardner (1985d) demonstrated, others may disapprove of the handicapper. However, this does not necessarily mean that he or she knows that. The self-handicapper may not actually receive direct negative feedback regarding his or her behavior. In particular, others may be reluctant to point out their recognition of the intentional nature of the handicap, and may simply forego social discourse instead. People typically do not provide direct feedback to others concerning the effectiveness of their self-presentations, particularly when the presentation is unfavorable (Blumberg, 1972; Tesser & Rosen, 1972, 1975). Instead, such disapproval may be diffused and communicated in a less contingent manner then might be assumed (Gotlib & Robinson, 1982). People seem unwilling to give direct and contingent negative feedback. Instead, negativity is "leaked" indirectly through nonverbal channels while audiences try to mask their disapproval of a presenter as best they can.

For example, Gotlib and Robinson (1982) had subjects interact with depressed and nondepressed target persons. They found that subjects were quite positive in terms of direct feedback (e.g., willingness to interact at a future time) toward depressed and nondepressed targets. However, more subtle and indirect measures indicated that subjects responded quite differently to depressed than to nondepressed targets. They showed more negative nonverbal reactions toward depressed targets, smiling less often and showing less pleasantness in facial expression. In addition, they revealed more negative paralinguistic cues in their conversations with depressed targets than with nondepressed ones.

Interestingly, individuals who engage in disapproval avoidance may be most likely to receive diffuse and noncontingent feedback regarding their social behaviors. Because of this, the disapproval avoider may conclude that there is something correspondingly broad and diffuse, but clearly objectionable, about his or her character. Such a conclusion would underscore an already tenuous and uncertain self concept, typical of the person most likely to engage in such avoidance behaviors at the outset.

The effectiveness of similar strategies is an empirical question at this time. Social comparison with less able others, redirecting the focus of evaluation to a less threatening dimension, and attempts to foster low evaluation standards may be more effective maneuvers. Yet we can speculate about some of the costs of these coping attempts also.

The individual who socially compares downward seeks to affiliate with others who adhere to low aspirations. The result may be a sense of dissatisfaction with a social network and a sense of unrealized potential. Likewise, the individual who fails strategically relinquishes successful performance, to some extent, and fosters a less favorable first impression and a more lasting negative evaluation on more objective (e.g., social comparison) indexes.

Finally, the individual who redirects attention to less threatening dimensions (e.g., the failing athlete who tries to switch focus to his academic prowess) foregoes evaluation on a subjectively valuable dimension. His or her self-esteem may be damaged in an important sense, at the same time the public persona is shored up. This is precisely the set of circumstances that fosters self-doubt (Arkin & Baumgardner, 1986). The individual foregoes gaining valuable information about an important dimension of ability, and opts instead to focus on less valuable information. In so doing, he enhances a sense of uncertainty about competencies he most likely deems important.

In addition to this loss of valuable information, those privy to such redirection efforts may, much like with self-handicapping, see through such a strategy and draw even more negative conclusions as a result. Thus, audiences perceptive of such self-presentations may view them as evidence of weakness or lack of ability. This in turn may eventuate in even more damage to an already tenuous conception of self.

INTEGRATION

It is obvious that individuals want to avoid the paralytic results of social disapproval. The embarrassment and shame that social disapproval provokes is so unpleasant because it is associated with a diminution in one's sense of self-worth (Modigliani, 1968) and with the recognition that one's presentation of self has been undermined by some external event (Goffman, 1967). Clearly, social disapproval is imbued with great significance.

Some common threads in this selective review of coping with disapproval have emerged. First, there was evidence that individuals are inclined toward two different means of coping with disapproval. With regard to the first means, individuals who possess a robust self concept seem prone to engage in such tacit, and more cognitive, denial strategies. Confident persons, who are presumably "psychologically healthy," are most likely to acquire self-deceptive "cognitive buffers" when faced with social disapproval. Interestingly, these coping mechanisms consist of self-deception and denial, both of which many clinicians and academicians have traditionally viewed as maladaptive. More contemporary research and theory point to the adaptive significance of misperceiving reality, however (e.g., Sackeim, 1983).

The picture that emerges for the more active strategies is markedly different. Strategies of self-handicapping, downward social comparison, and strategic failure seem most typical of the polar opposite, the individual who views herself in a negative light. Perhaps these less confident persons do not possess the cognitive buffers, such as self-deception and denial, and must therefore turn to more active and convincing means to avoid social disapproval. And, perhaps people with a precarious self concept are simply more cognizant of their shortcomings and therefore take a more active role in managing social evaluation.

Along these same lines, failure may simply present a more potent threat to low-esteem persons. Extreme precautions may therefore be necessary in order to circumvent this more serious threat. Thus, more active behaviors, such as self-handicapping and strategic failure, may be the only recourse; telling oneself (e.g., denying the prospect of disapproval) that failure is unlikely may not be convincing enough for these persons.

Finally, the effectiveness of these sorts of coping mechanisms is not always a given. The cognitive defenses, prevalent among those with a robust self concept, may be quite effective, unless carried to extreme. However, in the case of the more active strategies, such as self-handicapping, the self-presentational advantage is more questionable. For instance, although a handicap may diminish anxiety and have an enhancing effect because of this, it may be viewed quite negatively by others. In short, there is a tradeoff inherent in choosing such a strategy: although handicapping may provide an individual with a ready excuse for a poor performance, the irony is that others may be quick to recognize, and judge negatively, such a ploy.

REFERENCES

Arkin, R. M., & Baumgardner, A. H. (1985a). Self-handicapping. In J. H. Harvey & G. W. Weary (Eds.), *Attribution: Basic issues and applications* (pp. 169–202). New York: Academic Press.

Arkin, R. M., & Baumgardner, A. H. (1985b). *The facilitative effects of providing a self-handicap.* Unpublished manuscript, University of Missouri, Columbia and Virginia Polytechnic Institute and State University, Blacksburg, VA.

Arkin, R. M., & Baumgardner, A. H. (1985c). *The rejection of inconsistent feedback: Social anxiety and self-presentations in response to approval and disapproval from others.* Unpublished manuscript, University of Missouri, Columbia and Virginia Polytechnic Institute and State University, Blacksburg, VA.

Arkin, R. M., & Baumgardner, A. H. (1985d). *When self-handicapping fails to serve a purpose: Impressions of the strategic procrastinator.* Unpublished manuscript, University of Missouri, Columbia and Virginia Poltechnic Institute and State University, Blacksburg, VA.

Arkin, R. M., & Baumgardner, A. H. (1986). Self-presentation and self-evaluation: Processes of self-control and social-control. In R. Baumeister (Ed.), *The public self and private self.* (pp. 75–97) New York: Springer Verlag.

Arkin, R. M., Cooper, H. M., & Kolditz, T. (1980). A statistical review of the literature concerning the self-serving attribution bias in interpersonal situations. *Journal of Personality, 48,* 435–448.

Aronson, E., & Carlsmith, J. (1962). Performance expectancy as a determinant of actual performance. *Journal of Personality and Social Psychology, 65,* 178–182.

Baumeister, R. F., & Jones, E. E. (1978). When self-presentation is constrained by the target's knowledge. *Journal of Personality and Social Psychology, 36,* 608–618.

Baumgardner, A. H. (1985). *The strategy of failure: The role of social anxiety, expectations, and doubt.* Unpublished Doctoral Dissertation, University of Missouri-Columbia, Columbia, MO.

Baumgardner, A. H., & Levy, P. E. (1987). Interpersonal reactions to social approval and disapproval: The strategic regulation of affect. Unpublished manuscript, Virginia Polytechnic Institute and State University, Blacksburg, VA.

Baumgardner, A. H., Lake, E., & Arkin, R. M. (1985). Claiming mood as a self-handicap: The influence of spoiled and unspoiled public identities. *Personality and Social Psychology Bulletin, 11,* 349–357.

Beck, A. T. (1967). *Depression: Clinical, experimental, and theoretical aspects.* New York: Harper & Row.

Beck, A. T. (1976). *Cognitive therapy and the emotional disorders.* New York: International Universities Press.

Berglas, S., & Jones, E. E. (1978). Drug choice as a self-handicapping strategy in response to noncontingent success. *Journal of Personality and Social Psychology, 36,* 405–417.

Bers, S. A., & Rodin, J. (1984). Social comparison jealousy: A developmental and motivational study. *Journal of Personality and Social Psychology, 47,* 766–779.

Birney, R. C., Burdick, H., & Teevan, R. C. (1969). *Fear of failure.* New York: Van Nostrand-Reinhold.

Blumberg, H. H. (1972). Communication of interpersonal evaluations. *Journal of Personality and Social Psychology, 23,* 157–162.

Bradley, G. W. (1973). Self-serving biases in the attribution process: A reexamination of the fact or fiction question. *Journal of Personality and Social Psychology, 36,* 56–71.

Breznitz, S. (1983). The seven kinds of denial. In S. Breznitz (Ed.), *The denial of stress* (pp. 257–286). New York: International Universities Press.

Brickman, P., & Bulman, R. J. (1977). Pleasure and pain in social comparison. In J. M. Suls & R. L. Miller (Eds.), *Social comparison processes: Theoretical and empirical perspectives* (pp. 149–186). Washington, DC: Hemisphere.

Brodt, A., & Zimbardo, P. G. (1981). Modifying shyness related behavior through symptom misattribution. *Journal of Personality and Social Psychology, 41,* 437–449.

Cohen, A. (1959). Some implications of self-esteem for social influence. In C. Hovland & I. Janis (Eds.), *Personality and Persuasibility* (pp. 102–120). New Haven, CT: Yale University Press.

Cottrell, N. B., & Epley, S. W. (1977). Affiliation, social comparison, and socially mediated stress reduction. In J. M. Suls & R. L. Miller (Eds.), *Social comparison processes: Theoretical and empirical processes* (pp. 43–68). Washington, DC: Hemisphere.

Daly, J. A., & McCroskey, J. C. (Eds.). (1984). *Avoiding communication: Shyness, reticence, and communication apprehension.* Beverly Hills, CA: Sage.

Demos, R. (1960). Lying to oneself. *Journal of Philosophy, 57,* 588–595.

Douglas, W., & Gibbons, K. (1983). Inadequacy of voice recognition as a demonstration of self-deception. *Journal of Personality and Social Psychology, 44,* 589–592.

Erdelyi, M. (1974). A new look at the new look: Perceptual defense and vigilance. *Psychological Review, 81,* 1–24.

Finagrette, H. (1967). *On responsibility.* New York: Basic Books.

Friend, R. M., & Gilbert, J. (1973). Threat and fear of negative evaluation as determinants of locus of social comparison. *Journal of Personality, 41,* 328–340.

Goffman, E. (1967). *Interaction ritual.* New York: Anchor Books.

Gotlib, I. H., & Robinson, J. (1982). Responses to depressed individuals: Discrepancies between self-report and observer-rated behavior. *Journal of Abnormal Psychology, 91,* 231–240.

Greenberg, J., Pyszczynski, J., & Paisley, C. (1984). The effect of extrinsic incentives on the use of test anxiety as an attributional defense: Playing it cool when the stakes are high. *Journal of Personality and Social Psychology, 47,* 1136–1145.

Gruder, C. L. (1977). Choice of comparison persons in evaluating oneself. In J. M. Suls & R. L. Miller (Eds.), *Social comparison processes: Theoretical and empirical perspectives* (pp. 21–42). Washington, DC: Hemisphere.

Gur, R. C., & Sackeim, H. A. (1979). Self-deception: A concept in search of a phenomenon. *Journal of Personality and Social Psychology, 37,* 147–169.

Hakmiller, K. L. (1966). Threat as a determinant of downward comparison. *Journal of Experimental Social Psychology, Supplement, 1,* 32–39.

Harris, R. N., & Snyder, C. R. (1986). The role of uncertain self-esteem in self-handicapping. *Journal of Personality and Social Psychology, 51,* 451–458.

Jones, W., Cheek, J., & Buss, A. H. (1986). *A sourcebook on shyness: Research and treatment.* New York: Plenum Press.

Kolditz, T. A., & Arkin, R. M. (1982). An impression management interpretion of the "self-handicapping strategy." *Journal of Personality and Social Psychology, 43,* 492–502.

Lake, E. S., & Arkin, R. M. (1985). Reactions to objective and subjective interpersonal evaluations: The influence of social anxiety. *Journal of Social and Clinical Psychology, 3,* 143–160.

Langer, E. J., & Roth, J. (1975). Heads I win, tails it's chance: The illusion of control as a function of the sequence of outcomes in a purely chance task. *Journal of Personality and Social Psychology, 32,* 951–955.

Leary, M. (1983). *Understanding social anxiety: Social, personality, and clinical perspectives.* Beverly Hills, CA: Sage.

Leary, M. (1984). *Social anxiety and interpersonal concerns: Testing a self-presentational explanation.* Unpublished manuscript, Wake Forest University, Winston-Salem, N.C.

Lewinsohn, P. M., Mischel, W., Chaplin, W., & Barton, R. (1980). Social competence and depression: The role of illusory self-perceptions? *Journal of Abnormal Psychology, 89,* 203–212.

Martin, M. W. (Ed.). (1985). *Self-deception and self-understanding: New essays in philosophy and psychology.* Lawrence, KS: University Press of Kansas.

Mischel, W., Ebbesen, E. B., & Zeiss, A. M. (1973). Selective attention to the self: Situational and dispositional determinants. *Journal of Personality and Social Psychology, 27,* 129–142.

Mischel, W., Ebbeson, E. E., & Zeiss, A. M. (1976). Determinants of selective memory about the self. *Journal of Consulting and Clinical Psychology, 44,* 92–103.

Modigliani, A. (1968). Embarrassment and embarrassability. *Sociometry, 31,* 313–326.

Myers, D. G., & Ridl, J. (1979). Can we all be better than average? *Psychology Today, 12,* 89–98.

Nelson, R. E., & Craighead, W. E. (1977). Selective recall of positive and negative feedback, self-control behaviors, and depression. *Journal of Abnormal Psychology, 86,* 379–388.

Nicholls, J. G. (1984). Achievement motivation: Conceptions of ability, subjective experience, task choice, and performance. *Psychological Review, 91,* 328–346.

Peplau, L. A., & Perlman, D. (Eds.). (1982). *Loneliness: A sourcebook of current research, theory, and therapy.* New York: Wiley-Interscience.

Philips, G. M. (1968). Reticence: Pathology of the normal speaker. *Speech Monographs, 35,* 39–49.

Pyszczynski, T., & Greenberg, J. (in press). A biased hypothesis-testing model of motivated attributional distortion. In L. Berkowitz (Ed.), *Advances in experimental social psychology* (Vol. 20).

Quattrone, G. A., & Tversky, A. (1984). Causal versus diagnostic contingencies: On self-deception and on the voter's illusion. *Journal of Personality and Social Psychology, 46,* 237–248.

Rhodewalt, F., & Davidson, J. (1984). *Self-handicapping and subsequent performance: The role of outcome valence and attributional certainty.* Unpublished manuscript, University of Utah, Salt Lake City, UT.

Rogers, C. R. (1959). A theory of therapy, personality, and interpersonal relationships as developed in the client-centered framework. In S. Koch (Ed.), *Psychology: A study of science* (Vol. 3, pp. 184–256). New York: McGraw-Hill.

Ross, L., Greene, D., & House, P. (1977). The "false consensus effect": An egocentric bias in social perception and attribution processes. *Journal of Experimental Social Psychology, 13,* 279–301.

Roth, D. L., Snyder, C. R., & Pace, L. M. (1986). Dimensions of favorable self-presentation. *Journal of Personality and Social Psychology, 51,* 867–874.

Rothbaum, F., Weisz, J. R., & Snyder, S. S. (1982). Changing the world and changing the self: A two-process model of perceived control. *Journal of Personality and Social Psychology, 42,* 5–37.

Sackeim, H. A. (1983). Self-deception, self-esteem, and depression: The adaptive value of lying to oneself. In J. Masling (Ed.), *Empirical studies of psychoanalytic theories* (Vol. 1, pp. 101–157). Hillsdale, NJ: Erlbaum.

Sackeim, H. A., & Gur, R. C. (1979). Self-deception, other-deception, and self-reported psychopathology. *Journal of Consulting and Clinical Psychology, 47,* 213–215.

Salovey, P., & Rodin, J. (1984). Some antecedents and consequences of social-comparison jealousy. *Journal of Personality and Social Psychology, 47,* 780–792.

Shrauger, J. S. (1975). Responses to evaluation as a function of initial self-perceptions. *Psychological Bulletin, 82,* 581–596.

Shrauger, J. S. (1982). Selection and processing of self-evaluation information: Experimental evidence and clinical implications. In G. Weary & H. L. Mirels (Eds.), *Integration of clinical and social psychology* (pp. 128–153). New York: Oxford University Press.

Shrauger, J. S., & Schoeneman, T. J. (1979). Symbolic interactionist view of the self-concept: Through the looking glass darkly. *Psychological Bulletin, 86,* 549–573.

Smith, T. W., Snyder, C. R., & Handelsman, M. M. (1982). On the self-serving function of an academic wooden leg. *Journal of Personality and Social Psychology, 42,* 314–321.

Smith, T. W., Snyder, C. R., & Perkins, S. (1983). The self-serving function of hypochondriacal complaints. Physical symptoms as self-handicapping strategies. *Journal of Personality and Social Psychology, 44,* 787–797.

Snyder, C. R. (1978). The "illusion" of uniqueness. *Journal of Humanistic Psychology, 18,* 33–41.

Snyder, C. R., & Clair, M. S. (1977). Does insecurity breed acceptance? Effects of trait and situational insecurity on acceptance of positive and negative diagnostic feedback. *Journal of Consulting and Clinical Psychology, 45,* 843–850.

Snyder, C. R., & Fromkin, H. L. (1980). *Uniqueness: The human pursuit of difference.* New York: Plenum Press.

Snyder, C. R., & Smith, T. W.(1982). Symptoms as self-handicapping strategies: The virtues of old wind in a new bottle. In G. Weary & H. L. Mirels (Eds.), *Integration of clinical and social psychology* (pp. 104–127). New York: Oxford University Press.

Snyder, C. R., Shenkel, R. J., & Lowery, C. R. (1977). Acceptance of personality interpretations: The Barnum effect and beyond. *Journal of Consulting and Clinical Psychology, 45,* 104–114.

Snyder, C. R., Higgins, R. L., & Stucky, R. J. (1983). *Excuses: Masquerades in search of grace.* New York: Wiley.

Snyder, C. R., Smith, T. W., Augelli, R. W., & Ingram, R. E. (1985). On the self-serving function of social anxiety: Shyness as a self-handicapping strategy. *Journal of Personality and Social Psychology, 48,* 970–980.

Taylor, S. E. (1983). Adjustment to threatening events: A theory of cognitive adaptation. *American Psychologist, 38,* 1161–1173.

Taylor, S. E., Lichtman, R. R., & Wood, J. V. (1984). Attributions, beliefs in control, and adjustment to breast cancer. *Journal of Personality and Social Psychology, 46,* 489–502.

Tesser, A. (1980). *A self-evaluation maintenance model of social behavior.* Unpublished manuscript, University of Georgia.

Tesser, A., & Paulhus, D. (1983). The definition of self: Private and public self-evaluation management strategies. *Journal of Personality and Social Psychology, 44,* 672–682.

Tesser, A., & Rosen, S. (1972). Similarity of objective fate as a determinant of the reluctance to transmit unpleasant information: The MUM effect. *Journal of Personality and Social Psychology, 23,* 46–53.

Tesser, A., & Rosen, S. (1975). The reluctance to transmit bad news. In L. Berkowitz (Ed.), *Advances in experimental social psychology* (Vol. 8, pp. 193–232). NY: Academic Press.

Weinstein, N. D. (1980). Unrealistic optimism about future life events. *Journal of Personality and Social Psychology, 39,* 806–820.

Wills, T. A. (1981). Downward comparison principles in social psychology. *Psychological Bulletin, 90,* 245–251.

Wilson, S. R., & Benner, L. A. (1971). The effects of self-esteem and situation upon comparison choices during ability evaluation. *Sociometry, 34,* 381–397.

Wood, J. V., Taylor, S. E., & Lichtman, R. R. (1985). Social comparison in adjustment to breast cancer. *Journal of Personality and Social Psychology, 49,* 1169–1183.

Wortman, C. B., & Dunkel-Schetter, C. (1979). Interpersonal relationships and cancer: A theoretical analysis. *Journal of Social Issues, 35,* 120–155.

Wortman, C. B., Costanzo, P. R., & Witt, T. R. (1973). Effects of anticipated performance on the attributions of causality to self and others. *Journal of Personality and Social Psychology, 27,* 372–381.

Zuckerman, M. (1979). Attribution of success and failure revisited, or: The motivation bias is alive and well in attribution theory. *Journal of Personality, 47,* 245–287.

13

The Role of Similarity/Difference Information in Excuse-Making

C. R. SNYDER and ROBERT N. HARRIS

INTRODUCTION

Several years ago, the first author and his colleagues developed a theory regarding uniqueness-seeking behavior (see Snyder & Fromkin, 1980, for overview). Against a prevailing viewpoint that people always prefer others who are similar to themselves (i.e., the Donn Byrne, 1971, reinforcement theory of interpersonal attraction), it was proposed that a moderate amount of similarity was the most satisfactory state for people. In brief, uniqueness theory predicts that people find the state of extremely high similarity relative to others to be aversive, and therefore will strive to lessen their perceived and manifested sense of similarity to a more moderate level. The conclusion after conducting research pertaining to uniqueness theory was that the motive to reestablish some sense of specialness appears in many situations where people perceive their uniqueness to be threatened. Nevertheless, some fascinating circumstances where the uniqueness motive was reversed eventually led us to examine the topic of excuse-making.

This chapter is based, in part, on a convention paper presented by C. R. Snyder at the Midwestern Psychological Association, Chicago, May, 1985.

C. R. SNYDER AND ROBERT N. HARRIS • Graduate Training Program in Clinical Psychology, Department of Psychology, University of Kansas, Lawrence, KS 66045.

Interviews with research participants about situations that lessened their uniqueness needs revealed a common theme: if people believed that they were not doing well at something, they did not want to feel they were the only ones doing poorly. In other words, people would forego their uniqueness needs when they perceived themselves to be in a jam. Indeed, failure situations appeared to provide an important exception to the uniqueness motive. What is it about failure situations that fosters the person's use of similarity/difference information about themselves? This question, and the role of similarity/difference information in this process eventually became a focal point of a subsequent theory of excuse-making (Snyder, Higgins, & Stucky, 1983; Snyder, 1985c). We turn to this excuse theory and the role of similarity/difference information at this point.

EXCUSE THEORY

"Excuses are explanations or actions that lessen the negative implications of an actor's performance, thereby maintaining a positive image for oneself and others" (Snyder et al., 1983, p. 45). Several aspects of this definition are worthy of elaboration before examining the role of similarity/difference information in promulgating excuses. First, there obviously must be a person who is the author of the excuse. Second, a bad outcome of some sort must have occurred (or be anticipated). The outcome is bad in the sense that it does not meet either social or personal standards. Third, the person must be perceived as being "linked," that is, "responsible" for the bad outcome. (This responsibility linkage is a crucial component of excuse-making, and as such will be described in detail subsequently.) Fourth, it is assumed that the motivational basis for excuse-making is that people want to maintain a positive self-image. Fifth, this positive self-image is presumably preserved for both oneself and others. Although there are certainly instances in which excuses are aimed principally at the external audience of other people, in many instances excuses are also for the internal audience of oneself.

In order to understand the aforementioned definition of excuse-making, it is necessary to highlight the responsibility linkage. Interestingly, the similarity/difference type of information provides a useful framework for understanding the notion of responsibility. In this vein, the ideas of Harold Kelley (1967, 1971, 1973) can be readily applied to understand how a person may be perceived as being more or less responsible for an action. Kelley's analysis of the variance model details the causes that appear to covary with an effect over time. If a particular cause appears to fluctuate with a given effect, then that effect is attributed to that cause. More specifically, Kelley postulated that three types of similarity/difference information—consensus, consistency, and distinctiveness—are relevant in forming attributions regarding a person's responsible for an outcome.

Consensus information taps similarity/difference of behavior by one person in similar situations relative to the behaviors of other persons in that same situation. The lower the consensus, the more the person engaging in the behavior is seen as being responsible. For example, if the present chapter turns out poorly, we will be seen as quite responsible for this poor showing when the authors of other chapters are brilliant, stimulating, and witty.

Consistency information taps similarity/difference of behavior by one person in a given situation over time. The higher the consistency, the more the person engaging in the behavior is seen as being responsible. If we write a terrible chapter in this book, and follow it up with horrendous subsequent articles and chapters, then we will be held as being especially responsible for these poor writings.

Distinctiveness taps the similarity/difference of behavior by a person in one situation relative to other performance situations. The lower the distinctiveness, the greater is the perceived responsibility of the person engaging in the behavior. Consider our horrible chapter again. If we flub up this chapter, as well as other written work, our experiments, and our editorial duties, then we are especially responsible (we're not only lousy writers, but also lousy psychologists).

It should be emphasized that the similarity/difference information as advocated in Kelley's analysis of the variance model represents between- and within-subject "variance." The consensus notion reflects similarity/difference relative to other people (i.e., between subject), and the consistency and distinctiveness notions reflect similarity/difference relative to oneself in similar and dissimilar situations (i.e., within subject). The addition of the within- to the between-subject type of similarity/difference information helped to elucidate how people use such information in assigning responsibility for actions. In the subsequent presentation, it should also be noted that Kelley's original "cold" employment of attribution principles (i.e., how observers objectively assign responsibility for another person's actions) is utilized in a "hot" or motivated way (i.e., how actors intuitively know these rules and therefore use them to lessen their responsibility for bad actions).

TRANSFORMED RESPONSIBILITY EXCUSES ("YES, BUTS")

Once the person admits to having done something negative, transformed responsibility excuses are invoked in order to lessen the sense of condemnation for the bad act. As such, transformed responsibility excuses represent psychological information that may diminish the accountability of the actor for the bad act, thereby preserving a relatively positive self-image. The prototypical phrase for this is "Yes, but . . ." and the "but" is following by some sort of extenuating circumstance that lessens the negative repercussions of the "bad" act, thereby preserving the person's image.

Given the utility of Kelley's analysis of variance factors of consensus, consistency, and distinctiveness in defining the attributional responsibility for negative outcomes, we began our early analysis of transformed responsibility excuses by assuming that people also use the similarity/difference dynamics that are inherent in consensus, consistency, and distinctiveness information in order to lessen responsibility. This turned out to be a useful approach because all "Yes, but" excuses can be explained under the consensus, consistency, and distinctiveness dimensions. Each of these subtypes of transformed responsibility "Yes, but" excuses will be explored at this point.

Consensus-Raising Excuses

The similarity/difference dynamic inherent in consensus-raising excuses rests on comparing oneself in a given situation *with other people in that same situation.* The excuse-maker seeks to raise consensus by suggesting that others in the same situation also would do poorly. The inherent excuse logic here is that it must be something about the situation that causes the individual to fail, and therefore it is not the fault of the individual. Take our poor chapter, for example. We note to ourselves, and perhaps other people that the other authors also did not do such a stellar job with their chapters. In the degree to which we can convince ourselves and others that most of the authors in this book did not do too well, then our "responsibility" is lessened and our images maintained.

Consensus-raising excuses can take several forms. Each of these will be briefly presented.

Task Difficulty and Luck. A person may attribute his or her failures to the internal factors of ability and high effort, or to external factors, such as task difficulty and luck. Summaries of research on attributions after failure (e.g., Arkin, Cooper, & Kolditz, 1980; Zuckerman, 1979) reveal that people ascribe their outcomes to the external factors of task difficulty and luck. The consensus raising in these excuses is that an extremely hard task would make most everyone fail; likewise, bad luck can rear its powerful head at any point and produce failure for anyone.

Coercion. If someone or something else made us do the ill deed, then we can reason that most people would also be similarly influenced by these powerful outside forces. This type of excuse is especially prevalent when people have generated some harmful action toward other people (e.g., Brock & Buss, 1964; Harvey, Harris, & Barnes, 1975). Related research suggests that external audiences will hold the actor as being less responsible for his or her bad actions if that actor was not free to behave in another way, i.e., was coerced (Harvey *et al.*, 1975; Kruglanski & Cohen, 1973). In the filmed versions of the classic Stanley Milgram (1963, 1965) obedience studies, many persons who had seemingly given high electric shock to another person explained this by asserting "the experimenter made me do it." Elsewhere (Snyder *et al.*, 1983), this phenomenon was labeled the harm-choice deescalator in order to synopsize how transgressing people argue that they (and implicitly others in the same situation) had little or no choice in their action. The sense of choice is purposefully lessened when the outcome is bad. Examples abound in regard to such excuses. "He made me do it" or "I had to do it" statements emerge from the mouths of children and adults who find themselves in such predicaments.

Attributive Projection. This well-known clinical term reflects the process whereby a person who is made aware of some negative personal characteristic ascribes these shortcomings to other people also. Research corroborates this projection process (for reviews see Holmes, 1968, 1978). In a typical research paradigm, research participants, half of whom are given some negative performance or personality feedback, are then allowed to rate other people on the same performance or personality dimensions. Under such procedures, the persons given negative feedback are more likely to ascribe similar negative characteristics to other people. What is especially intriguing about this "misery loves company" excuse is that several studies actually show that such a process temporarily serves to reduce the stress and negative emotion related to the negative feedback (Bennett & Holmes, 1975; Burish & Houston, 1979; Holmes & Houston, 1971; Zemore & Greenough, 1973). These latter studies are noteworthy in that it is relatively rare to test whether excuse-like maneuvers affect people's emotional state and self-image.

Overall, therefore, research reveals that several different types of consensus-raising excuses occur. Research in our own laboratory, however, suggests that such consensus-raising excuses are very sensitive to external repudiation (e.g., Mehlman & Snyder, 1985). It appears that people will not publicly employ consensus raising if they sense that others around them (e.g., experts, experimenters, etc.) can rebut their excuse. Because consensus-raising excuses are often public in nature, excuse-makers may be prone to refrain from such protective strategies in order to avoid repudiation by knowledgeable observers or authorities. At the very least, there may have to be some reasonable probability that others would also do poorly in a given arena before the excuse-making person ventures into the public realm of verbalized consensus raising. This precaution does not apply, of course, when the excuse-maker employs the consensus-raising strategy in private. Future research may profitably focus on the private and public aspects of consensus-raising excuses. Furthermore, although some consensus-raising types of excuses (i.e. projection) do appear to reduce the stress of a failure as measured by state indexes of emotion, more research is needed in order to demonstrate their short- and long-term efficacy as a coping strategy. We will return to these points later when we discuss the therapeutic implications of consensus-raising excuses.

Consistency-Lowering Excuses

The similarity/difference dynamic of consistency/lowering excuses focuses upon a comparison of oneself in a given situation *with oneself in that same situation at previous or future time periods.* Excuse-makers seek to lower consistency by asserting that they previously have done better on the very task or situation where they have just failed; or, the excuse-makers can argue that they will do better in the future in the situation where they have just performed poorly. The underlying logic here is that there must have been something in the given situation at the time of the performance that generated the poor performance. For example, if we bungle the present chapter, we can recount (to ourselves and others) how we have written much better articles and chapters previously on this topic.

There are three general subtypes of consistency-lowering excuses, and these will briefly describe at this point.

Emphasizing Unusualness of Bad Performance. As this subheading implies, this first type of consistency-lowering excuse reflects a straightforward verbalization on the part of the poor performer that it is unlikely that he or she would perform similarly in the same performance arena on future occasions. As a test of this type of excuse in our laboratory (Mehlman & Snyder, 1985), college students were delivered either success or failure feedback on a purported test of intelligence. Subsequent self-report results indicated that in the failure relative to success condition, students felt they would be less likely to obtain the same score on future occasions. Additionally, when the failure condition students who were allowed to generate the consistency-lowering excuse were compared with failure condition subjects who were not allowed to engage in such excuse-making, the former group reported significantly less state anxiety and hostility. Thus, there appeared to be at least temporary emotional benefits related to the consistency-lowering excuse tactic.

Lowered Effort Expenditure. The basic phrase here is "I didn't really try." If the person did not try, then the cause of the poor performance remains ambiguous (Snyder & Wicklund, 1981). More specifically, the person (and others) do not have to conclude that deficiency in actual ability fueled a failure as long as full effort is not expended. Although effort is generally considered to reflect an internal attribution, lowered effort in particular actually externalizes the cause relative to some more central and important cause (e.g., "It's just that I didn't try hard, and its not because I'm stupid"). As Birney, Burdick, and Teevan (1969) put it:

> There is little one can do about bad luck and fatigue except to try to convince oneself and others that they are operative. But not trying is within the control of the individual, and we would expect a person who is particularly fearful of experiencing self-devaluation not to put out a maximum effort when involved in an achievement task. (p. 215)

Surveys of research reveal that persons who have experienced a failure situation are more likely to invoke lowered effort relative to persons who have experienced success (Zuckerman, 1979). Miller (1976) provided an example of this phenomenon by having college students take a social perceptiveness test (SPS) under instructions that engendered either high or low ego involvement; moreover, within each ego-involvement group, half of the students were given success and half were given failure feedback regarding their performance. The critical dependent variable was the question, "How hard did you try on the SPS?" The failure condition students reported working less hard, and this "didn't try" effect was especially marked for the failure students in the high involvement set.

A recent study in our laboratory adds further detail to the lowered effort excuse strategy. In this study (Harris & Snyder, 1986), certain and uncertain self-esteem college students were informed that they were to take a nonverbal test of intellectual ability. In anticipation of the test, students were allowed to practice (the effort measure). Results showed that it was not the absolute level of self-esteem (e.g., high or low) *per se,* but the level of uncertainty of self-esteem that influenced subjects' preparatory efforts. That is, male college students who were uncertain as compared to certain of their self-esteem (whether high or low esteem) practiced less as measured by practice items attempted and amount of time spent practicing. Further, for these uncertain-esteem males, a decrease in reported anxiety was associated with a smaller number of practice items attempted and less time spent practicing. Finally, the uncertain-esteem students also underestimated (as measured by self-report) time spent practicing, and this underestimation distortion process was associated with a decrease in anxiety for these students. Therefore, at least for the uncertain-esteem males in this study, the lowered effort excuse emerged in behavioral and self-report indexes; moreover, these excuses served to diminish the anxiety associated with the predicament of taking the ego-threatening test.

Lack of Intentionality. The classic "I didn't mean to . . ." emphasizes the fact that the person *cognitively* did not intend to perform poorly, and as such the poor performance in a given circumstance is framed as being unusual for the person in that particular arena. Theoretically, therefore, the situation rather than the person is described as being responsible for the action when lack of intention is invoked (Jones & Davis, 1965). Research to date on this question has focused on observers' reactions to the intentionality information. Not surprisingly, lessened intentionality on the part of people who have committed a transgression results in a more positive appraisal of such people by observers (e.g., Karniol, 1978; Rotenberg, 1980). Also, other studies reveal that the authors of unintended as compared to intended negative actions are perceived as being less responsible (Shaw, 1968; Shaw & Reitan, 1969; Sulzer & Burglass, 1968). Even children appear to assign less responsibility when lack of intentionality is involved (Darley & Zanna, 1982; Sedlak, 1979).

The aforementioned theory and results are consistent with the underlying premises of the legal system, which assigns the intentionality notion a central role in determining culpability and punishment. Lack of intentionality is inherent in pleas to fit of rage, drunkeness, and insanity (Slovenko, 1983; Tedeschi & Riess, 1981). What is noticeably lacking in regard to the intentionality variable, however, are studies investigating whether people in predicaments use such a strategy, and whether the absence of intentionality serves to protect the giver's self-image and emotional welfare.

Consistency-lowering excuses are less open to public scrutiny than consensus-raising excuses. Because the person uses his or her own behavior in consistency-lowering excuses as the basis of the similarity/difference dynamic, others are less likely to refute the excuse (unless, of course, the observers have seen the person repeatedly fail in a given situation). In our own laboratory, we have found that, after failure situations, people do generate consistency-lowering excuses, and these excuses appear to facilitate coping in that they temporarily reduce stress (Harris & Snyder, 1986; Mehlman & Snyder, 1985). Such consistency-lowering excuses may also play fairly well with external audiences because such audiences do not have access to the actuarial data regarding how poorly the excuse-giver has performed in the past. Also, external audiences may be somewhat sympathetic to consistency-lowering excuses because we have all had "off nights" (note also the consensus raising in this latter logic). In regard to lowered effort, however, the repeated use of this excuse may serve merely to perpetuate a personal and societal self-fulfilling label of laziness.

Distinctiveness-Raising Excuses

The similarity/difference dynamic of distinctiveness-raising excuses rests upon a comparison of oneself in a given situation *with oneself in other situations*. The excuse-maker increases distinctiveness by emphasizing the difference between the poor performance in one situation relative to the good performances in other situations. If our excuse-maker can highlight the good performances, then the particular type of situation that was associated with the poor performance is indicted; or at the very least, the poor performance is circumscribed. Back to our dismal chapter: by focusing on our virtues in other arenas (e.g., as clinicians or administrators), we protect the possibility that we are competent psychologists.

Attention Diversion. The example of calling attention to one's strengths in other arenas after failure situations has been observed empirically (e.g., Baumeister & Jones, 1978; Greenberg & Pyszczynski, 1985; Mehlman & Snyder, 1985). For example, after receiving failure as compared to success feedback on a purported intellectual test, college students in a failure condition were significantly more prone to assert that they would do much better on measures of intellectual performance other than the one they took (Mehlman & Snyder, 1985). This attention diversion excuse tactic also served to lessen the negative emotional state of those failure condition students in comparison to failure condition students who were given no such excuse opportunity (see also Greenberg & Pyszczynski, 1985). Again, therefore, there is at least some evidence for temporary emotional benefits for the excuse-maker.

The person who is especially prone to employ this attention diversion type of excuse may have other strengths. Therefore, this type of excuse-maker may inherently invoke idiosyncrasy credits (Hollander, 1958) for the good deeds that one has accrued in one's life. In other words, the person who has obtained credits for his or her actions in other situations may be "allowed" a bad performance in a given arena (Hollander, 1976).

Splitting. The splitting excuse appeals to the schizophrenic in all of us. That is, the transgressing person admits to a weakness or bad aspect of themselves (in one situation), but emphasizes that this is one small part of a much larger "good" side that appears in other situations. In this vein, Schlenker (1980) notes that apologies imply that an "event should not be considered a fair representation of what the actor is 'really like' as a person" (p. 154). Goffman (1971) suggested that apologies serve such a splitting function by emphasizing how the otherwise "good" person is sorry for the "bad" part of him or her. Regarding the generation of apologies by persons in predicaments, Schlenker and Darby (1981) found that increasingly negative predicaments elicited more complete apologizing behavior among college students. In terms of the eventual negative reactions by an external audience, research suggests that apologies and remorse generate a more benign response (Austin, Walster, & Utne, 1976; Bramel, Taub, & Blum, 1968; Darby & Schlenker, 1982). Whether such apologies serve the giver in either short- or long-term emotionally beneficial ways has not been reported.

Like consistency-lowering excuses, distinctiveness-raising excuses have the advantage of employing similarity/difference information that is more in the purview of the excuse-maker than the external audience. In other words, the excuse-maker is the most knowledgeable source about his or her better performances in other arenas. Returning to research in our laboratory, we have found that persons in failure situations will readily utilize distinctiveness-raising excuses, and that such tactics appear to lessen the short-term emotional aversiveness of the failure (Mehlman & Snyder, 1985). Because of the short-term emotional benefits of distinctiveness-raising (and consistency-lowering) excuses to research participants, it is intriguing to entertain the potential of such excuses for the therapeutic arena. This latter point will be examined subsequently in this chapter.

The Interaction of Consensus, Consistency, and Distinctiveness

For purposes of exposition, consensus-raising, consistency-lowering, and distinctiveness-raising excuses have been presented separately. In many instances, however, these excuses interact through the similarity/difference dynamic in order to lessen the transformed responsibility. An example may illustrate this assertion. Consider the seemingly "pure" consensus-raising excuse of "Yes, but he was playing so well that nobody could have beaten him today." This excuse also implicitly lowers consistency ("Yes, but I have done better when I have played him on other days."). Often, the consistency and distinctiveness information are intertwined. For example, the "I didn't mean to" excuse-maker is lowering the consistency of the bad behavior and raising the distinctiveness by alluding to his or her good side. As should also be readily apparent, the excuse-maker can appeal to the similarity and the difference ends of the similarity/difference dynamic. Thus, excuse-making may operate by emphasizing similarity relative to other people in the same situation, and differences relative to how a person behaves over time, and over situations.

SIMILARITY/DIFFERENCE EXCUSES AND COPING

Before we address the issue of the coping value of consensus-, consistency-, and distinctiveness-based excuses, it is first necessary to review the evidence pertaining to whether people indeed make such excuses, and for whom (i.e. what audience) are they made. Having addressed these issues briefly, the bulk of this remaining section will turn to a discussion of (a) whether such excuses "work" as a coping strategy, and (b) what role they may play in the psychotherapy process.

Do People Make Excuses Based on Similarity/Difference Information?

If we take a scorecard approach, the overall answer to the question posed at the beginning of this subsection is yes. Using consensus raising as a first example, there are (a) a large number of studies showing how people utilize task difficulty and bad luck excuses; (b) many studies showing attributive projection; and (c) a few studies corroborating the coercion type excuse. In the case of consistency-lowering excuses, there are (a) many studies showing lowered effort; (b) one study corroborating the tactic of reporting unusualness of the bad performance; and (c) no studies testing lack of intentionality (although several studies show that observers do react to lack of intentionality excuses). In regard to distinctiveness raising, there are (a) three studies supporting the attention diversion process; and (b) one study demonstrating splitting excuses.

Although the dilemmas engendered by the experimental procedures in the aforementioned studies may differ in specific content, the common thread is that the research participants, who are typically college students, have been placed in predicaments where they anticipate or experience some sense of failure. These failures then appear to ignite excuse making in experiment after experiment. Although future researchers would do well to employ samples other than college students, including males and females of differing ages, such studies are likely only to expand the generalizability of making excuses in response to failure. This latter conclusion—that people make excuses—would come as no surprise to professionals or laypeople. What is perhaps noteworthy, however, is the potential explanatory power of the similarity/difference dynamic in understanding how people make excuses.

Why the similarity/difference information provides a framework for many excuses may relate to the very role that such similarity/difference information plays in the development of one's self-concept. Throughout child and adult development, the comparison of one's thoughts, actions, words, and behaviors in general provides a mechanism for building and maintaining a self-concept. In this latter sense, and owing principally to Leon Festinger's (1954) influential early work, a common viewpoint is that people evaluate and "validate" their behavior by comparing it to the behavior of other persons and to their own previous behavior. In order to help learn the myriad lessons of life, therefore, it is useful to perceive how we are doing relative to others and to our own previous performances.

Although such social comparison is often an objective process in that we attempt to form accurate perceptions of how we are doing relative to others or ourselves, more recent theory and research would suggest that in certain situations we use or distort the social comparison information in order to protect our self-image (see Wills, 1981; Wills, this volume, for reviews). Failures represent one principal type of situation where the similiarity/difference information is employed in a motivated manner by people. Therefore, the fact that people initially objectively employ similarity/difference information in order to judge themselves (the Festinger perspective) and others (the Kelley perspective) suggests that this similarity/difference information should be a readily available framework for protecting one's image under ego-threatening circumstances.

Similarity/Difference Based Excuses For Self or Others?

The issue here is whether the similarity/difference based excuses serve the internal audience of oneself, the external audience of other people, or perhaps both. At a theoretical level, the external audience is important because functioning in society in general and interpersonal contexts in particular involves attention to one's image. In this vein, the essence of the symbolic interaction perspective (Cooley, 1922; Mead, 1934) involves seeing oneself as others do by "stepping into their shoes." Other people figuratively become "looking glasses" by which we see ourselves. More recently this general perspective has been captured under the term *impression management*, wherein the person is principally concerned with the external audience. Erving Goffman (1955, 1963, 1967) has described this impression management as acting in a manner so as to save face in front of others.

The theoretical case for examining the internal audience rests on the premise that people internalize the standards of important external audiences (e.g., parents, teachers, etc.). Whether the theory of moral development is psychodynamic (Freud, 1927), social learning (Bandura, 1977), or cognitive (Kohlberg, 1963; Piaget, 1926), however, all theories share the viewpoint that children adopt the perspective of external audiences.

As the brief overview of audience issues reveals, concerns with external and internal audiences become interwoven. This becomes further entangled when one considers the very nature of similarity/difference based excuses, which involves attention to both how one's bad outcomes relate to others' outcomes in the same situation (i.e., the between subject comparison), and one's outcomes in the same and different situations (i.e., the within subject comparisons).

Although the foregoing analysis suggests a simultaneous attention to internal and external audiences when making similarity/difference based excuses, it is also likely that certain predicaments accentuate the relative importance of the external as compared to internal concerns. This latter point will be examined again in a subsequent discussion of when and where excuses work. Unfortunately, the experiments to date do little to disentangle the audience issues related to excusing. Because the research participants are interacting directly with an experimenter or observers who are physically present, or they know that other people will see or evaluate their behavior (even if the research participants are "alone"), the external audience concerns are present to some degree. The best way to conceptualize the audience issue based on the actual research methodologies, therefore, is not to consider the audience as internal or external, but rather to view the degree of external audience concerns (from slight to extreme).

Do Similarity/Difference Excuses Work?

Beyond the conclusion that people make excuses for themselves and others, the next and more important set of issues pertains to the function or result of such excuses. As was noted in the earlier discussion of the assumptions of excuse theory, it is postulated that excuses serve in "maintaining a positive image for oneself and others." Some researchers have operationalized the "maintenance of positive image" by tapping into the emotional states of persons immediately before and after they have been given some sort of failure feedback. In a typical paradigm, the change in negative emotions (usually state anxiety, depression, or hostility) is monitored as a function of the person making or not making the excuse. To date, there are six reported studies in which experimenters give failure or no-failure feedback to people and then test for (a) the similarity/difference type of excuses, and (b) the change in state emotion as a result of making or not making the excuse. In each case the failure feedback people make more similarity/difference based excuses than do the no-failure feedback people; moreover, in each case, among failure groups, those allowed to make excuses evidenced a less negative emotional response in comparison to the failed persons who did not make excuses. Temporarily, therefore, such excuses do appear to lessen the negative emotional impact of predicaments.

The strength of the array of studies we have cited is that the authors tested the impact of the excuse-making on research participants' emotional states. The weakness is that the long-term effects of the excuse-making process on people are not explored. In some sense this criticism is diminished because excuses are a situation-specific strategy for dealing with particular failure. However, the failures may have long-term implications for people, and in this sense, it may be useful to ascertain the more enduring positive and negative repercussions of excuse making.

A second and different tact on the operationalization of the image-maintenance process involves an examination of external audiences' or judges' reactions to the similarity/difference based excuse. Judges' reactions typically involve ratings of how responsible the actor is perceived for his or her "bad" action. Generally, judges do rate actors as being less responsible for actions that truly are high in consensus (see Kassin, 1979). Relatedly, observers have been shown to hold people especially responsible for more negative actions (which by inference should have low consensus, Burger, 1981). To date, research has also revealed that excuses involving coercion, lack of effort, and apologies generate less perceived responsibility on the part of observers. Overall, therefore, external audiences appear initially to react to similarity/difference based excuses with lessened responsibility. Whether such excuses have longer-ranging effects on the external audiences' perceptions of responsibility is an unexplored question to date.

The question of whether the similarity/difference based excuse works needs to be further qualified by examining the role of the external audience. As a first example, it should be noted that people appear to lessen their excuse-making attributions for failure when in the presence of a very knowledgeable observer or expert (Arkin, Appelman, & Burger, 1980, Experiment 2; Arkin, Gabrenya, Appelman, & Cochran, 1979; Wells, Petty, Harkins, Kagehiro, & Harvey, 1977). In a recent study in our laboratory (Mehlman & Snyder, 1985), we took this question one step further by examining the emotional repercussions of either giving similarity/difference based excuses or not giving such excuses in the presence of a knowledgeable observer (a bogus lie detector device) or no such observer. Without the knowledgeable observer, the failed excuse-giving persons reported the usual lessened negative emotional responses relative to failure persons who did not give excuses. On the other hand, under the knowledgeable observer set, the failed excuse givers reported more negative emotion than the failure people who did not give excuses. These studies, taken further, suggest that under the attention of certain audiences, people will give less excuses, and if they do give excuses, will feel worse for doing so. Here, therefore, external audience concerns should clearly dominate the internal audience concerns.

There are other types of observers before whom excuses do not appear to lessen judged responsibility. If the observer perceives himself as being behaviorally or psychologically different from the actor who has performed the bad act, then that observer tends to hold the actor as being especially responsible (Burger, 1981; Chaikin & Darley, 1973; Shaver, 1970). In a similar vein, if the observer is very uninvolved and does not identify with the actor in the particular predicament, then greater responsibility is ascribed to the actor (Burger, 1981; Walster, 1966).

Just as there are certain people before whom one should not give excuses, there are certain roles that discourage excuse making (Tetlock, 1980). For example, teachers are expected to take responsibility for their students' inabilities to learn, and research corrobortes this (Ames, 1975; Beckman, 1973; Ross, Bierbrauer, & Polly, 1974). Consider another example. It would be hard to imagine the acceptable excuse that the surgeon would give for being late for brain surgery.

Yet another caveat in considering whether the similarity/difference excuse "works" relates to the excuses themselves. Excuses that are too big for the particular situation may cause extreme suspicion on the part of others (Snyder, 1985a, b, c; Snyder, Higgins, & Stucky, 1983). Likewise, excuses that are given too often may lose their credibility to external audiences, and may generate personal stress rather than reduce it (Snyder, 1984). In this latter vein, it has been argued that people who become highly aware that they are engaging in excuse-making lose any stress-reducing benefits because they become sensitized to the societal stigma attached to excuse-making (Snyder, 1985a). When excuses lose their subtlety, then personal and interpersonal benefits may backfire. In moderation, however, and within the boundaries established in this subsection, it appears that similarity/difference based excuses do work in that they temporarily reduce the failure-related stress and they preserve one's image in the eyes of others. It is in this context that excuses can be considered as a coping strategy. In the subsequent final section, we will address the coping role of such similarity/difference excuses in the psychotherapy arena.

Similarity/Differences Excuses and Psychotherapy

In the extreme, similarity/difference excuses merely serve to promulgate the distress experienced by people. An example of a psychotherapy client of the first author illustrates this phenomenon. A 45-year-old male came for psychotherapy because he was not getting along with his co-workers and family. His explanation for this dilemma was that at age 8 he was physically abused by his father. The father died shortly thereafter, and his mother remarried. The abuse, which evidently consisted of several severe spankings, remained vividly on his mind through his adult years. In fact, he told himself and even others around him (especially males at work), that the reason for his interpersonal problems was his abuse background. He also verbalized the belief that anyone with such a history would bear the scars and exhibit the same difficulties as he had (note the maladaptive consensus raising here). This excuse was used so frequently that others around him became angry and hostile when he continued to use it (this latter response only served to reinforce his view that others around him were hostile and abusive). He had settled in a vicious cycle wherein the more he attempted to excuse himself with his abuse explanation, the more that others became uncomfortable and uneasy around him; in turn, he felt more pressure and stress and again reinvoked his abuse explanation.

A first step in treatment involved delineating those situations where he most frequently used the excuse. Interpersonal situations where he felt evaluated and uncertain as to how he would be perceived appeared to elicit his need to utilize his self-diagnosis of abused person. Although he tenaciously held to this abuse diagnosis, over the first few sessions he better specified those situations that seemed to generate his uneasiness and accompanying abuse excuse. In particular, he was most threatened by circumstances where he was to interact with an older male, or a male authority figure. With this examination of the type of situation that most strongly provoked threat, he was able to lessen the perceived threat and therefore the apparent need to use the abuse excuse in all arenas. Thus, with women, and later with his family more generally, he gradually lessened his abuse-based excusing.

The next step in treatment involved building his skills in managing his stress, and assertion training in dealing with people. During this phase of treatment, a serendipitous event happened to this client. He watched a television show on abuse, where he learned that not everyone with a childhood background of abuse had sustained irreparable psychological damage during their subsequent adult years. Further, he learned that many of those who had suffered negative repercussions because of their abuse history were able to overcome their difficulties. This realization served to shatter his counterproductive high-consensus assumption about how everyone who had been abused was by necessity psychologically devastated for life. Over several months, therefore, this overexcuser diminished his excusing behavior and at the end of treatment he was even considering abandoning his self-diagnosis as an abused person.

This overexcuser case illustrates the potential seductive long-term effects of excuses. Namely, some people may get stuck in their self-label or diagnosis. The excuse that is stress-reducing and perhaps maintains our social image in the short term probably does not do so when overused. Indeed, this seductive pathway to chronic excusing has been called a "Faustian bargain" (Snyder, 1984). It is noteworthy in this regard that persons with psychological symptoms may be prone to emphasize strategically those symptoms in anticipation of stressful events (Snyder & Smith, 1982).[1] As such, the strategic accentuating of symptoms as self-handicaps has been shown in several studies of symptom groups in our laboratory. For example, test anxious (Smith, Snyder, & Handelsman, 1982), hypochondriacal (Smith, Snyder, & Perkins, 1983), and shy (Snyder, Smith, Augelli, & Ingram, 1985) persons have been shown to report their symptoms in an excuse-like manner in anticipation of an ego-threatening event. Whether the strategic self-handicapping use of such symptoms serves to alleviate stress or preserve one's image in the eyes of others is an untested proposition to date.

In contrast to the case study of the overexcuser cited earlier, there are also persons who use too few excuse-like coping responses. Consider, for example, the fairly common psychotherapy client perception in which one imagines that one is the only person who experiences a particular problem. A male college student who believed that his shyness was highly unusual provides a good example of this phenomenon. By the time he reached therapy with the first author, his increasing perception of the abnormality of his shyness and his isolation from people were increasingly interfering in his life. In the course of treatment, he was

---

[1]This is not meant to imply that nonsymptom groups may not at times also employ their symptoms as excuses (e.g., DeGree & Snyder, 1985), but rather that chronic and elevated symptom persons are more likely to do so.

given the "homework" task of placing himself in arenas (e.g., parties) where he would interact with people. When people would approach him, he was instructed to merely report his honest feelings about how social situations were anxiety provoking. Also, he was told to report freely that he was shy. As a result of this process, this person learned that many other people were also uncomfortable at parties and "just talking." He was no longer a freak and he was more willing to interact socially and to work on his social apprehension. The consensus-raising excuse operating in this instance is obviously that many other people are also somewhat shy and anxious interpersonally. Further, the excuse is based in reality (i.e., others actually are nervous in social settings).

The authors have also observed a similar consensus-raising excuse phenomenon in the group therapy setting. In such a group therapy context, by describing some secret problem in the presence of other group members, a client will usually be amazed to find that one or more of the other group members have also felt, thought, or done the same thing (or at least something similar). Yalom (1975) labels this *universality* in his examination of the curative factors in group psychotherapy. For the person who is very hard on himself or herself, the process of getting "skeletons out of the closet" in a group context provides the possible beginning for the adaptive "Yes, but others feel the same way I do" excuse strategy.

The shyness case, and the group therapy example, illustrate the potential utility of employing consensus-raising excuses in the therapy process. If one does this, it is important that the consensus be believable and vivid to the client (Kassin, 1979; Nisbett, Borgida, Crandall, & Reed, 1976). In this vein, the early studies on the possible therapeutic effects of consensus raising related to a psychological problem did not show any effects because the sense of consensus was not strongly imparted to people. For example, Nisbett *et al.* (1976) attempted to change college students' depression by employing consensus information. Results showed that groups of college students who were told that their "Sunday blues" were very common in the dormitories did not show any emotional benefits relative to a group of students who were given no such consensus-raising information. The major problem with this study pertains to the weakness of the consensus manipulation. In a subsequent study, where people were given more vivid and impactful consensus-related feedback, the feedback has shown beneficial effects. Wilson and Linville (1982) employed a combination of consensus-raising and consistency-lowering information in order to enhance the academic performance of college students. Relative to students who were given no consensus and consistency information, students who were informed that it was typical to perform poorly in the freshman year (i.e., the consensus-raising) and that students improved academically over their freshman, sophomore, junior, and senior years (i.e., the consistency-lowering) evidenced significantly improved grades and lower one-year dropout rates. Although the validity of the measures and the long-term strength of the Wilson and Linville results have been questioned (Block & Lanning, 1984), two subsequent replications have also shown beneficial effects of consensus-raising and consistency-lowering information on college students (Wilson & Linville, 1985).

Consistency-lowering and distinctiveness-raising excuses can also be implemented with client populations. The basic idea here is to help clients realize how they (a) have not always had a particular problem or may not have that problem in the future (i.e., consistency lowering), and (b) have other areas of strength outside of the particular problem arena (i.e., distinctiveness raising). By using personal norms regarding past behavior, or the imagined way one could be in the future, a consistency-lowering excuse enables a person at least to hope for change. Likewise, by helping people to acknowledge the personal norms of better performance in non-problem-related activities, a sense of hope is activated. At least two studies (Andrews Debus, 1978; Dweck, 1975) relate to the beneficial effects of consistency-lowering and distinctiveness-raising excuses. In these studies, people who were taught to explain their failures in terms of lowered effort (thus simultaneously lowering consistency and raising distinctiveness by alluding to other arenas where they have tried and succeeded) were more persistent in their subsequent attempts at tasks.

The obvious conclusion is that more research is needed in order to understand the possible beneficial therapeutic effects of similarity/difference based excuses. However, based on the available theoretical and research evidence, as well as our therapeutic experiences, we would like to offer the following brief conclusions about the usefulness of similarity/difference excuses in the therapeutic process. When mired in a problem, we believe that many clients lose sight of how to effectively use personal similarity/difference information to their advantage. With such clients, the therapist's job is to help them use such similarity/difference information as an excuse in order to move beyond these problems. In this vein, the similarity/difference based excuses provide a jump start that initiates the coping process. Thus, there are benefits to perceiving oneself in a positive light, and having others do so as well. To turn a twist on an old saying, "an ounce of image may be worth a pound of coping."

ACKNOWLEDGMENTS

The authors appreciate the input of Carol Ford and Karen Albright on this chapter.

REFERENCES

Ames, R. (1975). Teachers' attributions of responsibility: Some unexpected counterdefensive effects. *Journal of Educational Psychology, 67,* 668–676.

Andrews, G. R., & Debus, R. L. (1978). Persistence and the causal perception of failure: Modifying cognitive attributions. *Journal of Educational Psychology, 70,* 154–166.

Arkin, R. M., Appelman, A. J., & Burger, J. M. (1980). Social anxiety, self-presentation, and the self-serving bias in causal attributions. *Journal of Personality and Social Psychology, 38,* 23–35.

Arkin, R., Cooper, H., & Kolditz, T. (1980). A statistical review of the literature concerning the self-serving attribution bias in interpersonal influence situations. *Journal of Personality, 48,* 435–448.

Arkin, R. M., Gabrenya, W. K., Jr., Appelman, A. S., & Cochran, S. T. (1979). Self-presentation, self-monitoring, and the self-serving bias in causal attribution. *Personality and Social Psychology Bulletin, 5,* 73–76.

Austin, W., Walster, E., & Utne, M. K. (1976). Equity and the law: The effect of a harmdoer's "suffering in the act" on liking and assigning punishment. In L. Berkowitz & E. Walster (Eds.), *Advances in experimental social psychology* (Vol. 9, pp. 163–190). New York: Academic Press.

Bandura, A. (1977). *Social learning theory.* Englewood Cliffs, NJ: Prentice-Hall.

Baumeister, R. F., & Jones, E. E. (1978). When self-presentation is constrained by the target's knowledge: Consistency and compensation. *Journal of Personality and Social Psychology, 36,* 608–618.

Beckman, L. (1973). Teachers' and observers' perceptions of causality for a child's performance. *Journal of Educational Psychology, 65,* 198–204.

Bennett, D. H., & Holmes, D. S. (1975). Influences of denial (situational redefinition) and projection on anxiety associated with threat to self-esteem. *Journal of Personality and Social Psychology, 32,* 915–921.

Birney, R. C., Burdick, H., & Teevan, R. C. (1969). *Fear of failure.* New York: Van Nostrand-Reinhold.

Block, J., & Lanning, K. (1984). Attribution therapy requestioned: A secondary analysis of the Wilson-Linville study. *Journal of Personality and Social Psychology, 46,* 705–708.

Bramel, D., Taub, B., & Blum, B. (1968). An observer's reaction to the suffering of his enemy. *Journal of Personality and Social Psychology, 8,* 384–392.

Brock, T. C., & Buss, A. H. (1964). Effects of justification for aggression and communication with the victim on postaggression dissonance. *Journal of Abnormal and Social Psychology, 68,* 403–412.

Burger, J. M. (1981). Motivational biases in the attribution of responsibility for an accident: A meta-analysis of the defensive-attribution hypothesis. *Psychological Bulletin, 90,* 496–512.

Burish, T. G., & Houston, B. K. (1979). Causal projection, similarity projection, and coping with threat to self-esteem. *Journal of Personality, 47,* 57–70.

Byrne, D. (1971). *The attraction paradigm.* New York: Academic Press.

Chaiken, A. L., & Darley, J. M. (1973). Victim or perpetrator? Defensive attribution of responsibility and the need for order and justice. *Journal of Personality and Social Psychology, 25,* 268–275.

Cooley, C. H. (1922). *Human nature and the social order* (rev. ed.). New York: Scribners.

Darby, B. W., & Schlenker, B. R. (1982). Children's reactions to apologies. *Journal of Personality and Social Psychology, 43,* 742–753.

Darley, J. M., & Zanna, M. P. (1982). Making moral judgements. *American Scientist, 70,* 515–521.

DeGree, C. E., & Snyder, C. R. (1985). Adler's psychology (of use) today: Personal history of traumatic life events as a self-handicapping strategy. *Journal of Personality and Social Psychology, 40,* 1512–1519.

Dweck, C. S. (1975). The role of expectations and attributions in the alleviation of learned helplessness. *Journal of Personality and Social Psychology, 31,* 674–685.

Festinger, L. (1954). A theory of social comparison process. *Human Relations, 7,* 117–140.

Freud, S. (1927). *The ego and the id.* London: Hogarth Press.

Goffman, E. (1955). On facework. *Psychiatry, 18,* 213–231.

Goffman, E. (1963). *Stigma: Notes on the management of spoiled identity.* Englewood Cliffs, NJ: Prentice-Hall.

Goffman, E. (1967). *Interaction ritual: Essays on face-to-face behavior.* Garden City, NY: Doubleday.

Goffman, E. (1971). *Reactions in public.* New York: Basic Books.

Greenberg, J., & Pyszczynski, T. (1985). Compensatory self-inflation: A response to the threat to self-regard of public failure. *Journal of Personality and Social Psychology, 49,* 273–280.

Harris, R. N., & Snyder, C. R. (1986). The role of uncertain self-esteem in self-handicapping. *Journal of Personality and Social Psychology, 51,* 451–458.

Harvey, J. H., Harris, B., & Barnes, R. D. (1975). Actor-observer differences in the perceptions of responsibility and freedom. *Journal of Personality and Social Psychology, 32,* 22–28.

Hollander, E. P. (1958). Conformity, status, and idiosyncrasy credit. *Psychological Review, 65,* 117–127.

Hollander, E. P. (1976). *Principles and methods of social psychology.* New York: Oxford University Press.

Holmes, D. S. (1968). Dimensions of projection. *Psychological Bulletin, 69,* 248–268.

Holmes, D. S. (1978). Projection as a defense mechanism. *Psychological Bulletin, 85,* 677–688.

Holmes, D. S., & Houston, B. K. (1971). The defensive function of projection. *Journal of Personality and Social Psychology, 20,* 208–213.

Jones, E. E., & Davis, K. E. (1965). From acts to dispositions: The attribution process in person perception. In L. Berkowitz (Ed.), *Advances in Experimental Social Psychology* (Vol. 2, pp. 219–266). New York: Academic Press.

Karniol, R. (1978). Children's use of intention cues in evaluating behavior. *Psychological Bulletin, 85,* 76–85.

Kassin, S. M. (1979). Consensus information, prediction, and causal attribution: A review of the literature and issues. *Journal of Personality and Social Psychology, 37,* 1966–1981.

Kelley, H. H. (1967). Attribution theory in social psychology. In D. Levine (Ed.), *Nebraska Symposium on Motivation* (Vol. 15, pp. 192–240). Lincoln: University of Nebraska Press.

Kelley, H. H. (1971). *Attribution in social interaction.* New York: General Learning Press.

Kelley, H. H. (1973). The process of causal attribution. *American Psychologist, 28,* 107–128.

Kohlberg, L. (1963). Moral development and identification. In H. Stephenson (Ed.), *Child*

Psychology (pp. 277–332). (62nd yearbook of the National Society for the Study of Education) Chicago, IL: University of Chicago Press.

Kruglanski, A. W., & Cohen, M. (1973). Attributed freedom and personal causation. *Journal of Personality and Social Psychology, 26,* 245–260.

Mead, G. H. (1934). *Mind, self, and society.* Chicago, IL: University of Chicago Press.

Mehlman, R. C., & Snyder, C. R. (1985). Excuse theory: A test of the self-protective role of attributions. *Journal of Personality and Social Psychology, 49,* 994–1001.

Milgram, S. (1963). Behavioral study of obedience. *Journal of Abnormal and Social Psychology, 67,* 371–378.

Milgram, S. (1965). Some conditions to obedience and disobedience to authority. *Human Relations, 18,* 57–76.

Miller, D. T. (1976). Ego involvement and attribution for success and failure. *Journal of Personality and Social Psychology, 34,* 901–906.

Nisbett, R. E., Borgida, E., Crandall, R., & Reed, H. (1976). Popular induction: Information is not always informative. In J. S. Carroll & J. W. Payne (Eds.), *Cognitive and social behavior* (Vol. 2, pp. 227–236). Hillsdale, NJ: Erlbaum.

Piaget, J. (1926). *The language and thought of the child.* New York: Harcourt Brace.

Ross, L., Bierbrauer, G., & Polly, S. (1974). Attribution of educational outcomes by professional and non-professional instructors. *Journal of Personality and Social Psychology, 29,* 609–618.

Rotenberg, K. (1980). Children's use of intentionality in judgement of character and disposition. *Child Development, 51,* 282–284.

Schlenker, B. R. (1980). *Impression management.* Monterey, CA: Brooks/Cole.

Schlenker, B. R., & Darby, B. W. (1981). The use of apologies in social predicaments. *Social Psychology Quarterly, 44,* 271–278.

Sedlak, A. (1979). Developmental differences in understanding plans and evaluating actors. *Child Development, 50,* 536–560.

Shaver, K. G. (1970). Defensive attribution: Effects of severity and relevance on the responsibility assigned to an accident. *Journal of Personality and Social Psychology, 14,* 101–113.

Shaw, M. E. (1968). Attribution of responsibility by adolescents in two cultures. *Adolescence, 3,* 23–32.

Shaw, M. E., & Reitan, H. T. (1969). Attribution of responsibility as a basis for sanctioning behavior. *British Journal of Social and Clinical Psychology, 8,* 217–226.

Slovenko, R. (1983). The insanity defense in the wake of the Hinckley trial. *Rutgers Law Journal, 14,* 373–395.

Smith, T. W., Snyder, C. R., & Handelsman, M. M. (1982). On the self-serving function of an academic wooden leg: Test anxiety as a self-handicapping strategy. *Journal of Personality and Social Psychology, 42,* 314–321.

Smith, T. W., Snyder, C. R., & Perkins, S. C. (1983). The self-serving function of hypochondriacal complaints: Physical symptoms as self-handicapping strategies. *Journal of Personality and Social Psychology, 44,* 787–797.

Snyder, C. R. (1984). Excuses, excuses: They sometimes actually work to relieve the burden of blame. *Psychology Today, 18,* 50–55.

Snyder, C. R. (1985a). Collaborative companions: The relationship of self-deception and excuse making. In M. W. Martin (Ed.), *Self-deception and self-understanding* (pp. 35–51). Lawrence, KS: University Press of Kansas.

Snyder, C. R. (1985b). Excuses, excuses, excuses. *Leaders, 8,* 170–172.

Snyder, C. R. (1985c). The excuse: An amazing grace? In B. R. Schlenker (Ed.), *The self and social life* (pp. 235–260). New York: McGraw-Hill.

Snyder, C. R., & Fromkin, H. L. (1980). *Uniqueness: The human pursuit of difference.* New York: Plenum Press.

Snyder, C. R., & Smith, T. W. (1982). Symptoms as self-handicapping strategies: The virtues of old wine in a new bottle. In G. Weary & H. L. Mirels (Eds.), *Integrations of clinical and social psychology* (pp. 104–127). New York: Oxford University Press.

Snyder, M. L., & Wicklund, R. A. (1981). Attribute ambiguity. In J. H. Harvey, W. Ickes, & R. F. Kidd (Eds.), *New directions in attribution research* (Vol. 3, pp. 197–221). Hillsdale, NJ: Erlbaum.

Snyder, C. R., Higgins, R. L., & Stucky, R. J. (1983). *Excuses: Masquerades in search of grace.* New York: Wiley-Interscience.

Snyder, C. R., Smith, T. W., Augelli, R. W., & Ingram, R. E. (1985). On the self-serving function of social anxiety: Shyness as a self-handicapping strategy. *Journal of Personality and Psychology, 48,* 970–980.

Sulzer, J. L., & Burglass, R. K. (1968). Responsibility attribution, empathy and punitiveness. *Journal of Personality, 36,* 272–282.

Tedeschi, J. T., & Riess, M. (1981). Predicaments and impression management. In C. Antaki (Ed.), *Ordinary explanations of social behavior* (pp. 271–309). London: Academic Press.

Tetlock, P. E. (1980). Explaining teacher explanations of pupil performance: A self-presentation interpretation. *Social Psychology Quarterly, 43,* 283–290.

Walster, E. (1966). Assignment of responsibility for an accident. *Journal of Personality and Social Psychology, 3,* 73–79.

Wells, G. L., Petty, R. E., Harkins, S. G., Kagehiro, D., & Harvey, J. H. (1977). Anticipated discussion of interpretation eliminates actor differences in the attribution of causality. *Sociometry, 40,* 247–253.

Wills, T. A. (1981). Downward comparison principles in social psychology. *Psychological Bulletin, 90,* 245–271.

Wilson, T. D., & Linville, P. W. (1982). Improving the academic performance of college freshman: Attribution therapy revisited. *Journal of Personality and Social Psychology, 42,* 367–376.

Wilson, T. D., & Linville, P. W. (1985). Improving the performance of college freshmen with attributional techniques. *Journal of Personality and Social Psychology, 49,* 287–293.

Yalom, I. D. (1975). *The theory and practice of group psychotherapy.* New York: Basic Books.

Zemore, R., & Greenough, T. (1973). Reduction of ego threat following attributive projection. *Proceedings of the 81st Annual Convention of the American Psychological Association, 8,* 343–344.

Zuckerman, M. (1979). Attribution of success and failure revisited or: The motivational bias is alive and well in attribution theory. *Journal of Personality, 47,* 245–287.

VI

Overview Perspective

Perhaps it is fitting to close this final section of the book by returning to the Hindu fable of the blind men and the elephant that was described in Chapter 1. In the traditional version of this fable, six blind men each touch an elephant in a different place. And, as the story goes, there are six different theories about the elephant. Those theories, whether right or wrong, serve to foster an understanding of *part* of the elephant. In the preceding chapters, the authors probably would agree that this is precisely what they are doing—developing and testing models that are limited to particular aspects of the topic of coping with negative life events. Indeed, as was argued in Chapter 1, much of the productive work in this area should be and is advancing along the lines of mini- or middle-level theories (i.e., theories that attempt to address some circumscribed aspect of human behavior). However, at some point in the development of this field, a larger theoretical framework will undoubtedly evolve. For now, however, the best that we can hope to achieve is a taxonomy for defining the topic. To alter the Hindu fable a bit, imagine the possibility of one blind man who explored many of the different parts of the elephant. This new elaboration of the fable obviously would necessitate one person maping the entire body of the topic (coping with negative life events, in this case).

In the chapter in this section, B. Kent Houston has undertaken the elephantine task of providing a descriptive model that may be applied to the enormous literature on stress and coping. Unlike the other authors in this volume, whose perspectives could be explained principally under one of the four processes (i.e., effort expenditure, control/mastery, social comparison, and image maintenance), Houston's taxonomic approach is purposefully more overarching. First, he reviews the three possible definitions of stress, including a stimulus-based, an intervening-process, and a response-based definition. He concludes that the response-based definition is the most useful one, and in doing so, distinguishes between physiological and psychological stress. Psychological stress, which is defined as the "experience of negative feelings," is described in detail by Houston as he delineates the factors that elicit stress (e.g., thwarting of desires, unlearned aversive situations, and learned aversive situations). Next, an analysis of coping is undertaken. In this vein, coping is generally conceptualized as a response whose purpose is to diminish psychological stress. The various coping strategies are then examined under one of two rubrics: the covert, within-organism ones, and the overt, action-oriented ones. Finally, Houston closes with a discussion of the limitations, implications, and uses of this taxonomy.

14

Stress and Coping

B. KENT HOUSTON

INTRODUCTION

Stress and coping are topics of substantial current interest, and much has been said and could be said about these topics. In considering stress, it is important to define the term for purposes of clear communication and theory construction, yet it has been defined in numerous ways and is frequently used without a clear referent. One purpose of the present chapter, then, is to discuss the definitions of stress and to try to deal with some of the problems associated with traditional approaches to defining the concept by distinguishing psychological from physiological stress. In doing so, a phenomenological definition of psychological stress will be provided.

A discussion of what events cause stress follows naturally from a discussion of what stress is. Typically, in contemporary presentations on the topic, emphasis is given to a single class of events that lead to stress states or conditions. Such a view seems narrow because there probably are different kinds of events that lead to such states. The second purpose of the present chapter is to discuss three categories of events that potentially lead to psychological stress, or in other words, three categories of stressors. In doing so, it is intended to call attention to certain stressors that usually are not included when psychological stress is addressed, for instance, monotony, certain basically hard-wired aversive events, and endogeneous biological processes. Additionally, a focus on external

B. KENT HOUSTON • Department of Psychology, University of Kansas, Lawrence, KS 66045.

stressors is typical of contemporary, formal presentations on stress. In an attempt to balance the perspective on locus of stressors, attention here is given not only to external stressors but to internal stressors as well.

In discussions of coping, sometimes emphasis is given primarily to cognitive coping maneuvers. In other, broader presentations on the topic, a modest number of categories of cognitive and other coping responses are described. Even though worthwhile, such presentations do not adequately convey the multiplicity of ways in which people can cope. Therefore, the third purpose of the present chapter is to present an elaborated taxonomy of coping responses.

DEFINITIONS OF STRESS

The term *stress* has been used to refer to a variety of phenomena, some of which transcend the individual as the unit of analysis, such as ecosystem stress, economic stress, migration stress, social stress, etc. The focus here, however, is on stress as it relates to individuals.

The term stress as it applies to individuals has been defined in numerous ways. These definitions fit primarily into three categories, stimulus-based definitions, intervening-process definitions, and response-based definitions. Stimulus-based definitions focus on stimuli or situations that typically disturb or disrupt the individual. For example, Holmes and Rahe (1967) and colleagues (Homes & Masuda, 1974) define stress as a class of stimuli or situations that typically require adaptation or readjustment, like marriage, birth of a child, divorce, death of a loved one, etc. A major criticism of stimulus-based definitions is that people respond differently to the same potentially stressful situation (Cox, 1978; McGrath, 1970). Thus some people respond more, some less, and some not at all when faced with the objectively same situation.

Intervening process definitions of stress focus on some kind of process that occurs in between the stimulus situation that impinges on the individual and the potential responses of the individual to that situation. For example, both Cox (1978) and McGrath (1970) define stress as the imbalance between the perceived demands placed on an individual and his or her perceived capability to deal with the demands. Similarly, Lazarus and Folkman (1984) define stress as an encounter with the environment that is appraised by the individual as taxing his or her resources and endangering his or her well-being. One problem with these approaches to defining stress is that they focus primarily on external stressors whereas they give short shrift to internal stressors, such as disturbing thoughts, desires, memories, etc. Another problem with these approaches is that they do not readily accommodate the possibility that a disposition to respond to some stressors may be hard-wired or built into the organism (see Zajonc, 1984). A person's response to such stressors may be influenced little by the person's perceived resources or capability to deal with them. Finally, stress defined as an intervening process is more difficult to measure than stress defined as either stimulus situations or particular responses.

Response-based definitions focus on the state or condition of being disturbed. Such an approach focuses on phenomena that are the outcome of the objective aspects of the stressor(s), individual differences, and possible intervening processes. Thus this approach has the potential for deflecting the problems associated with stimulus-based and intervening process approaches to defining stress.

Most frequently, the condition of being disturbed is defined in terms of either a particular physiological response or a particular pattern of physiological responses, such as the general adaptation syndrome described by Selye (1956). A problem with a physiological response-based definition of stress is that the defining physiological response or response pattern may be associated with various conditions, for example, passion, exercise, fear, etc., that for other reasons we may not want to regard as comparable. For instance, the various physiological conditions vary in their psychological significance (see McGrath, 1970). In general, people are motivated to seek and prolong pleasurable conditions, such as passion, joy, etc., whereas they are motivated to avoid or terminate unpleasant conditions, like fear, anger, etc. Moreover, the latter conditions play a prominent role in psychopathology whereas the former do not.

To deal with the problem of differences between conditions in psychological significance, one might define stress in terms of unpleasant or negative feelings. Certainly feelings, particularly negative ones, are central and personal aspects of the occurrence of stress. The difficulty with this approach is that it overlooks physiological conditions that may not currently be reflected in people's feelings but that nonetheless may adversely affect their physiological well-being, for example, chronic exaggerated pituitary-adrenocortical arousal.

One way of dealing with the problems of defining stress solely in terms of physiological responses or solely in terms of affective responses is to distinguish between two overlapping stress concepts, physiological stress and psychological stress. Therefore, *physiological stress* is defined here as a physiological condition from which relief is needed for the organism's physiological well-being. Examples are lack of food, oxygen, and water, depletion of neurochemical transmitters in the brain, physical diseases, exaggerated sympathetic adrenomedullary activity, exaggerated pituitary adrenocortical activity, and so on.

Psychological stress is defined here as the experience of negative feelings. The domain of negative feelings that psychological stress encompasses will be discussed shortly. The term *negative feelings* is used in the present chapter instead of negative emotions to avoid an unnecessary dispute concerning the definition of emotion and whether some of the negative feelings that will be discussed as being encompassed by psychological stress qualify as emotions. (See Kleinginna and Kleinginna, 1981, for a summary of the heterogeneous ways in which emotion has been defined.)

Before moving on to a discussion of negative feelings, it should be reiterated that psychological and physiological stress are overlapping, although not completely overlapping concepts. Physiological stress may be associated with negative feelings, hence with psychological stress, but it may also be associated with positive feelings, such as joy, happiness, etc., or even with no particular affective state—recall the earlier example of chronic exaggerated pituitary adrenocortical arousal. Psychological stress (negative feelings) is typically associated with physiological stress, but there may be instances in which psychological stress occurs in the absence of physiological stress, for example, the initial stages of boredom.

Typically, the negative feelings discussed in the context of stress are feelings such as anxiety, fear, depression, anger, and the like. Sometimes pain is also mentioned (Bastiaans, 1978; Schalling, 1976). Perhaps pain is less likely to be discussed because it is intimately intertwined with physical sensations; hence, pain may seem less psychological than fear, depression, and anger. For many behavioral scientists, an event to be regarded as psychological has to be influenced by learning and past experience (see, for example, Lazarus, 1966, p. 395). However, it has been said that "pain is always a psychological event" (Merskey, 1975, p. 25), and it has been asserted that "the salient features of emotions (inputs from sensory systems, arousal, and cognitive processes) determine the experience of pain just as they determine the experience of other emotions" (Mandler, 1984, p. 294).

The position taken here is that psychological stress encompasses all negative feelings, not only fear, depression, anger and the like, but pain and the other negative feelings associated with physical sensations as well, for example, nausea, vertigo, etc. There are three reasons for taking this position. One is that negative feelings share a common feature by virtue of their being unpleasant experiences, and because the realm of experience is psychological, they are all unpleasant psychological phenomena. Second, there are commonalities in how people may contend or cope with negative feelings in general. For instance, individuals can try physically to avoid external situations or stressors that generate negative feelings, they can divert their attention from either stressors or negative feelings, they can ingest drugs to reduce negative feelings. More concretely, individuals can physically avoid or divert their attention from situations likely to be fear producing, pain producing, or nausea producing, they can try to divert their attention from fear, pain, or nausea, and they can ingest drugs to reduce fear, pain, or nausea. The third reason for taking the position that psychological stress encompasses negative feelings, no matter what their source, is that the common features of emotions (viz., inputs from sensory systems, arousal, and cognitive processes) probably apply not only to pain but to the other negative feelings associated with physical sensations as well, for example, hunger and nausea.

Some investigators might question whether enough cognitive processing goes into some of the negative feelings associated with physical sensations to qualify them as psychological phenomena or psychological stress. This, however, leads to an arbitrary decision as to how much cognitive processing is enough. In this vein, it is interesting to consider Lazarus' (1984) statement concerning the cognitive processing involved in transforming a sensory state (physical sensation) into an emotion. He states "the transformation necessary to produce an emotion out of sensory states is an appraisal that those states are favorable or damaging to one's well-being" (p. 126). It seems as if pain, nausea, hunger, thirst, and the like are states that should be appraised as being as damaging to one's well-being as anger, and no one would disagree that anger is a psychological phenomenon or is associated with stress. In sum, there presently does not appear to be a clear definition or other reason that would exclude negative feelings associated with physical sensations from being regarded as psychological phenomena or as candidates for psychological stress.

Psychological stress as defined here focuses exclusively on subjective responses. Thus, the criterion for determining whether individuals are experiencing psychological stress is whether they privately regard their feelings as unpleasant. I say "privately regard" because individuals' concerns about self-presentation can influence what they will publicly say about their feelings. This poses a problem for measuring psychological stress, but, then again, there are problems with measuring psychological stress or any other kind of stress no matter how it is defined.

A question that can be raised concerning this definition is whether people who seek experiences that appear to involve unpleasant feelings, such as horror movies, parachute jumping, and the like experience psychological stress. On the face of it, one would not expect people to seek unpleasant feelings. One perspective on this question is that if the people do not regard their feelings in such situations as unpleasant, then they are not experiencing psychological stress. Some people experience positive feelings in situations in which others, perhaps the majority of others, experience negative feelings. Another perspective on this question is that individuals may endure unpleasant feelings (psychological stress) in various situations in order to achieve some goal, for instance, the exhilaration of the free fall or the roller coaster ride, to enhance pleasure (as in masochistic behaviors), to protect or enhance one's self-image of being stoic or brave, to relieve boredom or achieve varied experience (cf. high sensation seeking), or in general to experience the positive feelings associated with situations about which the individual has ambivalent feelings.

Clearly, occasional very mild psychological stress has little consequence for the individual. For example, the annoyance one may experience as a result of a brief interaction at home or work or the brief, mild discomfort one may experience in one's gastro-intestinal system following a spicy meal has little consequence. However, it is of consequence for the individual if either the annoyance or discomfort is strong, enduring, or reoccurs repeatedly. Thus what is important for the individual, and needs to be kept in mind in discussing psychological stress, is negative feelings that are strong or amassed (i.e., a number of negative feelings are elicited at the same time or in a short time interval), or that, if also strong or amassed, are enduring or recurring.

POTENTIAL PSYCHOLOGICAL STRESSORS

What kinds of events lead to psychological stress? In other words, what kinds of stressors are there? Reference to the diagram in Figure 1 may assist in elucidating the discussion of kinds of stressors as well as the subsequent discussion of coping behaviors. A situation, whether internal or external, may be perceived in such a way as to lead to negative feelings (psychological stress). Alternately, a situation may be perceived in such a fashion as to lead to positive or neutral feelings.

Perception has been defined in various ways, but it is regarded here as a cognitive process whereby sensory input is transformed and meaning is assigned to it. If a situation is perceived in a way that leads to negative feelings, the situation is regarded as aversive. It is proposed here that there are three categories of stimulus situations that may give rise to such perception and therefore represent three kinds of potential psychological stressors. They are thwarting of desires, unlearned aversive stimulus

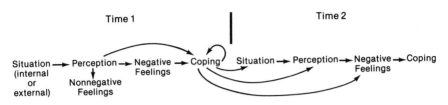

Figure 1. Schematization of psychological stress and coping.

situations, and learned aversive stimulus situations. Not only may encountering these stressors lead to negative feelings, but the anticipation or recollection of encountering them may also generate negative feelings. Lazarus (1966) aptly emphasized how anticipating an aversive event can be almost as bad if not as bad or worse than actually encountering the event.

The word *potential* is used in conjunction with psychological stressor because the response-based definition of stress employed here requires that an event cannot be regarded as a stressor without reference to the affective response it elicits. In addition, because psychological and physiological stress overlap, the events embodied in these three categories may lead to physiological stress as well.

It should be noted from the outset that a potentially stressful, real-life situation may involve events from more than one category of stressor as well as more than one event from any one category. For example, a medical procedure may involve pain-inducing stimuli (unlearned aversive stimuli), it may evoke fear and anger responses that were previously associated with medical procedures (hence it serves as a learned aversive stimulus situation), and it may thwart a person's desire to maintain dignity and be treated in a caring fashion.

This chapter will not attempt to link particular psychological stressors with particular negative feelings. Besides the characteristics of the stressor and individual learning histories, some of the variables that may be involved in the link between an external stressor and a particular feeling are perceived probability and controllability of the occurrence of the event (see Garber, Miller, & Abramsom, 1980), perceived cause of the event, and perception of whether occurrence of the event was justified or caused by someone's negligence or malice (see Averill, 1979). Also, individuals' affective responses to an event will be influenced quantitatively and/or qualitatively by their perception of their capacity for coping with the event (see Lazarus & Folkman, 1984) and their physiological arousal and feeling state prior to the event. Although these considerations are very important, they are beyond the scope of the present chapter.

Thwarting of Desires

The perception of the thwarting of one's desires is one category of potential psychological stressors. A desire means wanting or longing for something one does not have, keeping something one already has that one likes, or avoiding something one does not like. A desire may be learned or unlearned. Although the perception of the thwarting of a desire is the necessary ingredient for stressors in this category, the importance of the desire that is thwarted in a situation is paramount in influencing the meaning of that situation and the negative feelings generated. Whereas a car's running out of gas will thwart desires, running out of gas while driving to the emergency room will probably thwart more important desires, hence generate stronger as well as different negative feelings, than running out of gas while on a pleasure drive.

The traditional notion of frustration comes to mind when speaking of the thwarting of desires. Frustration involves the thwarting of desires that are being acted upon. However, the thwarting of desires, whether they are or are not being acted upon, may lead to negative feelings. For example, a person may have a desire for freedom, a desire to be healthy, or a desire to maintain job mobility, all desires about which the person may or may not be actively doing anything, yet the thwarting of these desires may produce negative feelings. The term *frustration* would be employed only in those instances in which desires that were being acted upon were thwarted. Thus frustration is a special instance of this category of stressors.

Perceived thwarting of desires as a category of psychological stressors is similar to Lazarus' (1966) formulation concerning the role that perceived thwarting of motives plays in psychological stress. There are three differences between the two formulations. A minor difference is in the use of the term *desire* rather than the term *motive*. The term motive implies that the organism is energized for action or is engaged in goal oriented action whereas the term desire does not necessarily imply either of these notions. As mentioned earlier, a person may desire or want something, and the perceived thwarting of the desire for this something may result in negative feelings whether or not the person is actually engaged in behavior to secure that goal. Thus the term desire seems more inclusive than motive. A second difference between Lazarus' formulation and the present one is the inclusion here of desires (motives in Lazarus' terminology) that Lazarus would probably not include. As an example, see the discussion in the following of desire for stimulation. The third difference between formulations, and perhaps the most important, is that it is asserted here that there are other categories of stressors besides thwarting of desires or motives that Lazarus (1966) not only did not include, namely, learned aversive stimuli, but would disagree with, namely, unlearned aversive stimuli (see Lazarus, 1984).

There is a myriad of desires the thwarting of which can lead to psychological stress. Some desires are fleeting; some are idiosyncratic. However, there are several common desires that are prominent when considering psychological stress. Even though common, some of these desires may be more prominent for some individuals than others. The desires for food, water, air, sensuality, preserving one's life, and avoiding pain and discomfort, are obvious, common desires, as is perhaps the desire to be loved (Maslow, 1970). The desire to maintain or enhance self-esteem is also prominent (Maslow, 1970). Thwarting this desire, as in a threat to self-esteem or loss of self-esteem, readily evokes negative feelings.

People seem to have a desire to control themselves, that is, their thoughts, feelings, and/or behaviors. Even the threat of losing control over thoughts, feelings, and behavior can lead to negative feelings. Illustrative of this notion is Freud's (1926) concept of neurotic anxiety wherein the threat of losing control over "unacceptable" impulses causes apprehension. The perceived thwarting of a desire to control one's self is an example of an internal situation leading to negative feelings.

People also seem to have a desire for controlling their external physical and interpersonal environments (see Langer, 1975) because such control is instrumental for satisfying other desires. The loss of such control or the threat of losing such control generates negative feelings.

People have been described as having a desire to complete behavioral and cognitive sequences. Under certain circumstances, interruption of sequences of behavior and sequences of thought have been hypothesized to lead to negative feelings (Mandler, 1984).

People have been described as having a desire for stimulation (see Zuckerman, 1978). Notions about a manipulation drive (Harlow, Harlow, & Meyer, 1950), a curiosity motive (Berlyne, 1960), and the like are congruent with this desire. Monotonous and unchallenging situations thwart the desire for stimulation and result in boredom, a negative feeling. Social isolation and sensory deprivation are more extreme examples of situations that thwart this desire, usually resulting in negative feelings. Curiously, monotony and boredom are typically neglected in presentations on psychological stress, although monotony on the job has been associated with negative feelings and the possibility of poor physical health (Levi, 1981). The neglect of monotony may stem from definitions of psychological stress that focus only on demanding, taxing, or potentially harmful experiences (e.g., Lazarus & Folkman, 1984; Sarason, 1984).

People seem to have a desire to organize their experiences into understandable, consistent, predictable systems. Uncertainties and lack of clarity about events can thwart this desire and lead to psychological stress (see Lazarus & Folkman, 1984). Starting college or a new job are mundane examples of situations that are characterized by uncertainties or lack of clarity, whereas being in a concentration camp is an extraordinary example of such situations (see Frankl, 1959).

Because values and beliefs are elements of how people organize their experiences, events that are inconsistent with people's values or beliefs, particularly if the latter are strong, will generate negative feelings. For example, if a person has a strong belief in justice, hearing that a confessed murderer or rapist was let off because of a legal technicality will generate negative feelings.

It is sometimes said that people are distressed when their attachments or commitments to people or things are threatened. For example, a disability may threaten a person's commitment to his or her work, an impending move may threaten a person's attachment to a home, neighborhood, or town. It is the position here that such situations involve the thwarting of desires, perhaps strong ones. Recall that one of the defining aspects of a desire is keeping something a person has and likes. A person or thing to which an individual is attached or committed represents something the individual wants to keep, and a situation that disrupts attachments or commitments thwarts the desire to keep that to which the person is attached or committed. Moreover, the stronger the attachment or commitment is to someone or something, the stronger the desire is to keep that someone or something, hence the stronger the negative feelings that will be generated if that desire is thwarted.

Unlearned Aversive Stimulus Situations

The second category of stressors is unlearned aversive stimulus situations. People seem to have built-in or "hard wired" dispositions to respond with negative feelings to certain stimulus situations, such as sudden loud noises, pain-inducing stimuli, and the like (see Zajonc, 1984). Thus the aversiveness of these stimuli is basically unlearned. To the extent that all sensory input is transformed and meaning is assigned to the sensory input, it can be said that the meaning attached to such stimuli is basically unlearned or built-in. It is not suggested here that the perception of such stimuli is entirely hard wired, at least in adults, but rather that it is largely hard wired, and nonintrinsic factors such as learning may influence the perception of such stimulus situations. Take, for example, the experience of pain. Such experience is influenced by the interpretation or meaning of the pain-inducing situation (Meichenbaum, Turk, & Burstein, 1975; Murray, 1975).

Generally, unlearned aversive stimuli can be categorized in terms of the sensory modality involved. Strong stimuli in any sensory modality can lead to negative feelings, namely, strong visual, olfactory, gustatory, auditory, kinesthetic (movement), or somasthetic (heat, cold, pressure, pain-producing) stimuli. Certain sensory stimuli besides strong ones can be identified that lead to negative feelings. Certain olfactory stimuli, like rotten eggs and decaying flesh, are aversive. Even moderate levels of stimuli that produce the sensations of bitter and sour produce negative feelings. Sudden noises, particularly if loud, can produce not only the startle response but the negative feelings associated with it. Intermittent as well as continuous noise, particularly if loud, can be aversive. Certain "screechy" sounds also are aversive. In addition, there may be unlearned aversive visual stimuli, such as spiders and snakes (Hebb, 1946), although controversy surrounds this notion (Delprato, 1980).

Intraorganismic processes may also give rise to negative feelings, although the stimuli and processes involved are less clear than those for the categories of unlearned aversive stimuli described above. Included here are (a) tissue needs that give rise to the feelings of hunger, thirst, fatigue, etc., (b) systemic infection, toxic conditions, etc., that may make a person feel nauseous, sick, etc., and (c) endocrine and metabolic anomalies and endogenous depletion of brain neurochemical transmitters that may influence affect.

It should be noted that the negative feelings that are evoked by intraorganismic processes may themselves serve as stressors. For example, feeling sick may elicit other negative feelings because it may thwart the desire to enjoy a vacation, to accomplish a task, etc.

Learned Aversive Stimulus Situations

The third category of stressors is learned aversive stimulus situations. People learn that certain stimulus situations are aversive, thus the meaning associated with such situations is learned. Such learning may occur via classical conditioning by virtue of the stimulus situation being paired with an unlearned aversive stimulus situation, another learned aversive stimulus situation, or the thwarting of a desire. Little Albert's experience (Watson & Rayner, 1920) is a classic example of a previously neutral stimulus (a rat) acquiring aversiveness by being paired with an unlearned aversive stimulus (loud noise). A previously neutral stimulus, such as a cave, could acquire aversiveness by being associated with a learned aversive stimulus, such as a rat for an individual like Little Albert. A previously neutral stimulus situation, like a group of people, may acquire aversiveness by being paired with the thwarting of a person's desire for justice, for example. Finally, stimulus situations may acquire aversiveness not only directly through the individual's own experience but vicariously, through observational learning. A class of small animals, a group of people, certain topics of conversation and the like may come to evoke negative feelings by virtue of an individual's observing other's reactions to them.

It should be pointed out that there are internal as well as external sources of learned aversive stimuli. For instance, a person may have learned to respond with negative feelings to the experience of other feelings. For example, a person may have learned to respond with anxiety or guilt when he or she experiences anger or sexual arousal. Moreover, images or memories of learned aversive stimulus situations, as internal representations of them, may evoke negative feelings. For example, merely thinking about a rat would evoke anxiety for a person like Little Albert. Finally, impulses to behave in ways that were punished in the past may evoke negative feelings. For example, aggressive impulses may evoke anxiety or guilt.

COPING

The responses that individuals employ to deal with psychological stress have been termed defenses or coping responses. Sometimes both terms have been used, the term defense being used for responses with certain features and the term coping for responses with other features (Haan, 1969; Menninger, 1963). Traditionally, the term *defense* has been used primarily with regard to a fairly narrow set of cognitive responses and is tied to psychodynamic theory. The term *coping* has the advantage of being applicable to a wider array of responses and has not been tied to a particular theory.

For research and clinical purposes, it is desirable to have a method of categorizing and describing coping responses. Several interesting classification systems have been proposed (e.g., Lazarus & Launier, 1978; Moos & Billings, 1982; Pearlin & Schooler, 1978), though none are very extensive. The purpose of this section is to present a classification system that is more extensive. Although described in terms of the foregoing definition of psychological stress and description of stressors, the classification scheme can for the most part stand by itself and is generally applicable to stimulus-, process-, or other response-based definitions of stress.

Coping is defined here as a response or responses whose purpose is to reduce or avoid psychological stress (negative feelings). It should be pointed out that such responses may or may not be successful in reducing psychological stress, for instance trying hard to distract one's self in the dentist's waiting room may not succeed in reducing one's apprehension. Moreover, coping responses may not be successful in the short run, but may be successful in the long run. For example, newly learned assertive behaviors used when interacting with a problematic person may require time and practice to have their intended effect. Similarly, a coping response may be successful in the short run but not in the long run. The wish-fulfilling thought on the part of an AIDS patient that a cure will soon be developed may reduce psychological stress for a time.

The adaptiveness or maladaptiveness of coping behavior is an issue separate from other considerations and requires several criteria by which it is judged, such as how realistic the coping behavior is, how acceptable is it to others, what are the short- and long-term consequences of it for other areas of functioning, etc.

It should also be pointed out that people may employ coping responses with or without being aware of doing so. Curiously, some authors state that responses must be consciously employed in order to qualify as coping responses (see, for instance, Stone & Neale, 1984). It seems reasonable that, like many overlearned behaviors, people may engage in habitual coping responses without being aware that they are doing so. Moreover, there is reason to believe that some cognitive coping behaviors occur without awareness (see Erdelyi, 1979).

In discussing the varieties of coping responses, no attempt will be made to describe the circumstances under which a particular response is likely to be made or will be effective if it is made. Such considerations, although very important, are beyond the scope of the present chapter.

Reference to Figure 1 will assist in discussing coping behaviors. As indicated in the figure, coping may be targeted on the external or internal stimulus situation, the perception of that situation, the ensuing negative feelings, or on coping processes or responses themselves. The arrow from perception to coping, bypassing negative feelings, reflects the notion that individuals may avoid negative feelings through learned coping responses.

Although depicted in the figure as somewhat of a static episode,

Table 1. Outline of Varieties of Coping Responses

Covert, within-organism
  Focus:
    Cognitive problem solving
      Cognitive planning
      Cognitive rehearsal
      Information seeking
    Cognitive control of negative affect
      Cognitive avoidance or escape
      Reinterpretation
    Facilitating cognitive or overt, action-oriented coping
Overt, action-oriented
  Focus:
    Aversive situation
      Avoidance or escape
      Actions on physical environment
      Actions on interpersonal environment
      Circumventing thwarting situations
    Negative affect
      General strategies
      Affect-specific responses
    Coping functioning
      Enhance coping resources
      Facilitate cognitive coping

coping is an ongoing, evolving process, as others have aptly pointed out (Lazarus & Folkman, 1984). Finally, it should be noted that in any real-life situation, more than one coping response may occur from the same or different categories.

An outline of the varieties of coping responses is presented in Table 1. There are two main classifications: covert, within-organism coping responses and overt, action-oriented coping responses. Within each classification, several types are indicated. Each type is further elaborated in the following.

For the sake of simplicity and symmetry, it would be preferable to identify parallel types of coping responses within the covert and overt divisions, for example, problem-solving responses within covert and overt divisions. However, this was not feasible, considering the possible multiple functions of some coping responses and the ambiguity surrounding the functions of other coping responses.

COVERT, WITHIN-ORGANISM COPING RESPONSES

The classification of covert coping refers to coping responses that occur within the organism and that are not directly observable. There are three types of covert, within-organism coping responses, those that focus on cognitive problem solving, cognitive control of negative affect, and facilitating other coping responses.

Cognitive Problem Solving

This type includes cognitive activities whose purpose is to modify the aversive stimulus situation (the problem), whether internal or external. Such activities may occur while anticipating, encountering, or following an aversive event. For example, a person may engage in problem-solving thinking prior to, during, or after taking an examination. Although such activity is more likely to occur in regard to modifiable events, it may be employed to think through alternatives following an unmodifiable event, for example, finding a new mate following the death of a spouse, finding new recreational activities, or a new vocation following a permanent disability. Although the notion of problem solving is most frequently associated with external aversive events, it may be employed with regard to internal aversive events as well, like thinking through how to deal with a recurrent unpleasant memory or with recurrent negative feelings.

There are three categories of cognitive problem-solving responses that need to be considered: cognitive planning, cognitive rehearsal, and information seeking.

Cognitive Planning. Cognitive planning involves mental formulations for dealing with problems. One kind of cognitive planning involves generating ideas concerning alternative courses of action for an aversive situation and evaluating the consequences of each alternative. For example, a person may believe that he or she is being unfairly treated by an immediate supervisor, so considers the alternatives and consequences of (a) confronting the supervisor, (b) quitting the job (escape), (c) going around the immediate supervisor to a higher authority, or (d) organizing other employees who feel the same way and either confronting the supervisor or going to a higher authority. As a consequence of this kind of cognitive process, no viable alternatives may be identified or the effort or risk of possible courses of action may be regarded as too great, and resignation may follow.

Another kind of cognitive planning involves identifying or setting intermediate goals in the course of pursuing long-term goals, for instance people may set intermediate goals in the course of their rehabilitation from a severe illness or injury. Another kind of cognitive planning is prioritizing, scheduling, and pacing activities, for example, to avoid or escape negative feelings associated with overload. A similar kind of cognitive planning involves prioritizing, scheduling, and pacing when dealing with aversive events (e.g., prioritizing and scheduling the trip to the dentist for a toothache, or the talk with the neighbor about his noisy dog).

Cognitive Rehearsal. Cognitive rehearsal, frequently intertwined with cognitive planning, involves going over in one's mind in some detail what may happen in a forthcoming situation, a sequence of behaviors or alternative sequences of behaviors for responding to the situation, and the likely reactions to the sequence(s) of behaviors. For example, a person may think about all the bad things that could happen in a situation, for example, prior to, during, and following surgery, and cognitively rehearse his or her responses to each possibility. Moreover, a person concerned about having a request turned down may mentally rehearse various ways of making the request as well as what to do if an attempt is not successful.

There is also a potentially less constructive use of cognitive rehearsal. People may think over and over again about the bad events that may occur in a situation, the possible negative consequences of their behaviors, or about having no viable course of action. Such individuals may be described as engaged in rumination or worry. Worry is an ambiguous term and may be applied to the constructive use of cognitive rehearsal as well as to dwelling solely on the negativity of the situation. It is not clear whether dwelling on the negativity of a situation represents coping as defined here. Such behavior may merely reflect an elaboration of the thoughts that are associated with the negative feelings about the aversive situation. It is easier to view such behavior as coping when dwelling on the negativity of the situation serves to divert the person's attention from other more aversive situations, reduces disappointment in a situation, serves as an excuse for not dealing well with a situation, etc.

Information Seeking. In contrast to seeking our information from the environment, which is an overt, action-oriented coping behavior, people may search their memories or think back to a similar situation in the past to draw information as to how to cope covertly or overtly with the present situation, or how to construe a situation if the present one is ambiguous. Ambiguity has been described as exacerbating psychological stress (Lazarus, 1966; Lazarus & Folkman, 1984), hence information that would reduce the ambiguity about an aversive situation should reduce psychological stress, although occasionally the situation may appear worse following clarification.

Cognitive Control of Negative Affect

This type of covert coping refers to cognitive activities aimed at reducing negative feelings by influencing the perception of an aversive situation, one's coping capacities, or the negative feelings themselves rather than by objectively modifying the aversive situation. Such responses may occur with or without a person's awareness and, depending on the criteria one might apply, they could be arrayed on a continuum ranging from rational/reasonable to irrational/unreasonable. Moreover, cognitive control responses may be used in anticipating, encountering, or following an aversive event. There are two categories of cognitive control coping responses that need to be considered, namely, cognitive avoidance or escape, and cognitive reinterpretation.

Cognitive Avoidance or Escape. The avoidance or escape category involves avoiding the cognizing of aversive stimuli or stopping the cognizing of aversive stimuli or negative feelings. A cue associated with an aversive event in the past may allow a person to avoid subsequently cognizing that event (see Dollard & Miller, 1950). Moreover, people may stop (escape) cognizing an aversive event or negative feeling by, for example, diverting their attention to something else. Concepts such as perceptual defense, attentional diversion, selective attention, and selective memory are subsumed under cognitive avoidance or escape. People may divert their attention from aversive events or negative feelings to innocuous or affectively positive external or internal stimulus events. In addition, people may divert their attention from a troublesome negative feeling, such as depression, by attending to external or internal events to generate another negative though more tolerable feeling, such as anger. This is similar to the traditional notion of defense via affect. The kinds of internal events that are likely to be useful in diverting attention and supplanting negative feelings are remembered or imagined events, particularly pleasurable ones.

Cognitive Reinterpretation. Cognitive reinterpretation involves attempting to reduce negative feelings by reinterpreting the aversive situation, the negative feelings themselves, or one's coping capacities. A person may reinterpret a situation as less aversive for a reason other than attempting to reduce negative feelings, but this then would not be said to be coping. For example, a person may respond with negative feelings to overhearing portions of a personally relevant conversation but have his or her feelings assuaged when one of the parties to the conversation volunteers the specifics of the objectively innocuous conversation.

With reference to the categories of stressors, a person may reinterpret learned and unlearned aversive stimulus events as being less aversive. Moreover, with regard to the thwarting of desires as a category of stressors, a person may reinterpret whether the desire is really thwarted or may reinterpret the strength of the desire that is perceived to be thwarted. For example, if individuals perceive their growing older as slowing them down in their desire to be successful in some endeavor, they may reinterpret their aging as not slowing them down or reinterpret their desire for success in terms of not really wanting to be successful.

The reinterpretation of aversive events may occur in the context of what might be regarded as wish-fulfilling fantasies. For example, Friedman, Mason, and Hamburg (1963) describe how a parent of a child dying of leukemia proceeded to make plans for college for the child, how another parent believed that the current drug being given the child would be a cure for the disease, and how yet another parent believed that discovery of a curative drug was imminent.

If people are personally responsible for an aversive event, whether past, present, or future, they may reinterpret the extent of their responsibility (see also Chap. 13 on excuses). For example, if a project a person has been working on turns out poorly, the person may attribute responsibility for the poor outcome to someone or something else. People may also reinterpret responsibility for future events (for example, "it's not my responsibility to deal with that") to avoid the anticipated burden of the situation or the possibility of a bad outcome. Not only may people reinterpret the extent to which they are responsible for some aversive event, but they may reinterpret what aspect of themselves was responsible. For example, some people are socially unsuccessful because they are unattractive. If they acknowlededged this, it would create negative feelings because it would thwart their desire to maintain or enhance self-esteem. Therefore, they may reinterpret the reason for their lack of social success in terms of not trying hard enough in social situations. Such a reinterpretation allows them to avoid the negative feelings that would ensue if they acknowledged that they are unattractive.

Sometimes people will reinterpret responsibility for events for which they personally are not responsible but that thwart particular desires concerning others. For example, people may reinterpret another person's responsibility for an aversive event in order to preserve their positive view of the other person.

People may also reinterpret their coping capacities. For example, people may exaggerate their capacities to cope, thereby facilitating a positive reinterpretation of an aversive situation. Alternately, people may denigrate their coping capacities to lessen their perceived responsibility for a bad outcome to a situation.

Reinterpretation of the negative feeling state may also occur. People may reinterpret their feelings as neutral or even positive. The latter traditionally has been referred to as reversal of affect.

Cognitive Responses to Facilitate other Coping Responses

People may spontaneously use or be taught to use thoughts (for example in the form of self-statements) to prompt and reinforce various cognitive coping responses, such as cognitive planning, rehearsal, avoidance, reinterpretation, etc., as well as overt coping behaviors, such as relaxation, deep breathing, etc. (see Meichenbaum, Turk, & Burstein, 1975). For example, when encountering a pain-inducing event, people can remind themselves to not think about the pain, to relax, to take a deep breath, etc.

OVERT, ACTION-ORIENTED COPING RESPONSES

This classification refers to coping responses that can be directly observed. Three types of overt, action-oriented coping responses can be distinguished—those that focus on the aversive situation, on negative feelings, and on coping.

Aversive Situation-Focused Coping

Responses of this type focus in some way on actively dealing with the aversive situation. Four categories of such responses may be identified: (a) avoidance or escape, (b) actions on the physical environment, (c) actions on the interpersonal environment, and (d) circumvention of thwarting situations.

Avoidance or Escape. There are several ways in which people can avoid or escape aversive situations. One is simply physically to avoid or escape aversive situations or the people or things that may cause aversive events. Thus people may leave (escape) an embarrassing social situation as well as avoid people who are likely to embarrass them. Leaving school, leaving the job, leaving the family, and the like, all reflected in the notion of changing life's circumstances, are but a few of innumerable examples of avoidance or escape.

Avoidance may occur in terms of time as well as space, as when people put off undergoing an aversive medical or dental procedure, beginning a burdensome task, making a conflictual decision, discussing a problem with a person, etc. One can facilitate avoidance in time by dealing with easier or more pleasurable situations or tasks.

Avoidance may also occur through inaction, for instance, avoiding embarrassment by not speaking up in a group, avoiding arguments and negative feelings by not bringing up certain topics of conversation with certain people, avoiding detection on the battle field by playing dead, etc. Besides avoidance or escape through not doing something, avoidance and escape can occur by stopping doing something, for instance by giving up or withdrawing from some course of action.

Avoidance may also take the form of delegating responsibility for a potentially aversive event (e.g., a burdensome task or a task on which a person may do poorly) to someone else.

So far, mention has been made of overt, action-oriented coping responses that are intended to allow a person to physically avoid or escape an aversive situation. There are also overt, action-oriented coping responses that are intended to allow a person psychologically to avoid or escape an aversive situation. Examples of this are fainting, sleep, and use of drugs, including alcohol.

Actions on Physical Environment. There are innumerable overt, action-oriented behaviors that serve to modify aversive situations in the physical environment. One's body is included here as a facet of the physical environment. Examples are fixing noisy or troublesome equipment, fixing up unpleasant surroundings, turning down loud sounds, taking a splinter out of one's hand, disarming a bomb, eating and drinking to remove hunger and thirst, etc.

Actions on Interpersonal Environment. Overt, action-oriented coping behaviors may be employed to influence other people in an attempt to reduce the aversiveness of situations. One kind of such coping focuses on people who may purposefully create an aversive situation, and coping behaviors are aimed at either reducing their capacity to create that situation or dissuading them from doing so. Examples of such coping are physical attack, verbal attack, including discrediting the source of unfavorable communications, negotiation, appeasement, ingratiation, indicating that one can blunt, deflect, or eliminate the aversive event, and indicating that one can retaliate. Another kind of coping behavior in this category focuses on people who are unwitting sources of negative feelings and whose aversiveness is due either to learning or the thwarting of desires, for example, interviewers, authority figures, etc. Numerous social behaviors may serve a coping function in such instances, such as smiling, talking, laughing, being humorous, submissive, ingratiating, etc. The exaggerated nature of social behaviors, such as laughing, talking, etc., may signal their use as coping responses.

Circumvention of Thwarting Situations. When a person or thing is responsible for the thwarting of a desire, a coping possibility is to go around or circumvent the obstacle. For instance, if a supervisor is not responsive to a person's grievance, the person can bypass the supervisor and deal with the supervisor's supervisor. People can circumvent obstacles in time as well as space. For instance, a person can wait until an obstacle has gone.

Negative-Affect-Focused Coping

Responses of the type focused on negative affect involve actively doing something to reduce negative feelings themselves. Two categories of such responses may be identified: (a) general strategies, and (b) affect-specific strategies.

General Strategies. There are many coping behaviors that are generally applicable to a wide array of negative feelings. The following are some of the many categories of such coping behaviors: (a) use of drugs, including alcohol; (b) fainting and sleep; (c) meditational exercises, prayer, and deep muscle relaxation; (d) vigorous physical activity, for example, aerobic exercise; (e) ventillating feelings like yelling or pounding a table when angry, having a "good cry," and the like; (f) joking; (g) use of self-reinforcers such as eating food and spending money; (h) seeking social support, like reassurance, physical comforting, love and attention from others, particularly significant others; (i) seeking pleasurable activities other than those just indicated, such as listening to or performing music, viewing or creating art, watching TV, going to the movies, engaging in sex or seeking other thrills, etc.; (j) seeking assistance for negative feelings from a friend, relative, religious counselor, physician, or mental health professional. One could speculate on and no doubt debate what factors are responsible for the psychological stress reducing effects of the coping behaviors in these categories. Factors common to many are attentional diversion (diverting one's attention from one's negative feelings or their cause), supplanting negative affect with neutral or positive affect, and reinterpretation of the aversive situation(s) in question. Reduction of physiological arousal is probably another factor common to some of the coping behaviors in these categories.

Affect-Specific Responses. There are certain coping responses that are closely if not exclusively associated with certain negative feelings. Expiating behaviors—doing good deeds, self-punishment, and the like—are associated with reducing guilt. Generating activity of various kinds is associated with relieving boredom. Working unusually hard on something in hope of doing well or working on something that one does well may reduce dysphoria due to lowered self-esteem. In either instance the intention of the coping behavior appears to be to increase self-esteem and thereby to lessen negative feelings.

Coping-Focused Coping Responses

There are two categories of coping responses that focus on coping functioning, namely, enhancing coping resources and facilitating cognitive coping responses.

Enhancing Coping Resources. This category involves acquiring coping behaviors or enhancing the effectiveness of one's coping responses or capacities. There are several kinds of such responses. One is learning behaviors that are perceived as important for coping with a class of aversive situations, like learning karate in hope of better coping with physical threats or learning how to carry on conversations in hope of better coping with anxiety-producing social situations. Closely allied with this kind of coping is practicing coping behaviors. One can practice behaviors that are perceived as helpful for coping whether the behaviors were recently acquired or not, such as practicing karate or practicing the giving of a potentially anxiety-provoking speech. Another kind of coping behavior of this category is acquiring physical implements to enhance one's capacity to modify or avoid aversive situations. Examples of this range from acquiring guns to enhance coping with threats of crime to acquiring stylish clothes to cope with social anxiety. People may alter the physical environment to enhance their capacity to avoid or escape an aversive situation or to attack those responsible for an aversive situation. Examples of this range from building bomb shelters and escape tunnels to installing booby traps.

People may gain assistance from others either informally or through joining an organization to enhance their capacity to (a) take action on the physical environment, such as fixing up a tenement, (b) take action on the interpersonal environment, for example, gaining allies to enhance one's capacity to attack or negotiate; (c) circumvent a thwarting situation, for example, organizing employees to try to circumvent a supervisor, or (d) avoid or escape an aversive situation, such as joining with others to escape confinement, escape the country, etc. Another way of enhancing coping resources is to enhance one's somatic resources prior to a potentially aversive event, like getting plenty of rest or exercise and eating properly prior to a period of excessive work, extended travel, and so forth.

Facilitating Cognitive Coping Responses. Various overt behaviors can augment or facilitate cognitive coping. Cognitive avoidance can be facilitated by reading, for example in the dentist's waiting room, by "getting busy" on various activities, and by many of the behaviors described in the section on general strategies of negative affect focused coping. Various overt behaviors from writing to gathering information can be performed to facilitate time management, prioritizing, and scheduling.

There are numerous things people can do to facilitate reinterpretation of aversive events, for instance, seeking the company of others who think similarly about the situation, trying to convince others of one's reinterpretation, gathering evidence to support the reinterpretation, or doing things, like drinking, to facilitate one's reinterpretation of one's capacity to cope. Drinking during an aversive situation may facilitate an enhanced reinterpretation of one's capacity to cope, whereas drinking prior to an aversive situation may facilitate denigrating one's capacity to cope. The latter may be termed self-handicapping.

People may actively seek information about aversive or potentially aversive situations. Such information may be useful in the various cognitive problem solving activities described earlier. The traditional notion of vigilance can be viewed as an active coping behavior directed at gaining information about the location and magnitude of aversive situations, which would assist in cognitive problem solving. Actively seeking information may also be useful in influencing reinterpretation of the aversiveness of the situation. Further, actively seeking information may be useful in reinterpreting one's feelings about an aversive situation, for instance a person may find that it is normal or all right to feel nervous about some pending aversive event—a medical procedure or leaving home for the first time. Also, information may be useful in indicating how to cope covertly or overtly with a potentially aversive situation, such as divorce, disability, the aversive aspects of beginning college or a new job.

COPING: CONCLUDING COMMENTS

In wrapping up this discussion of varieties of coping responses, two important points deserve to be reiterated. One is that coping is an ongoing, evolving process. For example, a person who has reinterpreted an aversive event in a particular way may subsequently try to facilitate that reinterpretation by seeking the company of others who think similarly or by trying to convince others to think similarly. In addition, the effectiveness or ineffectiveness of a coping behavior will influence the use of other coping behaviors. For example, after trying unsuccessfully to negotiate with a person who is responsible for an aversive situation, the individual may try to circumvent the person or escape the situation.

The second point to reiterate is that in real-life situations more than one coping response from the same or a different category of coping response may occur. For example, a person may cognitively avoid apprehensive feelings while engaging in cognitive problem solving, or people may work on gaining assistance from others to enhance their capacity to attack while at the same time trying to negotiate with or even appease an adversary.

CONCLUSIONS

It is important for clear communication and for theorizing about the diverse phenomena that get subsumed under the term stress that kinds of stress be specified. In particular, for talking about an individual it seems useful to distinguish psychological stress from physiological stress. However, the use of the term, stress, even if it is preceded by an adjective, suggests some commonality in the phenomena to which the term is applied. Perhaps the commonality is a state that if unrelieved *can* have negative short- or long-term consequences for that which experiences such a state, for example, a person, social group, or economic system. However, this or probably any other commonality is so vague that neither communication nor theory construction would be facilitated by its use. Thus it still seems desirable to precede the term stress with a modifier.

Despite what has been said earlier in this chapter, there are no doubt those readers who are still opposed to defining psychological stress in terms of negative feelings. Two additional comments about such a definition can be made. One is that the phenomenological definition of psychological stress proposed here is in keeping with a growing acceptance in contemporary behavioral science of studying covert psychological events. The second comment concerns pragmatics. Such a definition potentially makes measurement of psychological stress easier. If one adopts a stimulus-based definition of psychological stress, it is no easy matter to try systematically to assess the diversity of short- and long-term situations that may impinge on a person during a particular time. If one adopts an intervening-process definition of psychological stress, one is forced indirectly to measure those intervening processes, which can be inordinately difficult. Considering the aforementioned difficulties, measuring negative feelings seems much easier, although it is not without its own faults, as was mentioned earlier. In addition, measurement of negative feelings need not be complex; rather individuals can merely be asked whether what they are feeling is unpleasant. Thus people need not be able to articulate or complexly label their feelings.

It was intended that serious consideration be given to two notions regarding events that lead to negative feelings. One notion is that the events that a person regards as aversive probably can be arrayed on a continuum from those whose aversiveness is due exclusively to prior learning and experience to those whose aversiveness is influenced little by prior learning. To encourage consideration of this notion, categories of learned and unlearned aversive stimulus situations or stressors were proposed. Doing so, however, dichotomizes the continuum, and this unfortunately leads to loss of information and thus a loss of clarity about stressors. Nevertheless, I hope the reader will carefully consider the notion of such a continuum.

The second notion regarding events that lead to negative feelings is that some such events may be biological processes. Perhaps the emphasis on behavior and learning in the behavioral sciences has led us to overlook how biological processes can contribute to or cause psychological stress.

A presentation on stress and stressors is not complete without a discussion of how people deal with stress and stressors, or in other words, a discussion of coping. An attempt was made here to categorize the multiplicity of ways in which people can cope with psychological stress. Perhaps such a taxonomy will provide clinicians and/or researchers with a thought provoking framework with which to consider how clients, research participants, or people in general deal with psychologically stressful situations.

After perusing the presentation on coping responses, it might be asked "What responses are left that aren't coping responses?" In answer to this question it should be noted that many of the responses described may be employed in the pursuit of pleasure, hence would not be regarded as coping responses under such circumstances. For example, people may cognitively plan vacation trips, seek information about jobs in which they are interested, rehearse a sales pitch in hope of increasing its effectiveness, have a drink with friends, etc. Therefore the morphology of many responses will not identify whether they are coping responses; rather one needs to assess what motivates the responses. Thus depending on the circumstances, many responses may serve a pleasure seeking or a coping function—or both functions.

REFERENCES

Averill, J. R. (1979). Anger. In *Nebraska symposium on motivation, 1978* (pp. 1–80). Lincoln, NE: University of Nebraska Press.

Bastiaans, J. (1978). The optimal use of anxiety in the struggle for adaptation. In C. D. Spielberger & I. G. Sarason (Eds.), *Stress and anxiety* (Vol. 5, pp. 213–219). Washington, DC: Hemisphere.

Berlyne, D. E. (1960). *Conflict, arousal, and curiosity.* New York: McGraw-Hill.

Cox, T. (1978). *Stress.* Baltimore, MD: University Park Press.

Delprato, D. J. (1980). Hereditary determinants of fears and phobias: A critical review. *Behavior Therapy, 11,* 79–103.

Dollard, J., & Miller, N. E. (1950). *Personality and psychotherapy: An analysis in terms of learning, thinking, and culture.* New York: McGraw-Hill.

Erdelyi, M. H. (1979). Let's not sweep repression under the rug: Toward a cognitive psychology of repression. In J. F. Kohlstrom and F. J. Evans (Eds.), *Functional disorders of memory* (pp. 355–402). New York: Wiley.

Frankl, V. (1959). *Man's search for meaning.* Boston, MA: Beacon.

Freud, S. (1926). Inhibitions, symptoms and anxiety. In *The standard edition of the complete psychological works of Sigmund Freud* (Vol. 20, pp. 87–104). London: Hogarth Press.

Friedman, S. B., Mason, J. W., & Hamburg, D. A. (1963). Urinary 17-hydroxycorticosteroid levels in parents in children with neoplastic disease: A study of chronic psychological stress. *Psychosomatic Medicine, 25,* 364–376.

Garber, J., Miller, S. M., & Abramson, L. Y. (1980). On the distinction between anxiety and depression: Perceived control, certainty, and the probability of goal attainment. In J. Garber & M. E. P. Seligman (Eds.), *Human helplessness: Theory and application* (pp. 71–95). New York: Academic Press.

Haan, H. (1969). A tripartite model of ego functioning: Values and clinical research applications. *Journal of Nervous and Mental Disease, 148,* 14–30.

Harlow, J. F., Harlow, M. K., & Meyer, D. R. (1950). Learning motivated by a manipulation drive. *Journal of Experimental Psychology, 40,* 228–234.

Hebb, D. O. (1946). On the nature of fear. *Psychological Review, 53,* 259–276.

Holmes, T. H., & Masuda, M. (1974). Life changes and illness susceptibility. In B. S. Dohrenwend & B. P. Dohrenwend (Eds.), *Stressful life events: Their nature and effects* (pp. 45–72). New York: Wiley.

Holmes, T. H., & Rahe, R. H. (1967). The social readjustment rating scale. *Journal of Psychosomatic Research, 11,* 213–218.

Kleinginna, P. R., Jr., & Kleinginna, A. M. (1981). A categorized list of emotion definitions, with suggestions for a consensual definition. *Motivation and Emotion, 5,* 345–379.

Langer, E. J. (1975). The illusion of control. *Journal of Personality and Social Psychology, 32,* 311–328.

Lazarus, R. S. (1966). *Psychological stress and the coping process.* New York: McGraw-Hill.

Lazarus, R. S. (1984). On the primacy of cognition. *American Psychologist, 39,* 124–129.

Lazarus, R. S., & Folkman, S. (1984). *Stress, appraisal, and coping.* New York: Springer.

Lazarus, R. S., & Launier, R. (1978). Stress-related transactions between person and environment. In L. A. Pervin & M. Lewis (Eds.), *Theories of emotion: Vol. 1. Emotion: Theory, research, and experience* (pp. 287–327). New York: Academic Press.

Levi, L. (1981). *Preventing work stress.* Reading, MA: Addison-Wesley.

Mandler, G. (1984). *Mind and body: Psychology of emotion and stress.* New York: W. W. Norton.

Maslow, A. H. (1970). *Motivation and personality* (2nd ed.). New York: Harper & Row.

McGrath, J. E. (1970). A conceptual formulation for research on stress. In J. E. McGrath (Ed.), *Social and psychological factors in stress* (pp. 10–21). New York: Holt, Rinehart, & Winston.

Meichenbaum, D., Turk, D., & Burstein, S. (1975). The nature of coping with stress. In I.

G. Sarason and C. D. Spielberger (Eds.), *Stress and anxiety* (Vol. 2, pp. 337–360). Washington, DC: Hemisphere.

Menninger, K. (1963). *The vital balance: The life process in mental illness.* New York: Viking.

Merskey, H. (1975). Psychological aspects of pain. In M. Weisenberg (Ed.), *Pain: Clinical and experimental perspectives* (pp. 24–35). St. Louis, MO: Mosby.

Moos, R. H., & Billings, A. G. (1982). Conceptualizing and measuring coping resources and processes. In L. Goldberger & S. Breznitz (Eds.), *Handbook of stress: Theoretical and clinical aspects* (pp. 212–230). New York: The Free Press.

Murray, J. B. (1975). Psychology of the pain experience. In M. Weisenberg (Ed.), *Pain: Clinical and experimental perspectives* (pp. 36–44). St. Louis, MO: Mosby.

Pearlin, L. I., & Schooler, C. (1978). The structure of coping. *Journal of Health and Social Behavior, 19,* 2–21.

Sarason, I. G. (1984). Stress, anxiety, and cognitive interference: Reactions to tests. *Journal of Personality and Social Psychology, 46,* 929–938.

Schalling, D. (1976). Anxiety, pain, and coping. In I. G. Sarason & C. D. Spielberger (Eds.), *Stress and anxiety* (Vol. 3, pp. 49–71). Washington, DC: Hemisphere.

Selye, H. (1956). *The stress of life.* New York: McGraw-Hill.

Stone, A. A., & Neale, J. M. (1984). New measure of daily coping: Development and preliminary results. *Journal of Personality and Social Psychology, 46,* 892–906.

Watson, J. B., & Rayner, R. (1920). Conditioning emotional reactions. *Journal of Experimental Psychology, 3,* 1–14.

Zajonc, R. B. (1984). On the primacy of emotion. *American Psychologist, 39,* 117–123.

Zuckerman, M. (1978). Sensation seeking. In H. London & J. E. Exner, Jr. (Eds.), *Dimensions of personality* (pp. 487–559). New York: Wiley.

Author Index

Subject Index